P9-DLZ-962

MEMOIRS

by

KINGSLEY AMIS

Summit Books

NEW YORK · LONDON · TORONTO · SYDNEY · TOKYO · SINGAPORE

SUMMIT BOOKS
Simon & Schuster Building
Rockefeller Center
1230 Avenue of the Americas
New York, New York 10020

Copyright © 1991 by Kingsley Amis
All rights reserved
including the right of reproduction
in whole or in part in any form.
Originally published in Great Britain by Hutchinson.
SUMMIT BOOKS and colophon are trademarks
of Simon & Schuster Inc.
Manufactured in the United States of America

1   3   5   7   9   10   8   6   4   2

Library of Congress Cataloging in Publication data
Amis, Kingsley.
    Memoirs/by Kingsley Amis.
        p.   cm.
    Includes index.
        $25.00
    1. Amis, Kingsley—Biography.
2. Authors, English—20th century—Biography.
        I. Title.
    PR6001.M6Z47   1991
    828′.91409—dc20
[B]   91-18126
        CIP
    ISBN: 0-671-74909-9

All unattributed photographs come from the Amis
collection, copyright Hilly Kilmarnock

TO
HILLY
PHILIP, MARTIN, SALLY
JAIME AND ALI

ACKNOWLEDGEMENTS

I am grateful to Robert Conquest for permission to quote some of his poems and limericks, to the estate of Philip Larkin for the extracts from 'Aubade', 'Love Again' and for 'The Way We Live Now', and to the estate of Sir John Betjeman for 'Croydon'. I am also grateful to Anthony Thwaite, the editor of *Larkin at Sixty*, for permission to reproduce a version of my contribution to that collection. Some other extracts in this book appeared first in my collection, *What Became of Jane Austen?*

CONTENTS

MEMOIRS

PREFACE

It will be seen that this book consists not of a connected narrative but of a series of essays or sketches. Most of them are about individuals I have known more or less well. Most of the others are about self-contained episodes of my life, like my time in the army or my trip to Prague in 1966, though here again I have tried to focus on others rather than myself. I have done so not out of self-effacement but for several other reasons. Most writers lead dull lives whether or not those lives may be fun to lead, and are likely to be boring to read about in any detail. Writing directly about my own would anyway not appeal to me, even if I had a good memory for that kind of thing and had kept diaries with any persistence. For the periods of weeks or months that I have done so it was, as so often, only to relieve my feelings over some personal problem.

This leads me to one of my stronger reasons for attempting to keep myself away from centre stage. To publish an account of my own intimate, domestic, sexual experiences would hurt a number of people who have emotional claims on me, probably as much by my writing of good times as of bad, and I have no desire to cause pain, or further pain, to them or myself. And without any of that . . . Who would want to read about the time I had thinking up and writing one book or another and what I felt about its reviews, sales, translation into Catalan, or about how I spent my summer holidays in 1959?

Even as they are, there is probably quite enough about me in these pages, more than I intended or realise. And I have already written an account of myself in twenty or more volumes, most of them called novels. Novels they fully are, too, and those who know both them and me will also know that they are firmly unautobiographical, but at the same time every word of them inevitably says something about the kind of person I am. 'In vino veritas – I don't

know,' Anthony Powell once said to me, 'but in scribendo veritas
– a certainty.'

The kind of thing I have written here (allo- rather than autobiography) depends largely on a good memory for anecdotes and anecdotal detail, which I have. It is easy and tempting to improve
on reality in recounting them, which I have fairly conscientiously
eschewed in what follows, and in remembering them too, which I
can only hope I have mostly avoided. I have purposely invented or
changed nothing of substance. Of course, in the interests of speed
and of limiting dullness, I have invented dialogue, but nothing that
is material or is not the sort of thing that would have been said at
the relevant moment. If some of the total result reads like my fiction,
that does not point to its untruth, any more than plausible passages
in my fiction are necessarily taken from life.

It will save space further on if I say here that I was born in 1922
in South London and brought up in Norbury, S.W.16, the only
child of William Robert and Rosa Annie Amis. In 1940 the family
moved to Berkhamsted in Hertfordshire. From 1934 to 1941 I
attended the City of London School, first at its premises on the
Victoria Embankment, from September 1939 in Marlborough,
Wilts. In 1941-42 and 1945-49 I was at St John's College, Oxford
University. In 1942-45 I served in the army. In 1948 I married
Hilary Ann Bardwell, by whom I had three children, Philip (b.
1948), Martin (b. 1949) and Sally (b. 1954). In 1965 the marriage
ended in divorce and I married Elizabeth Jane Howard. She and I
ceased to live together in 1980 and this marriage too was subsequently dissolved.

From 1949 to 1961 I was an assistant lecturer, then a lecturer, in
English at the University College of Swansea. In 1958-59 I taught
Creative Writing at Princeton University. From 1961 to 1963 I was
Fellow and Director of Studies in English at Peterhouse, Cambridge
University, resigning in the latter year to become a free-lance writer.
For something over four months in 1967-68 I was a visiting professor
at Vanderbilt University, Nashville, Tennessee.

My chief works are listed elsewhere in this book. In addition, I
published *The Book of Bond*, under the pseudonym of Lt.-Col.
William ('Bill') Tanner, in 1965, and *Colonel Sun: a James Bond
adventure*, as Robert Markham, in 1968.

Primrose Hill,
May 1990

FAMILY

My FATHER'S FATHER was said to come from East Anglia, which at one time I took to be some remote and savage mountain or desert region. He was called officially Joseph James Amis, and in the family circle, sometimes perhaps with a hint of satire, known as Pater or Dadda. I can see him vividly as a small fat red-faced fellow with starting moist eyes and a straggly moustache which has confused itself in my mind with the 'Old Bill' style of the Great War. His nose had strong purple tints and, something I took to be unique to him, several isolated hairs an inch or two long sticking out from it here and there. He laughed frequently, with a great blaring or scraping sound of air blown through the back of the nose, but I find it hard to remember him smiling. I have only realised since preparing to write this how much I disliked and was repelled by him. Actually I saw little of him except at Christmas or an occasional birthday and that was quite enough for me. On one of the former he managed to give my cousin John and me one and the same tie as a present. A joke, possibly.

He enjoyed eating out, with I suspect plenty to drink, and I used to admire him, if for nothing else, for sticking his napkin in the neck of his shirt, then thought a vulgarity. At these feasts he was a great teller of jokes, typically without any preamble, to trap you into thinking you were hearing about some real event. One of these horrified me so much that I have never forgotten it. A Scotsman (I was still so young I had not heard about Scotsmen being supposed to be mean) took his wife out to dinner. Both ordered steak. The wife started eating hers at top speed, but the man left his untouched. 'Something wrong with the steak, sir?' – 'No no, I'm waiting for my wife's teeth.' I had not then heard of false teeth either, and imagined the living teeth being torn from the woman's jaws on the spot and inserted into her husband's. Except in greeting I cannot remember my grandfather addressing a word to me personally.

1

His house and chattels were more prosperous than my own parents'; they were situated at Purley in Surrey, quite a posh part and then, say about 1930, semi-rural, though already, I think, connected with London by the results of 'ribbon development'. It was perhaps a half-hour bus-ride from our own place in Norbury, S.W.16, halfway back towards London. The grandparental mansion was called Barchester, but any Trollopean overtones must have been in the mind of some previous owner. There were of course servants, as in any even mildly prosperous middle-class household of the time, but Mater (no feminine equivalent of Dadda for her) was a careful manager, so much so as to be a source of near-legend.

It may or may not have been true, for instance, that she would leave out two matches for the maids to light the gas in the mornings: one match might plausibly break, so the reasoning was imagined, while more than two would be an inducement to some sort of pyrotechnic revel. To save lavatory paper, Mater would cut up and hang up grocer's and similar bags on a hook, and one morning my Uncle Pres claimed to have cut his bottom on the lingering remains of an acid-drop, an incident taken up in one of my novels, the artist not being on oath. Being unable to recall a single meal or anything else eaten at Barchester, except at a Christmas or two, I can believe that Mater avoided entertaining where possible.

Dadda was a glass merchant or wholesaler, which meant he traded in glass or glassware, the kind you drank out of or less commonly ate off, and for years, my father told me, was doing well enough, until he began to be hit by mass-production. Dadda had a big line in unbreakable glass. This is or was of course not literally unbreakable, just unusually tough, held together, somebody once explained to me, by inner tension, and meant to survive, say, being knocked off a table on to a carpeted floor. If too severely struck it disintegrates in a flash, goes to powder rather than fragments, implodes with a loud report. It was in keeping with Dadda's style of not preluding his funny stories that he should have crept unseen into the family drawing-room one evening with an 'unbreakable' glass plate and, meaning doubtless no more than to cause a moment of wondering surprise by bouncing it across the carpet, caused it to burst in the fireplace like a hand-grenade thrown without warning. The incident did not shake a jokey, excitable, silly little man like him. Not long afterwards, holding up one of his horrible amber-brown 'Jacobean' tumblers, he asked an important American client if he would like to see something. When the man said he would indeed, Dadda

2

strode to the hearth and did his hand-grenade act all over again. I like to think that this demonstration did its tiny bit to bring on the decline of J. J. Amis & Co. at the hands of Woolworth's.

Dadda also figured in an attempt to obstruct or somehow muck up the marriage of Gladys Amis, his daughter and my aunt, to a Harvard professor named Ralph Foster, a distinguished scholar as I was later led to believe. Precision is difficult after sixty years, but my impression at the time was that the final attempt came on the very eve of the ceremony and that it was Mater's idea rather than Dadda's. I do remember that, summoned by Uncle Pres, my parents took off grim-faced on the fatal evening to help to talk Dadda/Mater out of their opposition. Since Gladys was over the age of consent, indeed over twenty-one, Ralph free to marry, etc., the old people could not have done much beyond acting like bloody pests and spoiling everybody's fun, but no child of my age then would have found anything out of the way about that. The surprising part was that, as far as I could understand the situation, my own mother and father seemed to be on the right side. For some reason nothing to do with the personalities of those involved, it seemed much more natural to me that Pres and my aunt Poppy should have supported Gladys and Ralph.

Anyway, virtue and sense triumphed, the marriage took place and the Fosters disappeared to America. Sadly soon, at the unfunny age of thirty-six, in fact, Ralph fell down dead of excitement ('nervous heart') at a baseball game, but had had time to produce two children, Bobbie and Rosemary.* Bobbie I hardly saw or remember, though Rosemary appeared with her mother on this side of the water as a girl of ten or twelve, bright and sweet but too young for my sexual purposes.

America had figured in my life earlier, with American uncles, aunts and cousins to be seen from my early childhood, and if I took any interest in family history I might well have been able to confirm my impression that most of the ancestral Amises had emigrated there, to Virginia, in the earlier nineteenth century. I can recall a very Dixie-style Uncle Tom (*sic*), probably a cousin of my grandfather's, and a cousin Uretta, whose curious name was said to have

---

* A version of this episode is recounted in my novel *The Old Devils*, chapter 9.

been the product of a dream. She called my grandmother 'Aunt Ju' (for Julia), and very odd it sounded in her accent.

On my father's side I had, or was aware I had, two uncles, one unmarried, two aunts, one the soon-absent Gladys, two cousins and nobody else, and saw not so very much of them, despite the short distances involved – not so remarkable perhaps in what was still the age before the motor-car for most people. The only one of these likely to interest a novelist, I suppose, was my younger uncle, Leslie. After Dadda had performed his last noteworthy act, by dying of a heart attack (at over seventy, but some said he was helped on his way by negligence), Leslie took over the care of Mater and the rump of J. J. Amis & Co. at something like the same time.

I was content to let J. J. Amis stay out of my life, but there were expeditions to the household Leslie and Mater had set up in Surrey, a little south of Purley in Warlingham. I liked Leslie, the only one of my senior paternal relatives to show me interest or affection. He was a smallish, good-looking man, with abundant straight dark hair he kept carefully ordered, a bond between us though unintended on his part; at that time my contemporaries and I paid enormous attention to our hair-arrangement. As I grew through adolescence I was able to picture his horrible life. His routine took him every weekday evening from the commuter station to the pub opposite, where he would tank up sufficiently to face Mater's company till her bedtime. After supper on lighter evenings he drove her to the same or another pub. Unwilling or unable to get out of the car, she would be fetched glasses of port, though whether he used to climb back aboard to drink beside her or returned to the pub for some sort of company I have never tried to discover. Mater was a large dreadful hairy-faced creature who lived to be nearly ninety and whom I loathed and feared in a way I had never felt towards Dadda.

It must have been about the time of the war that my father told me, in earnest confidence, that he had been visited at his office by my uncle Leslie. Dad was very grave.

'Do you know what he told me? He said he liked men. Wanted to [he may have brought himself to say] go to bed with them. What do you think of that?'

'I don't know what to say,' I answered truthfully. 'What did you tell him?'

'I said, "I take it you've seen a doctor?" '

Whatever any doctor might have said or done, Leslie turned out in the end not to have needed one much. When Mater finally died, terrifyingly late, Leslie realised what capital he had and went round the world on shipboard. The passage of a few years had made possible franker speech at home and my father felt able to tell me, with much amusement and fragments of envy and admiration, that, according to report, Leslie had fucked every female in sight. Evidently he went on doing so as long as he lasted, which sadly was not long, perhaps a couple of years.

For some reason I have always thought this a story ideally suited to the pen of Somerset Maugham, though he would have had to leave out the detail about Leslie's phantom homosexuality. I could bring it in if I were writing the events up as fiction: the presence of Mater had the effect of removing women from Leslie's whole world, but left his libido intact and questing. With her out of the way, his natural heterosexual drive was freed. Both Maugham and I, and plenty of others, could have worked in a couple of other touches I remember. On being invited to a bottle party – this, I suppose, would have been in the Twenties – Leslie had asked what was entailed and was told to take a bottle along. A bottle of what? Oh, anything. So in good faith he had turned up with a bottle of HP sauce. Then, during his Warlingham days, I noticed that he ate raw parsley in great quantities because, he said, of its richness in organic copper, though he failed to add what this compound was supposed to do for you. More likely it just grew profusely in his wretched garden.

Poor Leslie. Impressionistically, perhaps altogether falsely, I think I can recall him coming back into a pub near the village, where my parents and I, now of drinking age, were on a visit, after he had taken a glass of port to Mater in the car outside, and his painful look of attempted animation.

My mother's father was the only grandparent I cared for. He liked and collected books, real books, poetry books, had lined part of a room in his little Camberwell house with them. I wish there had been a time when he could have told me something of what he thought of these, but he died before his doing so would have meant anything much to me. I know what his wife, my Gran, thought of them from what my mother told me. Misguidedly, but by any reckoning harmlessly, he would read his favourite passages aloud to her and she would make faces and gestures at him while his head was lowered to the page, which helped to make me hate her very much. When Grandad died, or a couple of years after, I was hoping at least to inherit a decent part of his library, but Gran allowed me five volumes only, on condition I wrote 'from his grandfather's collection' on the flyleaf of each one. I took Coleridge, Byron, Shelley, Keats and Wordsworth, and have the Coleridge and the Keats still. Shamefully, I scribbled notes all over the Byron while lecturing on that poet twenty years later, and took it off my shelves.

To picture my Gran one has only to call to mind one of those horrible shrunken little old women dressed in black who used to sit on walls or outside shops on the Continent. Near her right eye she had an apparently bottomless black hole about the size of a pin's head which put an extra tiny horror into her kiss of greeting. Every week my mother and I would take the bus to Brixton and change for Camberwell, getting off for a turning off Coldharbour Lane, Lowth Road. In retrospect Lowth Road strikes me as the archetype of the place the hero of the rags-to-riches film swears at the age of ten to fight to be a thousand miles away from, though it was probably nowhere near as bad as that.

Gran would bring my mother up to date with family news, how Lily's cough was worse and Nell could not have long to go now. 'One thing the doctor said, she's got healing flesh. She heals so quick she healed round the radium needles.' Gran asked me an occasional question about school, always carefully pitching her remarks at someone a couple of years younger than me, and once or twice ridiculed toys I had brought with me. But the star of Lowth Road, my knockout relative, was my aunt Dora.

Dora was my mother's younger sister by some five years, dark, grey-eyed, pale and of a permanently disaffected expression, though she was always quite friendly to me. She wore no make-up or jewellery of any kind, then a rarity, and her general appearance was to dowdiness what Lowth Road, as I saw it, was to squalor. I never saw her in anything but a black jumper and black skirt. Uneasiness radiated from her, as far as me, anyway. While some sort of talk continued round her, she would pick up and dispose of every fragment of debris, fallen flower-petal, empty needle-packet, scrap of fluff, single human hair on any material. My mother smoked cigarettes and from time to time would light one, always shaking out the match beyond any doubt before dropping it in the rather fancy ashtray. At once Dora would jump to her feet, take the dead match into the adjoining scullery and hold it for a good half-minute under the running tap before dropping it in the sink-tidy. No notice was ever taken of this procedure, in the sense that nothing was said, though there was plenty I wanted to say. I asked my mother about it on the way home.

'Oh, she's just a bit funny. She worries a lot.'

'But anyone could have seen that match was out before she picked it up.'

'It's just her way. It doesn't mean anything.'

Again, it meant plenty to me: it meant my aunt Dora was off her head, and can have done little to alleviate the fears of madness which have worried me from time to time throughout my life, unnecessarily it seems on the whole. Dora was, of course, not mad or anywhere near it, but suffering from an anxiety neurosis with obsessions. This was not a phrase I could have expected my mother to know in 1932 or whenever it was; all the same I think she might have said a little more than she did. But reticence on all such topics was the way then.

It might be worth adding here that my mother felt an envy and resentment towards her sister that may have amounted almost to hatred. With her auburn hair and fine complexion my mother was a pretty woman, as was agreed by my schoolfellows, no kinder critics on such matters than schoolfellows anywhere. To my equally direct view, Dora was plain, and probably nothing more than fictional convention makes me think I can see from this distance something quite fine and clear in those grey eyes even while they stared. But anyway, Dora had been the one who got the fussing and the pretty frocks, as my mother more than once reminded me and my father. My mother had an attractive mezzo-soprano voice, which as far as I know she never displayed in public, but which I often heard at the musical evenings that were part of our social life before 1939. I never heard Dora sing, but it was affirmed that some music-teacher person had listened to both sisters, and according to the Amis side had pronounced my mother's voice the finer. But it had been Dora who had her voice trained.

And Dora sang in public all right. In the years before the Great War it was the custom for a professional singer, always I think a woman, to lead the singing of the National Anthem at the close of public functions, especially banquets, Livery Company dinners and the like. For that you got – Dora got – a free evening dress, a free dinner and five guineas. Not bad pay for 1910, and certainly enough to feel envious about.

Let that be. Once, in that small and remarkably oppressive

kitchen which gave a view of the back garden, Dora said to me, politely as ever,

'Would you mind moving your chair a little this way? Then I can see if there's anyone out there.' (As far as I remember there was no way in from the back.)

No doubt wondering why there might have been and what they would have been doing there, my mother asked some question about hooligans (not common in those days, even in S.E.5), burglars, etc.

'No, it's just there might be someone there and I'd want to be sure of seeing them if there were,' said Dora.

Soon afterwards my Gran asked me if I would like to go and play in the garden. I went at once, no doubt feeling I should be more comfortable out there and perhaps safer too. The place consisted of a short concrete strip and two flower-beds half a dozen feet wide with a median path of what were probably cinders bounded by scallop-shells, and a terminal wall or fence. To devise a game for one actually playable in this space would have taxed the ingenuity of an Edward de Bono, while playing in the intransitive sense of frolicking about was limited, largely by the thickly planted flowers that Dora assiduously tended and I can see still with unexpected vividness: marigolds, snapdragons, Michaelmas daisies, wallflowers, though not necessarily all at the same time. To this day the scent of wallflowers recalls to me most unwillingly that garden at 27 Lowth Road.

Dora also assiduously tended my grandmother, and however much could be said against the inside of the house it was always impeccably clean and tidy. She was her mother's support. There was a son, my uncle George, but he was never to be seen, a couple of times only by me, and literally all I can recall about him was that he had curly hair and was a postman, perhaps considered too proletarian to be on visiting terms with my parents.

On the excessively rare occasions when Dora's full name emerged it was not as Dora Lucas but (Mrs) Dora Mackness. She was separated from her husband. Mackness, known as Arthur, was another singer, a member of a concert party called The Roosters, well known for entertaining troops in the Great War. I have no dates for their marriage or separation, though I gathered they were not far apart. My father, who had no time at all for his mother-in-law, used to say that the old lady, missing Dora's services at home, had enticed her back there with colourful fantasies about what Arthur might have been, probably was, up to with all those mademoiselles from

Armentières when he was on tour. I find this more plausible now than I did when I was a young man.

There was certainly something funny about Dora, part of it to do with her mother. A few years ago my psychologist friend, the great Jim Durham, explained to me that the match-saturation and such things were items in a neurotic ritual designed to ensure the continuance of some satisfactory state of affairs, to be on the safe side, rather as the Aztecs would shed a few gallons of blood daily just to make certain the sun rose the following morning as usual. It always had so far and quite possibly the blood had nothing to do with it, but what proper fools they would look if they cut off the blood one fine day and no more days were forthcoming. In the case in question the object of the ritual, so I understood Jim to say, was to guarantee Dora's mother's survival. Leave that match in the ashtray and it just *might* . . .

Dora showed as much concern for her mother's life as could be reasonably demanded when, one night in 1940 or '41, a bomb fell near the house and she threw her body over the old woman's in protection, perhaps sustaining some injury. By this time I was old enough to see as little of those two as I wanted (i.e. zero) and have never heard what Dora did that was too funny to be tolerated and got her put into some institution, much as I should like to. She flourished in this place, putting her cooking skills to use and becoming a trusty in the kitchen. One day the news of her mother's death arrived and from that moment all her neurotic symptoms disappeared for ever, one of those events you can do little with except be mightily struck by it.

Having abruptly ceased to be a lunatic, Dora at the age of perhaps fifty was left with no place in society and nowhere to go. In a scene I should have greatly liked to witness, the hospital authorities, or one of them, pointed out to her that, these things being so, and her usefulness in the kitchen and canteen being substantial, perhaps the necessary paperwork could transfer her to, as it were, the production side. Dora accepted and began to rise in the system. I used to boast to my fellows of having the only mad aunt who had done so well in the asylum that they offered her a fellowship when she graduated.

I saw her once more after many years when she briefly visited me and my parents. She was physically altogether unrecognisable, small, headscarfed, wearing slacks, lively and friendly, and to me most repulsive in a new way. My mother reacted to her first coldly, then with direct hostility. It is not hindsight in me now, nor I hope the

9

pressure of cliché, that leads me to say I saw the emergence of a fraction of the resentment I have mentioned and sense of injured merit running back all those years, saw these things out in the open instead of merely inferring their presence. Such behaviour on my mother's part was most uncharacteristic, as was my father's upbraiding her for it after Dora had hastily left, especially such upbraiding in front of me.

Dora's ascent through the hierarchy of hospital catering continued until she was on the point of taking the top job in that sphere in one of the large London teaching hospitals, Guy's or Bart's, when she suddenly died, like Leslie all too cruelly soon after achieving her freedom. Not much more need be said of those two sad lives, except perhaps that if there is such a thing as progress it will surely have seen to it that these days neither could have turned out as it did.

When not reading *The Prelude* to his grimacing wife or serving gents' suitings at a chain outfitters' off Brixton Hill or playing the piano, my maternal grandfather might be playing the organ at the local chapel, having taught himself this art. The chapel was connected with the Baptist community centred at nearby Denmark Hill, a place probably better known today as the site of the celebrated and capacious Maudsley mental hospital. A tradition I have no reason to quarrel with says my mother and father first met as children in this chapel. No doubt they often met there subsequently but by the time I started taking an interest in such matters that community had long disintegrated. In the intervening decades English Baptists had defected in droves to the established Church. Two of them at least had defected further than that, and my mother and father had abandoned nearly all religious observances by the 1920s, though for a few years my mother liked to go to church at Christmas and on Armistice Day.

Laughably as I once saw it, they considered themselves religious apostates, which meant among other things that they gave me no religious instruction of any kind, although they were perfectly hospitable to what I got at school in that line. My father was determined I should not have any of that chapel stuff 'rammed down my throat', not even offered with gourmet sauce. He also incidentally refrained from ramming instruction in playing the piano, an abstention I have regretted for over fifty years. But – because it has to come in somewhere, and this paragraph may need a bit of livening up – he neither directly nor indirectly offered me any enlightenment at any stage about sex, with the exception of a short course of harangues about what happened, in some detail, to boys who played with themselves. Every ejaculation (though my father put it differently, I am sure) thinned the blood and the victim eventually fell into helpless insanity.

Before you start grinning, reader, if that's what you feel like doing, let me tell you that a chum told me how at his school each class as it approached puberty was taken on a little tour of the supposed masturbation-mania ward of the local mental hospital. I have had no opportunity of checking this story: the date would have been about 1945.

Having raised the question I thought it might be worth doing a little digging into the matter. Masturbation-maniacs belong to the realms of fantasy; schizophrenics, acute depressives and others unfortunately do not. It seems very likely that my chum, who was certainly not pulling my leg about what he thought he had seen, had been shown some of these poor creatures in their ward and had them passed off on him as victims of the dreaded habit. It seems likely too that this treatment was not uncommon, and if you find that hard to believe, reflect that most of you were not educated by men born in Victorian times or immediately after. It is just the sort of thing – isn't it? – that got the Victorians a bad name.

The Bible, or Black Book, of the wanking-kills school was the work of the celebrated William Acton (1813-75), who in the latter year published *The Functions and Disorders of the Reproductive Organs*. When these are misused in the way under discussion, says Acton, the complexion becomes pasty and riddled with acne (nice one!), the growth is stunted, *the blood is thinned*, the sufferer becomes unclean in his person, avoids his fellows and after other untoward experiences becomes blind and helpless. The stoutest – well, heart might be forgiven for quailing after a run-through of these points. Not that my father ever went quite that far.

I was sensible enough not to believe his warnings, which he topped up every so often, but to keep my disbelief to myself. Thereafter I went my own way under a pact of silence and dissimulation. This suited him, who despite his willingness to deliver warnings about madness was instinctively shy about these matters. Apart from the fact of my own existence, no sort of detail of his sexual life ever reached me until very late on. I have often been tempted to think that it was never a very active one, but experience teaches that nothing is likely to fall more wildly astray than this sort of judgement, even as regards contemporaries whom one knows intimately.

If it was silly and perhaps worse of my father to have given me the blood-thinning lectures, it was wrong of him not to have given me any version at all of what he might have called the facts of life. With a good deal of omission that with some justice would outrage a feminist, my working knowledge or stock of shoddily informed part-guesswork about them was in place by the time I was about seven, standard for my era, class, etc., and of course it was picked up from my mates. I see nothing very terrible about that. What was increasingly bloody in my case was that I was never given the all-clear, in other words my parents went on and on not making it all right for me to refer to physical sex or even to let it be seen that I knew about it.

I must have been fourteen when the woman next door made in my hearing some very mild reference to somebody's honeymoon or some such depravity. My mother gave her a fierce (and absurdly visible) shake of the head. This state of affairs gravely impeded parts of social communion with chums' parents and the like. I must have been sixteen before my mother said, 'Well, I suppose by now you know all there is to know about marriage and so on,' and I said, 'Yes, I think so, Mum.' I liked her too much to add, 'but you'd have made my life a good bit easier if you'd said something like that to me about six years ago.'

As I have already implied, sex instruction in the home is often – usually? I don't know – not instruction but a formal permit. But it must be given. I shall never forget the scene when it came to my turn. I swear it began with me hearing my wife saying somewhere out of shot, 'Your father wants to speak to you in his study' – a room big enough, say, to accommodate a full-grown rhinoceros, though without giving him much room to turn round.

Philip and Martin came in, their expressions quite blank, innocent in every possible way that the most expensive film-director could have put there. They were, I suppose, seven and six years old. The short monologue I gave them slipped out of my head afterwards at the first opportunity, though I know I did conscientiously get in a certain amount of what might be called hard anatomy and concrete nouns, although again I must have used the word 'thing' a good deal and talked about Dad planting a seed. Well, what would you? I have never loved and admired them more than for the unruffled calm and seriousness with which they heard me out. I knew they knew, they knew I knew they knew and so on to the end but never mind. They left in a silence that they courteously prolonged until they were out of all hearing. It was a couple of years before Philip confided to me that he had muttered, 'Hold on to your hat – he's going to tell us the big one' as the two made their way to my 'study'. But we did it. In no sphere is it truer that it is necessary to say what it is unnecessary to say.

To return to my father and his attempts to influence my sex-life: the date of his last veto of masturbation is unrecorded, but it must have been before 1939. In that year I became seventeen years old and was fast approaching a far deadlier threat: fornication territory, though like over 95 per cent (I should guess) of my mates I had not yet reached it. But in that year too the war came and whisked me off to Wiltshire as an evacuee schoolboy, soon to be translated to Oxford, not quite so soon, but soon enough, into the army. I am sure my father was sorry to lose my company, but the thought that my sex-life was at last beyond his ken must have softened the blow a little. Peace was shattered, however, by the great adultery explosion.

By a series of implausibilities and coincidences unacceptable in any kind of fiction or drama, reflecting moreover no kind of discredit on my father, he found out I was having an affair with a married woman. As well as really shocking him this put him in a fix. He could not withhold my pocket-money, which now derived from the army paymaster; he could not kick me out of the house, his own house where I was at the time on leave, with my mother, anxious for my company, also within its walls: the guilty woman was over 200 miles away. What he did was write me a letter, a paragraphed 500-worder with all the commas and much else in place: he could read and write. I am heartily glad not to have that letter by me now. I had let him down, he said, and here and there he made me feel I had. (Remember that this was 1943 and I was twenty-one.) More painful was his self-reproach at not having seen to it that my morality had been trained to resist such temptation. 'I'd ask you to give her up,' he said, 'if I thought you'd take the slightest notice,' which daunted me. Then he managed a snobbish insinuation about her and I immediately felt better.

So far it might seem that my father's religious activities were confined to the negative one of not ramming beliefs, etc., and the equally negative one, in a different sense, of preventing me from having a sex-life. (He also objected to the use of the name of Christ

13

as a swear-word – just inaccurate snobbery, really.) But all the Christian morality that went with the doctrine I suppose he thought he had thrown out, or at least kept quiet about, stayed in place: the conscientiousness, the patience, the frugality. He knew this some of the time. With all his theoretical disbelief or unbelief or, at least as likely, simple boredom, it was at the same time totally characteristic that, when plunged into unusually deep despair about my shortcomings, he was likely to put them down to my complete lack of religion. And I should not be truly his son if I had never felt that he had something there. And religion meant behaving like a pious Protestant. Matthew Arnold would have worried less about the survival of Christian ethics in an age without literal faith if he could have had a couple of chats with the old man.

In all this and much else my father was characteristic of his place and time – b. London 1889, d. Cambridge 1963. With Uncle Pres and Uncle Les he attended the City of London School, removed only a year or two ago from its century-old home on the Victoria Embankment. No university – Dadda's meanness, I suspect; instead, a City office. There is a popular theory that we show how strongly we react against a parent as a person by how strongly we dislike or oppose his way of life or occupation. It seems to break down in the present case. I only disliked quite small, fairly separate bits of my father and them not very strongly, not nearly enough to account for the trance of hatred and ennui the term 'City office' arouses in me. Anyway, there will be no more of it here. After a War spent tending airships in Scotland – a cushy one, if you like – he joined Colman's Mustard and stayed until his retirement. Finis.

For parts of the training he pushed my way I can only be heartily grateful. I cannot claim to be more honest and responsible and thrifty and industrious than most people, but I am pretty sure I would be less distinguished in these fields if I had been brought up quite outside the shadow of the chapel. On the other hand, as I came to sense the image in which my father was trying to mould my character and future I began to resist him, and we quarrelled violently at least every week or two for years. It was not, I think, that I was unusually intractable by nature, nor that he took less kindly than most men to having his deeply felt wishes flouted, or at least contested, by somebody he had power over. Certainly, he had embarked on parenthood comparatively late, so that by the time I started noticing that he could be wrong about things he was already in his middle forties and, perhaps, less resilient than earlier. He had not, moreover, re-embarked on parenthood, and this had the common effect of sharpening our conflict.

An only child is short not so much of allies, of potential sup- porters, as of means of dilution and diversion, simply another body to share the parental attention. This isolation may make him over- ready to defend his interests. For my own part, I had acquired from somewhere a very liberal helping of adolescent intellectual's arrogance, while inheriting in full measure my father's obstinacy. The last factor alone was enough to launch us regularly on one or another conversational collision course, immediately recognised as such by both, indeed by all, parties, but not to be deviated from at any price. There must, I suppose, be families where this doesn't happen.

What might very roughly be called art was a reliably productive cause of friction. Art, not a word or a concept my father had much truck with, consisted for him of Gilbert and Sullivan, the Edwardian ballads (virtually none of which ever came my way again) that he and my mother and their friends sang at the piano, West End stage successes in which musical comedies of the Lupino Lane, Leslie Henson/Fred Emney type came to predominate, and detective sto- ries by such as R. Austin Freeman, Francis Grierson and John Rhode from the middle part of the spectrum. This list, admittedly not exhaustive, seemed and seems to me woefully short, especially for somebody by nature neither stupid nor incurious. Anyway, I had my own ideas of what art consisted of.

The art that most reliably provided a domestic *casus belli* was music. This was partly because it was the one for which my father, in his way, a way I had no time for at all at that stage, really cared. He wanted me to like Gilbert and Sullivan and took me to *The Pirates of Penzance* and *The Yeomen of the Guard*; I meanly exaggerated my boredom. He tried to get me interested in those ballads; I disparaged their lyrics and wanted to know why there was no Schubert or Wolf (Wolf! Was I mad or just trendy?) under the lid of the piano-stool. I would go on to accuse him of not really liking music, to which he would retort, with annoying relevance, that that would come better from someone who, like him, could play some of the stuff. But a more important irritant was the nature of music itself. If I chose to frowst away a fine afternoon in an art gallery or to ruin my eyes over a book when I could have been out in the fresh air (working off the impulse to masturbate), then that – at any rate in my father's more tolerant moods – was up to me. Music kicked up a row, and

I really could not expect to have the damned wireless or gramophone blaring through the house all the hours there were and upsetting my mother. Especially that sort of music . . .

Actually it was most sorts. My father's catholic distaste ranged from Haydn to Troise and his Mandoliers, from Benny Goodman to Borodin. He was not content with just registering objection in each case: he would deliver a critical verdict, often in the form of an analogy. There was a piece of Duke Ellington's, for instance, I think from the *Black, Brown and Beige* suite – anyway, something about as far from primitivism as jazz had then got – which put my father in mind, or so he said, of a lot of savages dancing round a pot of human remains. *The Swan of Tuonela*, on the other hand, called up successive images of a small animal in pain and a large animal in pain. Perhaps it was the element of horrible truth in this which prevented me from seeing how funny it was and made me come up, as I surely must have done, with one of my blanket charges of dislike of all music.

These and a great many other problems might have been solved in a different kind of household and house and neighbourhood. Norbury, S.W.16 is not a place. When in the early part of the century the railways started building from London to the southern and south coast towns they put a station down every few miles, on the reasoning of various entrepreneurs that such places would form centres for the new population that would be coming to work in London and that houses, shops and so on would grow up round them. This proved correct. Norbury was one of the most isolated of these. It had to have a name, so that of Norbury Manor, somebody's not-all-that-nearby country house, was hung on it. Two-up-and-two-down by the hundreds of yards was the rule, and shops along the High Street (or 'main road'). No rubbish about roots for Norbury. (Stanley goes on a bit about this in my novel *Stanley and the Women* (part 2), though he recognises that absence of roots has its advantages. So do I.) The partition walls of no. 16 Buckingham Gardens were not specially thick, and most sounds went through them. And the room where one was in the evenings was naturally the one with the wireless in it.

Those who have grown up with the BBC Third Programme and Radio 3 might find it difficult to imagine how little music was broadcast in the Thirties. One would go months without a chance to hear individual works in even the standard repertoire. So I would very much want to listen to Brahms's Second Symphony any time it was available, and my father, after a day at the office and getting on for an hour's journey home, would very much not. And there we were.

The smallness of the house and of its successors was made mildly claustrophobic at times by my father's constant concern to stop me getting away from him, in several senses of the phrase. He and my mother could not have restricted my choice of friends, and my chances of seeing them, more unflaggingly if there had been a long family history of male prostitution or juvenile dipsomania. When I was at home, as when not at school I usually was, I kept finding that reading in public was deemed rude, while reading in private was anti-social. There was a thing called joining in the family circle that has left me with a lifelong non-enjoyment of sitting over the remains of a meal. This pattern persisted. Whenever, after my marriage, my family and I visited my parents or they came to stay, everything had to be done with everybody present: no recipe for getting the best out of people.

As if we had not had enough on our plates already, my father and I came to differ about politics. But I need spend no time on that: he was an ex-Liberal of the Lloyd George denomination who went Tory after the Great War and for years was active in his constituency and in the local Ratepayers' Association. I was a bloody little fool of a leftie who went on being one not only after asking 'What would happen if somebody voted against Stalin?' and being given the answer 'But who would ever want to?' but after deciding that that answer would not do. I often wonder what the old Dad would make of me if he could hear me holding forth about, say, the *Observer* in 1990.

What my father had wanted me to be was, of course, a version of William Robert Amis, a more successful version, not by any means least as a player of games. He was very much one himself in his sphere: he looked it with his medium height, stocky frame and some breadth of shoulder. If he had a passion it was not above all for Gilbert and Sullivan but for tennis and cricket. The former he played vigorously well into middle age; he knocked the Boys all over the field when they played the Parents at cricket and actively skippered the local side in his sixties. To the end he batted like a stylist, with a late cut I have never seen surpassed, and club cricket was good in those days. He wanted me to excel him and paid for individual coaching, quite an outlay for one in his position, and did his best to get me a trial for Surrey. But to his manfully concealed disappointment it came to nothing: my eye, especially my right eye, or perhaps just I, was no good.

And in my career too I was to have been a more successful version of him, for he got no further than a senior clerk's responsibilities and pay with the horrible mustard people, and considered himself a failure. He was never bitter about this, but meant to see to it that I had a better chance than he. Here he did the trick at considerable financial cost: scholarships notwithstanding, he had to go on supporting me and being deprived of a youth's earning capacity. At this point I will avail myself of a chance of confessing to a minor but contemptible lie I used until recently to tell, describing myself as a 'scholarship boy' all the way up the ladder. Well, actually Dad paid for my first year at the City of London School, gambling successfully that I would get a scholarship in the year that followed. That sounds a small thing but, as at least I had the grace to see from the beginning, it wasn't really. It would have been much out of character if, while showing pride and pleasure (and some incomprehension) at my first success as a writer, he should not have warned me that I must not make the mistake of thinking I could actually support myself and family in this fashion. Good advice as things were then.

Boredom, I am sorry to say, came to be my chief reaction to my father's company, though I did not want to feel like this and grew better at hiding it – I hope. As ageing people (among others) will, he would recount and reminisce without relevance: cricket, the City (oh God), friends he had made since I left home, a chap in the pub, a chap in the train. I am sure he on his side was not much entertained when, on request, I would tell him of my doings in a world as alien to him as that of commerce was to me. It is depressing to think how persistently dull and egotistical we can be to those we most value, and how restless and peevish we get when they do it back to us.

But this would be the wrong note on which to end this movement. The era of the quarrels was also, not surprisingly, the time of greatest intimacy. In those years my father would exploit a talent for physical clowning and mimicry that made him, on his day, one of the funniest men I have known. Every story called for the full deployment of facial, vocal and bodily resources, and was conscientiously acted out. My mother used the same techniques, so that at one stage I thought they were standard in anecdote-telling, and to this day find something lacking when they are not used. It is in mid-story that I see my father most clearly, quite a dapper figure in one of his grey or light-brown lounge suits (though he never could tie a tie properly), hobbling across the room in the style of some decrepit director of the firm, or forcing his face into lines of disquietingly silly uncouthness as he became the man next door.

I have said that my mother was by common consent an attractive woman. She was a great hit as the Empress of Abyssinia in what was probably 1936 or 1937 at the local Mock Lord Mayor's Banquet, an annual event staged by the constituency Conservative Association. (In ridiculous costume I had carried the Mace.) My father was an even greater hit, or at least made more noise, as Haile Selassie. He had a rowdy, babyish streak in him which caused him, when perfectly sober, to pretend to be a foreigner or deaf in trains and pubs. Looking back now, I think I see his own father in that idiosyncrasy.

Though she had plenty to say for herself, my mother was a quieter person in all ways. She was gentle, timid, suffering from 'nerves' in a way that Dora did not, with a heart weakness that killed her at sixty-six. My father and I used to laugh at her for her superstition, which was of the straightforward unlucky-thirteen-broken-mirrors-spilt-salt variety, including rare specimens like having to sit down for a moment if you returned to the house just after leaving it. I laughed on the other side of my face when I found by degrees that I had inherited this trait from her in a sort of novelettish form, causing horrible sentences like 'It was on the very morning that he received news of the Award that the agonising, incapacitating disease showed its first unmistakable sign' to come swimming into my head from nowhere at any hour of day or night. Give me magpies by the dozen instead.

Like most mothers of that time, mine was determined that the family should be 'regular', which meant she was in charge of the laxative department. The various ones we had to swallow illustrated to perfection the supposedly very English idea that, if something was really going to do you good, it must taste horrible: senna 'tea', California syrup of figs, worst of all Gregory powders. These last were rendered not much less horrible by being smeared with blackcurrant jam, a preserve I have avoided ever since. I cannot avoid the feeling that my recent mild trouble in the relevant area could be traced back to the aperient period.

My mother took what I still think was an excessively close interest in my general health and condition. Hilarious as it must seem to anybody who has set eyes on me in the last ten years or so, I was a thin little boy with a naturally small appetite. It worried my mother that she could see my breast-bone when I was stripped. She called in the nice old family doctor, who examined my fingernails, something I was reluctant to let him do, since I was biting them fiercely in those days. I was to discover later that the presence of white spots on or under the nail was supposed to indicate malnutrition. Dr Pringle evidently found none in my case and pronounced me 'a well-nourished child'.

This was not enough for Mum. She tried to beef me up with stuff like Parrish's Chemical Food, a fearful reddish liquid which was supposed to turn your teeth black unless you bypassed them by sucking it through a straw. More directly, she would sit opposite me at the dinner-table pushing forkful after forkful of food into my mouth, not an ideal way of encouraging the appetite – for solids, that is. Here again I feel I can spot a contributory cause of later developments. When I seemed too old for force-feeding I was allowed to eat what I could of what was in front of me with merely verbal encouragement. A custom developed whereby after some minutes I would say plaintively, 'Mum, would you sort it for me?' and she would divide the unconsumed portion into what I was allowed to leave and what I *must* eat. Oh dear. The thought of it makes me quail even now, and no waiter can hope for my friendship if he draws attention to my less-than-empty plate. But my mother was too obviously concerned for my welfare, too gentle, to arouse my resentment, only my fervent wish to get the meal over somehow.

It must be as true of my parents as it would be of any other married couple to say that neither ever 'looked at' another person of the opposite sex, and our circumstances made it most unlikely that any such thing could have happened without my having seen something of it. Nevertheless when I was about ten there was a mysterious priest called Steinmitz, also known, no less mysteriously, as Plunks, who seemed to be looking at my mother all right. He was always hanging round the place for no stated reason, bulky in clerical black, protuberant of eye and, according to the juvenile me, smelling of dirty apples, which I soon afterwards deduced meant drink. In a novel one could hardly have avoided making something of him, starting with his names. And what was a priest, a *Roman* priest, doing near my parents?

Later there was Uncle Tommy (no actual relative), a tall, handsome, entertaining Novocastrian with what seemed to me an impossibly elderly wife, jolly enough old girl as she was, known openly and appropriately as Fats. Tommy was always turning up unexpectedly and without Fats. Once he turned up as far away from S.W.16 as East Runton, the resort on the Norfolk coast where my parents and I were holidaying, typically allowing himself to be glimpsed as if by chance in the middle distance in the high street rather than approaching direct. The least absurdly inappropriate term for his relationship with my mother is perhaps that he was an admirer of hers, but the term quite fails to suggest the semi-detached, morning-coffee, 8.5 to Blackfriars, dinner-dance, carless and, by modern standards, almost drinkless world in which (I am quite sure) Uncle Tommy altogether refrained from laying a finger on my mother. No scope there for a sensitive study from me as a 'remembering' adult about anything in the hopeless inarticulate passion line. And just as well: children have no understanding of adults' lives and are not interested in them as such, and there is always something forced or false about their 'recollections' of such things. Or there would be if my kind of novelist tried it.

Much more importantly, Uncle Tommy brought me a Mars bar whenever he turned up. He also took in a literary review of the Jack-Squire-Jack-Priestley persuasion called *John o' London's Weekly* (which faded away in the Sixties) and owned what seemed to me a lot of books. One or two of them were in the Tauchnitz edition, a Continental imprint specialising in stuff considered too dirty by British publishers. I at once and regretfully established that *Lady Chatterley's Lover* was not among them, but that a then almost equally illustrious monument of supposed filth, Aldous Huxley's *Point Counterpoint*, was – in two volumes. Perhaps the greatest literary disappointment I have ever suffered was settling down with it for a whole uninterrupted afternoon of what I confidently foresaw as a banquet of obscenity, only to realise after not very long that the stuff was about as arousing as the *Magnet*, a number of which I hope I had had the sagacity to hold in reserve. Huxley's book was grown-up *in the wrong way*, never getting to the point. I have not looked at it since.

But I have digressed. Though a great jam-making, cricket-tea-preparing figure, my mother continued all her life as inveterate a reader as I was in my youth: a book was as much part of her accoutrements at home as handbag and knitting: no classics, but no 'slop' either – the names of Norah C. James and Ann Bridge come to mind. (Philip Larkin passed on a recommendation or two here.) This is probably quite unconnected with my own choice of vocation. But Mum probably did as much as anybody to set me going, though in other ways, not producing a sibling for me, restricting my choice of companions, having had a father with a literary bent, suggesting on rainy afternoons when I had no book or comic to read – quite innocently and without premeditation, I am sure – that I should do a bit of writing. She was a jolly little woman for all her 'nerves' and shortness of breath, fond of a giggle, a fag, a gin and tonic (no more than a couple) and, I am sorry to record, an occasional glass of Empire wine, Keystone or Big Tree, for the 'iron' in it. But she was more than that. It was that gentle creature who, when I rendered my first wife pregnant before our marriage, told my father not to be such a fool with his threats of excommunication and persuaded my future parents-in-law not to boycott the ceremony as they had been intending – the first of the appallingly long line of figures in my life whom I have come to value altogether more highly, to appreciate the uniqueness of, now they are gone.

She went in 1957, falling down dead of a first stroke. When Hilly and I went to the little house in Shrublands Avenue, Berkhamsted, it seemed outlandish, bizarre, to find Dad standing there by himself. 'Why did it have to happen?' he asked more than once, and got no answer. Afterwards, now retired, he came to live with us in Swansea. Of course he did. And of course we took him with us on our 1958-59 trip to America. He enjoyed himself there, but there was nothing for him to do in Swansea and, although he had often visited us there with my mother, he knew virtually nobody of his own generation. I stood by helplessly as he tried to construct an independent morning for himself, walking or taking the bus into the centre, buying the *Daily Telegraph* and doing as much as he could of its crossword in a coffee-shop, going to a pub for a single and solitary glass of light ale, then back to the house for lunch, after which he was glaringly at a loose end. He put up with this régime for a while before, saying he must find himself some sort of job, he took off for London.

The job he found himself was with a firm that made or sold domestic cleaning stuff like brushes and dusters, a come-down but better than idleness. He also found himself a couple of lady friends and, for him, was quite forthcoming about his relations with at any rate the first of them. I shall never forget the diffident pride with which he said to me,

'She's quite attractive, you know, to me at least. A good bit younger than me, of course. Well, a thing like that, when you get to my age, you wonder. Anyway, I wondered. But then . . . actually . . . well . . . yes!'

This was pleasing and touching. But his days were numbered by then. He developed what he thought, or said he thought, was an ulcer but turned out to be an inoperable cancer. The end came quickly: on 25th March 1963 he wrote me a cheerful letter in his customary neat and attractive hand, thanking me for getting him into a nursing-home in Cambridge, where I was still teaching at the university. On 18th April he died, leaving all his possessions, such as they were, to one of the lady friends, who refused to let any of them go, even claiming back the watch and wallet Hilly had passed on to Philip and Martin. So I have nothing of his but that last letter, and nothing of my mother's at all.

SCHOOLS

WHAT MAKES MANY children resemble little madmen is, as with the full-sized kind, not knowing what they may do next. They may look roughly like you and me or even perhaps nicer, give no untoward sign, but what are they thinking? My first impression of school is of far more children than I had ever seen before gathered into one place, all moving about and all shouting at the tops of their voices. The place was the playground of St Hilda's School (or quite likely 'College', to announce bourgeois respectability), surrounded by an impenetrable shrubbery.

'They [Mum and Dad] didn't say it was going to be like this,' I whimpered to myself as, wild-eyed or staring into vacancy, boys pelted or lumbered to and fro on unrevealed purposes. I wailed to one who seemed less intractable than the rest, 'Will you be my chum?' To this he responded by biting me in the arm, or that may have been the frowning fellow at his side. Then some fat old lady rang a hand-bell and, like a preview of part of an American prison movie, the inmates slouched into rough lines, muttering to themselves and still flashing wild glances to and fro.

That first plunge into school cannot really have been as bad as that, but it was as bewildering. There were girls at the place too, some of them big girls, while all the boys were little. By degrees I recovered from my nervousness and dislike. Nevertheless one does rather go through life constantly suffering from unpreparedness for how awful things are going to be, starting with human nature. I stayed at St Hilda's only a short time and made no friends. I remember none of my fellow-pupils except for a girl, one of the big ones, called Freda Roberts, and that only because she was once famously heard to fart. Among the mistresses Miss Crampton said 'le shat, the cat' as often as if for a bet, and I could not understand why some of my classmates seemed to be suppressing laughter at this. I fell in love with Miss Barr, whom I see now as a tall, Eton-cropped figure of improbable elegance. She took English, and it is here, perhaps, that we can date my first devotion to the glories of our literature.

Norbury College, a secondary school now utterly vanished, was just up the road. It was a biggish house with sheds, quite substantial sheds, built on as classrooms. It only ever had two famous alumni: me, and Derek Bentley, who was hanged on very dodgy grounds for his part in a famous murder of the 1950s. He would not have learnt the use of violence at the College, which was one of the most peaceable places I have ever known. There was an occasional fight in the playground – fists only, of course – but that may have been largely because what you do in playgrounds is fight, on the similar principle, seen more recently, that if you build a youth centre youths will come and riot at it: no centre, no rioting. And in any case it is really only quite small boys who behave like little madmen. By seven or eight they are usually tractable if not tamed, or so it was in those days. Further, at this sort of local day school the masters were much more important in one's life than the other boys, who were to be encountered uncurbed only for a few minutes at a time before and between long bursts of teaching, especially if you went home for lunch as I did. In those few minutes one might have picked up the odd bit of information or misinformation about sex or, of course, had a fight, but social life was lived almost entirely outside school.

I found my masters at Norbury College interesting enough. They included two unrelated Messrs Waller. 'Little' Mr Waller, who had a squeaky voice caused he said by too much choral singing as a boy, taught maths and got me interested, especially in algebra. For a short time, until literature took me over, I thought I might be a mathematician. 'Big' Mr Waller did little to speed the transition. He was supposed to teach us English, but found things like parsing and sentence-analysis disagreeable. He preferred reading books out to us and so did we. They were about the Great War ('I've copped it in the back, sir') or lethal espionage in Eastern Europe ('For God's sake shoot me and have done with it'). But I could get all that at home.

Big Mr Waller left after a time and Mr Ashley replaced him, a younger man with a direct eye who cared about poetry, including what was then fairly modern poetry (the Georgians), and made us write essays about things like Beauty. He made us write poetry, too. One such assignment was a poem in blank verse about the miracle of Santa Sophia at Constantinople. Mine was ninety-nine lines long and Mr Ashley said it was the best. For years afterwards I patronised him in retrospect and have only quite recently seen what I owe him for having helped to get me started. He was properly sarcastic about my first published work of fiction, a 300-word story called 'The Sacred Rhino of Uganda', when it came out in the school magazine. In it, a certain Captain Hartly [sic], evidently less well up in local lore than a 'veteran hunter' had any right to be, shot the rhino and was instantly set upon by some 'native worshippers' it had. He got away with his life, I forget how, but in that wordage surely a straightforward matter. These events were recounted in some taut impressionistic prose on which Mr Ashley was particularly hard: 'He clutches at his side . . . pitches forward . . . unconscious . . .' With this the initial, experimental period of my writing came to an end.

In 1934 I appeared at the City of London School, which my father and two uncles had likewise attended. It then occupied a large, rather oppressively dignified building on the Victoria Embankment. It had lots of corridors and a vast agoraphobic playground filled with self-possessed boys in black coats and striped trousers. At this time I was an undersized, law-abiding, timid person. Fear made me vomit on the first few mornings, but I quickly found that this was excessive. Nobody ever used me unkindly, except perhaps King (Science III), who at tuck-shop time every morning would greet me with 'Hallo, Curly' and ruffle my hair, which I currently wore in two brilliantined flaps. His bearing, the tone of his voice and the redness of his own hair quenched any thoughts of resistance. I was soon reconciled, however, and began to be fascinated by the vast free entertainment that school life usually represents and the social possibilities it offers, or offered at CLS. My fellows, I saw dimly, were drawn from a wide spectrum: accents varied from ones that discomforted me to ones that made me feel superior. But example at once taught me to put such attitudes aside. To be accepted you had only to be amiable; to be liked you needed pre-eminently to be able to raise the occasional laugh – but here the most vapid clowning served as well as wit. Like life, really.

Efficient mimics of the staff were especially highly regarded. I developed an imitation of the headmaster: 'Get it right, not wrong. Black, not white. Cat, not dog.' This measure had the double advantage of securing esteem from classmates and providing a counterpoise to the terrified veneration I felt for my original. For this was

26

the great F. R. Dale, a classical scholar in the best old style. To hear him read Greek verse, observing tonic accent, metrical ictus and the run of the meaning all at once, was to be given a distant view of some ideal beauty as well as to marvel at a virtuoso. When the BBC in due time wanted someone to read Homer aloud on the Third Programme, they chose him. He was human, too. If ever a kind of man vanished for good, his did.

As at every school one ever hears about, the masters were imitable eccentrics almost to a man. This can only partly be put down to the stylising effects teaching has on behaviour. What is also at work in this situation is the nature of the observer. To the pre-pubertal eye all grown-up behaviour is so fantastic as to defeat discrimination; the youth in his last year or two at school is already taking out naturalisation papers for the adult world. It is the boy in his earlier teens who sees that world with the delighted, faintly hostile astonishment of the tourist, who is entertained to the limits of endurance by its quaint tribal customs, its grotesque ritual dances, its capering, scowling, gesticulating witch-doctors. And if he later becomes a novelist he must strive to recapture, not indeed the undifferentiating vision of childhood, but the adolescent's coldly wondering stare. Not that that will be enough on its own.

However that may be, I shall never forget Mr Marsh sucking the earpiece of his glasses (you could borrow Auden and MacNeice off him, but I made nothing of them at that time, 1936-37), or Mr Penn accusing us all of having eaten his biscuits (there was to be rejoicing later when the locals among whom we had been evacuated took him for a German spy purely on the strength of his appearance and manner), or Mr Carruthers's imperturbability when Rumsey and I dropped from shoulder-height the suitcase full of broken glass – a long-treasured riot-mechanism – at the back of the room. I remember these things not as facts, but as little mental films with a complete set of sound-effects. The most noteworthy figure of all, I realise now, was Mr Copping, who played (one at a time) the flute and the double-bass, who spoke with an Attic Greek accent of the fifth century, who once captivated us all by replying with incomparable, table-turning deftness to a disingenuous question from Rigden about castration: 'I don't know whether any of you have ever been to a horse-fair,' the answer led off – I can hear those Periclean tones now. As I do so I marvel at the way the 1938 version of Mr Copping still seems older than the 1990 version of me, a trick of time which will no doubt always keep its hold.

27

But the man who actually taught me most, about English literature among other things, was the Rev. C. J. Ellingham. At that time two years were allotted for preparation for the long-vanished School Certificate; Mr Ellingham was confident that his part of the syllabus could be covered in one, and illicitly used the other to see that we did not remain totally ignorant of classical music, painting, and English poetry outside the official courses. Most of the poetry was of then recent years, though Mr Marsh's favourites were stopped short of. I had already discovered Housman for myself by the time in question, but Mr Ellingham gave me a profound and necessary shock by announcing that Housman was his favourite poet – this from a very unequivocal Christian: so I saw for ever that a poem is not a statement and the poet 'affirmeth nothing'. Not long afterwards I came to share Mr Ellingham's preference and eventually retain it even in face of Larkin's work.

In retrospect, I see that the Ellingham taste was not infallible. On one occasion he read us a dreadful piece of goo by the (I hope) now long-forgotten Richard Middleton from the 1920s, sincerely felt, no doubt:

> Man proposes, God in His time disposes,
>   And so I wander'd [sic] up to where you lay,
> A little rose among the little roses,
>   And no more dead than they.
>
> It seemed your childish feet were tired of straying,
>   You did not greet me from your flower-strewn bed,
> Yet still I knew that you were only playing –
>   Playing at being dead. (etc.)

and evidently expected us to admire it ('On a Dead Child'). I hope I wondered about it even then but cannot be sure.

A full account of Mr Ellingham would have to take note of the hint of rebellion against the divine will in this poem (line 1) also visible in the greater part of Housman's work. Other things besides. He was an admirer of the then much-admired *Seven Pillars of Wisdom* of T. E. Lawrence, lending me his copy with great precaution of brown-paper wrapping, etc. I decided after a brief inspection, being even more humble by nature then than I am now, that I was not well-read or clever enough to appreciate this work, whereas I have long since those days decided that it is a piece of pretentious

28

bullshit. On the other hand, Mr Ellingham was perhaps the very first to expose the mistranslations and illiteracies in Ezra Pound's 'adaptations' from Latin. He lent me and I found most readable an off-print of an article of his on the subject, but I have never been able to trace it.

I have sometimes suspected that Mr Ellingham did not greatly care for me. He saw through my affectations, found unconvincing my excuse for not playing games much (the school sports ground was at Grove Park, a horrible dog-leg journey from the parental home in those pre-car days), considered, probably rightly, that I pulled less than my weight in the primitive cottage half a dozen of us were to share when the school was evacuated to Wiltshire in 1939. But he knew I was clever, thought I might be some good some day and helped in more ways than he knew about. I never thanked him, but people never do, do they? Not properly.

My education, pursued with some obduracy by the masters, was filled out and humanised by the other boys. From Moses I learnt about Fats Waller and Charles Morgan; from Bateman, air-pistols and the dating of girls; from Lightfoot, Borodin and Rimsky-Korsakov; from Williams-Ashman, upper-middle-class life, comprising the possession of actual pictures (not reproductions) by living artists, the voluntary reading of *The Oxford Book of French Verse* and the notion of foreign travel. But at this distance it is people like Wybrow that I recall most vividly; Wybrow, that great rampager and iconoclast, loping through the cloisters with one hand ready to dart out in assault, the other clutched inward for defence, his whole being permanently gathered for the delivery of a jeering guffaw, his ravaged face and elbowing, shoving demeanour an advertisement of instinctive revolt. He treated me tolerantly enough and got into the habit of yelling 'Hiya, Sergeant Delius' when I appeared, in dual allusion to my OTC rank and my imitation of the composer 'three months before the end' – a popular request-item at that time. Whenever I remember Wybrow I am saddened at the thought of all that pulsating violence going to waste in commerce or trade, instead of enlivening the cultural pages of a Sunday newspaper. I suppose I envied him his air of being completely his own man.

At the age of fourteen, like everyone else, I was drafted into what I had nowadays better spell out as the Officers' Training Corps. (A despised minority of pacifists and other freaks was allowed to opt for the Boy Scouts.) We put on uniform twice a week; we drilled; we did weapon training; we went on field-days and a couple of weeks' camp in the summer; we went to a rifle-range; we even had a miniature range of our own in which we fired .22″ rounds out of .303″ rifles – I was good at that, becoming a First-Class Shot. There was a great occasion when a contingent from the school marched in the Lord Mayor's Show. For quite some time I thought that if I failed to become a writer I would go into the army. (Even in later years, or at least up to 1980 when I published my novel *Russian Hide-and-Seek*, the military life continued to cast something of a spell.)

The only fly in the OTC ointment, in fact two flies in one, was the Regimental Sergeant-Major. This was a man in his forties, I suppose, who had presumably been a long-serving warrant officer or NCO. He was intelligent, witty and an anti-semite. This last did not make him popular. Once I was standing next to my friend Richenberg in the front rank of some squad or other when the RSM strolled by. At that moment Richenberg was guilty of something appalling like having an epaulette-button undone. The RSM stopped in front of him.

'What's your name, boy?' – though he knew perfectly well.

'Richenberg, sir.'

'What's your religion?'

'Jewish, sir.'

I find it hard to describe what happened at that; I suppose there is no such thing as an audible hush or a silent intake of breath, but it was as if every Gentile in hearing turned white. Whatever it was, the RSM caught it and had the sense to pass on. Nobody at the school had told me not to behave in the sort of way he had; I just knew, like everyone else.

The RSM's other fly-like aspect was that of being a wildly flaunting homosexual. I have no idea what kind of success he had, nor where he had it, if any – the armoury, among the racks of SMLE rifles? In the miniature range? A mystery of more general interest is why nobody ever grasses on these people – they never did in those days, at least. Or nearly never. There was a maths master who shared the RSM's tastes. His procedures were remarkably direct. At that school each boy had a large individual desk at which two could sit if they squeezed up, which was quite legitimately done when a master was, say, helping a boy with some written work. This master would help boys towards a different end, all the way and on the spot, so to speak. Then one afternoon the porter summoned him in mid-class to the headmaster and he was never seen again. He had an unusual name and I saw his obituary only a couple of years ago, commemorating a distinguished career in some branch of theoretical physics. Naturally I looked with interest for details of his activities before he launched himself on that career and came upon only a sentence that began, 'Finding that schoolteaching was not his métier, he . . .' Good old CLS.

I moved into the sixth form, which meant I could use the front entrance on the Embankment, go out to lunch at the Lyons' near Blackfriars Bridge, and be harangued slightly by Mr Copping, in his aspect as my junior housemaster, for hardly ever turning up at the sports ground. I explained about the difficulties of access and that went down all right, Mr Copping himself being no great devotee of the leather. Nobody else cared whether I so much as looked at a football, 'houses' at such day-schools being nothing more than lists of names with which team games within the school can be organised. I used the time so saved to establish that certain avocations and interests were not for me: I had no graphic gift of any kind, the theatre was boring (though the cinema was not), you could keep Dadaism and all that, architecture ought to be comprehensively done away with.

I also wrote a bit of poetry; a long thing called 'Prelude' was foisted on the magazine editor. It was a kind of suburbanite's *Waste Land* tizzied up with bits of Wilde. Shorter pieces, of appalling pretentiousness and affectation, soon followed, including a prose 'poem' that drew Mr Ellingham's proper contempt. In the same issue there was a story about the war in Spain by the secretary of the school branch of the League of Nations Union. I joined this organisation. Meetings were held in concert with the City of London School for Girls.

It was a great surprise when, in the summer of 1939, one or two people suggested to me that there might be going to be a war with Germany. I had not had time to think this over when we were abruptly evacuated to Marlborough. The haversack rations in the train were delicious, far better than those we had got used to on OTC field days. Out of the window, everything began to look very countrified and was still looking it as we drew into Marlborough, which turned out to be in Wiltshire. Accommodation was hastily organised: billets in the town for the majority, barns with army-type beds in them for a select band that included me. During the next few days I ate about twenty tins of sweetened condensed milk, the discarded residue of my companions' train rations. They seemed to find this an odd thing to do on my part.

My appetite sharpened by the country air, I also ate a good deal in the dining-hall of Marlborough College, an institution few of us had previously had cause to know about. After one such meal, at which the sixth-formers had acted as waiters (in anticipation of Christmas Day in the army), I was standing talking to Richenberg near the front gate of the college. A fifth-former called Horwood, whom we both knew slightly, came over to us.

'You've heard, have you?' he asked. 'He's taken Danzig and bombed Warsaw.'

'Are you sure?'

'Just came over the wireless. I got it off one of the cooks.'

After a moment, Richenberg said, 'Well, anyway, I should imagine we've got a fair chance of beating him.'

'A fair chance?' I was puzzled. 'We'll wipe him up.'

They both looked at me. 'They reckon his air force is pretty hot,' said Horwood. 'And his tanks.'

'Well, we've got an air force and tanks, haven't we?'

'Not like he's got, according to what I read.'

'The Polish army isn't mechanised,' said Richenberg.

'But we've been sending them stuff for months now.'

'We haven't got enough stuff for ourselves.'

'Oh, nonsense,' I said.

One of them changed the subject, probably to what school life might henceforth be like, a question, with its attachments of home-sickness and selfish anxiety, that interested me more than our military supplies to Poland. At the time, the colloquy I have tried to re-create did not have on me the effect it should have had. I did not reflect that Horwood, a boy with no pretensions to being 'well informed', might be considered to have shown me up as naïve and complacent. Nor did I sneer retrospectively at those of my parents' friends who knew people at the office who had got chatting in the train to chaps who had been told confidentially by someone in the know that Germany's economy would not stand a sixth-months' war, or who had been drinking at the golf club with a fellow whose brother-in-law had driven his car into – guess what? – a cardboard tank on a road near Hamburg. But, after all, the Poles, not to mention the French, were at the moment still in the field.

With commendable speed, the City of London School tackled the dual task of turning itself into a boarding-school and using the same classrooms, sports fields and courts, chapel, sanatorium and goodness knows what else as another boarding-school already in occupation. None of the masters showed signs of the appalling extra burden of work, replete with boredom and irritation, they must have had to shoulder. The boys, at any rate, were happy as the result of novel surroundings, welcoming and indulgent treatment from their billet landladies and a whole new world of illegality to explore. They received little comfort or friendliness from the Marlborough College boys, who remained, apart from some contact between squash champions and the like, entirely aloof.

The unlooked-for descent of five or six hundred London day-boys, many of them noisy and tatterdemalion, was no gift from the gods, but after a time some host-like gestures, in the form of joint debates or even individual invitations to tea, might reasonably have been expected. None were made to my knowledge in the five terms I was at school in Marlborough. During that period I spent two minutes in conversation with Marlborough boys; they were acquainted with Richenberg, now captain of the school. When I look back on that whole situation, it seems to me very surprising, and I would give a lot to be able to see, in retrospect, the figure of Wybrow ranging contumeliously across the front court of the college, kicking a Marlborough prefect's rolled umbrella out of his hand or jostling an important parent at the gate. But he had left us before we moved.

These reflections, like so many others, did not occur to me at the time. I was busy finding out that organised games, even if approached late in life, were enjoyable and could be fitted plausibly enough into a mode of existence that also included Mozart and Louis Armstrong. I joined the chapel choir, and singing in four-part harmony soon revealed itself as the apex of non-sensual pleasures, one I have been able to obtain too rarely since leaving school. The rural attractions were tremendous, imparting a kind of zest to adolescent melancholy, and for many years my every attempt to visualise a generic country scene would call up some image of Marlborough. The barn where I ate all the condensed milk was soon evacuated; five of us, under the wardenship of Mr Ellingham, were established in a small cottage on the Bath road. Heated only by the living-room fire, it was the coldest building I have ever lived in, far worse than anything in the army, and this in the winter of 1940-41.

One night at least in the bedroom I shared with Richenberg the urine froze in the chamber-pot.

But there were recompenses. Conversations took place with Richenberg and Rose, not to speak of the great Ellingham himself, that afforded an optimistic preview of the university. It was in this direction that our lives were now bending themselves, and there, in due course, we eventually departed, my two companions going into residence in October 1940, myself in the following April. I was delayed, I would have pleaded, by having switched from Classics to English.

And there, for a long time, I would have been content to leave the matter. Not now. However dull it may sound to the uninitiated, I have to put it in the record that, with things as they then stood, I could have walked into a medium-grade classical scholarship, of which there were plenty at Oxford and Cambridge. There were then, my memory says, just two awards in English at Cambridge and two more at Oxford, a scholarship at Christ Church and an exhibition at St John's. After heaven knows how much special provision, extra work, and breaking precedent for me at CLS, my foolhardy wishes were accommodated and I was put forward in English. (I like to think that Mr Ellingham had something to do with that decision.) I got the exhibition at St John's. I cannot in this space explain what I owe to the school for letting me, against its better judgement, have my way, but it is large, and ever since I have been a little hard on anyone who might try to attack the 'inflexibility', 'dogmatism', etc., of the English educational system, as it was then and for so many years.

'Life at a large day-school in a large city,' I once wrote, 'embodies a freedom which I should guess to be unique, a freedom based on heterogeneity. Where there is no [social] orthodoxy there can be no conformity and no intolerance. This was certainly true of the City of London School. I have never in my life known a community where factions of any kind were less in evidence, where differences of class, upbringing, income group and religion counted for so little. In particular, although perhaps fifteen per cent of the boys were Jewish, not a single instance of even the mildest anti-semitism [with the exception noted earlier] came to my attention in the seven years I was a pupil there. The academic teaching was of a standard not easily to be surpassed, but more important still was that lesson about how to regard one's fellows, a lesson not delivered but enacted. Thanks indeed for that.'

SCHOOLS

I wrote the above in 1958 about the period 1934-41. I wonder, merely wonder, how much of it is still true of the School at its new home in Queen Victoria Street.

OXFORD

I WENT UP to Oxford in the spring of 1941 in impeccably proletarian style, being driven over from my parents' house in Berkhamsted by the family butcher in his battered Morris, and approaching the wrong way up Plough Lane. I had only visited the city once before in my life, to sit for and win an exhibition – a kind of cut-price scholarship – at St John's College. Coming as I did from a comparatively lowly school, I was allotted a nasty little pair of rooms in the top corner of the front quad. There was a sitting-room about big enough to throw a party for six, and a bedroom with a bed, a cupboard and a wash-stand in it. I knew nobody in the college and, scattered round the other colleges, fewer than a dozen 'men' (as they had now become) whom I had known at school. They very soon and decently threw a sherry party for me.

Having virtually never drunk anything stronger than beer before, I was not really prepared for this. I drank a lot of sherry; well, I suppose not much more than half a bottle. Since I seemed to feel not so very different from usual with it inside me, I thought perhaps I was going to turn out to have a head for drink. Emerging into the fresh air of Broad Street undeceived me. Everything was luminous with wonder, but it took me I have no idea how long to progress the hundred yards or so round the necessary corner from Balliol and to get up the stairs to my room.

Here, quite soon I expect, two young men knocked, came in and found me sitting in my armchair.

'We represent the Oxford University Conservative Association,' said one of them, then, perhaps noting the chamber-pot I was holding on my lap, added, 'but perhaps we had better return at a more convenient time.'

This initial blaze of glory did not last, was untypical. After a year and a half of war smart Oxford, anything like the Oxford to be seen in *Brideshead Revisited*, was shut for the duration, much of it never

36

to reopen. Everything, including the materials for posh lunches, etc., cigarettes, clothes, coal, was rationed or in short supply. Even if it had not been, I would have been far too hard up for most of it. I reverted to beer, though that too could be hard to find, always ate in college and so on, though I was fool enough to join the Oxford Union Society, for one term only, at the incredible outlay of £1. 10s. I attended some debates, but decided their style was not for me on witnessing the following exchange:

Worthy dullard: 'This situation is too grave to be handled with kid gloves.'

The Secretary, ringing his bell and interrupting, as the rules permitted: 'On a point of information, kid gloves are very vulgar,' this causing the loudest laughter I ever heard in the chamber where future prime ministers were alleged to have made their first flights.

I had also joined the 'student' branch of the Communist Party, in which at that time high positions were held by John (then 'Jack') Terraine, now a military historian, and Iris Murdoch, now Iris Murdoch and a pal for decades. Belonging was at least cheap and it involved girls, not very nice-looking ones, though, most of them, but it also meant reading, or trying to read, Marx, Lenin and Plekhanov (aargh), going to 'study groups' and meetings, *speaking* at meetings, on balance a poor return for having, in this most banal of ways, rebelled against my father (these words too probably deserve their inverted commas), and the only useful lesson I learnt, for later, was the cunning and the unquenchable assiduity with which Communists infiltrate other groups, non-political (religious, for instance) as well as political.

Another body I joined, not so voluntarily, was the STC. (If you failed to join you were called up into the ranks in short order.) Oxford must have been an administrators' nightmare then, with so many dons away on some form of war service, and a new intake of undergraduates appearing every term instead of the normal once a year in the autumn. One thing was plain, however, and that was that sooner or later nearly all undergraduates would be in uniform. I was used to the STC from school, though I could have thought of better ways to use my time at Oxford than getting into a uniform a day and a half a week and drilling. There was a hell of a lot of actual drilling, which is economical of space, equipment, instructors and preparation. But actually I was quite good at it, and there was a wealth of satisfaction in hearing Sergeant-Major Reid, a Scots Guardsman who, by believable repute, had killed fifteen Germans at Dunkirk with his bayonet, bawl at Lord This of Magdalen or the Hon. That of Christ Church, 'You're the worst bloody soldier I've ever seen, sir! Now get down to the hut and back *at the double!*'

My own college was short on lords. It was rich, or so it was said, but no richness ever seemed to percolate as far down as us. On a second glance I found I did know, or had met, one of its undergraduates, a certain Norman Iles. We had shared digs at Cambridge the previous year in vain pursuit of the same scholarship. He at once introduced me to the man with whom (under the doubling-up system wartime had brought) he shared a tutor, one Philip Larkin, whose first action was to offer me a cigarette, the equivalent in those days of a glass of rare malt whisky. Norman, large, large-faced, out of condition, with an air of half-serious hostility to the world in general, to any received idea, but unaffectionate tolerance towards individuals of his own standing, had the stronger personality of the two. It was hard to say what he thought he was doing at Oxford at all, except that the system had propelled him there along with the rest of us, certainly not to acquire an education or pursue an interest in the English literature he was ostensibly studying. He was a kind of ideal bad undergraduate, cutting lectures, not delivering essays, doing what he could to undermine the academic outlook by representing the university as a place where charlatans lorded it over ambitious or apathetic noodles, supplementing this image by one of a bad college man, stealing coal or 'borrowing' jam (severely rationed) and other consumables out of neighbours' rooms.

Nevertheless Norman became the centre of a sort of circle that included Philip, me, and three or four more semi- and would-be drunks in and outside St John's. Perhaps his underlying attraction was that of the cynic or nihilist who gives others a guilty pleasure by going much further than they would have dared to go on their own. And Norman had plenty of ridicule to spare for himself. Pub-crawling was the favoured, almost the only possible, social activity, now and then too strenuous to suit me. There was not unlimited beer, but you had to drink it as long as it was there. Spirits were rare, but they went down too whether you really wanted them or not – occasionally they would come up again, not only in my case. Jazz, something of a passion for others of us, notably Philip, really left Norman cold; indeed it would be hard to name anything that he actually liked or enjoyed.

It was interesting, not to say startling, that he passed his required exams and, while by nature one of the STC's most dedicated foes, received a high-grade certificate qualifying him for officer training. Matters returned to normal, or Norman-normal, when, as he told me, he was quite soon sent to a special place reserved for unemployable officers. After the war he was to do relief work in Poland. I cannot resist adding that I last heard of him in 1986, when he sent me a whole book he had written called *Who Really Killed Cock Robin?* offering to 'restore' nursery rhymes and carols to their original versions (invariably sexual) and revealing on one jacket-flap that the character Baa, Baa, Black Sheep is really a promiscuous girl, on the other that the author had become a full-time artist.* As a character says of the hero in Philip's novel *Jill*, 'one of those mysteries that are not worth solving.'

I have said that in those wartime Oxford days new faces appeared every term. One belonged to E.D.L. du Cann, at once known as Duke, soon famous as wag and prankster. He had a sports jacket with a sort of poacher's pocket just wide enough to carry a 10″ gramophone record. Other people would 'borrow' it, and I feel rather bad about saying that some of the Oxford shops lost several deleted jazz discs by this route. (I was much envied for the rare Sidney Bechet disc I walked out with.) Duke's set-piece was an imitation – it was a great time for imitations – of part of a Soviet propaganda film called *In the Rear of the Enemy*, full of small arms fire and shell noises. He had rooms above another jazz lover, Graham Parkes, who would play himself this or that record to cheer him through working on a Greek prose. There was a particular Louis Armstrong piece called 'Bessie Couldn't Help It' in which Louis sings at one point:

> A boy kissed Bessie in a Buick last night;
> My, oh my, how she smirked [?] with delight . . .

and follows it with a kind of gurgle of indescribable lasciviousness. Graham told us that every time the vocal approached this stage Duke would come rushing down the stairs, pause outside in silence until Louis had done his gurgle and then return whence he had come. It was a treat in later years to recall this sort of thing when

---

*To my amazement, what must have been a reprint of this book was reviewed four years later in the *Sunday Telegraph*, unfavourably, I was relieved to see, but at some length.

the Rt. Hon. Edward du Cann was being statesmanlike about party or country on the TV screen.

The army claimed me in the summer of 1942, but I was briefly in Oxford again the following year, Headington actually, in what is now the seat of Robert Maxwell. Some chums, including Philip, were still about, and it was with a small group of these that I contrived my own humiliation if ever a man did. On our way to the Horse and Jockey, we were passing a Military Police office when, with immense bravado, I stuck my hands into my trouser pockets. Within seconds a red-capped corporal appeared.

'Would you speak to the DPM [Deputy Provost-Marshal] a minute, sir?'

'Oh Christ. Where is he?'

He was a major, not very old. 'How long have you been commissioned?'

'Three weeks, sir.'

'M'm.' He looked over at the chums, who were making no effort at all to efface themselves. 'I must reprimand you for your sloppy and unsoldierly behaviour just now and advise you strongly not to repeat it. But perhaps the second part of that is unnecessary.' There was a hint of his finding something funny in the situation that eluded me completely. But when I had given him the most cracking salute I knew how and he had turned back towards his office, I hope I had the sense to thank my lucky stars that it had been that DPM I had encountered and not any of a wide variety of others.

In October 1945 it was the merest good luck that landed me in England, between seeing the Hun put in his place and what could have been a spell of a year or so giving a hand at various points East, where the war was over but plenty of disagreeable things remained to be done, in the course of which one might have got shot by Communists or just died of some tropical disease, as had befallen one of my college mates. During my twenty-eight days' disembarkation-embarkation leave in the UK, a telegram arrived summoning me to the regimental depot at Thirsk, in Yorkshire, there to receive something called a Class 'B' Release, the result of a wise government measure to get scholarship boys and other talented fellows like me back at top speed into civilian life and the tasks of peace. I remember Louis Armstrong's 'Tight Like This' was playing on the wireless at the time and I turned the volume up.

At Thirsk, I caused a lot of satisfying resentment among Class 'A' men, some of them old sweats of twenty-five, who were themselves bound for the jungle and assumed at the sight of my green youth that that was my destination too. Like a sentimental fool I handed in my revolver, instead of hanging on to it and flogging it later to some rascal, and went off in my demob suit. This was at any rate better than the demob shirt, the sort printed on one side of the material only. I reached Oxford just nicely in time for the start of the autumn term, more than ready to throw myself into the tasks of peace. In my case these were to be headed by not working, getting drunk and pursuing young women.

I was allotted a handsome set of rooms in the rather dismal so-called New Quad, now emptied of the civil servants – potato administrators, it was said – who had occupied it during the war, but had left at least one trace of their stay in the form of a contraceptive machine affixed to a lavatory wall. There came a night when two others and I kicked this device off its mounting – it takes three to do that – and chained it to the bars of a window of Somerville, the women's college just up the Woodstock Road. None of us could have explained why we went to this considerable trouble. Boredom, conceivably. After the bustle of wartime, Oxford had barely had a chance to start returning to some sort of peacetime self. It had a depopulated air, certainly for such as me. Nearly all of those who had come up with me in 1940-41 – Philip for one – had either graduated and departed or were still Class 'A'-ing like mad in Burma.

This is by way of partly explaining what brought me up against John Wain, a junior Fellow of St John's who had slotted in his three years of undergraduate residence while I had been away at the war. He had been found unfit for military service (lungs), like Philip again (eyes), like others who when counted in with those who had craftily evaded service elsewhere (like Dylan Thomas) made up quite a total, and suggest as part of an answer to the old question, 'Why were the Great War poets better than the Second War lot?' – 'Because a good half of the Second lot managed to stay out of it.' I digress, however.

John came to Oxford once or twice a week as a diversion from his other post at Reading University. The two of us were soon meeting fairly regularly for a pint-and-pie lunch, usually at the Eagle and Child ('Bird and Baby'), the St John's pub on the far side of St Giles. I found him most attractive, lightly caustic with a voice and manner to match, knowledgeable, wordly-wise, a budding academic without the crap. He knew lots of people in Oxford, including dons, a branch of humanity with whom my own social contact so far had been a couple of chokingly sedate port-and-walnuts sessions as a Senior Common Room guest. John was a lover of jazz and knew about it. He was full of stories, like the one about the sherry-bottle that held something other than sherry. The inconvenience of his rooms in Reading had led him to pee habitually into a bottle last thing at night, emptying it first thing in the morning. Once, about to hand some guests glasses of what was meant to be Tio Pepe, he had noticed at the last moment that this was not so, and deduced in the nick of time that what had gone down the pan that morning was the Tio Pepe. 'Hold it,' he had blurted – 'this isn't good enough for you – it's piss, in fact. Have some gin instead.'

So far so good. Only his walking-stick, among the able-bodied surely a warning signal in the same category as facial hair, and a tendency to tweed hats, made me uneasy. He also seemed, though three years younger than the twenty-five-year-old me, to comport himself like somebody in his forties – like a don, in fact. I should not complain too irritably about that, because it was John who pushed me in the academic direction myself, inciting me to go for my First, pointing me towards a provincial college lectureship and away from the suburban schoolmaster's job I had vaguely envisaged. (Whether he was right or not, for me and the world, is another matter.) He also encouraged me to try to be some sort of proper writer instead of the dabbler I had largely been, though he once generously wrote that the process had been the other way round. And when later the time came and he somehow got the job of presenting a BBC radio series of programmes of new writing, it was, I seem to remember, a piece of me, of *Lucky Jim*, that opened the first broadcast.

All this and more disposed me in John's favour. Other things failed to do so. There was to be an early small one in the summer of 1953 when each of us had a first novel in the press. I was taking a caravan holiday with my family by the Thames at Pangbourne, not far from where John had a cottage. One afternoon there he shook me considerably by reading aloud a portion of his own novel. My first reaction to what I heard was that it seemed to be of a certain banality of conception and style, not extreme but marked and consistent; my second, that this could not in the nature of things be the case, with John being so well up in everything, and that therefore the novel I had myself written must all be on some dismayingly wrong, outmoded track. I was thus well softened up for what followed.

'What advance are you getting on your book?'

'A hundred quid,' I said with what a little earlier would have been some complacency, having been assured, truly or not, that the standard rate for an unknown's first novel was £75.

'Oh. I'm getting two hundred and fifty for mine.' He leaned forward. 'You see – mine isn't Joe Soap's first novel.'

Ah, well of course that would account for it. There was a good left-and-right follow-up in 1958 or '59 in New York, where an amiable American academic called Harvey Breit, victim of the popular falsehood that Englishmen like meeting other Englishmen in the States, and knowing both John and me to like jazz, got us together in Eddie Condon's Club. John opened by asking me,

'Are you working on anything at the moment?'

This way of putting the matter suggests fast and economically that the one questioned is a mere part-timer, dashing off a rondeau or epigram should the spirit move him, otherwise selling antique furniture or sitting on his bum. 'Yes,' I said.

'Oh. What is it?'

Could it have been a monograph on the fauna of Kentucky? 'A novel,' I said with restraint, not adding 'actually' or 'called *Fuck You*'.

John gave me a sly, old-pals' wink. 'Make it a good one this time, eh?' he said.

'I suppose that's what we're all trying to do,' I said, in an attempt to piss on him and sound humble at once.

'Eddie told me Benny Morton was hoping to drop by around ten,' said Breit.

Not much later, John said, 'Kingsley, you're always going on about what nice people the Welsh are. I'm afraid I didn't take much notice at first, but then just recently I've run into some of them and I rather agree with you. You ought to write a novel about them one of these days.'

'My second novel [published a couple of years earlier] is set in Wales,' I said, telling him nothing he had not known already.

He gave me another sly wink. 'M'm, but, well, a proper one – you know.'

'There's Cutty Cutshall just going up on to the stand now,' said Breit.

The one-Englishman-putting-another-down-in-America dialogue

has become as much a convention of the US-UK genre as the screen scene in Restoration comedy, and this one was hardly to be got steamed up about. Another piece of John's wit, however, struck me as a little heavy.

Several times after moving to Swansea I had asked him to come and stay. He never came, so, as one does, I stopped asking him. Later, perhaps years later, some third party, whose own views on proper behaviour could themselves have done with a lick of paint, told me John had confided to him that the reason for the declined invitations was his fear that Hilly would 'break down his bedroom door' to get her hands on him. The reader must take it from me that that had never been her way, and even if it had been, she had assured me with repeated emphasis that many and many a door would have had to fall before she got to John's. Too angry to have the sense to keep my mouth shut, I faced him with the story. Instead of denying it, he remarked that it showed a grave deficiency in my informant's sense of humour. From that moment I considered myself released from any duty to keep to myself what I thought of his books, a specially handy dispensation when his Life of Johnson came out in 1974.

I have two endings to this rancorous little digression, one long, one short, neither my own. The longer one has the jovial Magnus Magnusson preparing with me a brief sound radio broadcast. 'I don't want to run through the whole works,' he said, 'but I would just like to rehairss the links. You know some of you writers can be very prickly, difficult fellows and we don't want there to be any ill feeling. Now, when I introduce you I propose to say, "Kingsley Amis, probably best known to listeners for his *Lucky Jim* and other comic novels, is in the studio with a batch of recent science fiction . . ." That all right with you, Kingsley? Good. The thing is, the other day we had John Wain on the programme, who I believe is a friend of yours . . .'

'I've known him for years,' I said.

'And what I said about him to start with was, "I suppose I can best introduce John Wain to listeners by calling him the poor man's Kingsley Amis." And you know he got quite stroppy. Threatened to walk out of the studio and all that. As I say, you writers can be very difficult. Like prima donnas. Anyway, we're not going to have that trouble this time.'

'Well, the poor man's anything doesn't sound all that good,' I said, 'especially when followed by the name of a feared, hated and more successful rival' – I spoke the last dozen words only in my head. 'Poor man's Dickens, poor man's Hemingway, anyone.'

'No,' said Magnus. 'I see what you mean. I should have thought of that.'

It was Philip Larkin, looking up from as it might have been an advertisement of one of John's later books, who said, 'Isn't England a marvellous free, open country? Take a fellow like old John Wain, now. No advantages of birth or position or wealth or energy or charm or looks or talent – nothing, and look where he is now. Where else but in England could a thing like that happen? You know, a few years ago I think he got to be Professor of Poetry at Oxford. Just imagine.'

Whither it is high time we returned. After a period in 1945-46 engaged in the kind of self-indulgence referred to earlier, and fending off the man (an ex-major, it was said) who tried to persuade me to rejoin the Communist Party, I suppose I might be said to have got down to some serious work. I attended lectures, most assiduously those of the repulsive but necessary Tolkien mentioned elsewhere, also visited a succession of tutors offering instruction in the same part of the syllabus, the almost-universally disliked area that included philology, the structure and history of the language, and the literature of the period roughly up to the death of Chaucer in 1400. Just writing those last few phrases, the bare thought of when Chaucer died or that he lived at all, has brought me a strong whiff of the depression the thing itself regularly brought me. To go through all of it, even a bit of it, would kill me.

And yet since those days, since I left the academic profession some fifteen years later, since my own works began to be studied at universities alongside those of other living writers, and to be written upon by those who taught at such places – well, I have become pretty sure that I and others had things the wrong way round, that philology, however laborious, is a valid subject of academic study, and those post-Chaucerian poems and plays and novels we turned to with such relief are not. They are to be approached instead in the spirit of self-cultivation and entertainment. Ask yourself whether our literature has improved or declined since it began to be studied as a university subject. Start with English poetry.

But – to return again – I had no such thoughts in my head as I bashed my way through Shakespeare, Spenser, Milton, Wordsworth and the rest of them. I more or less had to leave out Donne, finding him intolerably convoluted, and betted successfully that there would

45

be in that paper a Marvell or Herbert question I could answer. In the end I got there battered and bleeding, but clutching the necessary First. Ironically, and for once the term fits, I got my highest marks on the Old English paper; I have never written anything finer in its way than my answer to the question 'Why is *The Battle of Maldon* [a fragment of 'ape's bumfodder' written about the year 1000] made much of?', a positive firework-display of hypocrisy and affectation.

With only a vacation to draw breath, I plunged into the famous B.Litt., repulsive stuff in a different sense, with lectures put in on the Oxford principle of fending prospective candidates off by the prospect of intrinsic boredom combined with entire practical uselessness. I remember nothing more than my mere attendance at a course on the history of English studies given by the narcotic David Nichol Smith, except for the little thrill of horror I felt on learning that 'English studies' had begun with a contentious bishop as early as the sixteenth century, *before Shakespeare*. Better than *Beowulf*, though.

All this exam stuff is necessary, was necessary, to suggest how Oxford had been changing, certainly since 1939, perhaps longer, a change accelerated but not, I think, caused by the war. Elegance (foppery) was losing ground to purposefulness (philistinism). In *Brideshead Revisited*, the novel par excellence of pre-war Oxford, though written in retrospect and not published till 1945, nobody ever seems to go near an exam even in thought, let alone deed – simply being there at the university was the point of going to it. In 1946-48 it was sometimes as if exams filled the world.

Not all the time. The change I have noticed was never more than partial and was even reversed here and there, though in order to count for anything you still had to be good at something (in the theatre, usually) more than just being extravagant and showing off, but then again a combination of the three was naturally telling. Some mention of Kenneth Tynan is obviously inevitable at this point.

Ken came up to Oxford in the October of 1945, just as I did back from the army, and the mere sight of his velvet suits, damask shirts, etc., in the bar of the Randolph Hotel, even perhaps the sound of his voice, was enough to suggest that, as Philip Larkin wrote of this period, 'all that was starting up again.' Besides flamboyance and wit, Ken was a man of great generosity, not least to me, trying to help me to get published as well as buying me, among many others, drinks, and we became excellent friends after a fashion, even coming to collaborate on a television programme. But I never felt at home in his preferred world of the theatre magnified into a way of life, so to speak, indeed in any part of the general trendy-left-wing, showbiz-Zen-Buddhism, pot-smoking, bullfight-cult, international-American, 'happening' sub-culture that, thanks largely to him, characterised post-war Oxford and soon spread to parts of London, and I saw almost nothing of him for some years before his death in 1980 at the age of fifty-three.

In May 1946 I met Hilary (always Hilly) Bardwell, a student at the Ruskin School of Art, and here we come to one of those difficult bits. I said in my preface that I intended to leave out as much as possible of potentially hurtful topics, and here is the biggest of such omissions. In the relevant parts of what follows I mean without apology to be severely reticent and factual, after just one mention of the word love.

My life was now quite different, not least in my moving out of college in 1947 and into digs. I had done nothing at all to decorate or otherwise 'impose my personality upon' that set of rooms in the New Quad, beyond glueing to the wall above the always-empty fireplace an over-enlarged photograph of the clarinettist Pee Wee Russell, with a typed caption adapted from the last stanza of Tennyson's poem, 'To Virgil':

> I salute thee, Pee Wee Russell,
> I that loved thee since my day began,
> Wielder of the wildest measure
> ever moulded by the lips of man.

There were three others in Miss Butler's lodging-house at 19 St John Street: a talkative Welshman with psoriasis, another Welshman called Meacock who once found the time when not in the pub to give me a phial of powder that rendered my feet forever unsmelly (provided originally by the British Army in the Far East), and an extravagantly handsome Lothario type – a Freemason, I remember – who used illicitly to smuggle girls into his bed-sitter. He told me two things I have never forgotten. One was that at the end of a dazzling career in classics, in which he had won every award in sight, he thought he was just beginning to acquire some dim idea of what the Greek tragedians might actually have been saying and doing; the other that, grievous as it might be not to have a fuck when you wanted one, that was nothing compared with having a

47

fuck when you didn't want one. We heard later that he had made a fortune selling children's shoes in Australia. Miss Butler liked us all and had thought we were gentlemen, but showed herself very disappointed the day after a party of ours to which we had invited her. The staple drink was a firkin of Benskin's bitter laced with laboratory alcohol provided by Meacock.

This was the era when the tones of Bunny Berigan's record of 'I Can't Get Started' seemed to come floating out of every window between Beaumont Street and Wellington Square. Hilly and I ate midday at the 'British Restaurant' in Gloucester Green or the one in St Aldate's (1s. 3d. for shepherd's pie and rice pudding), in the evening often an omelette (meat, cheese, vegetable or plain) at the Chinese, also known as the Stowaway. We went to what was in effect the OU Jazz Club and even danced at it. We went punting, took coach trips to London, had all the fun of being brassily cheated at St Giles's fair. Hilly impressed me by being rejected as not readily hypnotisable at a so-called hypnotist's stage show, and in a different way by washing her hair and her smalls in the Randolph and, much to my trepidation, in the bath-house at St John's.

When Hilly and I got married we went first of all to a one-room flat in Norham Road, Summertown, North Oxford, a sunny and spacious time and place. She would beat me at halma before I hurried off to a lecture or an exam in Oxford proper. We had room enough for only one companion, a small, dapper but dignified ginger cat called Winkie. He would come for walks with us on fine evenings like a dog, leaping and darting through the hedges and trees but always coming when he was called. He was an implacable hunter and it was a lucky moth that got out of the flat once in, though he sometimes needed help to reach trickily placed ones.

Winkie came with us when about May 1948 we moved to Marriner's Cottage in Eynsham, a village half a dozen miles from Oxford on the Witney road with a stone bridge over the river, a fishmonger strong on sprats, a good bus service to Gloucester Green, and a village green where they held a fair. At it, a very pregnant Hilly got stuck in the whirligig upside down. The cottage itself was not only next to the pub (which had a real parrot in it) but part of the same block. It had a stone-flagged passage from front to rear and a walled garden with rambling roses, hollyhocks, a walnut tree and the best gooseberries I have ever tasted. Some evenings, encouraged by a saucer of milk, a hedgehog came visiting.

Here to have tea with us, to drink, perhaps to play records, came among others Philip Larkin and Ruth (the bespectacled girl from 'Wild Oats'), John Postgate, son of Raymond, rising physicist and amateur Dixieland trumpeter ('master of the furtive style', as a contemporary unkindly put it), and J. B. Leishman, scholar, don, in fact one of my ex-tutors and a shining exception to their general run, a man of great sweetness and extraordinariness. He was an authority on Rilke and Donne – the first luckily never came up in my life, the second, unluckily, he never persuaded me to warm to. Leishman came bicycling out to tea with us several times, a folded map tied with parcel-twine to the thigh of his plus-fours – or were they breeches? He was a solitary, a bachelor, not homosexual, not sexual at all, a man I wanted to get to know better, but I could find no way of doing so. What he thought of me as a pupil I have no idea; the only comment of his I remember hearing was that I was punctual. One day, so we heard, he rode his bike off a precipice on some mountain on the Continent.

By the following summer, change was drawing unpleasantly close. The government grant that I had rather impudently stretched out for four years was about to dry up. I was job-hunting, scanning the English vacancies in the *Times Educational Supplement* (no *Higher* one then), rushing off to interviews at Bristol, Birmingham, God knows where, running into the same set of competing faces every time minus one, that of the successful candidate for the previous post of its kind. The K. Amises, four of them now, left Marriner's Cottage willy-nilly and distributed themselves among the two sets of what had become grandparents. There was no farewell moment, though of all places I have ever lived in, this deserved one; we just found we were not living there any more.

So I will contrive such a moment here, a party at the cottage, not any kind of valedictory gesture, just the only one of its kind I was able to give at (or near) Oxford. Ken Tynan was there with some of his train. James Michie brought his blonde 'Barbara James' (see p. 109). Randolph comics like Niko the Greek, Randolph wits like Stanley Parker, collegiate jazz musicians like Paddy Latham (guitar), writers like Barry Harmer, Arthur Boyars and others of even lesser note, groupies associated with the Playhouse, the Experimental Theatre Club, the *Cherwell* – along they all came. There was rather a lot of noise, some drunkenness, a little fornication, no serious damage, no neighbours' complaints. In fact by more recent standards it was as harmless as a walk round St John's garden. Innocent, too, in a way, though Tynan and his henchmen were working on that.

I suppose this was as close as I ever got to glittering, at Oxford or anywhere else. Just as well, perhaps. But to sneer at glittering comes rather too easy to those like myself who could never have afforded to go in for it on any kind of regular basis. Poor moralist, and what art thou?

PHILIP LARKIN

I HAVE THOUGHT it all right to reprint here a version of the piece I wrote for the volume *Larkin at Sixty* (ed. Anthony Thwaite) in 1982, when the poet still had three years to live. I append to it some reflections that it would not have been proper, in one sense or another, to publish in Philip Larkin's lifetime or in the immediate aftermath of his death.

Soon after arriving at St John's College, Oxford in April 1941 I met somebody who, a trifle comically I thought at the time, was called Philip Larkin. I was most impressed with his self-confidence when he told me not very long afterwards that he had once come across, in some writers' manual, a list of names not to be given to serious characters, and found 'Larkin' on it. His clothes too seemed to me not very serious: tweed jacket, wine-coloured trousers, check shirt, bow tie – no commonplaces then. I had already gathered that this sort of thing was no sign of any particular artistic bent; even in our own college there were almost enough velvet-waistcoated barbarians to suggest the opposite. But in my suburban way I considered it was flashy of him to go on like that, though I would have had to admit that the effect was neat, the shoes clean, the tie carefully chosen and knotted. He always dressed well and smartly, also appropriately, whether in undergraduate informals or the senior librarian's 'good' suits.

He had a biggish nose, a fresh complexion and a head of rather nice, fine light-brown hair that was already, though he was only eighteen then, showing signs of recession. It was again not much later that he said his grandfather had been bald as a coot at twenty-eight. ('He used to wear a cap in the house. He looked ridiculous.') Before I grew too fond of him to see him in any such light, Philip struck me as a little ridiculous in appearance, anyway outlandish, unlikely, on one's hasty summing-up, to be attractive to girls.

At our first meeting, which I remember as much less dramatically

51

satisfying than the account he gives in his introduction to the 1964 edition of *Jill*, he was instantly affable, to be seen as one who erected no barriers. But there was about him a barrier not of his own making, a painful stammer that impeded conversation, not so much by slowing it down as by discouraging inessentials. I thought a good deal about this stammer, which had a not very watchable facial accompaniment, but never managed to see it as a plausible symptom or symbol of anything. As Philip grew older, it receded to vanishing-point, as these things do.

Otherwise, Philip was to outward view an almost aggressively normal undergraduate of the non-highbrow, non-sherry-sipping sort, hard-swearing, hard-belching, etc., treating the college dons as fodder for obscene clerihews and the porter as a comic ogre, imitating Tolkien, getting me to imitate Lord David Cecil, wholly gregarious, going to the English Club, admittedly, but treating its sessions as incidents in beery nights out and/or targets for more derision, being fined by the Dean (I wish we had more than the tiny but exact glimpse of this near the start of 'Dockery and Son'). I have since thought that some of this was a little strained and overdone, as if to repel any attempt at intimacy. The solitary creature of later years, unable to get through the day without spending a good part of it by himself, let alone the author of (say) 'First Sight', was invisible to me then; most likely I was not looking hard enough.

Philip's exterior of a non-games-playing hearty wobbled rather over jazz. I was ready to meet him halfway, having like most other youngsters of the period come as far as Benny Goodman, Artie Shaw and others, treating the stuff as one more indisputably good thing along with films, cricket, science fiction, the wireless and all that. With Philip the music was a preoccupation, a passion, as it was for numbers of his and our friends and as it soon became for me. I cannot improve on his description (in the introductions to *Jill* and *All What Jazz*) of the part it played in our lives; I will just add that our heroes were the white Chicagoans, Count Basie's band, Bix Beiderbecke, Sidney Bechet, Henry Allen, Muggsy Spanier, Fats Waller, early Armstrong and early Ellington – amazing that there were early bits of them by 1941 – and our heroines Bessie Smith, Billie Holiday, Rosetta Howard ('I'm the queen of everything') and Cleo Brown. All gone now.

About this time the OU Rhythm Club organised a series of concerts, but the material was not much to our liking: George Shearing, Cyril Blake's band from Jig's Club in Soho, the seven-year-old

Victor Feldman. Much more congenial, to me, were the sessions at the Victoria Arms in Walton Street, since converted to the uses of the Oxford University Press. Here, in a small dingy room usually empty or nearly so, there was a battered but well-tuned piano which Philip could be persuaded to play. He did so with some proficiency in an unemphatic style that in my memory sounds as much like Jimmy Yancey's as anyone's. The result was graceful, clear, melodic and often faintly sad, the Larkin of 'Coming', if you will, rather than of 'Whatever Happened?' ('How did you learn?' – 'Years of trying.') He stuck as a rule to the twelve-bar blues form, which was fine with the rest of us – it was our favourite too. If there were no outsiders present I would sometimes sing, or rather bawl, a series of lyrics culled from records; 'Locksley Hall Blues' (Tennyson-Larkin) was an exception.

Nevertheless, resist it as we might, the syllabus of the Oxford English School forced itself upon us both and on others: lectures to attend, essays to write and above all books to read, texts, plays, poems. No enthusiasm was aroused. All Old English and nearly all Middle English works produced hatred and weariness in everybody who studied them. The former carried the redoubled impediment of having Tolkien, incoherent and often inaudible, lecturing on it. Nobody had a good word to say for *Beowulf*, *The Wanderer*, *The Dream of the Rood*, *Cynewulf and Cyneheard*. Philip had less than none. If ever a man spoke for his generation it was when, mentioning some piece of what he called in a letter to me 'ape's bumfodder', he said, 'I can just about stand learning the filthy lingo it's written in. What gets me down is being expected to *admire* the bloody stuff.' So far, as I say, so standard, but he would have commanded less general support for his equally hard line on Middle English literature, in which others could find a few admirable or at least tolerable bits, mostly by Chaucer. When it came to works in Modern (post-1500) English, he was on his own.

I have no recollection of ever hearing Philip admit to having enjoyed, or again to be ready to tolerate, any author or book he studied, with the possible exception of Shakespeare. He was at best silent on those who, from the evidence of his own work, might have been expected to appeal to him: Collins, Crabbe, Clare. (The compulsory part of the syllabus stopped before it reached Christina Rossetti, let alone Hardy.) During the summer vacation of that year I worked my way through *The Faerie Queene*. Like most of us, I think, I resented having to read it at the required pace, but without being likely to repeat the experience I was quite glad to have been forced into it. Not so Philip. I had used the college library copy (principle as well as finance dictated that you never bought a book merely because you were going to be examined on it). At the foot of the last page of the text he had written in pencil in his unmistakable, beautiful, spacious hand:

First I thought Troilus and Criseyde was the most *boring* poem in English. Then I thought Beowulf was. Then I thought Paradise Lost was. Now I *know* that The Faerie Queene is the *dullest thing out. Blast* it.

(When I queried the uncharacteristically non-alcoholic language with him, he retorted that he had not dared to aggravate his offence by writing down the words he was thinking.)

I must not give the impression that such judgements were offered in talk and then to any extent answered. Whatever one made of it in private, most people at Oxford, not just Philip, treated literature in this sense as a pure commodity, a matter for evasion and fraud, confidence trickery to filch a degree. Reading it and going to lectures on it was how you prepared for the only significant event, the coming battle of wits with the examiners. (Philip was to retain a low view of the academic study of literature.)

If special attention was given to the Romantics, it did not reflect esteem. Each was brought up and dismissed in two short lines in 'Revaluation', another blues; they all signed on as Bill Wordsworth and his Hot Six – Wordsworth (tmb) with 'Lord' Byron (tpt), Percy Shelley (sop), Johnny Keats (alto and clt), Sam 'Tea' Coleridge (pno), Jimmy Hogg (bs), Bob Southey (ds). (There was a Café Royal Quintet, I remember, with 'Baron' Corvo on xylophone.) Shelley was singled out for a form of travesty in which nothing was altered but much added: 'Music,' began one of Philip's, 'when soft *silly* voices, that have been talking *piss*, die, Vibrates, like a . . .'

I need not go on. If syllabus-literature was to be avoided wherever possible, writers beyond its scope could be all right, though of course not as exciting and discussable as Pee Wee Russell or Johnny Hodges. I saw at once that Philip was much more closely concerned here than I had been. He quickened my interest in or even introduced me to the work of Auden (above all), Isherwood, Betjeman, Anthony Powell, Montherlant (a lonely foreigner) and Henry Green, to *The Rock Pool* (Connolly), *At Swim-Two-Birds* (Flann O'Brien) and *The Senior Commoner* (Julian Hall), a wonderful marsh-light of a novel whose influence in 1946 or so was to help to render unpublishable the predecessor of *Lucky Jim*.

I was well enough aware that Philip wrote poetry, but so did I, so did half the people one talked to – superficially, it was no more than might have been expected from the likes of us. But, much to my envy, Philip had poems published in undergraduate magazines. I published two of them myself in the OU Labour Club *Bulletin*, which I edited for a term in 1942, and was censured for bourgeois obscurantism by the Committee. How odd – the poems were quite straightforward, said Philip, glossing with a pair of very direct monosyllables the first two nouns in the line 'The steeples and the fanlights of a dream'. This remark reached an unaccustomed depth and seriousness in our conversations about the craft of poetry. In my experience, poets who are any good only discuss their work as a reaction to criticism or if they need advice on technical points. Philip had had no criticism then and he had never needed advice on technical points.

In that year and a bit, Philip Larkin was not the leading Oxford poet; that position was held by Sidney Keyes or Michael Meyer or John Heath-Stubbs. When *Eight Oxford Poets*, edited by the first two, appeared in 1941, Philip was not represented; it appeared since that Keyes, who might well have known that Philip considered him a third-rate personage, left him out with some deliberation. This was annoying, but no great matter, for at that stage of his life his main intention was to become a novelist. (It was I who had decided to be a poet.)

Parts of what was to become Philip's first novel, *Jill*, not published until 1946, were already in existence in those mid-war years. One part, the Willow Gables fantasy, had come to independent life as a kind of pastiche of schoolgirl stories with super-soft porn undertones. (The belatedly published poem, 'The School in August', belonged to it and gives the flavour.) When I read the finished novel, I was amazed at the skill that half concealed the utter incongruity of that episode with the rest of the material. There was another, deeper division between the experiences of the hero, John Kemp, in wartime Oxford, instantly attributable to the Philip I knew, visible Philip, and on the other side Kemp's fantasy life, dreamy, romantic, sensitive, the work of someone I had never known before, invisible Philip. I found them hard, if not impossible, to reconcile – well, so had the author.

I had read, with permission, the early pages and even offered suggestions. One of them got 'Cold it looked, cold and deserted' changed to 'It looked cold and deserted'. I saw little of *A Girl in Winter* before publication, but was consulted in some detail in the early 1950s over what would have been Philip's third novel, a serio-comic account of the gradual involvement of a rising young executive in the motor industry, Sam Wagstaff, with a working-class girl he knocks down in his car coming home from the factory. Why this promising idea was abandoned, why its more ambitious successor went the same way, is obscure to me, but I suspect, alongside much else, the workings of that underrated agency in human affairs, fear of failure. No poem of Philip's preferred length lays your head on the block in the way any novel does.

I got to know Philip better after we had both left Oxford; there, I had usually seen him as one of a group. In 1946 or so I went and stayed with him at his parents' house in Warwick. My chief memory of that visit is reading a manuscript, or rather typescript, book of his early, unpublished poems. A page near the front said,

The present edition is limited to 1 copy.
This is no. 1

(Anybody else I knew would at least have taken carbons to give his chums.) The poems, mostly written I suppose in his late teens, evoked Auden, though not at all directly. It was uncomfortably clear to me that every one of them was better than any that I, aged twenty-four, had written. By then he had published *The North Ship*, and I had been sufficiently impressed, if left rather cold, by that, but it was these poems that he had never published that told me how good he was and would be.

In 1948 or so I went and stayed with him at his digs in Leicester. There he was in a house smelling of liniment, with a landlady who resembled a battered old squirrel and a dough-faced physicist co-lodger. On the Saturday morning he had to go into college and took me ('hope you won't mind – they're all right really') to the common room for a quick coffee. I looked round a couple of times and said to myself, 'Christ, somebody ought to do something with this.' Not that it was awful – well, only a bit; it was strange and sort of *developed*, a whole mode of existence no one had got on to from outside, like the SS in 1940, say. I would do something with it.

Jim Dixon's surname has something to do with ordinariness, but at the outset had much more to do with Dixon Drive, the street where Philip's digs were. Yes, for a short time I was to tell his story. The fact that, as it turned out, Dixon resembles Larkin in not the smallest particular, not even in place of origin, witnesses to the transmuting power of art. Philip came into *Lucky Jim* in quite another way. In 1950 or so I sent him my sprawling first draft and got back what amounted to a synopsis of the first third of the structure and other things besides. He decimated the characters that, in carried-away style, I had poured into the tale without care for the plot: local magnate Sir George Wettling, cricket-loving Philip Orchard, vivacious American visitor Teddy Wilson. He helped me to make a proper start. And I never even bought him a lunch! – not then, anyway.

In 1976 or so he and I were in a taxi on our way to a drink in London. I said into a silence, without premeditation,

'What chance of the Nobel?'

'Oh, that's gone,' he said with gloomy decisiveness. 'I thought they might be keeping it warm for a chap like me – you know, a chap who never *writes* anything or *does* anything or *says* anything. But now I find they've just given it to an Eyetie bugger [presumably Eugenio Montale, awarded the prize in the previous year] who never *writes* anything or *does* anything or *says* anything. No, that's *gone.*'

After a pause, I asked, 'What about the Laureateship?'

'I dream about that sometimes,' he said in the same tone, '*and wake up screaming.* Nah, with any luck they'll pass me over.'*

End of conversation. What made me laugh about it was that Philip had spoken altogether naturally. Few other people would have had the self-mastery to exclude from their manner any trace of facetiousness or other defensive reaction when quizzed about such matters. He always knew where he stood, never fooled himself or said anything he did not mean; when he told you he felt something, you

---

*This is what I printed in 1982, but it is fiction. When asked about the Laureateship, Philip actually said something like, 'Oh, Christ, that's in my lap, I've no hope of getting out of that bugger,' though, as we later saw, he did. That was what I put in my original typescript, which I let him see, and took it out at his request – 'Makes me look a bit of an arrogant shit.' Indeed.

I chuckled quietly when I saw 'his' answer to the Laureateship question quoted here and there as a 'Saying of the Week'.

could be quite sure he did feel it – a priceless asset to a poet, and a poet of feeling and mood at that. The same quality ensured that when he had nothing to say he said nothing, a turn of mind that helped him not to write any bad poems.

I am grateful for having known Philip Larkin for so many years, not only because he is my favourite poet – well, next to Housman (must try to be honest too), but because he was Philip. Although his manner quietened since those Oxford days, he continued to treat the world with jovial acerbity, a sense that the fools and charlatans, the Pounds and Picassos and many of their living heirs were doomed by their own absurdity. All this belied the sober, triste style of his photographs – well, there were gloomy moments, at least they would have been if they had not been so funny, about the TUC or the state of jazz or having to pay bills, or death, of course. He was the most enlivening companion I have ever known and the best letter-writer; to the end a glimpse of the Hull postmark brought that familiar tiny tingle of excitement and optimism, like a reminder of youth.

The sight of that Hull postmark was the nearest I got to the place at any time during the thirty years he was Librarian at the university there, though I had gone and stayed with him when he was working in Wellington, Leicester (as I have said) and finally Belfast, where I briefly considered applying for a job. At first it was neurotic upsets of my own that put me off going to Hull; for a later and longer period it was Philip himself. Just as I was thinking – in the late Seventies, perhaps – that I might invite myself up there, he wrote in a letter that John Wain had done just that (expletive deleted), a clear discouragement to me, as I fancied then, but am not so sure now.

Philip was cutting himself off, or rather, since he was quite ready to see me, even stay with me, in Swansea, London and Barnet, he was developing his policy of keeping his life and friends in strict compartments. After his death I was mildly amazed to find evidence (for instance at the exhibition of his memorabilia at University College, London) of several close friendships and long copious correspondences he had enjoyed with people I had never heard of. Hull, in particular the university library, was his castle, though I had noticed he let in a television team that included John Betjeman.

By then he had long cast off the pretence that he hated being a librarian, had only become and gone on being one because he had to be something, was pretty useless at it. I was once sitting behind a newspaper in the Swansea common room while two engineers, i.e. lecturers in engineering, therefore by common consent philistines, chatted together. One was telling the other about a recent visit to Hull. I pricked up my ears. The chap was full of praise for everything he had seen, 'especially the library. This fellow Larkin there [neither of the two, clearly, had any idea of what else Philip did] has transformed the place. Designed a new building to hold a million volumes. Oh, a real live wire, *myn*.' When I told Philip about this he showed, not the gratification I had unthinkingly expected, but the look of a man whose guilty secret has been revealed.

He was becoming respectable, at any rate in the places where it showed. This was something of a new departure for him. In the past he had been capable of a kind of recklessness that was beyond me. Of course I and others joined in when at the end of a beery evening he pissed on the fire in the St John's junior common room. I would never have followed his example in – well, some time in the Forties he had been visiting Bruce Montgomery in Shrewsbury, where the latter was schoolmastering. In those days, before he started making real money, Bruce had been a beer-drinker, a fanatical one by Philip's account, setting a cruel pace and insisting on being closely followed. After a prolonged session, the pair had the hardihood to attend a meeting of the school literary society. Philip found himself in the chair furthest from the door with hundreds of boys, many sitting on the floor, between him and any exit. Quite soon after everybody was settled a tremendous desire to urinate came upon him. Finding he could not face causing the upheaval that must have attended his leaving the room, and reasoning, if that is the word, that he was wearing a lot of clothes, including, in those days of fuel rationing, a heavy overcoat, he decided to rely on their absorbent qualities and intentionally pissed himself. It turned out that he had miscalculated, and under his chair there rapidly formed a pool of . . .

Round about here, rather late on, I thought, Philip broke off telling me this story and said he wished he had never started on it. He went on to extract from me some sort of promise not to go round repeating it, which I interpreted as a ban on any sort of publication. But now I consider myself released from that undertaking, in rather the same spirit as I have allowed his letters to me to be published in Anthony Thwaite's collection.

Much to my regret I have managed to lose, in divorces, changes of house, etc., everything he wrote to me before 1967 and quite a bit from since then. But I remember, from one of the lost letters of probably the Fifties, a poem that shows him to have had a talent for light verse comparable with Bob Conquest's, though different in approach and, to our loss, not so often exercised.

THE WAY WE LIVE NOW

(to be recited in a clear Welsh voice)

I let a fart in the street and a woman looked round;
I pissed on the fire, and got myself covered with ash;
I had half an hour with a whore and came out in a rash,
So I let my sperm fall in the brim of an old hat I found.

I vomited over my shoes in the bogs at the Pheasant;
I slipped in the road, and came down with my hand on some
                                                              slime;
Life is performing these actions time after time
Till Death makes our body smell worse than it does at present.

That too I am fairly sure Philip would not have wanted to see published in his lifetime, perhaps ever, but I think it comes in well here, before we get down to the serious stuff.

Philip was close about money. He scrupulously bought his round, paid his share, but it would have been quite unlike him to pick up the whole tab on impulse instead of the previously agreed half. His letters were full of references to the amount a meal or a holiday had cost him, his talk too. As well as being unattractive, this had its comic side, as when at a party of Bob's I saw Philip talking with finger-wagging earnestness to my son Martin, who was registering all he said. In the ambient uproar I could not hear what the topic was, but supposed, or at least thought there was a fair chance, that it was something like life and literature.

'Oh no,' said Martin when I asked him afterwards. 'All about bills.'

'Bills?'

'The bills he keeps having to pay. "The day after I get the bloody *electricity* bill I get the pissing *paper* bill, and the day after that the sodding *gas* bill." He seemed to take them all personally, as if no one else ever got them.'

Philip wrote in another lost letter, again probably of the Fifties, about his dislike of taking girls out and so having to waste money on them: 'I don't – I *don't* – want to [do that] and spend circa £5 when I can toss off in five minutes, free, and have the rest of the evening to myself.' That may be comic too, but only at first sight. Without, I hope, being boringly 'deep' or analytical, I see Philip's closeness (good word) about money as springing from a general reluctance to let go of anything he felt belonged to him or was part of him. Hence, perhaps, his love of solitude, which increased as he grew older, though he diagnosed and justified it in himself in, for instance, a poem of the early 1950s, 'Best Society', which was never published in his lifetime. And from there his resistance to marriage – 'meaning you promise to give someone half your money for the rest of your life and not to fuck anyone else' – is almost too easily reached.

As to Philip's sex-life, I thought it was not so unlike that of others of our contemporaries until round about the end of the Fifties, when I stopped hearing much about it. Was it then or earlier, I wonder, that he remarked to me, again half joking, whole earnest, 'Sex is too wonderful to be shared with anybody else'? But his desire persisted, as is shown in that painfully honest, also unpublished poem, 'Love Again', written in 1979. Here the poet wonders why 'it never worked for me', and finds no satisfactory answer:

> Something to do with violence
> A long way back, and wrong rewards,
> And arrogant eternity.

(*Violence?*) And something to do with emotional parsimony, and that fear of failure which I mentioned earlier in another context. Fear of success too, perhaps, coming out as inviting failure: see 'Letter to a Friend about Girls' (written in 1959). And what about painful honesty, refusal to fool himself? He once complained to me that X, one of his girls, was not attractive enough. All right to go to bed with, I said. He burst out almost savagely, 'Oh Christ, when she's *naked*, with just a gold chain round her neck, she's attractive *then* all right!' Sorry, I wanted to say, but I didn't arrange it like that. He said in a letter that, coming in late one night, he had picked up a photograph of Y, who was certainly attractive and to spare when fully dressed, and gazed at it in mingled tenderness, lust and dissatisfaction, the last-named emotion deriving from her facial resemblance, as he always saw it, to the comedian Stan Laurel. An element of selective blindness, of self-deception, is perhaps necessary if sexual matters are to 'work' for anybody.

Apart from coming to it next, I imply no special connection between the foregoing and what is regarded with some justice as the great Larkin theme: death and the fear of death. It finds its clearest and most memorable expression in the poem 'Aubade' (1977), which, though it occupies less than two full pages of the *Collected Poems*, he himself must have considered particularly important, since he published it separately as a little pamphlet. It came in a mildly decorative envelope with no lettering on it anywhere, nothing; same with the cardboard cover of the pamphlet itself. I would find it hard to say just why I find this so like Philip, but I do.

Anyway: in 'Aubade' the poet speaks of waking at four a.m. and being unable thereafter to think of anything but his inevitably approaching death:

> the dread
> Of dying, *and being dead*,
> Flashes afresh to hold and horrify.

My italics. On first reading these words, I at once remembered a conversation that ended with Philip saying, 'I'm not only [or perhaps 'not so much'] frightened of dying,' then shouting, 'I'm afraid of being dead!' And he goes on in the poem to make a show of tackling the answer to those who say (his italics):

> *No rational being*
> *Can fear a thing it will not feel*, not seeing
> That this is what we fear – no sight, no sound,
> No touch or taste or smell, nothing to think with,
> Nothing to love or link with,
> The anaesthetic from which none come round.

Here, tellingly, with the rhyme think with/link with, his skill deserts him for a moment, and there is a smug finality in the last line. This fear had arisen in conversation too, and I should have told him then and there not to be a bloody fool – if you can't think you can't realise you haven't any senses and aren't anywhere, and don't tell me again it'll be different from before you were born because (though you had nothing to think with then either) you could pass the time by looking forward to your birth. I *know* the paths of glory and everything else lead but to the grave. And on first reading 'Aubade' I should have found a way of telling you that depression among the middle-aged and elderly is common in the early morning and activity disperses it, as you tell us in your last stanza, so if you feel as bad as you say then fucking get up, or if it's too early or something then put the light on and read Dick Francis. This poem is not to be borne in mind while reading the magnificent ones about the run-up to death, which comes when we have plenty to think with and about.

Philip got through his own run-up with the bravery and reticence he decried in 'Aubade'. I knew of course he was ill, but not how ill: his last letter to me, written or rather dictated the day he went into hospital for the last time and ten days before his death, talks like earlier ones merely of 'tests', exhorts me not to 'get unduly alarmed', chats about Dylan and Caitlin Thomas and Jelly Roll Morton. But I think he had known all, or enough, about it for months. He had held out against the idea of my coming up to see him, even with Hilly, of whom he was very fond, even when I said we would arrive when he said and leave when he said and bring food and drink. He pleaded exhaustion, though that letter is perfectly coherent and normal, and funny. I understood his refusal better when I looked again at 'Aubade' and saw as if for the first time that after 'Courage is no good' there follows 'It means not scaring others.'

On 9th December 1985, Hilly and I went up for Philip's funeral. Andrew and Jan Motion, Blake Morrison and Charles Monteith travelled with us. We were met at the station, well outside Hull, by Terence Weldon, Philip's solicitor, who took us to his house, gave us food and drink, got us to the church, also outside Hull. It was packed. At the graveside I spoke to Philip's sister and niece, who had come to Swansea thirty years before to pick him up after visiting us. I remembered with amusement how that earlier meeting had not been part of the plan, how Philip had always said he could not stand children and had never got on with his niece, then aged seven or eight, and how he had been moderately disconcerted by her obvious pleasure at seeing him again.

The word went round that visitors to the house in Newland Park, Hull, would not be welcome, so I never saw where he had lived for ten years or even the city itself. Back at the Weldons' that cold, misty afternoon, we were about to leave for the station when we found that the mist had cleared just enough for the Humber Bridge, whose opening in 1981 Philip had celebrated in a splendid occasional poem, to become partly visible. The tops of its towers made a beautiful and eerie sight, my most vivid memory of that day.

What I have written above about Philip's 'closeness' and inclination to solitude or solitariness, emphasised from early middle age onwards by progressive deafness, is not exaggerated, but I must close the second half of this memoir as I closed the first, by emphasising his tendencies in the opposite direction. As I wrote in a notice just after his death, 'he was too warm, too humorous, too genuinely sociable – as well as having been a little awkwardly so – to settle into withdrawal,' and, I might have added, too devoted to his job, which was a good half of his life at Hull.

More recently, I got hold of a cassette of the 'Desert Island Discs' programme he made in 1976. Here, asked straight off if he was a gregarious man, he said he had come to the conclusion that he probably was: 'I should be very happy [on a desert island] for about twenty-four hours, and fairly happy for another forty-eight hours, but after that I suspect I should miss people and society in general.' But perhaps there was little real contradiction: yes to company, talk (especially over a drink), jollity, friendship, even affection, no to intimacy, to 'the awful daring of a moment's surrender'.

My sorrow at his death and my abiding sense of loss is tinged with regret. He was my best friend and I never saw enough of him or knew him as well as I wanted to. If I had, I might have been able to tell him, among other things, that he was a wonderful poet whose work would last. But as it is I have to fall back on hoping he knew I thought so.

JAZZ

BORN IN 1922, I suppose I was one of the first British generation to whom jazz was a completely natural thing, not new, not a fad, not exotic, and certainly not in any way unrespectable, or suspect because 'negroid'. Older people were against it then, an added recommendation. As I grew up a little I found that a lot of what I had thought of as jazz was really dance music, or suspect because 'commercial'. I have already described how when I reached Oxford my enthusiasm soared and my knowledge expanded, chiefly under the influence of Philip Larkin. Jazz became a part of my life and still is. Every morning at home I play half a dozen tracks on my little tape recorder, mostly taken from radio broadcasts or off old 78s. Today for instance it was a couple of ferocious Dixieland numbers I taped so long ago that I have forgotten what the band was, 'Drop Down Mama' by Sleepy John Estes, a blues singer too obscure for an entry even in the monumental *New Grove Dictionary of Jazz*, a couple of Joe Turners with Pete Johnson at the piano and one of Muggsy Spanier's so-called Great Sixteen. Tomorrow perhaps Artie Shaw. Why not? How uncommercial he seems now that he belongs to a vanished world!

Because . . . In 1941, my first year at Oxford, I discovered that jazz could be not only entertaining and enlivening but emotionally moving too, if never quite as much so as parts of some classical works. I was particularly struck by what we called the Banks sides, twelve of them cut in 1932 by a small band that included the trumpeter Henry Allen, the clarinettist and tenor saxophonist Pee Wee Russell and, on four of the twelve, Fats Waller, whom most readers even today, nearly half a century after his death, will have heard of. Banks himself was the singer, a sort of counter-tenor, not very jazzy perhaps by some standards but fascinating to me, especially in the words he sang. I had not known then that such singers would have in their memory several hundred blues verses which, in their allotted minute or so, they would sing a few of more or less at random. I thought Banks was performing connected songs or poems of a kind of awesome surrealism. This certainly applied to 'Spider Crawl':

> Oh see that spider crawling up that wall . . .
> Let me be your little dog till the big dog comes . . .
> The graveyard sure is a mean old place . . .
> My gal is just like a weeping willow tree . . .

Trumpet and clarinet wove magic flourishes and arabesques between the lines. Philip had a copy, I had none and could not get one: the record was deleted, out of print. So much did this one piece come to mean to me that when, in 1943 or so, it again became available, I at once bought it, even though I was in the army and had nowhere to play it. I kept it on the table by my camp-bed just to look at, an icon not even to be picked up unnecessarily for fear of scratching it. No classical rarity can ever have been as rare as that in any sense.*

That tiny story will have to do duty for an account of the impact the stuff made on me, serve instead of a list of the Armstrongs and Bixes and works of the Chicago Rhythm Kings we played and replayed, substitute for an analysis of its appeal, simple, strong, melodic, as Bruce Montgomery always used to insist, rather than rhythmical. To catch an earful was to enter a world of as yet uncharted, un-written-about romance, innocent, almost naïve. I should have been horrified if I could have known that in that very year of 1941 'modern' jazz, in the shape of what Charlie Parker and Dizzy Gillespie were beginning to play, was to begin the slow but sure destruction of the music I had just begun to love.

'Spider Crawl', like three of the other Banks sides, is a blues,

---

*In the early or middle Fifties Banks went on tour. This took him to among other places Belfast, where Philip Larkin, still nursing the unconquerable hope, went to one of his performances. Philip found he bore no audible resemblance whatever to the Banks of 1932. The sole point of interest, and that social or anthropological rather than musical, came late, when Banks announced he would end with a vocal impression by way of tribute to the man 'who has done most to express the spirit of my race!' Not Louis Armstrong, not even Paul Robeson, but Al Jolson singing 'Mama' or a comparable horror.

which is to say it consists of short choruses of twelve bars each, using as simple a chord-sequence as can be imagined, virtually confined to the chords of the tonic, the sub-dominant and the dominant seventh. Other standard jazz tunes used sequences not much more complicated. According to an account given a thousand times, Parker and his followers craved for something more demanding, more adventurous (oh dear), and wrote and played tunes in which the chord changed every *beat* – more fun to play. More fun, any fun, to listen to? Very much not to this pair of ears.

Other enemies, unperceived as such at the time, were moving in on our jazz, my jazz, from different directions, or were soon to do so. Its audience expanded. (As Isaiah Berlin said of something else, 'It's becoming popular? It must be in decline.') There were jazz concerts. Appearance before an enthusiastic audience – it always is enthusiastic – deforms the music by encouraging the exhibitionism often latent in the performers and instigates stuff that may be fun to watch but is dull to listen to – long drum solos, double-bass solos. The long-playing record, perhaps the deadliest blow, was invented in 1948, doing away with the concentration and concision enforced by the 78 record with its three-plus minutes, purposely selected in the first place, no doubt, to fit the average dance-hall number. Jazz critics, journals, university courses came along and helped to kill it with respectability.

For a number of years after 1941 and even 1948 the thing held together, because many of the original musicians were still very much around and playing in the old way; Henry Allen, for instance, had been born in 1908, Russell in 1906. But by the time I got to the States in 1958 the disarray was perceptible. Some of the old crowd were dead, jazz performers being a short-lived lot; some had got out; some had 'adapted'. The ones who were still there and playing seemed to have let part of the fire go out of them. Hilly spotted this at once and wrote in her diary, after the first of several visits we made to Eddie Condon's Club in East 56th Street, NYC, in December 1958 (passing through those portals was like entering Valhalla): 'The band played good Chicago-style stuff but didn't at any time touch the greatness of so many of our old records.'

Among those present and performing that evening was the black trumpeter Rex Stewart (1907-67), some of whose earlier work we knew from records at home. Though a good and very accomplished performer he had always had a tendency to show off his technique, and by now he was evidently going further, tap-dancing as he played, bursting into song, shouting mildly lewd remarks and making animal and other noises with his trumpet. There could hardly have been a better illustration of my comment just now on the hazards of playing jazz before an audience, though it is true that Americans up to that time and perhaps later tended to regard jazz as a branch of vaudeville more than puristic Europeans like me would. But like the others' his playing was simply not as good as we knew it had been.

Later Rex came and chatted with us for a few minutes, a squat chunky fellow rather resembling a black Tibor Szamuely with a short beard. He said of Duke Ellington, in whose band he had played for eleven years, that he was a difficult, domineering man to work under, though he admired him as much as a musician could whose hero was Sibelius. I call him Rex here because I was later to get to know him a bit and we lunched and drank together a couple of times in New York. I found him genial, cynical, mildly disparaging of some others, complaining for instance, justly enough I suppose, that Armstrong had long been lost to Hollywood. When we talked further about his years with Ellington I asked him if he and the others in the band had known that King George VI* had had a collection of every Ellington record on its original American label. 'Oh, we knew,' he said, 'and when we were refused hotel service in Tennessee or South Carolina we'd say to each other, "Well, George likes us, George likes us." '

Rex turned up as leader of a group that a jazz-loving publisher called Sandy Richardson assembled specially for Hilly and me at his house in Hopewell, Pa. – he, Sandy, had earlier taken us to hear Wilbur de Paris and his band play their 'New New Orleans' music, which was good because of the old New Orleans bits still to be heard in it, not because of any of the newness. Anyway, Rex had with him, among others, the clarinettist Buster Bailey, the trombonist J. C. Higginbotham, and another trumpeter called Joe Thomas. The party and the music began in the garden. I did not and never had cared much for Bailey's style, finding it too blandly mechanical, but he redeemed himself slightly by his startling resemblance to Colonel Nasser, then President of the United Arab Republic, and

---

*That was the story then, but it seems much more likely that the royal Ellington fan was the King's brother, Prince George, Duke of Kent, whose collection must perforce have been incomplete, since he had died in an aeroplane crash in 1942.

his enthusiastic tomming (tomming is or was the buttering-up of whites by a black) – 'Ain't he the most, Kingsley!' he would bawl as other musicians finished their solos. I had thought Higginbotham the greatest of all trombonists; I had shaken his hand with more reverence than that of W. H. Auden on a different occasion, but that evening he was not on top form or more lastingly in decline. Thomas, whom I had been looking forward to hearing, had turned up too drunk to play. 'Pops Bechet just died,' he said in mitigation, and this had indeed happened, though, as I have this moment discovered, a full month earlier. By his general demeanour Thomas seemed to be suggesting that I had had some hand in this sad event, or at least was concealing my satisfaction at it. But he soon forgot about that after another drink.

The evening was enjoyable, exciting and disappointing at once. When it got too chilly outside we crowded into Sandy's cottage and the band went on playing in a room no bigger than a spacious kitchen. Rex began 'talking through his horn' and made his trumpet say recognisably, 'Get me another drink for the love of Mike' and other, less drawing-room expressions. Well, it was a party, I told myself.

I attended a jazz concert at Lambertville, N. J., at which both Duke Ellington's orchestra and the Johnny Dankworth band from England performed. The audience were generous to the visitors without apparent insincerity and Cleo Laine was splendid, never better, much applauded; I had a small, ridiculous moment of relish when she sang 'I don't stand a ghost of a chance with you' using the long British A in 'chance'. And the Ellington band were a national institution. And yet . . . My feelings were crystallised by a visit to Birdland not long before we sailed for home. I have tried to blot out of my mind most of what they played, but the sound of Miles Davis's trumpet, introverted, gloomy, sour in both senses, refuses to go away. I had heard the future, and it sounded horrible.

In 1961 the American musicologist Henry Pleasants published a short book, *Death of a Music?* (Gollancz), which demonstrated to my satisfaction that when a music, or a kind of music, loses all connection with song and, in the second place, with dancing, it also loses its audience and is doomed. The music of Pleasants's title was serious music, classical, whatever you like to call it. The last third of his book consists of a substantial rider arguing that jazz, or American music as he would prefer to have it known, having retained its links with song, was the music of the future and would take over the kind of audience that modern serious music had lost. When I ran into Pleasants some twenty years later in England I asked him, 'In the light of what's happened since, you wouldn't say that about jazz any more, would you?' – 'No,' he said, 'absolutely not,' and we went on to agree that it had gone the same way as its elder brother and was lost.

Totally. Only the name survives (I am leaving out more or less worthy pastiches of what we once had). Good going in a sense, to have got from Monteverdi to John Cage in – what? Forty years? The Hot Five to Ornette Coleman? Nothing makes me feel more thoroughly old than to realise that there is nothing but a bloody great hole where quite an important part of my life once was. I mean, poetry, the novel and much more besides have gone off all right, but they have not *vanished* (except as it might be for pastiches of bygone writers).

One of the last jazzmen, the once-great Wild Bill Davison, turned up in London in May 1989, a little old man of eighty-three who when I went to see him was sitting in a kimono eating a bowl of what looked like chop-suey. He was at the start of a UK tour with Art Hodes, an eighty-four-year-old pianist who was terrible forty years ago (Philip Larkin remarked of him that he sounded as if he had three hands and didn't know what to do with any of them). With them there was to be a presumably British group called John Petters' Dixielanders in a show called *The Legends of American Dixieland*. I stayed away, probably wisely in view of the sadly dull record of some of his recent work he presented me with. In the November of the same year Davison died in California.

I never heard in the flesh or met my great hero, Pee Wee Russell, when I had the chance in 1959. But that was no doubt just as well too, because he had 'adapted' or at any rate gone off, as records of his had shown.*

On my newish equipment I can hear the notes of the music on the Banks sides at least as well as ever, but not the things I used to hear.

---

*He had never recovered his old fire after a serious illness half a dozen years before.

BRUCE MONTGOMERY

I MUST FIRST have seen Bruce Montgomery on my first morning in St John's in 1941 coming out of his staircase in the front quad to go to the bath-house. (In those antediluvian days you had to walk across the open for these purposes, in some cases what could have been a hundred yards.) I felt rather like a recruit getting his first sight of a full colonel in red tabs, spurs, etc.: here was an *undergraduate*, the real thing. This man, along with an indefinable and daunting air of maturity, had a sweep of wavy auburn hair, a silk dressing-gown in some non-primary shade and a walk that looked eccentric and mincing, though I found out later that it was the result of a severe congenital deformity in both feet that could still result in a joint going 'out' without warning.

When more fully attired, he inclined to a fancy-waistcoated, suède-shoed style with cigarette-holders and rings. They made me uneasy, especially the last two items, which at about this time were apparently compulsory for villains in British films. Even Philip Larkin, himself no ascetic in matters of dress, disapproved.

'I don't care for those rings of Bruce's,' he said. 'They're flashy.'

'Yes, and foreign.'

'Yes, and common.'

But in those early days I saw little of Bruce, who had come up in 1940, a couple of terms ahead of me. I did see a bit of him, odd as it may sound, in the college chapel. As well as reading modern languages, he was organ scholar, i.e. organist and choirmaster. I had enjoyed singing in the choir at school and joined this one for a time. It was not a success: I was the only undergraduate there apart from Bruce himself, and among those mere seven or eight voices my incapacity with anything not wholly elementary was all too evident. I soon stopped going. Bruce told me later, not quite apologetically enough to suit me, that he had thought my interest was in him in a very personal way.

I stayed the course in a larger choir also under Bruce's baton, that of the OU Musicians' Club. The work I remember us performing was *The Rio Grande** by Constant Lambert, a great hero of Bruce's. It was the latter (I think) who had re-scored this work, originally for brass, percussion, solo piano and strings, by adapting the brass and string parts for a second piano. The result was probably a general success; it certainly was for me, and *The Rio Grande* remains to this day the only musical work I can validly claim real knowledge of.

Bruce was like many (I sometimes used to think it was most) of my Oxford contemporaries in being unfit for military service. I was A1, not even A(x)1 Psychopathic, the enviable distinction of another composer of my acquaintance, and was hauled off into khaki in 1942. A couple of pages, far too little, prefixed to the 1964 edition of Philip Larkin's novel *Jill* fill in a bare touch of that later wartime Bruce I missed, and give a tiny glimpse of what Philip calls 'Bruce's modern-languages-Playhouse-classical-music-Randolph ambience', the last being perhaps the most marked – in those days Bruce was already a hotel-bar man while the rest of us were largely still pub men. Now, both almost in their last term, the two became close friends. Like me, Philip had found Bruce a little intimidating at the start, though he was the gentlest of souls (I only saw him angry once, when I had stigmatised Malcolm Arnold's overture *Beckus the Dandiprat* as marred by fake jollity). But there would remain something formidable, at least, about a man who, as Bruce apparently had, had written a book called *Romanticism and the World Crisis*, possessed a grand piano and had painted a picture that was hanging on the wall of the sitting-room in his lodgings. I would have given something to see that.

When I got back to Oxford in 1945 it was to find that things had not stood still in my absence. In particular, Bruce was already launched on both his two careers. His first novel, *The Case of the Gilded Fly*, had been written in a single Oxford vacation (with a J nib and silver pen-holder, according to Philip) and published in 1944 under the pseudonym of Edmund Crispin. I was consumed with admiration and envy of this achievement, especially envy. Now

---

*Knowing him to have been a close friend of Lambert's I played records of this work to Anthony Powell in Swansea, and was astonished when he went to bed halfway through.

I am keeping literary criticism out of this book as far as possible, but if *Gilded Fly* is a rather bad novel, if not something worse, then something ought to be said of that here. At two vital points, those involving the crime itself and the dénouement, the author introduces grotesque improbabilities. This would matter less if it were not for the constant flippancy and facetiousness of the style, an excessive striving after high spirits or their effect. There are good things, as reviewers say, in all his novels, of which the best is *The Moving Toyshop*, but I now find them unreadable. They came out yearly until 1952. Perhaps I am merely imagining that when I saw that the 1953 volume, *Beware of the Trains*, was to be a collection of short stories, I thought, 'Oh dear, not just a gathering of old scraps, I hope.' Anyway, it turned out to be the last of the series.

This is to look a little ahead. So it is time to say something of his career as a composer. I have to take the word of others that he wrote some very good church music, and he produced some other works for small forces, though I saw or heard nothing of his in that line after about 1950. Before then he had gone into film music, writing the score for the enduringly popular *Doctor in the House*, a score that might have attracted more attention than it did if a technical defect had not seen to it that the music itself remained practically inaudible throughout. After that – I am bringing this part of the story forward into the 1960s now – he wrote a good deal more music for the British cinema, including, little as one may enjoy recording the fact, several of the *Carry On* series and never, I think, rising very high in the hierarchy of British film composers.

What he certainly failed to do, much to my own disappointment, was to write more than the first act (if as much) of a projected and fully planned grand opera to my libretto, *To Move the Passions* – the only libretto, I should guess, to have been written in the consonantal rhyme or chime Wilfred Owen used in poems of his like 'Strange Meeting'. It was to have been a costume piece set in the musical world of eighteenth-century London, with a plot about a decent middle-aged composer, a nasty pushy young composer, and the young ingénue they were both pursuing. Virtue and middle age were to have triumphed. Also featured were Three Critics, who sang in a stricter metre various platitudes about Nature and the poetical Imitation thereof derived from the course on Augustan literary theory I was giving in my lectures at Swansea at the time. Then, mysteriously, the project went cold, but the mystery was soon cleared up when Bruce revealed that he had 'had to' cannibalise the existing music for a film score that had been running late. (Not a *Carry On* film, I hope.)

Passions was not the only failed or aborted Montgomery-Amis musical collaboration. In fact we actually completed, as far as I could tell, a one-act chamber opera to be called *Amberley Hall*, another costume piece. There were only three characters, a lady, her husband and her aspiring lover. It had one dramatic twist I still think was jolly clever, whereby the lover wants to get caught somewhere near getting his way and the husband doesn't want to know, so the latter stands impassively in front of the necessary screen while the lover thumps and clumps away behind it. It was never performed that I heard of. Until the other day I thought that the coronation anthem ('The Century's Crown') we wrote together had similarly remained on paper, but it seems it *was* performed, by the Glasgow Choral Union and the Scottish National Orchestra on 3rd June 1953 in Glasgow. A long way from Swansea.

If this brief memoir is a little patchier and less organised than some of the others, it suits the subject and the circumstances. I would not say I spent a higher proportion of my time with Bruce drunk than I did with anyone else, just that it seemed like that. He loved treats, not big parties so much as four-hour lunches, and he was the first of us to be able to afford them. After a brief period of schoolmastering in Shrewsbury described by Philip, who visited him there, as beer-drinking interrupted by brief bursts of teaching, Bruce was suddenly in the world of success you read about in the papers, there with the first gin-and-tonics and Jaguars. He was said to move among starlets, pursuing Muriel Pavlow, pronouncing 'Diana Dors' without the final S and making us feel he knew something. He was overpoweringly generous, taking me to see Silvana Mangano in *Bitter Rice* and Constance Shacklock in *Rosenkavalier*, quite likely on the same day. He introduced me to the greatest detective-story writer in the world, John Dickson Carr, at the most drunken institution in the world, the International Musicians' Association, now defunct. And all this time he was working, giving concerts and recitals, turning out books.

Then, as so often years after the event or lack of one, things seemed to have changed. The books had stopped coming out. Short stories I doubt if he would have passed a couple of years earlier appeared in the evening papers. Once, referring to his own books, which he seldom did, he said firmly, 'They're drivel,' with a straight look at me which I dodged.* You heard very little about the film music now. Bruce began a sort of shadow-career as an anthologist of science fiction, with *Best SF* (1955), *Best SF Two* (1956) and five more. Excellent anthologies they were, and ahead of their time, and they did a lot for science fiction, but that was all. Then there was *Best Tales of Terror* and *Best Tales of Terror Two*. Then there was a collection of some of his perfunctory short stories. Finally came the novel we had all been rightly dreading, *The Glimpses of the Moon*, and his death in the following year, 1978.

I had lost any real touch with him for some time before that. After about 1960 he drew in his horns and rarely ventured from his house at Totnes in Devon. Unexpectedly for one so much at home in the hotel bar and with lavish living generally, he was no traveller, perhaps through caution on account of that dislocating joint of his, perhaps because by now he was getting hard up. I visited him once in Totnes in the Sixties. He worked hard to make the weekend a success, but was handicapped by the effects of drink and also by having forgotten he had invited my brother-in-law as well as Jane and me, which he undoubtedly had. Afterwards I wondered a bit how he spent his time pretty well cut off down there, except in drinking and playing the piano, but I have always been too much of a townee to be much good at imagining a semi-rural existence.

The last time I saw Bruce was in London in 1973 at and after a science-fiction lunch. By the end of the lunch itself I had had enough to drink, thank you, but he had not, he said, so as his guest on so many previous occasions I felt I had to take him to a Strand drinking-club I belonged to, where we luckily found a reasonably private corner. Here he quickly and revoltingly showed that he had, after all, had enough, in fact rather more. I asked him if he would like some black coffee, tea, anything of that sort. 'No, I'll have the same again, please,' he said not very distinctly – 'a large Scotch and water.' Not much penetration was needed to see that some sort of point of no return had been reached.

Uncountable times in those late years I would be summoned to the telephone – 'Bruce on the line' – 'Oh, God.' What could not really be called a conversation but could certainly be called an

---

*Philip to me another time, referring to the links between Gervase Fen, Crispin's detective, and W. G. Moore, a don at St John's: 'At least you and I aren't in old Bruce's *bad books*.'

embarrassment, lasting up to ten minutes, would follow, with me asking in an eager prefectorial tone how he was and what he was up to and when he was coming to London, and him unable to say anything intelligible at all. The last of these, I think, came when I was staying in the country, and I addressed my remarks to the image of an actor grotesquely playing the crucified Jesus on the turned-down TV set near by.

He did finally marry, and Ann seemed devoted to him, but I saw too little of her and of them together to say more. He grew plump early, worried about his health, was not very attractive to women but found lovable by them, with beautiful manners when not falling down drunk, speaking often in a tone of jolly asperity, generous to a degree that would earn a hundred blessings. And what happened to him was very simple and dreadful. He had two genuine and precocious talents which both dried up quite quickly and completely when he was about thirty. It must have been about then that, never one to talk about himself, he said to me almost matter-of-factly, 'I can see no point in anything any more and don't get any fun out of anything I do.' How are you supposed to handle that, lots of money now and some fame and nothing to say? Drinking yourself to death is one solution. That process from the same kind of point took Dylan Thomas twenty years; it took Bruce twenty-seven. There have been others.

But it seems too depressing to end like that. Let me tag on the lyric of a little song he wrote about 1950, I suppose, and as far as I know never published or even wrote down, though he would sing it on request in a light, plaintive, front-of-the-mouth tenor. I remember all the lines except one, which is also where my memory of the tune briefly gives out, though I am sure a sympathetic pianist and I could soon run up something adequate. As a whole it may or may not be any good. It is too full of Bruce and memories of Bruce for me to be able to tell.

> Why should the swallow return,
>> Why should the spring come all over again,
>> Now we're no longer together, and when
> My poor heart has so much to learn?

> Why should the roses unfold,
>> Now you have thrown our love away,

Just like a flower you wore one day,
Until it grew withered and old?

There's no reason
Why any season
    Should happen, if love can die;
[The dead leaves fell in the autumn rain]*
    And I found we'd kissed and you'd said goodbye.

Winter has turned into spring,
    Summer is here, but oh what can I say?
    Wherever you are you're too far away
For summer to mean anything.

*'Restored' line.

THE ARMY

THE BRITISH ARMY has been compared to many other institutions – school, lunatic asylum, prison and so on – but one parallel that has never been drawn before, I think, is with a society of the kind you read about in some science-fiction stories, a world much like our own in general appearance but with some of the rules changed or removed, a logic only partly coinciding with that of our own world, and some unpredictable areas where logic seems missing altogether or to point opposite ways at once. To learn to live with it is not just a matter of acquiring facts but of developing an intuition, a feel, not to be satisfactorily or directly communicated in words. It would be rash to dismiss anything said of it or in it as myth, the pack-board tale, for instance.

There was a thing called a small pack which you wore on certain occasions fixed by a system of straps between your shoulder-blades (so that of course you could not take anything out of it or put anything into it without dismantling the system of straps), containing various articles designed to assist eating, etc. They could not by any natural means be made to fit smoothly and neatly into the exact square-oblong shape of the pack. But you could be put on a charge, formally accused of a misdemeanour, for having a misshapen pack. The only way of devising a perfectly flat, right-angled pack was by using pack-boards, plywood rectangles cut to size and shape. But you could be put on a charge for using pack-boards. Checkmate, what?

Nobody I met in 1942-45 had ever seen any of this happen. It was told, like much else, of the Guards or a certain posh regiment or some other distant beings. But it was widely believed, by many perhaps in a semi-mystical sense, as some Christians say they 'believe' in the resurrection of the body. To dismiss it as fantasy, on the other hand, or to believe in it as a device for, say, breaking a soldier's spirit, would be equally mistaken. I am not sure about it myself. One of the things the army does for you is to enlarge your concept of human nature and of what is possible.

So, for instance, I believed without hesitation when I was told by a cadet who had been a lance-corporal in the Grenadiers (they probably called him something else there, but he wore a single chevron) about the coal-buckets. In every barrack-room there was a perfectly burnished bucket with pieces of filed-down, varnished coal shaped to sit on top of its contents like a flat stretch of gleaming black crazy paving. I saw with my own eyes men put on charges for not polishing their boots when the Army Council had expressly forbidden the polishing of boots but the Colonel liked polished boots. And I believe the story of how our military police stopped the theft of phials of penicillin by female dock-workers in Naples; they hit suspected smugglers over the head with a copy of the *Manual of Military Law*, thus dislodging the secreted container. People who have not been in the army take the story for myth.

I think I first noticed this faint but immanent unreality in my first week of service when I was sitting in the NAAFI reading a paper-back. (The only other thing to do was go and see the film of *Hellzapoppin'*, which I had already done once that day and three times that week.)

'What you reading then?' asked a long-service NCO near by.

'Story about the army.' (By Gerald Kersh, I remember.)

'What's it like? I mean does he understand the army, the fellow who wrote it?'

'Well, I've just come to a bit where the sergeant in front of the squad asks a bloke why he's wearing shoes, and the bloke says he's excused boots, and the sergeant says, oh, excused marching, and the bloke says no, just excused boots.'

The NCO nodded and sniffed. 'He understands the bloody army,' he said.

My enlistment via benefit of university meant I only spent a couple of months in the ranks before joining an OCTU (Officer Cadet Training Unit), and this handicapped me to the end in my own understanding of the army. My service with the OTC at school and STC at Oxford, however, helped, though mostly in more practical ways. I looked a goon and a bleeding civvy in uniform, but boy, could I drill a squad. I once amazed and, if such a thing had been possible, impressed the chief OCTU drill sergeant by a virtuoso display in a space no bigger than a Nissen hut. Here I took thirty squaddies through all the prescribed evolutions – 'Squad-will-retire . . . about . . . TURN . . . squad-will-move-to-the-left-in-threes . . . left . . . TURN . . . squad-will-advance . . .' – at top speed and with all the multifarious errors avoided without sign of difficulty. This won me some general respect.

My mathematical abilities helped too: they had got me into the Signals in the first place, later took me on an advanced wireless course that included the first trials of a line-of-sight telegraphy (unsuccessful) and of the ancestor of the telex machine (successful) and qualified me to operate a radio link with Moscow if need be. I passed out with a Q2, equivalent to a Third in a degree course, and, encountering the army at its rawest and most wayward, never touched a wireless set again. In this training period I also did a great deal of what the army had desperately longed for Signals to do, 'learning to fight as infantry'. I once described some of this in a short story of 1962 in words that fit my present point too well to be altered:

> . . . the cross-country runs, the musketry competitions, the three-day infantry-tactics schemes with smoke-bombs and a real barrage, the twelve-mile route-marches in respirators which had seemed in retrospect to show a curious power of inverted prophecy when the unit completed its role in the European theatre of war without having had to walk a step or fire a shot.

But that kind of thing was liable to happen to anybody and this is supposed to be a personal account. So, then: at the end of June 1944, I got to Normandy as part of the large and lavishly equipped Signal unit entrusted with the communications of British Second Army headquarters (Second Army Signals).

My fellow-officers were a mixed lot, though as far as I was concerned they seemed to share a low level of general culture. There were men who had been Post Office engineers or warrant officers in the Regular Army; I could see the point of them all right. There were some odds and sods like me who knew a bit of maths or physics. And there were, perhaps the majority, what a character in another short story of mine called, rather harshly perhaps, 'a bunch of ignorant jumped-up so-called bloody gentlemen from the Territorial Army', bank managers, local solicitors, estate agents, Rotary Club types. It was these who tended to occupy the senior positions, which was unfortunate, or so I thought. The Colonel was a large, self-assertive fellow whom I suspected of hoping to be mistaken (in a poor light, so to speak) for a Regular soldier. I never discovered his civilian occupation, but it cannot have been anything involving specialised knowledge, perhaps some form of civil administration or shopkeeping. Two senior captains performed acolyte roles, one running the disciplinary, regimental side of life, which included being nasty to subalterns like me, the other, a Fleet Street man in peacetime, acting as fixer with black-market clothing and food, whisky, cigarettes, etc. The technical side, the apparatus that ran the line and radio systems on which the entire role of the unit depended, was organised by a small, ungregarious ex-PO major who, with his junior technicians, saw to it that Second Army Signals actually carried out the job it had been designed for.

Many times the Colonel insisted that we must regard the Mess as our home, or at least a club, where all were in some sense equal. For some months before the Normandy invasion that Mess had been housed in Headington Hill Hall near Oxford, the present home of Sir Robert Maxwell, which is the sort of thing that gets called ironical these days. Anyway, for a little while I was green enough to believe the Colonel, who after dinner would say things to me like,

'Well, Bill [my standard name in the army], I expect a Communist like you must be jolly glad to think of your old friend Uncle Joe Stalin taking over Poland and Czechoslovakia and all those other places we went to war for, when he sees his way clear.'

'All those places will be allowed to have proper democratic elections, sir,' I would say, 'to decide what kind of government they want after the war.'

'And you're really a big enough fool to believe that, are you, Oxford degree and the rest of it?'

I would make some more or less meaningless remark about fools with or without degrees, and it would probably seem to pass unnoticed or unheeded, but then a day or two later I would be quite likely to find in Unit orders that my section was called upon to supply the duty jeep a week or so before its turn was due to come round.

Then another evening the Adjutant would say, shortly after I had assured him that the *Warsaw Concerto* was a piece of worthless commercialism, that he expected what I really liked was those lumps of stone mucked about with by that fellow Epstein, was it, and those pictures of girls with both their eyes on the same side of their nose.

'No, I can't bear anything like that,' I would answer truthfully, perhaps over-emphatically.

'Funny, I should have thought that sort of thing would be right up your street, Bill.'

The Adjutant looked as if he had not believed my disavowal. Anyway, when the following week a snap inspection of my section transport was held, my mind went back to the *Warsaw*-Epstein conversation. For a moment I suspected him of punishing me, not for anything I had said or done, but for what he (wrongly, but never mind that) believed I believed. Then I decided that that would have been too feminine a reaction on his part, that I was getting paranoid, etc. Very likely. The atmosphere of that Mess was certainly not one to discourage paranoia.

One event I wish I had noted more closely was a Unit Dance in '43 or '44 where, of course, these creatures would have been consciously trying to behave like gentlemen, in many cases with their wives present. They were not too bad, I suppose, no worse than average, better in the case of some non-followers of the Colonel – noisy, drunken or trying to become so, uncouthly convivial, frankly on the look-out for sex in the case of the unmarrieds, just like me, in fact. Beer, gin-and-It and Scotch flowed. At a late stage I was half-witness to a scene involving the Adjutant, his wife, who was blonde, a little bit horse-faced but harmless, the other Colonel-acolyte and an odd hanger-on and female or so, seven or eight persons in all.

'I've told her often enough,' the Adjutant was saying. 'It's not my fault there isn't any kid after nearly ten years. I'm doing my part when the time comes round. It's her who's not doing hers. Must be.'

'I think we could go into this another time, Ted,' said his friend.

'I'm not having her sitting there and saying that's right, we haven't got a kid but nobody seems to know why,' said the Adjutant. 'It's *her fault* and that's an end of it. *I* can manage what the book says you have to do. *She's* the one who unfortunately can't perform the necessary. Everybody got that?'

His wife, with her hands over her face, had certainly got that. Why she was still sitting there I could not imagine. Nor could I think of anything anybody could have done. Ticking a man off for maltreating his wife in public is notoriously delicate, especially if the man is the senior among a group of officers.

'*Barren*. That's what it used to be called. I expect they've dreamed up some new fancy high-falutin name for it now.'

I forget what happened after that. I think I was overtaken by one of those horrible moments of suspicion apt to strike a young man at such times, that what he had just seen is a sample of what life, grown-up life in the real world of earning a living and having a family, is actually like, and that what he has tried to believe up to now has been based on reading too much poetry, etc.

Anyway, any occasion like that, any occasion at all, eating in a building, sleeping in a building, were not features of life across the Channel. There was no sex to be had there, or none that I could find. There was no beer, and of course no whisky even if I could have afforded it. But there was some stuff called burgundy, which I found I liked after all, the last phrase meaning a few years after my mother had tried to make me drink Keystone or Big Tree 'burgundy' from Australia or South Africa to put health-giving iron into my blood. Nor was this all, as it proved.

Not only through being French, and Normans too, the local population were on the whole disagreeable. They had some excuse, in that their life had been at any rate reasonably tranquil before all these intruders started dropping shells and bombs into their farms and fields, and the Germans had been relatively lenient to the Normans to encourage their traditional hostility to the authority of Paris. British soldiers who took soap from door to door in the hope of bartering it for bacon got many a black look, though admittedly quite a lot of bacon too. Some got more.

The received wisdom was that you stood a better chance if the farmer had white hair, i.e. was old enough to have served alongside the Tommies in the Great War. One afternoon, Sergeant Lally, Corporal Beavis and I were out on a bartering expedition of more than ordinary importance. Beavis was not of the Royal Signals but of the Army Catering Corps, was indeed the senior of the two cooks serving my section of about forty men, a good cook too as they went. It had been felt that his expert eye directed at a farm larder would be more useful than, say, an instrument-mechanic's. The first farmer we came to had white hair. He greeted us cordially and the bartering went well enough. When it was done, I had the fine sight of the patron emerging from his cellar carrying a bottle off which he was blowing dust. We were soon settled in his comfortable parlour drinking its contents, which tasted to me incredibly strong and not wholly pleasant. The stuff was called Calvados, of which none of us three English had ever heard. (Neither had anybody else outside Normandy, as I later discovered.) With a shared vocabulary of fifty words or so, conversation was not brisk, but it was pleasant to sit back and gaze out at the farmer's luxuriant sunlit apple-orchard, getting drunk for the first time for many days. Or starting to: it seemed not very long before Beavis left the room, in search, I assumed, of a latrine. But no: he soon came running into view in the orchard, jumping over tussocks and fallen branches and shouting, 'Look at me! Look at me! I'm a horse! I'm a horse! Whee-ee-ee-ee-ee-ee!'

It took him two days in bed to get over that, during which time of course he could cook nothing. But a rare stroke of good fortune had seen to it that, while Beavis could in normal times cook everything but porridge, the other cook, Private Lindsay from Glasgow, could cook nothing but it, and that supremely well. For those two days the section feasted on porridge, and if you think you would tire of it long before the end, you have not tasted porridge made with Normandy cream with more Normandy cream poured over it ad libitum. (Admittedly, one sometimes longed for a mug of tea without milk.)

At night there was much air activity. I mention this only to record an interesting psychological consensus. Like my colleagues I slept in a small individual canvas tent, near a slit trench in which it was considered bad form to take shelter. Nor was there more than minimal danger, though my own side did get quite near killing me with an unexploded anti-aircraft shell. But the noise was immense at times. I found myself lying on my back in my camp-bed with my tin hat, supposedly proof against shrapnel, on my head. After a couple of minutes' thought I would transfer the hat to the area that included my genitals. A couple of minutes' more thought, and the hat was back on my head. Still more thought – back down to the balls. Yet more thought . . . at some stage I would get fed up with the fandango and fall asleep. Coyly mentioning it one morning at breakfast in the Mess tent as a possibly amusing quirk, I was greeted with a roar of agreement, sympathy, relief – 'Thank God somebody's said it at last!' All my brother officers without exception regularly went through the same routine. As regards which end of the anatomy the protective steel came to rest (if not on the floor), a distinct majority thought they favoured the head. And they talk about British distrust of the intellect!

The headquarters had arrived in sufficient quantity by now, and as far as we were concerned the war could start. My duties were those of signalmaster, or rather one of a round-the-clock trio of these presiding over what was in effect a military post office. We saw to the transmission, reception and delivery of all service messages passing out of, into and through the headquarters, using line communication, wireless and despatch rider but not, to universal and often-voiced regret, carrier pigeon. In practice, many hours of duty were spent answering telephone calls from the staff or staffs around one – quartermasters, operations officers, adjutants, engineers, gunners, RAF liaison men, American liaison men, lawyers, padres, Kinema, Phantom. It was nothing at all compared to being shot at, but since nearly all these calls were inquiries made in a chiding spirit at best, and virtually every caller was senior in rank to a mere lieutenant, it was not relaxing either. Four (mostly undeserved) ballockings in a row from, say, a general-staff brigadier, an Airborne full colonel, the Signals brigade major and the Deputy Provost-Marshal made one, well, feel one could do with a cup of tea.

At such times I would try to think of what I had been told by a New Zealander captain of Intelligence I once sat next to (in the officers' bog). Noting my Signals shoulder-flashes he said, 'This ought to cheer you up. The other day we captured the signalmaster's diary of a Jerry corps. The Resistance had all his land-lines cut on D-Day bar two, one to Commander-in-Chief West and another to an independent parachute brigade that happened to be around. That was the lot.'

I uttered perhaps the most heartfelt 'Christ!' of all my military career. I almost felt sorry for those German signals subalterns and captains, telling Field-Marshal Rundstedt that no, he still could not telephone any of those divisions (and of course he could not speak to them over the air either), but he could have a chat with a lot of parachutists any time he felt like it. For the rest of the day I could have faced almost cheerfully the telephonic presence of the biggest shit on the entire staff, Colonel the Lord Glenarthur, but he failed to show – probably having it off in Bayeux.

Then came the August breakout from the beachhead and all was movement – pack up, off to the next place, set up and take over control from the rear party, wait to be leapfrogged and taken over from, pack up, etc. It went well with Normandy tummy (acute diarrhoea and fever), heavy continuous rain and arriving after dark in a field you had not seen in the light and where no latrines had been dug, but it still beat being killed. I saw a lot of people whom that had happened to around Falaise, so recently that there had been no time even to bulldoze some to the roadside. Like life-sized dolls, everyone said, as everyone always has. The horses – for outside the panzer and motorised divisions much German transport, unlike British or American, was still unmechanised – seemed almost more pitiful, rigid in the shafts with their upper lips drawn above their teeth as if in continuing pain. The dead cows smelt worst.

By the autumn things had slowed down, certainly as far as my part of the unit, now Rear Second Army Signals, was concerned, or more likely those six or so months' experience together had seasoned us, made us as near an efficient military organism as a bunch of mainly duration-only young men, well sprinkled with hopelessly unsoldierly technicians, had a reasonable chance of becoming. Ennui had time to set in. Here is as good a place as any for me to give some idea, not of a day in the life of a junior Signals officer on active service, which would be too tedious for you or me to bear, but of an hour or so, a couple of glimpses in the present tense 'Berlin Diary' style of Christopher Isherwood, whose *Goodbye to Berlin* had been popular in the Oxford of my time. So –

I am sitting in the ante-room of the Officers' Mess drinking tea after lunch. It used to be a Belgian 'bourgeois' drawing-room and no doubt will be again. There are a divan, two sofas and a peculiar double armchair, high-backed, like part of a railway-carriage seat. In the corner is a massive stove, armoured with green tiles. It is far too big for the room, and when it is working, even in the coldest weather, the air is nearly too hot to breathe. On the walls, which seem hung with low-grade parchment, are a number of pictures. One is of the four most uninteresting chrysanthemums I have ever seen in my life; most of the remainder are landscapes, the small ones in fussy frames, the larger reminiscent of the landscape targets used in weapon-training. A faint breeze stirs the muslin curtains, but it is very hot.

I have just come off morning shift, so it is late and I am alone. I sip my tea, which smells of tented NAAFIs, and feel drowsy, also randy in an undirected way, entirely theoretical, as if the desire could never under any circumstances connect with any real woman. Persons of this sex are in any case hardly ever seen these days except at a distance. The view from the window is bounded on one side by the Command Group Vehicle, which sounds quite grand for a lorry festooned with aerials and needing a few dents hammered out and a lick of paint – and on the other by the hen-house where the Mess's looted chickens live. Through the lilac bush I can see the officers' latrine, towards which the second-in-command, in private life an (I hope) unsuccessful insurance executive, is walking, kicking feebly at grass-tufts. A jeep with no exhaust roars past in a cloud of dust. I begin thinking about the varied smells that pervade the area: that of mingled rum and burning cardboard from the cookhouse rubbish, those of the hen-house and the piggery, setting one another off, the fainter whiff from the latrine, the scent of the lilac that competes unsuccessfully with all the others.

My batman/driver, in his capacity as a mess servant, comes in and starts laying out the cups and saucers for tea. I get up, wander round the room, noting the sideboard, which looks as if it might have had some ecclesiastical purpose. Through its glass doors can be seen sets of fancy drinking-glasses, tumblers, ponies, goblets stained royal blue and blood-red. As I pass I bang my head on the lampshade, which at its lowest point is no more than five feet from the floor. A draggled gilded tassel hangs from its centre. It is almost completely opaque. Above it are three lesser shades of frosted glass; you can have the big shade, or the lesser shades, or all four lit up as you wish; with the lot going there is nearly enough light to read by at night. My eyelids sag. I must go out or fall into a snooze. I go out. The farmer's not quite completely unattractive daughter might come in to water the garden.

The thought of Sammy Quick drifts into my mind, Sammy the famous drunk, commissioned from staff-sergeant in 1939, a fixture at Southern Command when I was there briefly in 1943. I remember how Sammy would go into Salisbury after dinner on his own, get full of booze and pass out walking back to West Harnham camp on the canal path; how he had thought it safer to stay and booze in the Mess, and woken up at dawn in the kitchen garden under the runner beans; how he had taken to getting pissed in his bedroom in the commandeered semi-detached near by, and woken up very stiff on the floor; how, the week I was posted, he had settled for climbing into bed at eight p.m. with a bottle of Scotch. I wonder, not for long, how Sammy Quick is getting on now.

A few hours later I am at my desk near the rear wall of the signal office. From it I can see nearly everything that is going on, such as it is. At the other end of the room there are two six-foot tables laid end to end; these are called the counter. When orderlies from the Staff come in with messages for transmission they give them to one or other of the clerks who sit facing them. I watch the clerks' industrious backs: on the left Cpl Green empties a large tray full of 'traffic' (messages in transit) received from other formations; on my right Cpls Lattimore and Smailes push traffic out to be sent by teleprinter or wireless. Sgt Lee at his table makes up packets of messages for the DR runs; Cpl Marvin faces enormous racks of expired traffic, noting on a sheet each time of clearance. Tennyson, the locations clerk, is almost completely hidden by a wooden palisade on which he hangs a huge file stiffened with metal, which is supposed to show where every unit in the army lives at this moment.

Just at this side of the counter there is a window leading to the teleprinter vehicle which is backed up against it in the school yard. Operators clatter up and down the empty spares boxes which form steps to it. From inside it comes the rattle of the machines and an almost continuous sound of swearing. Davies pokes his head out and says, 'Can't read Army Troops again.'

He goes to the blackboard at the far end of the room, crosses through the chalked tick signifying the Troops printer and picks up Marvin's telephone, getting through with surprising speed. 'Test? Can't read Army Troops. All sorts of odd bloody letters. Book it out, will you? And for Christ's sake see it stays in this time. There's quite a bit for them piled up.'

My own telephone rings. 'Signalmaster? I want an SDR to go to Brussels for me leaving immediately.'

'Who's speaking, please, sir?'

'Lord Glenarthur,' says the other with a hint of impatience at my not having instantly recognised him by distinctive sound quality alone. 'You understand me? A special . . . despatch . . . rider,' he says, spelling it out for the thick. 'Immediately. Send him across to my caravan.'

By regulation, an SDR is supposed to be used only to fetch or carry packets, maps, or other military objects needed too urgently to wait for the twice- or three-times-daily DR service.

'I have two SDRs out already, sir. Couldn't we hang on for the next – '

'Are you refusing to obey my order?'

'No, sir.'

So a third poor bugger will be off soon on a 150-mile trip, most of it in the dark, to fetch some urgently needed military object like a parcel of clean washing or a dozen of cognac. I have tried more than once to get the Signals brigadier to do something about Lord Glenarthur and his SDRs, but the Staff are the Staff, another order of being from the rest of us. Well, they cannot last for ever.

I spent part of that winter billeted in a Belgian farmhouse, quite comfortably, with a cow, perhaps more than one, sleeping in the next room. I grew to like hearing and feeling her moving about and snuffling to herself. I spent much shorter periods in Brussels, but one of them was a whole forty-eight hours' leave.

You stayed at a reasonably swagger hotel that had been turned into an officers' club, not an arduous exercise. In its bars and lounges, senior British officers entertained local suppliers of black-market goods or unofficial exchangers of the millions of francs they had made selling food and petrol to civilians. I shared a nice little twin-bedded room with another, Joe by name, a captain in the Royal Tank Regiment, three or four years older than I. He was all right, by which I most immediately mean that his sole objectives for this operation were drink and women; if going and looking at a picture or a building crossed his mind, he gave no sign of it. We arrived too late for dinner, so it was a quick snack and straight out to those places where his objectives and mine might be found. Drink was expensive and served in slow tempo; as for women, I saw none that I might have been caught looking at even when very drunk who was not accompanied by at least one British officer in service dress smoking a cigarette.

In the end, Joe and I found ourselves rather miserably sitting by a window in a small café on the point of closing for the night, three-parts drunk, true, but of course with no company but each other's. I noted at the other end of the bar a rather pretty waitress chatting to the barman, who was doing something with his till and money. She was obviously about to leave, which would bring her past us.

Joe had shown that he knew some French, so I said to him – I still think rather brilliantly, 'Thou art a scholar; speak to it, Horatio.'

'Eh?' he said.

'Ask her to bring a pal along to that club place at midday tomorrow. Too late for her to start looking for one now.'

Joe got that part all right. Within half a minute he was talking away, doing well too, or so I thought till the girl looked out of the window and said something urgent that sent him dashing for the door, calling to me to follow him.

In less than another half-minute we were evidently pursuing a tram along the street. It gave out sparks and honked at us.

'This is the last one that goes to our part of town,' explained Joe as we ran. In those days you could talk as you ran. 'She spotted it out of the window.'

'Bit of luck. Is she going to turn up tomorrow, do you think?'

'Don't see why not.'

I could see any number of reasons, but by now we were using all our attention on climbing on to the tram. What I saw of the other people in it, and of the district through which we were passing, had the effect of arousing in me some doubt about the wisdom of our current enterprise. Well, she probably won't come, I thought.

But she did, looking even better than the previous evening. But then again she had with her a short dark-haired girl with a long nose and other features to match. There goes yours, cunt, I thought to myself unphilosophically, rehearsing Joe's seniority in rank and years and his share in arranging matters.

'Well, you seem to have got yourself a nice blonde, Joe,' I said with hypocritical cheerfulness.

'Oh no, I like the little dark one,' he said.

'You like the . . . Well now, shall we have a drink?'

We ordered one, and the blonde was explaining that her name was Joanne Duerinckx, and looking better yet as she carefully wrote it down for my benefit, when a man of about thirty whose name I never learnt, a moustached captain in some infantry regiment, insinuated himself into our party. He very soon set about making up to Joanne – in French, needless to say. I began to feel out of things, nor did I feel any distance back into them when he started talking to her about me. What he said most often began with some phrase meaning roughly, 'You don't want to bother with,' and went on with perhaps three words that sounded like 'ce petit vierge,' whose exact meaning, though not their general drift, was unclear to me at that time. Nice while it lasted, cunt. Unable to think of anything else to do, I tried to look bored, which required no great effort on my part. With matters still unresolved the girls now took their leave, saying they had to work that afternoon, but would be back in the evening. With rare self-command I decided to put that out of my mind until it came.

'Shall we have another drink?' asked the infantryman.

We did, more than one. They were called gin and french, and like much else that weekend I had not come across them before. They seemed to be such that you could drink a lot of them without getting drunk, or too drunk, or feeling too drunk. As far as I remember nobody mentioned lunch, or perhaps there were bits of things on the table or something. After some time, the infantryman asked,

'You chaps game for a stroll round the brothels this afternoon?'

What could I have done? We came out of the hotel, which faced on to a very classy boulevard, and turned up the first side-street along, one with what I thought had a distinctly tatty appearance. Not more than fifty yards up it there was a near-replica of a lower-to-middle-grade English pub.

'We'll just have a peek in here,' said the infantryman.

In here it looked much as it had out there, the kind of place where a labourer of that period would have taken his mate, for a couple of pints after work. Quite a few of such seemed to be so engaged, wearing caps, overalls, etc., à la Middlesbrough or Gateshead. Even the word GUINNESS was to be seen here and there. Huh, I thought, preparing to about-turn, fat lot clever-dick really knows about the way they go on in these parts.

'I'll just have a quick word,' he said, accosting the middle-aged, rather stuffy-looking barmaid.

In an incredibly short space of time I was sitting in an upstairs parlour, furnished rather like a seaside boarding-house at, say, Frinton, with a young lady on my knee wearing only her underclothes. Well, I say a young lady – she was a young-enough lady with not a hell of a lot to spare. Joe and the other chap were similarly accommodated. For a reason I have now forgotten I at once took from my jacket pocket my week's 2-oz chocolate ration, which I had been carrying about with some intention equally lost to memory. It was put away for later, perhaps as an unexpected treat for a favourite grandchild. The infantryman now called for an exhibition; this was a word I could make out without difficulty but without understanding in any deep sense.

In due course this too was made clear. 'My' girl took the passive role, which I thought in some way better, less heinous. The proceedings either bored Joe or aroused him to a frenzy of desire, for he led his partner into another room before they were concluded. The latter seemed to me unlikely, but one never knows, and he had after all preferred the look of 'the little dark one' to Joanne's.

I will draw a veil over the rest of the goings-on. Nothing of note occurred, though despite all those gin and frenches, what I had in theory gone there for in the first place – that occurred satisfactorily. It was preceded by a longish solo dance round the room with one leg in and one out of my trousers, which made the tart laugh a lot;

very Continental, that touch, I thought to myself. We parted on friendly terms. I cannot of course remember how much I paid or how much a 1944/5 Belgian franc might be worth in modern values, but when the infantryman reappeared he said we had not been overcharged. I suppose he might be envied for knowing.

When we had made our way back through the totally incurious throng of drinkers and regained the street, I suddenly felt like the knight-at-arms, so haggard and so woebegone, palely loitering and so on, though there were admittedly differences in the circumstances. Was I mad? I hurried the few yards back to the hotel and took a long hot shower that laid strong emphasis on carbolic soap.

'You'd better get a move on,' said Joe. 'We're meeting those two girls in the bar in twenty minutes.'

'Oh, Christ.'

Nearly all the rest of the evening has departed from my memory. The moustached infantry captain had vanished, nor did I inquire after him. Presumably we had dinner somewhere, if only for the sake of the blokes, who had eaten nothing since breakfast but a possible bar snack. I do remember us ending up four in a bed. Well, there was only one, and it was a good big one, and no cross-pollination was called for or took place.

'Tu crois que je suis enivrée, n'est-ce pas?' asked Joanne at one point.

'Non, non,' I retorted gallantly and untruthfully.

'Si, mais je suis simplement gaie,' she said.

I know it looks pretty crummy, and half the world would have to be changed before it would look any different, but I thought it sounded good then, and I still do.

For some days after getting back to my unit, my feelings about that forty-eight were, I suppose, pleasure and self-satisfaction mixed in with bits of guilt and shame. Then a new component was added when an acute itching, accompanied by red spots, began in an intimate area. I went very quickly to the MO, a scholarly-looking, almost donnish RAMC major in his forties.

'Doctor, I think I may have – '

'Right, drop your pants.'

He took literally one look, gave my penis a kind of comradely flip and said, 'Scabies, also known as the itch. Caused by a mite that burrows under your skin. Uncomfortable but harmless. We'll soon have him out. Corporal Clough!' He gave some instructions, then went on, 'A forty-eight in Brussels, I presume. People find it hard to keep themselves clean in wartime. Mix with one another more than usual, too. Oh, and a word of advice for the future. Next time you're afraid you've got what you were afraid you'd got, just remember that if you wonder whether you've got it or not, you haven't got it. That ought to go on Daily Orders. Now if you'll just sit over there, Corporal Clough will minister to you. Come back every day for a week and you'll be clear.'

Corporal Clough brought a small pudding-basin with some pleasant, cooling white stuff in it and a shaving-brush, and anointed my itchy parts. He had worked on the books page of a Northern newspaper in civilian life, and while he daubed my genitals we had some discussion of Virginia Woolf, Arnold Bennett and others, almost my first on such subjects since donning uniform. On the last day the MO pronounced me fit and said quite kindly, 'Try to be a bit choosier next time, eh? I don't want to see you again.'

But he did, in the front quad of St John's at Oxford in the October of that year, as we stood about waiting to go in to Hall. Like me he was of course clad in civilian clothes and wearing a gown. Well, at least I saw him. I went and stood close enough to him for long enough for him to have recognised me if he had been going to. No reaction. I suppose he would have been rather more likely to know my john thomas again than my face, though in the circumstances not much more. He was the college doctor with the dining rights that went with that position. Anyway, the sight of him brought a sharp but momentary reminder of Joanne and of the insoluble question of whether I had picked up the scabies from the tart or from her and, if the former, whether I had left a touch of it with her. I hoped not. What else?

To return now, not to the last days of war but to the first of peace. VE Day on 8th May 1945 filled north-western Europe with hundreds of thousands of suddenly idle British soldiers (among many others). Those of us in the Royal Signals were not idle, just less busy, since soldiers who no longer have to fight still have to be fed and have their boots mended, and communications about these and God knows what other matters must still be exchanged. At the same time, fighting and other soldiery were still required to deal with Japan. One result of this was that, with the serious business over in Europe, female soldiers, ATS (members of the Auxiliary Territorial Service), began to be sent over there to free men for service in the Far East. Nowhere were these females more appropriate and inevitable than in the kind of signal office in which I was still earning my pay. Mixed shifts operated teleprinters, assembled despatch-rider deliveries, routed messages. This last process meant passing each on its way by the regular route, the quickest, if possible direct, if not via another unit or signal office. The information needed for doing this was readily visible and only very modest intellectual abilities were needed to get it right, certainly not even the humblest of skills.

Nevertheless, one fine morning Private Armitage, who was not even much to look at, routed some query about surplus three-tonner canopies via a disbanded mobile bath unit in Holland. I summoned her to my office, which as far as I remember was an area of floor marked off by crates of obsolete line-transmission equipment, and told her mildly – I know it was mildly because now that the Western war was won no message in the entire theatre could be of any real consequence to anyone – the correct way to route messages to that destination, and would she see it was done like that in future, and she said she would and left me.

That evening in the Mess the ATS officer, a smart, rather pretty, efficient-seeming young woman, said to me, 'What's this I hear about you being beastly to one of my girls?'

I was horrified and bewildered. Thoughts of mistaken identity mingled with memories of the short lecture in which the Colonel (not the same Colonel as the one who had thought I was a Communist) had promised his officers a flogging if they or any of their men treated any of our attached ATS with less than perfect correctness. 'What?' I said.

'You gave poor little Joy Armitage such a brutal ticking-off that she completely broke down.'

Speaking in a sort of undertone, as if fearful of being overheard, I said, 'I told her she'd made a mistake which she admitted and said she wouldn't do it again and that was all. I certainly wasn't brutal. And where did she have this breakdown? Did anybody see her?'

'She obviously went off on her own and had a good cry.'

'I see.' I considered quickly. 'I admit I may have spoken a little more sharply than was strictly necessary,' I said, feigning contrition as well as lying.

That mollified the ATS subaltern, but she still said, 'I think you should apologise to her.'

'I should have to get the Colonel's permission to apologise to an Other Rank and I don't think he'd give it.'

But I could easily imagine a few of the things he would have said to me. Still, the matter passed, though not from my mind. That minuscular incident taught me more about women than anything that had happened to me in Brussels and some other places too. It was not a matter of my having been brutal or even sharp, but right when Pte Armitage was wrong, and right in an objective, unarguable way, and both she and I had known about it. Enough.

Not far away, women by the hundred were having the time of their lives. This was Germany, not Allied territory liberated from the enemy, and until about the time I am writing of, perhaps even later, Allied troops were forbidden to 'fraternise' with all German nationals over the age of five, the most massive incitement to paedophilia I have ever come across, though doubtless an inadvertent one. So if you wanted a screw you either went for an 'enemy alien' of your choice and ran the risk of a court-martial (and not in theory either, as was discovered by an RAF padre known to me) or competed with ninety-nine or so other Allied soldiers for a member of the ATS. This had some bizarre, even faintly horrifying results. Women who had all their lives made men avert their gaze in revulsion or pity suddenly found themselves being fought over, if not with actual broken bottles, then still with sincere ferocity by sergeants who had known service over half the globe. Diffidence and other emotions kept me out of it.

Presently the signal office was moved or closed down, and I found myself with my diminishing section – men were being posted back to England every day in ones and twos – in a small market town with nothing to do. Sometimes we sat on the veranda of the little hotel we occupied and watched the girls riding by on their bicycles.

'Guten Morgen,' said an unusually pretty one, smiling.

'Lucky fucking saddle,' called Driver Thompson gallantly.

CQMS Hadlett, an old India hand, was standing next to me. 'I'd rather sleep with her with no clothes on than you in your best suit, sir,' he said.

'But of course you . . .' I began, and stopped. I had come to another of the Q's catch-phrases. He had a particularly rich store of them, but one or another was liable to pop up at any time from the long-service sergeants and warrant officers. They were surviving examples of what must in the past have been a huge stock pervading army life and other parts of 'low' life, now surely all forgotten. There would have been one or more for every detail or moment of a soldier's day, concretising it, ironising it. 'Are you waiting to see

me, sergeant-major?' – 'No, sir, I'm just standing here for a bet.'
Not much that has been written on the subject in general is satisfactory. Even the great Eric Partridge never understood 'cheap at half
the price', which performs exactly the same semantic somersault as
the Q's remark. I wish I had made a note of some of the more
extraordinary, specifically military ones I heard. They would have
reflected one aspect of what would have to be called something like
army culture, the property and product of a kind of person rarely
met with by most of those who read books, a very intelligent,
humorous man with only rudimentary education. All different now.
Q Hadlett's grandson will be a university graduate, if that means
having had a more than rudimentary education.

Finally the section itself was disbanded. Before I left, I exerted
myself so far as to hold a poll in which the types declared their
preferences among the four nationalities we had come into contact
with in our progress across northern Europe. The Dutch, assisted by
my own vote, came out as the most popular, quite closely followed, I
was sorry to see, by the Germans. Then there was a long gap to the
Belgians, and a short one to the French at the bottom. I would have
reluctantly promoted the Belgians and had the French and Germans
sharing third place.

I was sent to a so-called Reinforcement Holding Unit (RHU) in
a place called Minden in Westphalia, where our chaps had thrashed
the French in the Seven Years' War. Several hundred other British
officers with nothing to do were also there, waiting for someone to
send them somewhere else and eventually to England. Nobody
thought of looking round the town, not even for half an hour. The
batmen (or 'soldier servants' as the nobs called them) had very
thoughtfully assembled a little library of pornography, or of what a
hopeful man might have assumed to be pornography, to alleviate
our respective solitudes. One of them brought it into my room –
there was barely an armful of it – for me to choose from. I rather
cunningly asked him what my predecessors had made of the various
items.

'Well, this fellow Frank Harris,' he said, 'he's like the most
popular. They all reckon it's a load of bullshit, but who cares?
Spinning a yarn's the point, eh?'

'What about this one?' I asked with some real interest, pointing
to a Tauchnitz edition of *Lady Chatterley's Lover*. 'Quite famous,
I've been told.'

'Oh, that,' said the batman with some disdain. 'They reckon that's a pack of lies too, but not in the same way.'

'Well, it is supposed to be a novel.'

'Eh? They reckon – how did one of them put it – he reckoned the fellow was trying to take him for a ride. Something to do with the way he talked. And not enough, you know, going on, he said. Captain in the Ox and Bucks, he was. Funny-looking bloke with an eyeglass. Now these two, they're quite popular.'

One of these two was called *The Dawn of Married Love*, the other title I forget, but both were by a Dr Rennie McAndrew, and I knew where I was, in vital-book territory familiar from smallish advertisements in the *New Statesman* and other forward-looking organs. They drew to attention treatises by Marie Stopes and her peers that explained 'family planning', homosexuality and simply how to fuck. Dr McAndrew was presumably exploring the third of these fields. I picked up *The Dawn of Married Love* and pretended to look briefly through it. 'I think I'll start with this one,' I said.

It would be hard to explain, let alone justify, to anyone under about forty-five the eagerness with which, in those days, grown men as well as boys would fasten on anything in printed form that even remotely evoked the sexual act or the female body. The *Encyclopaedia Britannica* article on 'Reproduction' in any public or of course school library (and how do I know that, reader?) was certain to be in shreds, and not as a result of the activities of people in bona fide search of information. If references to It could somehow be passed off, even more legitimately offered, as scientific or educational, authority was satisfied, or at least acquiesced. Hence the vital books, Marie Stopes and now Rennie McAndrew.

The foregoing is intended to suggest that I was not actually being abnormal, at least not statistically so, in the emotion with which I approached *The Dawn of Married Love*. As well as being something called a sexologist, Dr McAndrew turned out to be something like a Scottish Presbyterian. It had to be admitted that he handled the balancing act imposed on him with some skill and tact. He also took into account what few writers on this general theme used to put on their agenda, that an act of sex does not simply begin like, say, a ride on a motor-bike: there have to be preliminaries. Information, advice, tips on these were what the vital-book reader hoped, against all his experience, one day to find. The learned doctor suggested that dances were good places for meeting and legitimately taking hold of girls, but as among the ancient authors the going-over here of established material was part of the genre. Sitting-out time was particularly propitious, said Dr McAndrew. Then, there, you could make approaches. Ah! Tips! I have to confess to improving very slightly on reality by saying that one recto ended,

> For example, say to the girl you are sitting with,
> 'Can you tell me which is the longer, a man's

and the following verso went on,

> arm or a girl's waist?' She will of course reply that she does not know, which gives you your cue to say, 'Then, let us put it to the test!'

And I never even tried it out!

I was grateful to the good doctor for being easy to laugh at and so saving me from the slight sense of humiliation which usually descends when such a work is finally laid aside. One other tip I did remember, laughing at it in a good-naturedly superior way for what I took as its artlessness. It ran something like:

> Airs and graces, fine clothes and such, may make their appeal for a time, but no girl worth having will be interested for long in a man who is not right grounded in his work.

I now find this a genuine tip, an excellent piece of serious advice which I commend to my younger readers. It will either be unnecessary or have come too late for my older ones. Dr McAndrew also recommended questing men to keep themselves clean.

My literary conscience took me next, or next but one, to *Lady Chatterley's Lover*, of which I read some forty or fifty pages, wishing most of the time I could find that eyeglassed captain in the Ox and Bucks and tell him how much I agreed with him. I did not find it necessary to extend my acquaintance with the work when I put my name down to have the ban taken off it in 1960.

Then, probably in August 1945, I was off again, on a railway journey of a few hundred miles to an RHU in Bruges on the Belgian coast, where everything, even the RHU, looked much nicer. I knew I should have gone round looking at churches and bridges, but as in Brussels there seemed to be too many soldiers about. And I was on to other things, trying unsuccessfully to write a story about an eccentric major on the admin staff there and, equally unsuccessfully, to pursue a nurse in Queen Alexandra's service, but successfully finding drinking companions among old mates from Second Army. The apathy of the past weeks lifted when Japan surrendered and it was suddenly peacetime again. In one sense, an important sense, I was back where I had been as a schoolboy in 1939.

But I had not quite finished with Second Army Signals. One day in 1975 or so I got a letter addressed to 'Dear Bill' from someone I remembered well and with liking as Lance-Corporal Waddington, inviting me to a reunion of some part of the unit, perhaps the telegraph-operating (signal-office) company of which my section had formed a part. The venue was one of those assembly-room places off Edgware Road 'with the look of a rather expensive canteen' as I described it in the longish poem I wrote on the subject. Reunions are dodgy undertakings, like formal dinners or luncheons in that they can suddenly set you wondering if anybody at all among those present is enjoying himself to the smallest degree, plus some pitfalls of their own. But of course I turned up, out of curiosity I said to myself, but also to see again others I had liked besides Les Waddington.

That hope was to a large extent dashed. Rule one about such affairs is that three-quarters of those you had most hoped to see have stayed away. Then there was the hand-of-time stuff which would have surprised nobody who, say, has encountered someone early in life and then again later: greyer, balder, fatter, uglier, *older* – yes, that was how the poor buggers looked. And they were duller, too, most of them. The shine and cheerfulness of youth can appear at first blush very like real vitality, even wit. Time will lay bare the disappointing truth, as, in a rather different way, many husbands have found. And in our case what had brought us together before had been over for thirty years.

Well, so it goes. But it was more dismal to realise that I had not looked at any of them closely enough before, had seen only super-ficial differences where there were real substantial ones, had missed the fact that Signalman X and Driver Y were amiable bores while Corporal Hazel was lively, amusing, to be listened to. And, oh God, we do that all the time, go through life not properly noticing people or valuing them as they deserve. Not even those we love? A large Scotch, please.

The ex-Adjutant, little changed in appearance, showed up late and alone among the other officers. We chatted for some minutes, during which he tried unsuccessfully to take the piss out of me for being a writer. As I gazed into his tinted bifocals, I thought to myself that I had found one exception, one person I had looked at closely enough. I forbore to ask him after his family.

LORD DAVID CECIL

OF ALL THE lecturers I have heard, Lord David Cecil gave the most accomplished performance. You could have reached that conclusion almost without entering the lecture-hall, from noting the proportion of women doing so, likely to be greater than that of men where most arts subjects were concerned, but greater yet when Lord David was 'on'. Most of the audience as a whole were indeed going in the first place to a performance, which I think now meant that they were missing something.

For much of male Oxford, especially undergraduate male Oxford, Lord David was a bit of a joke, one with a touch of lower-middle-class resentment often lurking in it. It was not so much the dramatic, Leslie-Howard good looks, nor even the clothes, which were not particularly extravagant, but the mannerisms, the mobile head and floating hands, and above all the *voice*. John Wain got a lot of both matter and manner with his imitation (appropriated by me without acknowledgement until now) of the opening of a standard Cecil lecture: 'Laze . . . laze and gentlemen, when we say a man looks like a poet . . . dough mean . . . looks like Chauthah . . . dough mean . . . looks like Dvyden . . . dough mean . . . looks like *Theckthpyum* [or something else barely recognisable as "Shakespeare"] . . . Mean looks like Shelley [pronounced "Thellem" or thereabouts]. Matthew Arnold [then prestissimo] called Shelley beautiful ineffectual angel Matthew Arnold had face [rallentando] like a *horth*. But my subject this morning is not the poet Shelley. Jane . . . Austen . . .'

To some he was a caricature of an Oxford don; to some a forthright homosexual; to some, especially foreigners, both. Once on some British Council do I was grimly doing my best to entertain a bunch of foreign visitors to Oxford when one of them, a middle-aged man who was probably a Belgian schoolteacher, said to me,

'Zis man Ce*ceel*, he is a feghee uh?'

101

'I'm sorry, he's what?'

After several fruitless repetitions the chap said with some irritation, 'A *fairghee*, an ommosexual.'

Without needing to think I said, 'Oh no. Not at all. I've never heard that. It's just his manner. A lot of upper-class Englishmen go on like it. Means nothing.'

'Oh, I see, I was awfully wrong,' said the Belgian in what I supposed he thought sounded like poofter-speak. 'I beg your pardon.' To him I was clearly trying to cover up for one of my mates.

Anthony Powell laughed a great deal when I told him this story. 'Nobody less!' he said firmly. 'And I ought to know, seeing I was his fag at Eton. Nobody less!' He almost screeched in his emphasis, leading me to suspect the existence of some marvellous illustrative scandal, but none was divulged.

To digress for a moment: lecturers at Oxford, and doubtless elsewhere, could be divided into the hard and the soft, like cops. The hard men gave you information, usually about language, Old and Middle English, strong verbs, vowel shifts and fearful old poems like *The Dream of the Rood* and *The Owl and the Nightingale*, and what they gave you was likely to reappear in the relevant parts of the final examination. The hardest lecturer I ever heard, and the worst technically, in delivery and so on, was J. R. R. Tolkien, but you sat through him because his explanation of the anomalous form 'hraergtrafum' was likely to be called for as the answer to a 'gobbet' on the paper. The soft men offered you civilised discourse with perhaps some critical interpretation and ideas about the past. The only reputable hard-soft merchant was C. S. Lewis, also the best lecturer I ever heard. What you printably called David Nichol Smith, who according to Wain would take half a minute to tell the class that Pope and Swift were friends, I am not sure. Anyway, to come back to Lord David, he was the softest of the soft, and undergraduates set on getting good degrees, not necessarily an amiable group throughout, tended to give him a short trial followed by a prolonged go-by.

My first approach to Lord David closer than across a lecture-room came when I set out to take my B.Litt. degree in 1948. Shorn of any talk about maturing of the mind, broadening (or focusing) of the critical sensibility, etc., the object of getting this second degree was to give oneself the edge, when it came to finding an academic job, over those with a mere B.A. or M.A. (See also 'Oxford'.) It was of interest that, although you had to get through quite a lot of genuine work in the process, nobody had ever been known to fail this inquisition. So widely held was the assumption of automatic success that, having narrowly missed a job in Prague, I was to be accepted when the time came as an assistant lecturer at the University College of Swansea with my course only half done. Ah, but the second part was a thesis of about 40,000 words, and for a thesis you had to have a supervisor, and my supervisor, drawn out of who knows what hat, was to be Lord David Cecil.

The Instructions to Candidates for the B.Litt. told me that the supervisor would 'normally' make contact with the candidate twice in each term. When by the middle of the second term no contact of any kind, normal or abnormal, had been made, I thought that with my first part coming to an end and my grant set to run out I had better make a move myself. I went round to New College on a weekday morning and asked at the porter's lodge.

'You're looking for *who*, sir?' he asked, as if I had inquired about the Shah of Persia. When he was sure he had heard me correctly he summoned a nearby colleague and pointed me out to him as a curiosity. 'Look, here's a young gentleman looking for Lord David Cecil!' Then, turning back to me and chuckling intermittently, he went on, 'Oh no, sir. Lord David? Oh, you'd have to get up very early in the morning to get hold of him. Oh dear, oh dear. Lord David in college, well I never did.'

I consulted another don I had got to know a bit, a youngish one as dons went, F. W. Bateson of Corpus, who looked bucolic and donnish in about equal measure, which was right for one who had been, perhaps at that time still was, agricultural correspondent of the then *New Statesman and Nation*. He was a bit leftie in a sort of Bevanish way, which was all right with me at that stage. Since I had little idea of what I wanted to research into, except that I had a fondness for the Pre-Raphaelites, and he was interested in the development of the poetry-reading public, how its taste was formed, we cobbled up between us a subject about English poetry between 1850 and 1900 and the Victorian readership. Bateson would be my supervisor – he assured me that swapping over from Lord David's insubstantial stewardship was a mere matter of form, in fact of *a* form, which he would have to sign, which, clearly enough, involved finding him.

At this point, I think that very day, I had a stroke of luck: I *saw* him walking down Broad Street. Perhaps the excitement, perhaps trepidation, has transfigured him in my memory to something not far from Clint Eastwood in his Western garb – a kind of Stetson was certainly present and something more curious than ordinary shoes. Before he could supernaturally vanish I rushed up to him outside Blackwell's bookshop. He raised his eyebrows at me.

'Oh, Lord David, do excuse me – I'm one of your B.Litt. people.'

'Oh, how awful!' he cried – verbatim – 'I'd quite forgotten.'

I gave my name and struggled on, 'I wanted to, er, ask you to, er . . .'

He offered me no help at all as I explained what I wanted, but I managed, and I had him trapped nearly on the corner of the Broad and Parks Road, with New College just across the way. During our move there I attempted some sort of apology which he brushed aside. The actual business, the finding then the filling-in of the vital form, went off with surprising ease; he probably had a desk-compartment with a coded label meaning FORMS FOR FUCKING FOOLS WHO ARE FED UP WITH ME JUST POCKETING MY FEE AND WANT A SERIOUS SUPERVISOR. Anyway, it was done.

Thankfully shutting the Cecil study door behind me I had not taken more than a pace or two before falling over a small boy of five or six playing on the passage floor with some toy vehicle. He looked up at me and said confidently,

'This is a broken lorry. Will you guard it while I go and find somebody to come and repair it?'

'I'm afraid I must be getting back to Hall,' I said.

With a long percussive sigh at my denseness or intractability, he repeated his earlier speech exactly as before.

'I have to be going,' I said, starting to move.

All the resources of the International Phonetic Alphabet would be inadequate to do more than suggest the noise he made then. It was another and even longer sigh with a kind of descending moan in it expressing irritation, disappointment, dissatisfaction with the general scheme of things and finally a kind of philosophical resignation, as if nothing much better could realistically be expected from a person of my kidney or class.*

* This must have been Lord David's younger son, Hugh, whom I encountered the other day in the Garrick bar with his elder brother, Jonathan. Hugh, now a lecturer in history at Leeds University, turned out to be not only nice but preternaturally normal. So, with the exception of his being an actor by profession, did Jonathan. I wondered which of them it had been (if either), who, asked at a much earlier age what he intended to do when he grew up, replied, 'I'm going to be a neurotic like Daddy,' but I remained silent on the matter.

Well, I started researching and went off to Swansea to write up the results in the intervals of teaching and thinking about *Lucky Jim*. I dare say it was not a very good thesis, though it turned up among other things some interesting material – interesting to me, at least – about D. G. Rossetti and his unexpected insistence on entertainment as an essential quality of poetry ('good poetry is bound to be *amusing*'), and what I thought the best book on that whole circle, the far from unknown but rare *Memorials of Edward Burne-Jones* by 'G. B.-J.', his wife Georgiana, Kipling's aunt. One of my failures was to present myself as an indefatigable, endlessly curious and imaginative researcher. For instance, having joyfully come across an American scholar's book on the literary career of Swinburne, which gave me every fact I needed, I came totally clean about him and it, instead of cunningly offering the results as those of patient, widespread personal digging. But that kind of thing was a trifle compared with the shock of coming up to Oxford for my viva in the wake of my thesis in original typescript and three carbons (try typing a page or two in that style one day) and finding myself confronted by an examining board of two, Lord David Cecil (chairman) and a junior don of his college.

I was too disconcerted to be angry at the time, though I was a little cross afterwards that Lord David had not declared what was surely an interest in the matter and stood down. A sort of viva began. I had opened my introduction by outlining what I took to be the normal or average process whereby a poet's work reaches the public – written in the first place with a few friends or an individual in mind, reaching a small group of sympathisers, moving out to a wider circle, etc. To save having to say 'usually' or 'often' or 'in some cases' or 'perhaps' and all those all the time I had prefixed to this statement some formula like 'Let me now outline this supposedly normal process. A poet writes in the first place for his close friends.' Lord David read that much aloud and then snapped as if personally offended, 'Do you mean *alwith*?'

'No, sir,' I said, 'and in fact if you go on to the next sentence you'll see that I specifically say I don't mean always and propose to take note of cases where it doesn't apply.'

'*Oh*,' he said, if anything more affronted than ever, as if I had somehow concealed this information from him until that very moment.

If I had not failed my degree before entering the room, which is quite possible, I certainly had by then, and without having gone on to say what I felt, which was something like, 'and if you were less fucking conceited and lazy you might have been able to notice that for yourself.' As a final point of interest, I noticed that, with old-world discourtesy, the chairman of the examination board had not bothered to rub out the pencilled marginalia he had made on the top copy. The only intelligible word appearing there was ALWAYS embellished with exclamation-marks and question-marks. There were more question-marks and assorted squiggles on the rest of the Introduction (a short section) and I think a few more on some closely following pages. Nothing further.

I left it at that. I had my assistant lectureship, which was all that really counted. Indeed I doubt if anybody even noticed when the thesis and thus the degree went down the drain, and if, as I suspected then and still think very likely, I had been caught in a spot of academic crossfire, there was nothing I could do about it, even find out about it, from Swansea.

In following years it was a constant treat to run into Lord David at this or that literary function in London and be greeted by him with a slightly nervous geniality, which became more than slightly nervous when I happened to bump into him soon after some hoax or pseudonymous attack on him with which I might have been (but unfortunately was not) associated. I tried to put on an expression designed to confirm his suspicions, but he probably thought I was nothing more than drunk, which I may well have been besides.

For some time both before and after our small academic association I had taken Lord David Cecil as summing up in his person, his attitude to the university and his view of literature a great deal that had got Oxford a bad name. I once heard him quoted as having said that if he were to find out that (as it might have been) Henry James despised him or that Thackeray held a low opinion of him he would not have turned a hair, but if he felt that Jane Austen regarded him with contempt he would have been thoroughly daunted or something similar. My informant said with some heat that he would have given a good deal to see the mincemeat that Jane Austen would have made out of that brand of aristocratic selfishness, and although no great lover of hers myself I said something similar on my own account, even if I snarled a little less than he had when I said it.

And yet, looking back, some of Cecil's writings, especially the early ones, are not negligible, the book on Melbourne has a good name with those interested in Melbourne, and *The Stricken Deer* really has something to say about Cowper, true as it may be that the full line of Cowper's that furnishes the title ('I was a stricken deer, that left the herd') seems comically inappropriate to the author. But at least Lord David encouraged one to think of literature as something affording pleasure and some insight into human life rather than material for theory and polemic, Lamb (another Cecil hero) before Leavis even if Lamb gets you down in his way as much as he does me. People have enjoyed learning from *The Stricken Deer* who never saw that ridiculous hat or heard that nanny-goat squeal.

JAMES MICHIE

I GOT TO know James Michie when we were both students in the
English School at Oxford in 1948, I having returned from war
service, he having come up straight from school. I have forgotten
how we first met, but I have a very clear picture of the two of us
sitting in the sunlight on the patch of grass outside the Radcliffe
Camera reading room, inside which we were to spend many hours
of drudgery. As we sat we each held a piece of paper.

'I'm sorry, but I seem to have another poem here.'

'I've got one too.'

'All right, you go first.'

During what cannot have been more than five or six weeks I
produced about the same number of poems, which can hardly sound
a lot but is about twice my average yearly output over my poetry-
writing life. James produced about as many. Nothing like it has
happened to me before or since. I wish I knew what was at work.
It was not competition, more mutual example. We read and criti-
cised, but the criticism was confined to technical points of style and
the overall aim was clarity, as we instantly and tacitly agreed.

More to my present purpose, I thought James's poems were not
only at least as good as mine but somehow more promising. (And I
was twenty-six and he was twenty-one.) As I had – correctly – sensed
when looking at some of Philip Larkin's poems a couple of years
earlier, so I – wrongly, alas – thought I detected in these of James's
a great new poetic talent spreading its wings, though in my view he
did become a good, intelligent and much underrated poet. His
'Arizona Nature Myth' is a piece of masterly invention.

However: in those earlier days Basil Blackwell published a yearly
anthology of mainly undergraduate verse selected by a pair of undergraduate editors and called *Oxford Poetry* plus the year. 'What about
us doing the 1949 one?' I asked James one fine morning.

'How do we fix that?'

108

'Well, we could try just going into the bookshop and asking.'

'What are our qualifications?'

'We're poets, aren't we?'

I like to think that this piece of effrontery was uncharacteristic of me. Anyway, it worked, chiefly because neither of the men we spoke to could think of a reason for turning us down. The poems we assembled were mostly undistinguished. James smuggled one in by his girlfriend under the name of 'Barbara James', not as a piece of corruption – her poem was no worse than several of the others – but because to attach her real surname to the situation described in it might have caused parental outrage. By tradition, not perhaps a very good one, the editors were allowed to include a few specimens of their own work. As I saw very soon and clearly after the publication of the little volume, my own contributions were absolutely terrible – three clumsy, lifeless, nothing-to-say imitations of the Auden he-sonnet (e.g. 'Rimbaud') cleverly disguised by being she-sonnets instead, and never reprinted. James's poems were embarrassingly better, among his cleverest though he was never just a clever poet. But the star of the show, our discovery, was Elizabeth Jennings, despite the fact that she was to write better than she did there and, as far as I remember, made no special impression on critics.

In that very year, 1949, James's and my paths diverged, mine to Swansea, his either then or later to London. His poetic career seemed to prosper, unlike my own. When I saw him on my trips to London he produced a succession of West Indian girlfriends. The first I thought remarkably attractive, with European-like looks that would have allowed her to pass as a Spaniard or Sicilian, had she wanted to. Then, rather to my surprise, he turned up married to a different girl, less good-looking to my taste and unmistakably of Negro descent. I have always suspected in a nasty way that this characteristic gave her the advantage over the first one of being more annoying to (I think) Weybridge, anyway to his parents and what they 'stood for', though I doubt if he would ever have put it like that himself. Which reminds me to say that what James has always 'stood for' is pacifism, a creed I find personally abhorrent. I tried once to explain to him that in the event of a war, his and every other pacifist's only moral course would be suicide, but he was unimpressed.

In later years I saw less of him. A book of verse, *Possible Laughter*, appeared in 1959, but had no successor. I was a little disappointed by the collection, partly because it omitted or altered, for the worse in my view, poems I remembered from earlier. One began to think of James as a publisher rather than as a poet. Our encounters were rare and fleeting but they always ended with that disgusting formula, 'We must have lunch some time.' Then, not particularly soon after one of these, he rang me up out of the blue. The year would have been 1979.

'You know that lunch we're always promising each other we're going to have? Well, this time let's really have it. Have you got a free day next week?'

This ought to have put me on my guard at once. An old lunching hand like me should have seen clearly that the suggestion put in these circumstances must mean that James wanted something from me. But I said, 'Sure,' and we were on.

The restaurant, his choice, did set a faint uneasiness stirring. It was not new, was in Old Compton Street, had a French name and was previously unknown to me. At one o'clock, or a little later, it was far from full.

After some minutes James said a little casually, 'I was thinking the other day that there are an awful lot of bloody good short poems in the language.'

'Shakespeare's songs kind of thing?'

'Not only those. Less well-known ones but still bloody good.'

'Some bloody bad ones too. All those crappy epigrams.'

'I wasn't thinking of them. Songs from other plays. Lots of seventeenth-century stuff. And modern stuff too. Quite a bit of Browning. And Americans. There's a lot of good short American things, especially this century.'

'Not my field, I'm afraid. Anyway, how short is short? There are more sonnets than anybody would know what to do with.'

He frowned. 'I think they'd rather overshadow the other poems. I think you'd have to keep sonnets completely out of any sort of collection of short pieces.'

'How would you manage that?'

'Well, quite simply. Limit the length to thirteen lines.'

'Sounds a bit arbitrary. And what exactly are you – '

'I have actually been doing quite a lot of thinking about this and what I think there's room for is an anthology of short poems – short meaning thirteen lines or less – that would go down very well with people who like a bit of poetry but don't want to find themselves confronted with *The Dunciad* or *The Idylls of the King*. It would be great fun putting it together.'

Even now I failed to see quite where this was tending. Perhaps I was distracted by the food, which was just about eatable but peculiar, possibly an early bit of nouvelle. 'Yes, it would,' I said.

A great revelation seemed to strike James. 'And you – the very man! Of course! You've just edited this anthology of light verse for the Oxford Press.' (Which was why I was so sure of the year earlier on.) 'Done very well with it, too.' He said in formal tones, '*The Oxford Book of Short Poems*, edited by Kingsley Amis and yours truly. Anthologies are all the rage these days. This one would really grab them. Go down especially well in the States.'

Rather than anything about pennies dropping with resounding crashes I thought fuck you a considerable amount, chum – we've known each other well and long enough for you to have come straight to the point. But then he was a publisher, or perhaps he had stopped being one by this time. Anyway, I passed over this detail because the project immediately appealed to me. With my mind already starting to buzz I agreed. I would approach the OUP. Good. So the object of the exercise had been achieved and we could settle down to gossip, attacking George Steiner and the Arts Council, things like that.

After a bit, James said, 'Do you still write any poems these days?'

'Well, just the odd one.'

'Me too. I've had about fifteen or sixteen out in magazines over the years, not enough for a volume, never will have I don't suppose. I was thinking, that *Possible Laughter* book of mine's been out of print for ages, I might bring it out again with these extra ones thrown in.'

'Good idea,' I said heartily.

'If I could get a publisher. I suppose you wouldn't fancy giving me a hand in finding one?'

'Well really, I don't see why anybody should listen to – '

Most of this dialogue, as in other places here, is of course an approximation, but the next six words are exact, and with them I lost my sense of humour for some minutes. 'In fact it just so happens,' he said, and he was not trying to be funny, 'that I have photostats of those extra poems with me now.' And he took them out of his pocket and proffered them.

Before I knew what I was doing I had taken them from him and also some tenuous sort of commission. I further ended up paying for the lunch – James, I found later, is feared all over London as the fellow who gets the other fellow to pay. Right at the end, with receipt and change before me, I tried to strike back by suggesting he should treat us to an extra brandy. He demurred, on the grounds that such an arrangement would confuse the management, but memory suggests I successfully counter-demurred.

The Michie poems could obviously wait. The Shorter Poems were a different matter. I went to the OUP and they were quite keen, accepting the thirteen-line limitation, even paying an advance. They were only a wee bit doubtful that we would be able to find enough decent poems to fill a decent-sized book, but James, who was going to make the Americans his special province, put their minds at rest on that one.

I spent long afternoons in the London Library, combing the works of poets from George Gascoigne to Theodore Wratislaw. One of the incidental discoveries I made was that, while very nearly all the songs in Shakespeare's plays made splendid or at least adequate short poems in their own right, the same could not be said of more than a handful of songs in plays by other writers of that general period. These turned out to be either undetachable from their spoken contexts or simply not much good, or both, naturally, so I had come across yet another way, perhaps a little less well known than it should be, in which the Bard surpassed his contemporaries.

Another discovery, or suspicion that began to dawn on me as I read on, was that the OUP's doubts about there being enough possible poems for a book of the present kind, intermittently shared by me from the outset, were going to be justified. I mentioned this to James. He was still confident: I had not seen any of his Americans yet. There came the time when we got together, pooled our findings and considered future prospects. Quite soon I was convinced that a book of the size required could only be made by lowering the standard of merit in some proposed contributions to a lower level than I was prepared to accept. I thereupon withdrew from the project. The OUP were very cross with me, I think with some reason: I had received payment (which they did not demand back) to do a job, and although I had got through a good deal of useful work I had not completed that job. The book came out finally under the editorship of James and another and was not, I believe, very much of a success.

That left the poems, James's poems. I had grown less and less inclined to do anything about getting them published, but felt I could not actually do nothing all. An admirable compromise, I thought, between doing nothing and doing nearly nothing presented itself when I ran into an old friend, Charles Monteith of Faber's. After explaining the circumstances I asked him if he thought there were any possibilities for such a volume.

'No,' said Charles.

Nor apparently have there been. I grieve at the non-flowering of that talent that I thought I had seen so clearly on the way in 1948, and find it a sad come-down that James should be doing the *Spectator* literary competition every week. But I still read the old fellow's accomplished and elegant translations.

SHRINKS

Others might find it hard to believe, and yet others might well mutter something about bullies always being cowards, but I would regard myself as of a nervous disposition, most likely a legacy from my mother, with perhaps a premature dropping of the baby-sitter not helping – my own fault, the result of saying vaingloriously I was quite old enough to do without one. As other little boys have fancied, a horrible man might climb a ladder into my bedroom and murder me, presumably for the mere hell of it. Not so long after he was out of the way the vacancy was filled, as happens with nervous people, but filled with what in cases like mine are sometimes called fears of depersonalisation. I would cease to seem real to myself. The wartime black-out helped them on.

I say this much by way of introduction not to further self-analysis but to analysts, psychologists, mind-doctors, whatever you call them. The first one I went to see was called Armstrong and he worked at the Littlemore mental hospital near Oxford. I trusted him on sight, perhaps because he really was a trustworthy man, perhaps because he was the first member of his profession I had encountered. He asked me a lot of questions and said at the end, 'From what you've told me I can't tell you you'll never go mad, any more than I can tell you you'll never break your leg, but I can tell you there's no sign of it at the moment.' End of session and course of treatment and suspension of neurosis.

I suppose I was twenty-four at this time and, with a few momentary lurches on dark nights, stayed cured for ten years or so. Then I started getting frightened of nothing in particular about bedtime. I found that contemplating my sleeping children would keep me on my trolley, and then that the job could be done much more simply and surely by a couple of Mogadons. No recourse to shrink needed.

Then, suddenly, after about another ten years of just steering clear of empty lifts and such things, there was need again. A then newish wife and I had moved to Barnet in Hertfordshire, about ten miles from London – too far for taxis, etc., or so it was said. For some time there was no trouble, only inconvenience, until one afternoon I found myself stuck in an otherwise seemingly empty tube train for ten minutes or so outside Barnet station, above ground but effectively in solitary confinement. Thereafter I had to manage my travelling back and forth so that there were always people about for certain, which in practice meant going for the rush-hours. Off to another student of the mind.

I have forgotten the exact order they came in, but one from the 1970s practised in Windsor. After several overground train journeys to and fro, and the asking and answering of innumerable questions, I was told with admirable promptitude and honesty that there was nothing this fellow could do for me. Then I found myself making a series of long bus journeys to a hospital south of the river – a very educative experience if you travel on the top deck – and a young and amiable South African called Hafner.

Dr Hafner told me he specialised in my particular affliction, had indeed written most of a book on it – agoraphobia. I said I thought that what I had had sounded to me, with my vague lay knowledge, more like claustrophobia, fear of being shut up. No, he explained, agoraphobia was not fear of open spaces, as I had surmised, but of going out, of public premises, etc. He had had women patients who had not dared to go out of their house for years, could shrink in terror from the idea of entering a supermarket. I retorted that I was quite fond of going out, and any objection I might have to supermarkets was aesthetic or social. Well, some of these women patients of his were frightened of getting into buses, had refused to do so until he started treating them. But I had come here by bus, and . . . The first session ended about then. Dr Hafner gave me large parts of the typescript of his book to take away and read. I would find it all put much more clearly there.

I settled down to those pages with some eagerness. They were lucidly written, with no overuse of technical terms, though the various narratives were monotonous and repetitive, might indeed all have described the experiences of the same person. He had per-suaded lots of frightened old people to go into the street with him, to accompany him into supermarkets (what was special about them?) and even travel by bus with him in attendance. That was the first part of the treatment and it was usually successful; I think it was called deconditioning. Part II was markedly less so, consisting as it did of him going on being encouraging and everything but not actually going with the old ladies (they nearly all were old ladies) on their expeditions. 'It was most remarkable,' he wrote – I paraphrase from memory – 'how many patients relapsed, often totally, and were soon in need of further deconditioning.'

Remarkable, I wanted to yell, and did say to him more quietly at our next interview, 'Surely what would have been remarkable would have been their *not* relapsing. There you were with your syringe of intravenous Valium, enough to calm a runaway horse, and you were *there*, a doctor, ready to help, to explain they weren't mad, just upset, and then next time there you weren't.' He shook his head: I had missed some vital point. To be fair to him, it was not then, but at some other point during our talks, that he remarked I had entered his office smelling very strongly of drink. I explained that that was because before coming down to see him I had given myself a jolly good lunch at my club. 'I empathise very heartily with that,' he said with a smile, but I think he meant that he thought the drink had been resorted to in order to nerve me for the ordeal of the journey by dreaded bus, rather than the ordeal of talking and listening to him.

That was about the last I saw of Dr Hafner. My next chap was somebody with such a wonderful name for his part that when I came to put a bit of him into a book I was afraid to put the name in for fear of strictures of sub-Dickensianism. I might explain that I always try to avoid putting real people into books – you either have to start changing them the moment they appear or you ruin and throw off balance everything they come into or affect in any way. But Dr Wooster, so spelt in life, was too good to be denied a few lines in my novel, *Jake's Thing*, put into the mouth of a minor character, Ivor, and the result is too à propos to be left out here. Ivor, with his phobia about the Underground, makes a preliminary expedition from Warren Street to Hampstead accompanied by his shrink and gets on fine (shades of Dr Hafner). Next day, according to plan, he makes the return trip on his own and is absolutely terrified. This surprises the psychiatrist very much, but he has an explanation.

Ivor, like me, was an only child; his mother, like mine, had had a difficult confinement and a decision was taken against a further pregnancy. What in particular, he was asked, had frightened him in the Tube? As in an experience of my own on Hampstead station, no train was signalled and Ivor was hit by the fear of being down there for ever. Ah, there was the connection, said the shrink: Ivor being afraid of nothing arriving in his Underground was the result of his mother's fear of something arriving in her Underground. This cheered Ivor up, making him think he might be a bit peculiar, but at least he was not so bloody barmy as to come up with that. My own response had been to get up and walk out of Dr Wooster's consulting-room, ignoring his protestations that we were on the verge of uncovering the mystery, and never return.

Freudianism has probably been instrumental in fewer deaths than Nazism or Marxism, though it is surely one of the great pernicious doctrines of our century with its denial of free will and personal responsibility. But it is of course enormous fun, combining the discovery of curious information about people's inner selves with the clue-chasing, puzzle-solving pleasures of the old-fashioned detective story, solving or seeming to solve where other forms of therapy seem merely to uncover more questions.

The detective-story comparison is made in an entertaining but in parts harrowing book, *Breakdown* by Stuart Sutherland, the account of a total depressive illness suffered by an academic psychologist/psychiatrist, full of material about the various techniques and procedures used in the treatment of mental illness and also not sparing of intimate personal detail. I met the author – socially – a couple of times. Though pleasant enough, he failed to strike me as, say, somebody I would pick out of a group of strangers as likely to be among the sanest present. It struck me too, as it had when I was reading his book, that while it was no business of mine he seemed to my lay understanding to have got his academic and personal lives rather closely intertwined. On one of our get-togethers he put down four, possibly five large gins in not much, if anything at all, over the hour. When another seemed in prospect I asked him where he was staying in London, for we were standing in the bar of the Garrick Club at the time.

'Oh, I'm driving back to Brighton in a couple of minutes,' he said, no doubt facetiously.

He taught at the university there as head of department and as far as I know still does.

Curing or even alleviating my phobias was eventually given up as a bad (and expensive) job. Or rather I lost all fear of the Underground by never going down it again and being driven or taking taxis instead. By this time my wife and I were quartered in Hampstead. Various difficulties had arisen between us which I will not go into, and among those we went to for assistance was a certain Dr Cobb. I think he called himself a psychologist, but what he really was, at least in his dealings with us, was a sort of highbrow marriage counsellor.

One glance at his hat, which was of the round, rough, tufty sort affected by middle-class people in television series about village life, was enough to assure me that nothing of which I could make the slightest use was going to come out from under it. So we were having trouble with our marriage, were we? Well, being nicer to each other would help, of course. Finding out what the other one liked to eat, where he or she liked going for the evening, etc., and acting on it could not fail to be useful. Specific tasks were set, the performance of which by one of us must surely please the other. What about friends? I felt quite sorry for him when he fell back on textbook tricks like not opening the conversation, easily countered by at once becoming engrossed in a book. My growing boredom with the whole enterprise, which I suppose I could have tried harder to conceal, he mistook for surly defensiveness – perhaps it *was* surly defensiveness. If so he failed to break it down. When I stopped him coming I had put up two blacks, one for surly d. and the other for stopping him coming. Or I think I had. He never said anything so definite. At least he was not a Freudian.

Just the other day I went on my doctor's advice to another shrink, for depression this time. I had asked the doctor for a pot of pills for that, but the ones he gave me he said I must only use occasionally, and they made hardly any difference anyway, because he is a good doctor and good doctors never give you anti-depressants that stop you feeling depressed, just as most of them won't give you sleeping pills that make you sleep. So I went to the recommended psychologist, a lay one, i.e. not a qualified doctor, i.e. a quack, though I have or had no particular feelings about that.

The bouts of depression came in the afternoons, so he suggested that I should find things to occupy myself at that time. I could not face work, I told him, and reading was no good. Had I any besetting worries? None that would not be about normal in a sixty-seven-year-old man with an irritable bowel. What things, interests, people had dropped out of my life in the last few years? Well, my wife had left me, an old friend I rarely saw had died, and I played classical music less often on the gramophone. I should potter about, he said, administer things. I told him I had nothing to potter about with or administer. Had I any interest in the theatre? None whatsoever; I

118

had not been for over ten years. Might I go to the cinema? On my own? To see what?

I could find nothing in any of this that I would not have been perfectly well capable of thinking of to ask him if our positions had been reversed, i.e. me being the one with the large room in Wimpole Street. He gave me the sort of advice a kindly parson might offer a despondent parishioner free. At the end of our third and last meeting he asked me to keep a tally of my alcoholic intake (to what end?) and to go to bed later and get up and read if necessary to combat the sleeplessness that was worrying me. I had explained clearly that, although I might suffer from sleeplessness now and again, it caused me no worry at all, just boredom touched with gloom. I suppose he thought he was going to do better with a non-existent worry about sleeplessness than about a real depression. I wonder what we would have got on to had there been a next time.

Physical disease is treatable and curable; some mad people are also curable, chiefly by drugs, and if nobody seems to know how they work, who cares? But the poor old neurotic might just as well spend his money on booze and sex magazines. The only certain cure for arachnophobia is to spend twenty-four hours a day in a space-suit, with a qualified person standing by holding a flame-thrower and a half-litre tranquilliser injector, just to be on the safe side.

I have noticed that women rather like going to see shrinks whereas men tend not to. But then women are keener on going on holidays than men. Merely an observation.

SWANSEA

'WHAT MADE YOU choose Swansea?' people who remember I spent twelve years there still sometimes ask me. What is only slightly less uninteresting, though a scrap more to the purpose, is what made Swansea choose me. The original question calls up an image of an Oxford First in faultless tweeds lazily turning over notices of vacancies in English assistant lectureships all over the kingdom, before quirkily deciding that Swansea might be amusing. The reality was a penurious fellow with a wife, two children, one (Philip) of a year and a bit, one of a few weeks (Martin) born in the August of the year, 1949, I was appointed in the October of, half a thesis and no alternative, Swansea being the last unfilled English post of that academic year. In fact, the Welsh as a whole being even lazier than the English, they had all gone off on their long vacations before getting round to filling the post, and I signed on and took up my duties in the week in which the term had actually started.

There seemed to be quite a few duties. They consisted chiefly of giving lectures, and these required substantial preparation. If you think you can talk for fifty minutes, to an audience capable of asking questions, about a text you may not have read recently (or at all) after a look through it the previous evening and knocking together a few notes, just try it and see. Many, even most, lecturers live partly, even mostly, on what they have told last year's class; I had no such stored fat. Fair enough, but it limited the time I had to spare for things like exploring and house-hunting. I lived for most of a term in digs with an eccentric Irish Latinist in his thirties called Willie Smyth and a landlady who had waved hair, kept a spaniel called Sandy and was the sort of woman who could not be dissuaded from drawing the sitting-room curtains to stop the sun putting the fire out.

A Dubliner and a furious cigarette-smoker, Willie had three passions. One was radio; he had been in RAF Signals during the war.

Here we were in accord, though from different directions. He liked making and refining radio receivers; I liked the music he received on them. Another Willie thing was, of course, Latin, putting him rather on his own in a classics department full of Graecists and, within a few years, under a professor who favoured teaching the classics in translation. For a perfectly sane man, Willie had a poor sense of other people and large parts of the modern world, and sometimes seemed to think that Latin still occupied the place it had had in the Middle Ages. There was a well-attested story of his conversation with the fellow laying the carpet in a friend's house. Willie's discourse had included quotations from both Latin and Greek. The Greek ones, as an obvious courtesy, he translated; the Latin he had left in their native state, as one gentleman to another. His third passion was for trams, buses and motor-coaches. By arrangement, any amendment in the Dublin public-transport time-tables was at once sent him, and he was of course a subscriber to *Bus and Coach*. In a way that reminds me as I write this of John Braine, Willie knew there was something funny about this, but he would not allow it to be openly thought of as funny as others might, and nobody would ever have teased him about it. I have wondered more than once if the so-called Mumbles train, really a glorified double tram, running from central Swansea round the bay to Mumbles pier, might not have helped to make Willie 'choose Swansea'. It was then the oldest passenger railway in the British Isles, opened in 1807 and not (stupidly) closed down till 1960.

There were sporadic attempts, going back before my arrival, to get Willie a girl. He was ugly, but we see every day that that need be no bar. Far worse, he was pedantic, pernickety, letting nothing inaccurate or of uncertain meaning go by – not an aphrodisiac quality. He was a natural bachelor or, should you prefer it, his libido was inadequate to overcome his inhibitions. Once quite a decent-looking girl was very nearly got. Willie went to stay with her and her parents, near Aberystwyth I think. When he came back the deal was off. The family wireless had gone wrong; Willie with his knowledge examined it, found and replaced a faulty component, and the set was restored. Fatally, he was offered no money. His labour, he explained, he was of course prepared to supply free, but to be expected to pay for the component (which might have cost a couple of bob) was *inadmissible*.

All this was later. Old Willie was not a bad digs-mate for those two or three months, though to have his always startling unspectacled face as my first sight every morning – like many local houses this one had had its bathroom tacked on to the outside of the small bedroom – was no gift of the gods. It was quite a decent little house, looking on to the green that surrounds the vile concrete Guildhall with its tall unimposing clock-tower and inside, safely out of sight, the vast panels Frank Brangwyn had constructed for, and had turned down by, the House of Lords. Willie moved out of the house soon after I did, and out of this life too soon after that at the age of fifty-eight.

By the end of that first term I was settled in that little English Department. The tolerance and amiability of Professor W. D. Thomas, Miss Westcott, James 'Jo' Bartley and David Sims gave me quite a false idea of what life was going to be like on this side of the academic counter. The college itself was little at that time, a Victorian Gothic mansion, a straggle of sheds rather like those at Norbury College (these were full of scientists), some one-storey lecture-rooms and a couple of grander or larger but not horrible structures. All this was at one corner of a large park facing the great sweep of Swansea Bay and forming – then – the most attractive university setting I have ever seen. The staff, meaning not the cleaners and porters as at Oxford but the senior members of the college, seemed all right at least, accommodating several ordinary human beings as well as a number of old-style Welsh dodderers who had been around since 1922, when the place was founded, and a bunch of intellectual cavemen (or so they were usually regarded) who formed the engineering and other banausic departments.

Of the students I will say little, enough and to spare having been written on the subject in general over the past thirty years or more. But this I will say: already in 1949 there were quite enough there in the university who should not have been there, in the sense that they were not capable of benefiting from that kind of education. They had not wanted to be there and did not know what to do when they got there. And it was in 1960, before 'expansion' had taken off, that I wrote of university students that 'more will mean worse' (not 'means worse', which suggests some phantom law of nature). But enough. I met many good students, whose quality did not diminish over my years at Swansea, only the amount they were required to know in order to get a degree. And of course we need lots of technicians and technologists and what-not, and we get them from technical colleges which you may give any fanciful titles you please.

One of the men who was really serious about destroying the universities and turning them into vocational training centres was J. S., later Sir John, later Lord Fulton, who as Principal of the University College of Swansea must have been slightly responsible for 'choosing me', being an Oxford-Balliol-Lindsay-sociological-philistine man himself and probably taking me for one of the same. It is a law of academic as much as of any other kind of life that the enemy are united in knowing what they want while the decent chaps are divided and unsure. Fulton, whose declared objective it was to bring our universities into accordance with the needs of our society (perhaps the earliest use of a phrase since grown odiously familiar), said in an interview that 3,000 was about right for the complement of a 'new' university, and a couple of years later everybody was saying the same. And look at it now. You can always raise the numbers if you lower the standard. No doubt the present-day college at Swansea, which I never go near, is no worse than anywhere else.

That is as much as I feel like saying here about the hard part, the strictly academic part and, to be serious, the serious part. On my arrival I had been full of advanced ideas, partly American-derived, of what was involved in teaching students English literature; Professor Thomas knew that if you could give most of them a fair idea of what the writers were saying you were doing about as much as could be expected; for some you could do more, but there would never be many of them. After a time I began to see what he meant. Bartley and Sims instantly became drinking companions with interests much like my own. Miss Westcott was a middle-aged spinster of sweetness and natural propriety who nevertheless knew well enough what the rest of us were like. The ease with which one avoided swearing in front of her, the readiness with which expressions like 'Good gracious!' sprang to one's lips in her presence, was a perpetual wonder.

Jo Bartley was an Ulsterman who, with a Second to live down, had taught in India, one of whom it could be justly said, 'Now that's what I *call* a drinking man' and a smoker to rival Willie Smyth. He liked food too, also women, doing his job and researching among obscure plays. This last interest produced his memorial, one of the funniest books I have ever read, *Teague, Shenkin and Sawney, being an historical study of the earlier Irish, Welsh and Scottish characters in English plays* (chiefly eighteenth-century). From it you may learn, for instance, the significance of Flamineo's reference in *The White Devil* to a poisoner who, for his masterpiece, 'was once minded to have prepared a deadly vapour from a Spaniard's fart, that should

123

have poisoned all Dublin.' *Teague* (pub. Cork University Press, 1954) must also be an excessively rare book. Some enterprising publisher should take it up. It can never date.

Some of those who knew how right-wing Jo was might have been surprised at his hospitality to other races. Owing to some wifely manoeuvre I found myself taking the six-year-old Philip and the five-year-old Martin to a tea-party Jo was throwing for some African students.* Staring as venomously as I could at each child in turn, I said, 'You are going to meet some men who do not look like us. They are called Africans. Got it? Africans. What are they called? Philip?' – 'Africans.' – 'Martin?' – 'Africans.' – 'Right.' After various threats I led them into the Bartleys' house.

The two principal Africans were Mr Donka, who was thin, very dark purple and of matt finish, and Mr Dakur, who was stout, very dark brown and shiny. Unaware of anything I was saying or having said to me I nodded, smiled, other things too no doubt, while my sons stared as unblinkingly as the human eye can normally manage at Mr Donka and Mr Dakur. Philip seemed to favour Mr Dakur, Martin to be more taken by Mr Donka. In the end it happened in no more than a couple of minutes, when Martin said to Mr Donka,

'You've got a black face.'

Mr Donka burst out laughing. 'If Martin comes to my country, Martin's face too will become black,' and of course, so far from a relief of tension, there was an immediate upsurge of the general embarrassment that had only been simmering quietly away before. Resolving at once to show how little of a figure of fun I found Mr

---

* It was not on this occasion that Jo Bartley recited to me the verse that follows, but it must go in somewhere before he escapes from my narrative. He always claimed that he wrote it, and I have never come across it from any other source. So here goes.

> He who is wounded in the stones
>   Or has his privy member cut off,
> Shall, when he rises from his bones,
>   Be from the joys of heaven shut off.
>
> At this one need feel no surprise,
>   For heaven's chief delight amour is;
> It would be hell to get no rise
>   While lolling in the laps of houris.

Donka and how jolly equal I felt with him, and being what I now see as very repulsive, I began a round-table discussion with him about the world situation.

'I suppose you have your problems at home, just like us,' I said. 'Different ones, of course. I mean more . . .'

Mr Donka immediately turned grave. 'Oh, lamentable,' he said. 'Yes, we have a great many problems, but the worst is undoubtedly superstition.'

'Oh? What sort of thing do you mean?'

'I'll give you a typical instance. Are you fond of whisky?'

'Well, yes, I suppose I am, quite.'

'But you wouldn't want to go on drinking it indefinitely, one bottle after another. You just couldn't do it, any more than I could. Well, I have a friend at home who can, and it doesn't affect him. He never gets drunk. And, you know, those foolish people believe he just gets rid of it all with the power of his brain. He *thinks* it away, they believe. How could you be more superstitious than to believe a thing like that?'

I muttered that it indeed sounded absurd.

'Whereas the fact of the matter is that he puts his arm against the wall very quietly and lets the whisky run down it and away by a trick he learnt.'

'What sort of trick?'

'You expect him to tell me that for nothing, or anyone else?' Mr Donka laughed at my simplicity. 'But there it is, and the superstitious people believe he does it with the power of his brain. That's the sort of backwardness you're up against in my country.'

'I can see it must make life very difficult.'

David Sims was thoroughly Welsh without going on about it. He came from New Tredegar, a mining village on the border of what I suppose is now Gwent and a largely Welsh-speaking area perhaps even now, though Welshmen are given to sentimental exaggeration, to put it no lower, about their command of Welsh. Anyway, there was enough English about even in David's childhood for a sympathetic neighbour to call, 'Shit myself, have you?' when he arrived home from school in a state.

Soon David became my closest friend in Swansea. We were both interested in literature, a rarity then as now, and also in commoner pursuits. In retrospect our ruling obsession, with cash as tight as it was, seems to have been getting enough cigarette money or its equivalent. I went for herbs to eke out tobacco, uncannily like

Dixon in *Lucky Jim*. David preferred what were known as nips, which in this context meant the remnants of tobacco left unsmoked in a cigarette-butt. These he would roll up in a fag-paper and smoke. You had to really care for nicotine to endure, let alone enjoy, the result, especially when one's own nips ran out and those of friends, or not even friends, were resorted to. Once, not meeting my eye, David confessed to me he had re-rolled and smoked up all the nips left at the end of the day in the Common Room ashtrays.

We found a more rational, though not that much more pleasant, way of supplementing our income one year by marking all the scripts, some 800 in total, of one of the English papers in a Joint Welsh Board school examination. Realising that this project meant solitude, silence, and dropping everything else, we loaded the scripts (sixteen pages each) into a trunk and took them up on the bus to New Tredegar, where David's widowed mother would look after us. There in the cottage parlour, one of us each side of the fireplace, we sat for something like nine hours a day and marked, our only relief a glass of Guinness late every evening at the pub in Bargoed down the road.

I will not weary the reader, though I promise I easily could, with details of what we read and what we did about it. Badly framed questions, badly trained examinees, saw to it that far too many candidates adopted the saturation technique whereby a question about, say, Pope's technique is interpreted to mean, 'Put down everything you can remember about Pope and some of your shots may hit.' We tried really hard to be 'objective', not to mind vile but just-readable handwriting, spelling that was no worse than poor, sentences less than intolerably ugly or incoherent, above all the information that Chaucer was a perpetual fountain of good sense, or that Wordsworth got away from eighteenth-century poetic diction. Nevertheless, your 357th appraisal of somebody's thoughts on the descriptive power of 'The Eve of St Agnes' is unlikely to be as objective as your first. And you have opinions, which you cannot hang up with your raincoat and put on again when you leave. But I expect David and I were as fair as most of the other examiners in that year or any other, there remains no practicable fairer system if there are to be examinations at all, and it may be of interest to see what we and our colleagues were actually doing.

This was inevitably and merely to put the candidates in what seemed to be the right order of competence and knowledge. The examiner could have nothing to do with 'standards', with how many pass or fail. That was decided not by him but by the Board, who would say in effect, 'We will pass 70 per cent of candidates,' and the examiner arranged his marks to ensure that overall result. So when 75 per cent passed the following year, it meant not that the questions were 5 per cent easier, and certainly not that the candidates had all suddenly become 5 per cent cleverer. The Board had merely decided that 75 per cent should pass. Intelligence, competence stay the same; all you can do is monkey with percentages, usually for political reasons. This is unchangeable and inseparable from the examination system. Another unchangeable fact is that nobody can really put his head into our (or probably any other) educational arrangements without a twinge of fear for the survival of the nation.

I take us now outside the classroom and into the domestic scene. By our first Christmas in Swansea in 1949, the twenty-one-year-old Hilly, two small fiends of sixteen and four months respectively called Philip and Martin, and I had become installed in a sort of flat with good hefty steps punctuated by right-angle bends for the twin pram to be lugged up to the front door. Martin slept in a drawer. The airing-cupboard, a most necessary amenity, was a tea-chest lined with towels and warmed with hot-water bottles. The electric stove, a much-feared Baby Belling, gave you shocks when you tried to fry bacon on it. I mention these details not because they were unusual, but because something like them was the lot of all one's colleagues. An assistant lecturer earned £300 a year, which was not a lot of money even in those days – about £4,200 at today's values (a contemporary assistant lecturer is paid £12,000).

Similar tribulations in similar settings followed, including part of a derelict shop with an outside sink fed by successive kettles (see photograph), and a couple of rooms with none at all, just a wash-hand basin. (There was a much-shared bathroom with a quivering geyser if you could stand it.) During our stay here, Hilly would go every week night and wash up at the café of the neighbouring Tivoli cinema not far along the sea-front, from which she would bring back an ample supply of scraps for her Alsatian. Her tips were usually enough to buy the Alsatian a bottle of beer on her way home for him to drink with his supper. He would have been baby-sitting, writing his lecture and wishing he had not been too grand to accept the newsagent's offer of a bit of cash for packing Christmas annuals.

Then Hilly inherited £5,000 and the world was changed. Suddenly we had a house, a whole house within a stone's throw of that Cwmdonkin Drive that Dylan Thomas had been the Rimbaud of, a car, a refrigerator, a washing-machine – even a kitchen cabinet and a cupboard *from Heal's*. There was a furnace that heated everything, so that the nappies no longer sported little singed triangles where they had been dried on the fire-guard. I symbolically bought myself one of those grand metal cigarette-machines, all cogs and rollers, not to use, really, more just to look at from time to time. But my most precious acquisition was a room of my own, a *study*, unattractive enough, with an outlook on to the wall of the house next door, tiny, but big enough for me, a table and chair, and a typewriter. I sat down and started writing *Lucky Jim*.

You can write a lecture in a room with small children in it or running in and out of it, and the American poet Hart Crane is said to have been unable to write his poems without the victrola playing, but most people require solitude and relative quiet for anything in your creative bracket. In the previous year or more I had written one poem, not a very good one either. If I were in the business of encouraging young writers, which I most certainly am not, I would do it by a system of earmarked grants providing the aspirant with a place of his own to work in. Those needing to have such a facility provided for them would be fewer than in my day. Actually the really needy writers are old, not young, but bugger them.

One effect of being rescued from lecturer's penury was that we were now residents of a recognisable neighbourhood with some leisure to observe it. And to be observed by it – a lot. The dialogue on one's first visit to a shop was heavily ritualised, as on mine to that of Ferguson (never mind the Jock surname, boyo) the tobacconist, a round-faced, unsmiling but amiable enough fellow. When our transactions were done he said to me,

'You're not from these parts, are you?'

'No. London.'

'Got a job here, have you?'

'Yes.'

'At the college?'

'Yes' – and so it went on through was I married, any children, what were they, how old were they, how old was *I*, where was I living, how long had I been living in Wales, what other parts of Wales did I know, a CV by question and answer, impossible to resist or resent. The result of this innocent curiosity, or what went with it, was a neighbourliness not quite like anything we had found in England. Also present, and surely connected, was a readiness to give bad service with a smile, as hard to resent as the curiosity –

how could you complain with conviction about a wheel coming off a toy lorry on the day of purchase when the shop-assistant had just asked after the little boy's whooping-cough? It was characteristic that when we bought an electric heater that hummed like a small train as soon as it was switched on, Mr Bevan, who had taken rather a long time to getting round to calling on us, should have remarked on hearing it perform, 'You two have got good years [ears], haven't you?' After more delay, he arranged a substitute as a magnanimous concession to our eccentricity – after all, we were from London.

But the story that sums up this aspect of the Welsh character, and more, concerns Mrs Professor Morgan and the grocery order. On seeing that she had assembled a pile of goods that amounted to more than she could conveniently carry, the assistant said,

'Have you you [your] car with you, Mrs Morgan, or has the professor taken it down to the college today? Oh well, that being so I suggest we deliver your purchases for you, all right?'

Mrs Morgan was mightily pleased, though after about four days with nothing in sight her pleasure had abated.

When reprehended on the telephone, the manager said, 'But Mrs Morgan, this stow [store] has not operated a delivery service since 1939.'

'In that case, what did your assistant mean by his suggestion?'

'Well . . . I suppose he was only trying to be helpful.'

A Welsh pupil of mine in the early 1960s told me, when I met him again in the early 1980s, that he had gone round telling this story throughout that interval as a perfect summary of the Welsh character. But before I embark on that rich topic I had better make it plain that such first-hand knowledge as I have is derived almost entirely from residence and work in Swansea 1949-61, with a year off in America 1958-59, but including yearly visits of up to a month since 1982 and a few forays into West Wales and North Wales. To set this down is more than dull scrupulosity. Welshmen at any rate will probably not think it so. They more than most Englishmen have feelings about their own bit of the country, and the first question one of them asks another is always, 'What part of Wales do you come from?'

I think the first thing to get understood is that most Welshmen's sense of nationality or nationhood is correspondingly rather weak, weaker than the Scots' and of course far weaker than that of the Irish, with whom they feel no special affinity as supposed fellow-Celts. Many are not aware of themselves as particularly different from the English, use 'English' to include 'Welsh' except when the distinction has point, as over sport, and cannot be bothered to use 'British' to cover the two. Many Welshmen from my part of Wales and the southern counties generally are of English descent, after all, as plenty of place-names and surnames will show, legacies of the influx of labour from across the border and the Bristol Channel to the industrial areas in the nineteenth century. (It is a nice little fact that the population of the old borough of Swansea in 1801 was 6,099.) I once asked a MORI-poll average Welshman from my part what he thought of Wales and was told, 'That's an easy one, boy. Anything that's for this country I'm for.' Asked a minute later what he thought of England, he stared as at a moron and said, 'I just told you, boy. Anything that's for this country I'm for.' Here is one of the reasons why Plaid Cymru, the Welsh Nationalists, will never be a mass party.

National feeling in Wales is reserved for matters within the Principality, between the southern, mostly English-speaking post-industrial majority and the rural minority, considerably Welsh-speaking, in the north. To South Walians, northerners are primitive, rustic, also sly and treacherous, rather like the stock English view of the Welsh in general. With nothing in religion or history at work, the prejudice is mild, if not playful. But it is still there. I shall never forget the charming delicacy with which our hosts at dinner once explained that we would be meeting the Caradocs later. They're very nice people really, you know, charming. Very cultivated. They're, er . . . [Nudists, I wondered? Mithraists? Cannibals?] . . . North Walians. And whatever the immediate reasons, I shall never cease to find it odd that a state on the other side of the world should end up with the firmly dissociative title of New *South* Wales.

However: with all the overlaps and similarities, I see the character of my kind of Welsh people as something distinctive. When I first met them I was struck by differences from the English; at a later stage these seemed less important or noticeable; now I am aware of the differences again. I am fond of the English and also admire and approve of them. Nevertheless, I cannot help noticing that Welsh people are friendlier and easier to get on with. Their reputation for deviousness is very largely undeserved – by which small caveat is meant that the commonness of this failing is no greater in Wales than in England, but just that there is something *about* the Welsh variety I find specially repulsive. Their appearance of, their name for greater direct dishonesty means nothing more than that they will skin you no more nor less than the English will, but they are more likely to look pleasant as they do it. I wish I could remember which fabulously rich man it was that moved a few miles from the south of France to Italy in his last years, saying in explanation that he preferred to be cheated with a smile. He would have had a similar case for moving from England to Wales.

The Welsh are warm-hearted, which shows in a pure form, with no potential gain in prospect, in their affectionate treatment of children, far more reminiscent of Italy or Spain than England. In fact, if I were drafting an indictment of the English, I could do a lot worse than start there, going on up to the refusal of the upper-class English to shake hands on introduction or after a passage of time, an important constituent of the very important and peculiarly English institution of the 'snub', that loser of empires. But this is a large subject.

Behind all this again lie vague chunks of history, to do with the incredibly early Act of Union between England and Wales in 1536 (England and Scotland 1707), the consequent lack of a national Church and legal system, the lack of a Welsh nobility and gentry, the lack of a Welsh middle class until comparatively recently, and at the end of it all something approaching the lack of a Welsh class hierarchy. Ferguson the tobacconist could never have talked to me like that in England, with such unthinking freedom and lack of offensiveness, nor I to him. The difference is hard to define from inside, but a sensitive English visitor will spot it at once.

Whatever the causes, I would still rather enter a room of randomly picked Welsh strangers than a comparable hodge-podge composed entirely of English. I would rather deal with a Welsh stranger, from an official to a shop-assistant, than an English one. (In Swansea market in 1987 I suddenly wondered what was making everybody so nice to me, until I realised what country I was in.) And if circumstances made it possible, I would choose to be nursed in illness by a Welshwoman.

The next matter is no business of mine and I do not, as before, pretend to anything like a knowledge of the full facts, but I admit to mild irritation whenever Welsh nationalism makes one of its deservedly rare appearances in news or talk. It presents a false picture, both on purpose, so to speak, and unconsciously. In no sense can it or does it speak for Wales. It is an entirely peripheral movement, indeed not a 'movement' at all. Its supporters tend to be ministers of religion, college people and schoolteachers, members of the Welsh BBC. According to one theory, the thing would not have got off the ground even its couple of inches if the BBC, setting itself up in Wales about 1920, had not understandably but mistakenly stipulated that all employees should be Welsh-speaking, thus at once confining itself to what in South Wales had for decades been a minority and, among the better educated, often a faction. The classical kind of Welsh it has pledged itself to revive is not the impure kind, full of English loan-words and loan-constructions, still naturally spoken in parts of the country. The bilingual public signs that infest an English-speaking town like Swansea were not there in my time, when there were still quite a few genuine Welsh-speakers about. The bloody things are a joke, with TACSI set up next to TAXI and even BEICS next to CYCLES. The words that matter, like DANGER and STOP and NO RIGHT TURN, are in English only. The overwhelming power of the Labour Party in Wales will never . . .

But enough. A neat transition, and an overdue lightening of tone, is provided by a comment on the point by a very eminent Welshman indeed, the poet Dylan Thomas. In the course of an unpardonably long interview with him in, I seem to remember, the pages of *Adam*, the literary and artistic review conducted, for the last three-quarters of a century or so, by that old windbag Miron Grindea, Thomas was asked his opinion of Welsh nationalism. Here, for the first and only time, the fog of suffocating solemnity was penetrated by Thomas's reply, for which the interviewer fell back on reported speech: Mr Thomas answered the question in three words, of which the second and third were 'Welsh nationalism'. He never again rose to such heights.

Anyway, while I was in Wales I encountered the poet in the flesh, and of course many times before and since through the printed and spoken word, spoken because he is still very much a subject of talk in the Principality and doubtless to an extent all over the world. (His posthumous yearly income amounts to about £80,000.) So much is this so, and so common among those Welsh who would not think of themselves as literary people, that I consider I have done well to defer mention of him here for so long. Apart from just one poem, 'The Hunchback in the Park', which distinguishes itself from all the rest of his poetic output by not being about him, and a few isolated lines from other poems – 'And death shall have no dominion', 'Deep with the first dead lies London's daughter' – he strikes me as a very bad poet indeed, or else a brilliant one in a mode that is anathema to me. Either way he is a pernicious figure, one who has helped to get Wales and Welsh poetry a bad name and generally done lasting harm to both. The general picture he draws of the place and the people, in *Under Milk Wood* and elsewhere, is false, sentimentalising, melodramatising, sensationalising, ingratiating. But – once more – this is not a work of literary criticism.*

I met Dylan Thomas on a single evening in the spring of 1951, when he had accepted an invitation to give a talk to the English Society of the College. The secretary of the society, a pupil of mine, asked me if I would like to come along to the pub and meet Thomas before the official proceedings opened. I said I would like to very much, for although I had lost all my earlier enthusiasm for his writing I had heard a great deal, not only in Swansea, of his abilities as a talker and entertainer of his friends. I arranged with my wife and some of our own friends that we would try to get Thomas back into the pub after his talk and thereafter to our house just up the street from there. I got down to the pub about six, feeling expectant.

The foregoing paragraph is based on a brief account I wrote of this meeting in the *Spectator* in 1957. If I had known about him then what I have since learnt, I would still have turned up, but with different expectations. For one thing, I would certainly not have entertained the idea of getting him along to my house then or at any other time, indeed would have done my best to conceal its location from him. I will now go on with a version of what I went on to write then, cut and amended where necessary.

Thomas was already in the pub, a glass of light ale before him and a half-circle of students round him. The impression he made was of apathy as much as anything. Also in attendance was, I said in 1957, a Welsh painter of small eminence whom I called Griffiths. In fact this person was a Welsh poet of small eminence by the name of John Ormond Thomas and later known professionally, I understand, as John Ormond. In the course of the session he told us several times that he had that day driven down from his house in Merionethshire (north Wales, now part of Gwynedd) on purpose to see Thomas, whom he had known, he said more than once, for several years. Thomas seemed very sedate, nothing like the great pub performer of legend. He was putting the light ales down

* Any reader who happens to be interested will find the matter explored a little further in my novel, *The Old Devils*, pp. 14–15, 224–25 et passim, where somebody called 'Brydan' does duty in this aspect for 'Dylan'.

regularly but without hurry. After some uninspired talk about his recent visit to America, he announced, in his clear, slow, slightly haughty, cut-glass Welsh voice, 'I've just come back from Persia, where I've been pouring water on troubled oil.'

Making what was in those days my stock retort to the prepared epigram, I said boyishly, 'I say, I must go and write that down.' What I should have said, I now realise, was something much more like: 'What? What are you talking about? That means nothing, and it isn't funny or clever, it's infantile playing with words, like that silly line of yours about the man in the wind and the man in the west moon. Or the phrase in that story about Highlanders being piping hot. They weren't hot or piping hot, but saying so is *a bit naughty*, I agree. *Taff.*'

Instead of this we had an exchange of limericks. For this sort of thing to be fun, the limericks have to be good, ingenious, original and especially in mixed company, which this was, not scatological or distasteful (containing references to vomiting, for instance). These conditions were met only fitfully on this occasion. The time to be getting along to the meeting came none too soon. Thomas jumped up and bought a number of bottles of beer, two of which he stuffed into his coat pockets. He gave the others to J. O. Thomas to carry. 'No need to worry, boy,' the latter kept saying. 'Plenty of time afterwards.'

'I've been caught like that before.'

I realise now that this tenacious sticking to beer when spirits would obviously have been more portable confirms in a small way the view that Thomas was a natural beer-drinker, like many. But with a smaller capacity than many, perhaps the only defect in himself he seems to have noticed: there is a note of mortification in his remark to 'Dai' below. Anyway, he was finished off by all the bourbon they gave him in America, culminating in the famous eighteen straight whiskeys just before his death; but that was a good two and a half years later.

The bottles were still in Thomas's pockets – he checked this several times – when in due course he sat rather balefully facing his audience in a room in the Students' Union up the hill. About fifty or sixty people had turned up; students and lecturers from the college mainly, but with a good sprinkling of persons who looked as if they were implicated in some way with the local Bookmen's Society. With a puzzled expression, as if wondering who its author could be, Thomas took from his breast pocket and sorted through an ample typescript, which had evidently been used many times before. (And why not? But I thought differently then.)

His first words were, 'I can't manage a proper talk. I might just manage an improper one.' Some of the female Bookmen glanced at one another apprehensively. What followed was partly run-of-the-mill stuff about his 1950 reading-lecturing tour of the US, featuring crew-cut sophomores and women's literary clubs in pedestrian vein, and partly the impressionistic maundering, full of strings of compound adjectives and puns, he over-indulged in his broadcasts. Then he read some poems.

Of his own I remember 'Fern Hill' the best, a fine performance given the kind of poem it is, but for the most part he read the work of other poets: Auden's 'The Unknown Citizen', Plomer's 'The Flying Bum' (the Bookmen got a little glassy-eyed over that one) and Yeats's 'Lapis Lazuli'. His voice was magnificent, and his belief in what he read seemed absolute, yet there was something vaguely disconcerting about it too, not only to me. This feeling was crystallised when he came to the end of the Yeats. He went normally enough, if rather slowly, as far as:

> Their eyes mid many wrinkles, their eyes,
> Their ancient, glittering eyes . . .

and then fell silent for a full ten seconds. This, as can readily be checked, is a very long time, and since that baleful glare at his audience did not flicker, nor his frame move a hair's breadth, it certainly bore its full value on this occasion. Eventually his mouth dropped slowly and widely open, his lips crinkled like a child's who is going to cry, and he said in a tremulous half-whisper:

> '. . . *are gay.*'

He held it for another ten seconds or so, still staring and immobile, his mouth still open and crinkled. It was magnificent and the silence in the room was absolute, but . . . (So 1957. Actually of course it was bloody awful, a piece of naked showing-off and an insult to Yeats and to poetry.)

I will cut the account short at that point. There was a return to the pub but still no pub performance. Perhaps he thought we were not worth it. Very likely we really were not worth it. Who cares? One has to record that many and varied people found him delightful company. That man is not all bad who said of his wife and the state she had been in earlier that day, as he did to Peter Quennell, 'Methought I saw my late espousèd saint passed out on the bathroom floor.'

Thomas was an outstandingly unpleasant man, one who cheated and stole from his friends and peed on their carpets. At the start he boozed a lot because it fitted his image of a poet, rather than out of any real thirst or need: Mary Morgan – I have never seen this anecdote reprinted – found an old local drinking-companion to whom he had confessed as much: 'I wish I knew where you put it, Dai; I can't keep up with you.' But for the last eight years or more of his short life he had something to drink about. That famous description of himself as 'the Rimbaud of Cwmdonkin Drive' is sad and awful more than funny. He knew Rimbaud had stopped writing poetry for good at the age of nineteen. Nearly all of Thomas's best work was written or drafted by the same age. He had a final burst of energy about 1944, but nothing after. And he was too sharp not to see it. Whatever the deficiencies of his character, he cannot be blamed too severely for reaching for the bottle (rather than for the revolver), as a reaction to the creative misfortune I compare to that of my late friend Bruce Montgomery.

Thomas and his wife Caitlin, an Irishwoman, not a Welshwoman, were nevertheless an ideally matched couple. To his strong inclination to live off others, she brought a personal disagreeableness all her own and a purer egotism, one that calls for others' attention not through wit or other quality, but just by being there. In this book I stick to my own experience as far as possible, but I cannot resist mentioning and warmly commending a book she wrote a few years ago in association with somebody called George Tremlett, previously known as a biographer of pop stars. *Caitlin* (an excellent title) is the funniest piece of semi-conscious self-revelation I have ever read, and incidentally very informative about Thomas and their life together. She hated Augustus John because whenever she went to see him, which was almost daily for several weeks, he raped her. Things like that.

Several times after her husband's death, I found myself unable to avoid running into her in Swansea and London. Once indeed I somehow let myself in for standing her and the three children, Llewelyn, Aeronwy and Colm, lunch at the Wig and Pen in the

Strand. The three youngsters, though not in every case of the highest moral character, were agreeable enough, but I could see, quite helplessly, Caitlin limbering up for an attack on my complacency, insensitivity, etc. It came at the end of the meal, followed by an abrupt stormy exit. This was of course designed to evade the necessity of saying fawning, fulsome, grovelling things like Thank you. Aeronwy thanked me. She knew.

As a very late PS on the Thomas topic, which has probably been running too long already, let me just add that when Elizabeth Reitell, who as a woman in her early thirties had been Thomas's last attachment and confidante and helper in his final weeks in New York, visited Swansea in 1988, she kept up the old traditions by behaving rudely and inconsiderately to the proprietors and staff of the nice little family hotel that had been found for her, and leaving her bedroom in a state in which one would not have wished to find it.

To revert to the early or middle 1950s. In many ways this was our best time. Even my salary, like everybody else's, went up. We had drink *in the house*, which I remember as Philip Larkin's criterion of prosperity. People came to stay: Powells, Gales, Kilmartins, Karl Millers, Henry Fairlies. Hilly and I went to places, more and more to London as my literary life got going. A trip to America became a distant possibility. One day I might even find myself at a grander university. Without our seeming to will it or quite know it, Swansea was beginning to be somewhere on the way to somewhere else instead of a base, a home.

I miss it constantly and I miss those days. I have a favourite sentimentalised picture of the life there when I began to feel part of it. The scene is the Bryn-y-Mor pub near the old hospital, and Jack Thomas the landlord, the only man I have ever met with a real quiff (curl plastered down on forehead), is doling out the snacks and bottles of Double Diamond. It is Thursday lunchtime, with a late lecture at 2.30. Around me are local tradespeople, the fellows from the estate agent's and the garage, Jo Bartley, David Sims, Willie Smyth, one or two others. Later I will be taking the first-year Honours through 'Thyrsis', fourteen or fifteen of them at the most. All is peace. Often I wish I had never left, but that is meaningless, like all such wishes, because everything in that picture has disappeared.

Jane and Swansea turned out not to get on well together. While she and I were associated I was mostly out of touch with the place, though not with friends I had made while living there, notably

Stuart Thomas and his wife Eve, who for some years had a flat in Onslow Square in South Kensington. It was here that, some time in the Sixties, they gave a party for Daniel Jones, Swansea composer and lifelong friend of Dylan Thomas. The occasion was the first, possibly also the last, performance of Dan's opera, *The Knife*, at Sadler's Wells. It must have seemed to him then an important step on the road from being a Swansea composer to being a composer.

No doubt thinking that the words of an opera libretto are of little importance, Dan had seen to this one himself. Eschewing Welsh themes, clearly as part of his image-remoulding drive, he had concocted a sort of Western, with a fight in a bar and fatal stabbing as the climax of Act I. At the start of Act II, the curtain was snatched up to reveal the town gaol, with the sheriff and his deputy sitting boots-up and smoking stogies at the desk and the unjustly incarcerated hero weltering behind bars. Over a string tremolo, the sheriff (baritone) stretched credulity by singing in recitative style,

'I don't like it . . . the town's too quiet . . .'

This crowning or plumbing banality was suitably followed by a lynching or a rescue or one of those. The audience, mostly Welsh, was and remained respectful in a way that I feebly hoped no ordinary audience at any old lousy new opera would have been. That was depressing, I suppose, but I was more engaged, while being driven back to Onslow Square, by trying to think of something not unkind and not glaringly untrue to tell Dan.

Shaking his leaden hand, I said when the moment came, 'Well, Dan, I thought I could hear the tones of your master coming through what you wrote there.'

He waited mutely in his porcine way.

'Handel,' I said.

If I had said, 'Old Evans Parry Parry-Evans of Llantwit Major after his stroke,' Dan could not have looked more blockishly fed up. Christ, what more do you want, you arrogant *bugger*, I asked him silently, and also in silence revealed what he could go and do.

I saw little of him after that evening. But I saw a great deal of Stuart and Eve and their bungalow in Mumbles. There, summer after summer, I have spent a tranquil, planless three or four weeks, working for an hour and a bit every morning (just right) while Stuart went to his office and did some of what solicitors do, being swept off to the unchanging Yacht Club (a little Garrick beyond Wales) by the great bay, or joining an occasional minibus trip inland – no outdoor stuff. In the more distant past, Stuart and Eve saw me through some nasty bits by the same means as, before and ever since, they have used in making the good bits better: the application of much kindness, good sense, whisky and hilarity. Thanks chiefly to them, Swansea has again become what it was further back still in my life: the piece of earth I know best, better than any part of London, and feel most at home in.

ROBERT CONQUEST

My FIRST CONTACT with this extraordinary man was by letter, over a different sort of letter I had written defending him against an old shag (in Conquestian phrase*) called Herbert Palmer, who had taken a pedantic/illiterate swipe at him in the *Listener*. The epistolary introduction was appropriate to one who is by far the most assiduous letter-writer I have ever known, most fortunately for me since he settled in California ten years ago.

This move was actually a return to the land of his fathers, or at least his father, a native Virginian who married an Englishwoman during the Great War. Bob is an American, something to be borne in mind in any attempt to understand him (as Tony Powell has always insisted), though British in many ways, including accent and having gone to Winchester (school) and Magdalen College, Oxford. In 1939, he characteristically lost his dual American/British nationality by joining up in the Ox & Bucks Light Infantry. (The American passport was later restored.)

But this is not a potted biography of him, so I take you to our first meeting, at the PEN Club in Chelsea, where a party was being thrown to launch something called *New Poems 1951* in which Bob and I figured. It was about my first literary party; as a shot in my campaign to infiltrate that kind of world, I had come up from Swansea specially for it; I knew nobody there except, tenuously, Robert Conquest. We soon marked each other down and stayed in conversation, I think throughout; I certainly remember meeting no one else. He had with him his (second) wife, Tatiana, a strikingly attractive Bulgarian in a large hat who said very little, and that not easy to follow in her English. (John Wain was to report that she

*So I have long thought, but he generously attributes it to me.

had asked him what he heard as, 'Do you know many boys?', which he found rather defeating until 'boys' was clarified as 'poets'.)

Bob, however, had as usual plenty to say. In my memory, these forty years later, it consisted mainly of a recitation from memory of the entire text of *Mexican Pete*, his sequel to *Eskimo Nell*, not *Eskimo Nell* itself, of which of course I possessed a copy, though at least one commentator has made that inept confusion. More than one has made a more serious confusion by taking the original poem as a blast of male chauvinism, machismo, misogyny, etc. In fact, like its successor, it is an ingenious and wonderfully sustained *lampoon* on all that. For the interested, who will remember that *Eskimo Nell* has as its climax the total sexual rout and humiliation of the hero, Dead-Eyed Dick, the sequel tells how its eponymous hero, Dick's erstwhile comrade, returns to the scene to exact his revenge, which he accomplishes with the aid of what he has learnt at Bangelstein's College of Sexual Knowledge in the snows of far Tibet, where

> It won't be a neuter you'll get as a tutor, but our oldest, randiest priest,
> Who knows every appliance of sexual science and the mystic smut of
>   the East,
> For this old fogey is a Yogi, and often he will pass whole
> Years in pursuit of the Absolute just gazing up his asshole.

But

> If you wish to read of each foul misdeed Pete performed on the way to
>   college,
> Just look up 'Mexican' in the *Oxford Lexicon of Criminal Sexual
>   Knowledge*.
> It will also mention his long detention in a sexual maniacs' home,
> Where he did time for the nauseous crime of fucking the Pope of Rome.

I spent the evening, or a couple of hours of it, laughing continuously and getting very drunk on Dry Martinis, of which I then knew little. When everyone had left but the three of us, Bob courteously invited me out to dinner, but I had enough vestigial sense to realise I would have my work cut out to get back as I was, even though 'back' meant not to Swansea but to Harwell, near Didcot, where Hilly and I were to stay the night with her parents. I might just digress a moment to add that my memories of what happened after I left the PEN comprise walking down or up King's Road, which was incandescent with magic, sitting in a train trying and failing to read the first page of a detective novel I had read the whole of more than once before, and waking with a start to see a sign saying DIDCOT *decelerating* past the window, while two black men opposite stared at me in wonder and concern.

The chief content of that first meeting with Bob was typical too. He was then and has remained a 'serious' poet, publishing his *New and Collected Poems* in 1988, but while recognising here the flair and skill he brings to everything he writes, with a few treasured exceptions I admire more than I am moved; I might put it accurately enough by hazarding that his Americanness comes out in this role, and admitting that American poetry of this century holds little appeal for me. I insist that where he excels is in his light verse.

Here Bob is thoroughly British, or English, and I am thoroughly at home, finding indeed nothing better or more congenial in the language than what he has written in this genre. This stretches from *Mexican Pete* through such satirical works of 'Ted Pauker' as 'A Grouchy Good Night to the Academic Year' and 'Garland for a Propagandist' (pastiches of Praed and 'The Vicar of Bray' aimed respectively at the modern university and Stalinist apparatchiks) to the famous limericks. Some of these, along with the Pauker poems, I included in my anthology, *The New Oxford Book of Light Verse* (1978). The limericks appeared under the pseudonym of Victor Gray, an anagram of G. R. A. Victory, Bob's full Christian names being George Robert Acworth.* That small selection excluded, for one reason or another, some of his best work in the form. I take the opportunity of rectifying a part of that omission here. I may say that I contributed the second line of the first one myself.

> The first man to fuck little Sophie [or whom you will]
> Has just won the Krafft-Ebing Trophy,
>   Plus ten thousand quid,
>   Which, for what the chap did,
> Will be widely denounced as a low fee.

*His third pseudonym in that volume was that of Stuart Howard-Jones, supposed author of 'Hibernia', a brief satire on Ireland couched in such a vein that I felt it prudent to give H-J's dates as 1904-74.

Said Edna St Vincent Millay:
'At the poetry-reading today,
    They dragged Robert Frost off –
    But not till he'd tossed off,
And that was as good as a play.'

ALL THE WORLD'S A STAGE

Seven ages: first puking and mewling;
Then very pissed off with one's schooling;
    Then fucks; and then fights;
    Then judging chaps' rights;
Then sitting in slippers; then drooling.

A favourite of Larkin's: 'sure sign of genius – I knew it by heart
after one reading.'

A usage that's seldom got right
Is when to say shit and when shite,
    And many a chap
    Will fall back on crap,
Which is vulgar, evasive, and trite.

There was a young fellow called Shit,
A name he disliked quite a bit,
    So he's changed it to Shite,
    A step in the right
Direction, one has to admit.

That snobbish surrealist, Garsall,
Once did himself up in a parcel;
    He addressed it 'Lord Garsall,
    The Keep, Garsall Castle'
And mailed it first-class up his arsehole.

There was a clockmaster of Lyme,
Whose balls had a very sweet chime,
    And when *he* set his cock
    For seven o'clock,
It always got up dead on time.

143

MEMOIRS

AT THE ZOO

There was plenty of good-natured chaff
When I popped in to fuck the giraffe,
    And the PRZS
    Could hardly suppress
A dry professorial laugh.

Bob's short light verse extends beyond the limerick to such small gems as

When the earl pulled out his bloody great tool at tea
    To do the page-boy wrong,
His chaplain cried in incredulity,
    'How long, O Lord, how long!'

All these show the careful and conscientious craftsmanship, the delight in overcoming self-imposed difficulties without apparent effort, gracefully, that light verse demands if it is to succeed, a 'capacity for taking enormous pains in relation to any enterprise in hand' – Tony Powell again, who sees this capacity as a part of Bob's Americanness. Anyway, something of this general bent is perhaps to be seen in another activity of Bob's, easier illustrated than defined. So: where Philip Larkin and I had thought it funny enough to spend half a minute inventing characters called Emeritus Professor 'Stuffy' Tupper and his wife Poppy, Bob went away and produced a whole enormous family of Tuppers, including Whirly (the helicopter pioneer) and Bangy and Bashy (the wrestling twins), plus a distant Scottish branch, the Bell-Tuppers,* including Willie, Canny, Woody, Musty, Mighty et no doubt al.

Then again Philip and I went no further with Nick the Greek and his friend Shun the Chinese than such utterances as 'For Nick, eh, Shun?' (on the arrival of a pretty girl). Bob put in some work and gave us such pregnant dialogues as:

'So, we've been sold as slaves in Tunis, Nick!'
'Yes – remember to call your master "Bey", Shun.'

and

*Bob disclaims these and suggests Martin Amis as the source.

'I heard your parents were attacked by a couple of footpads, Nick.'
'Yes – Pa's assailant escaped, but I brought Ma's to bay, Shun,'

and more. Some male readers may care to extend for themselves the gallery Bob and I built up, starting with coke-soaker, kirk-sacker, cox-hooker et al., or add to the series that included far-kin households (the familial arrangements of an Amazonian tribe who abhor any form of intercourse with close relatives, but strike up lasting attachments with distant cousins and such). Women readers are likely to find such undertakings childish in the extreme.

But harmless. That could not quite be said, perhaps, of another outlet for Bob's capacity for enormous pains, unusual ones anyway, in the matter of practical joking. Some of that, a small sample, came my way in the early 1950s in the form of an official-looking envelope addressed to 'Lieut. K. W. Amis, R. Signals, Class "B" Reserve Call-up (Malaya)'. The nasty turn that gave me hardly outlasted a glance at the contents. Philip Larkin suffered a good deal longer. Always a devotee of girlie mags (we all were, but he led the field), Philip had mentioned to Bob receiving a postal circular about tits and had wondered where the sender had found his name and address. 'I hope I don't get into trouble,' his letter had gone on to say. Bob arranged that he should think he had.

A letter on government paper, as from the Vice Squad, Scotland Yard, arrived on the Hull breakfast-table, the heading, 'Regina v. Art Studies Ltd.' Proceedings were being taken in the matter of the above, said the writer, under the Obscene Publications Act 1921, also Regina v. Abse (1959) and Regina v. Logue (1962). No decision had been taken as to whether to prosecute Larkin as well, but his attendance as a witness might be required. All for now.

The distinguished poet fled to his solicitor's office and stayed there all day. Nothing more happened, except that he sent Bob his £10 bill for taking up the man's time. Bob paid up, of course. His manner showed no remorse when he discussed the incident with me. The solicitor should have known, or soon found out, that the Act and the cases were fictitious, he said. I suppose I said to myself that I could see the funny side, and then rather stiffly that it would never have done if we had all been built the same.

In deliberately inverse order I now set down something about Bob's real or proper concern, a sufficiently serious one as a writer on politics and authority on the Eastern bloc, particularly the USSR and its internal history. His political position has come to be on the libertarian Right, and he has always been implacably anti-Soviet, an unfashionable stance for an intellectual and poet in those early 1950s days. In those same days I was some sort of man of the Left, and this brought us into mild conflict. Some time later he was to point out that, while very 'progressive' on the subject of colonialism and other matters I was ignorant of, I was a sound reactionary about education, of which I had some understanding and experience. From my own and others' example he formulated his famous First Law, which runs, 'Generally speaking, everybody is reactionary on subjects he knows about.' (The Second Law, more recent, says, 'Every organisation appears to be headed by secret agents of its opponents.')

When I first met him, Bob was working in the Foreign Office – something to do with Eastern Europe. He never said anything about this and was pretty close about other aspects of his career. He left the FO after a time (in 1956, it appears) and took up a Fellowship at the London School of Economics. There he began to write the books that were to make him famous and throw light into places where none had been before: *The Soviet Deportation of Nationalities* (later *The Nation Killers*), *The Harvest of Sorrow* (on the crushing of the peasantry in 1930-33), and the best known, *The Great Terror* (Stalin's purges in 1936-38).

For many years *The Great Terror* was ignored where possible or dismissed as propaganda. Then, in 1988, favourable references to it began to appear in the Soviet media. The following year, instalments of the full text started coming out in the official publication *Neva*.

Recently an American publisher suggested a new edition of the book. 'What about a new title, Bob? We won't pretend it's a new book, but a new title would be good. What do you say?'

Bob answered in terms that get a lot of his character into small compass. 'Well, perhaps *I Told You So, You Fucking Fools*. How's that?'

After some thought, the publisher said, 'Yeah. But Bob, I don't see us swinging the fucking.'

To return to earlier days. Apart from politics, where after I had noticed events in Hungary in 1956 Bob and I were in broad agreement, we were drawn together by our shared interest in science fiction. He was one of the first members of the British Interplanetary Society, and published a novel in the genre, *A World of Difference*, in 1955. It featured a verse-writing computer, with profuse specimens given, and of course a 'Poet' class of space cruisers that included the *Jennings, Larkin, Enright, Amis, Gunn* and *Holloway*. From 1961 to 1966 Bob and I collaborated on the editing of five science-fiction anthologies, *Spectrum – Spectrum V*, and in 1965 on a straight novel, *The Egyptologists*, which greatly annoyed some women with its battle-of-the sexes plot (in fact the women came out of it one up on the men) and amused others, recently the great Ruth Rendell.

In the middle and later 1960s, when we were both settled in or near London, Amis–Conquest contact was easier and more frequent. This was the period of the so-called Fascist lunches at Bertorellis' Restaurant in Charlotte Street. More or less regular attenders included, besides R.C. and K.A., Tony Hartley, Tibor Szamuely, John Braine, Tony Powell, Donald (C.) Watt, Russell Lewis, Bernard Levin (at first) and the American journalist Cy Friedin, with an occasional MP, Nick Ridley, Tony Buck, as guest. Contrary to rumour, no plot or project was ever even suggested at that table, but I learnt quite a lot of history and politics now and then, before the rounds of grappa started.

Before I met him and for some years afterwards, Bob suffered from difficulties with girls, including wives. He will not, I hope, mind my saying that his marriage to Tatiana did not run as smoothly as it might have. I remember sitting one lunch-time in Mon Plaisir, the restaurant in Monmouth Street (not my choice of venue, let it be said), talking faster and faster about the weather to Tony Hartley while Tatiana performed a kind of sentry-go on the pavement outside, bashing the window with her umbrella as she passed and repassed. On another occasion a group of us were gathered in the bar of the Marlborough Arms in Torrington Place, the *Spectator* pub in the days when the journal was still operating round the corner in Gower Street. The session had started soon after evening opening-time and gone on rather. Before it broke up Bob got all the rest of us to sign a piece of paper certifying that we had spent the previous couple of hours in his company.

'What's this bloody thing for?' I asked him.

'To show Tatiana. To prove I haven't been with some other female.'

You poor bugger, I naturally thought. But in time I became aware of a pattern that has since become quite familiar to me from contemplating other marriages. The male observer's first impression is of his fellow-male having to put up with a good deal in the way of harrying or chivvying from his wife. Then as the outsider's familiarity grows he finds the husband doing his fair share of chivvying or harrying in return. Thus one morning after Hilly and I had spent the night at the Conquest house in Hampstead, hard by the old Bull and Bush, he drove us and his wife into the centre of things in their small car. Tatiana, in front next to Bob, was admittedly being a bit irritating, rabbiting on, perhaps urging a change of route or destination. For a few minutes he held his peace, then remarked in a calm, not at all unfriendly tone,

'Darling, of course I have no control over what enters your silly head, but I do wish you'd keep your pissy little comments to yourself.'

I felt Hilly stiffen in the seat beside me. I probably stiffened too. She and I were still fairly young in those days. (Not that we were without our own conflicts.)

Eventually Bob and Tatiana were divorced. A third marriage ended similarly. Some time later, after a trip to America – he was always off there – he produced a pretty and amiable Texan girlfriend, Liddie Wingate, twenty-seven years his junior. They lived in a flat in South Kensington and I visited them there. Then one day Bob said to me,

'Liddie and I are going to get married.'

I answered in pure astonishment, not shock or anything of the sort, 'Bob, you can't do that. Not *again*.'

'Well, I thought – one for the road.'

The marriage took place and as I write has lasted ten years without any strain visible to me. I will only say, without all censoriousness, that when it comes to shopping – frequency, duration, devotion – Liddie beats hollow all other women I have ever known. Boy, can and does she shop.

I will end this with two diverse anecdotes. Years ago there was a public lavatory (gents) immediately outside the Marlborough, needless to say much used by its patrons, others too. One day Bob and I were descending the lavatory steps when without warning he bawled,

'All right, Sergeant, get your notebook at the ready.'

I had only just stopped myself from crying out in terror when four or five little men appeared below and dashed past us up the steps. There was never a time when you could be quite sure Bob would not do something like that.

He was a generous and discreet flat-lender and of great usefulness to me in my unregenerate days. Normally I would avail myself of his basement pad in Eaton Place in Chelsea, but one time for some reason he had taken a service flat elsewhere which I borrowed. I got to it rather ahead of time and went in to find it, as expected, empty. At the same moment the disembodied voice of Bob said 'Lucky sod,' in allusion to a then recent poem of mine which began, 'All fixed: early arrival at the flat/Lent by a friend, whose note says *Lucky sod*;' as I realised when my feet were back on the floor. He had set up a tape triggered by the opening of door or lock. No one else I know would ever have dreamt of going to that trouble. Never was Bob's 'capacity for taking enormous pains' illustrated to better, or rather more striking effect. Incidentally the full Tony P sentence ends, 'particularly in the concerns of friendship'. Well, yes.

No: I will end finally with a clerihew of Bob's that says or illustrates more about him than any words of mine could.

> Mr and Mrs Pankhurst
> Wanted to wank Hirst;
> He said, 'Should anyone call,
> Shout out, "No ball!" '

ANTHONY POWELL

THE FIRST NOVEL of Anthony Powell's that I read, on Philip Larkin's recommendation, was his third, *From a View to a Death*, first published in 1933; I got to it in 1941 or '42. I immediately recognised a talent and a way of looking at the world that were utterly congenial to me, even though the bit of the world being looked at, with its butlers, country houses, etc., was quite outside my experience. After the war I got hold of the others and had read with delight and anticipation the first two volumes of the *Music of Time* sequence. Then in the summer of 1953 my very first book review, of a collection of James Thurber's stories, appeared in the *Spectator*. In it I made the point, which I still consider a fair one, that in America they go in for funny writers, like Thurber, while over here we seem to produce serious writers who are also funny, like 'Mr Anthony Powell' – you called people 'Mr' in print in those days.

This unexpectedly led to a letter from Tony, an invitation to lunch at the Ivy, and eventually to the first of a long series of visits to his house near Frome. Much to Hilly's and my relief, the place, though grand in style, was of modest size and contained no butlers or analogous persons, in fact nobody but Tony himself and his wife Violet – actually Lady Violet, we found, but as unswanky a Lady as could be imagined. Someone came in to cook, but Tony regularly put on a butcher's apron and prepared Sunday lunch, always the same dish, a satisfyingly pungent curry complete with fried banana and Bombay duck. At first we were shy of asking the Powells to our far from grand Swansea establishment, but took Violet's reference to having had to sleep on a trunk once at George Orwell's place as a (deliberate?) go-ahead signal. So they came to us, and returned for more. Violet would leave a ten-shilling note on the guest-bedroom mantelpiece for the bedmaker and Hilly would appreciatively pocket it.

At the Chantry, the Frome house, the ladies had breakfast in bed, the gents went to the dining-room. One morning in 1973 I went in there to find Tony already at the table.

He looked up from his newspaper and said, 'No more Auden,' adding when I looked blank, 'W. H. Auden is dead.'

'Oh,' I said. 'Well. Quite a blow,' or some similar banality.

'I'm *delighted* that *shit* has gone,' said Tony with an emphasis and in a tone of detestation that made me jump slightly. 'It should have happened years ago.' Feeling perhaps some elucidation might be called for, he went on not much more mildly, 'Scuttling off to America in 1939 with his boyfriend like a . . . like a . . .'

I have forgotten what it was that Auden had scuttled off like but I never knew Tony before or since to show the kind or intensity of emotion he showed then. It might tickle what he would very likely call another 'side' of him, the superstitious, occult-fancying side, to hear that in the middle of setting down this brief exchange I went out into the hall here and found a misdirected letter with a return address in Auden Place, N.W.1, on the back.

A third side, the opposite in a way of side 1, had been revealed many years before, probably in 1955, when the third *Music of Time* volume, *The Acceptance World*, was published. I was invited by BBC radio to subject Tony to a long interview on what in those days would have been the Third Programme. I must have turned up a couple of minutes late; anyway, when I arrived there was Tony with two or three BBC people in attendance. He and I greeted each other by our Christian names and at once the BBC faces fell in disappointment, almost disgust. It was not hard to guess that the interview had been intended to consist of a lower-class malcontent (the label of Angry Young Man had not yet been promulgated in 1955) having a good go at somebody whom he would see as an upper-class git; there was to be a more or less frank admission of this expectation in the *Radio Times*.

The producer had yet to appear, but his name was mentioned, only to escape me at once.

'Is he black, do you know?' Tony asked me not very softly.

'I really have no idea.' I sounded pompous even to myself.

When he, the producer, did appear he was as white as your hat, but his manner carried a touch of the autocratic. We all trooped off to the studio and Tony and I took our places each side of a microphone with the producer looking in at us through glass from the next room. Before starting to record we were to rehearse the opening.

I led off by saying how jolly good Tony's books were and then, as a means of getting the conversation going, started quoting, reading out, what the reviewer in the *Observer* had said about *The Acceptance World*. After a minute or less a light flashed on or off and the producer's voice boomed something at us from a loudspeaker. He bustled in, clearly dissatisfied.

'You're sticking too closely to the paper,' he told me.

I explained that I had about finished with the *Observer* and would soon be –

'No no, I mean you're sticking to the actual novels, the text.'

'I thought that was what we were supposed to be discussing,' I said.

'No no, that's not what I want. I want something about the status of the novel in general, its place in society and so on.'

Tony said, 'We don't care what you want. We're going to do what we want. And if you don't like it we're walking out of this studio. Now.'

What impressed me about this utterance, even more than its style and content, was its placid, conversational delivery. That's the upper classes for you, I thought to myself; I might have been able to summon the guts to say something along those lines, but I should have had to lose my temper to do it. Anyway, that short speech of Tony's knocked all the fight out of the producer.

'There's no need to take that tone,' he said.

'Oh, good,' said Tony appreciatively.

After a short pause the producer said, 'Carry on as you were doing,' and left us to it.

We took him at his word, and were both quite pleased with the result. The producer said he was too, probably satisfied just to have shown his flag.

When the *Music of Time* sequence was complete in 1975, with *Hearing Secret Harmonies*, I wrote and read a huge lecture, again over BBC radio (but with a different producer), on the thing as a whole. Putting it together involved, of course, slow and careful reading of each volume and the taking of copious notes. This had the distressing side-effect on me of making the books unrereadable, so far at any rate, though I mean to return to the charge in the not-too-distant future. I ought to have foreseen this, having published a short book on the works of Ian Fleming, *The James Bond Dossier*, in 1965, with a roughly comparable amount of work required and the same lasting result. But most people will think this a less lamentable deprivation.

In the course of my *Music of Time* lecture I said something about the individual volumes being like novels, each with a distinguishable theme or subject – entering the adult world, marriage, the coming of war, etc. – while the sequence as a whole was more like life, in a way more realistic, than its components, with for instance characters such as the painter Barnby coming and going haphazardly. Thinking about this more recently has suggested the odd conclusion that, if a comparison can be ventured, I am a more literary novelist than Tony. Two tiny incidents seem to me to bear this out.

In one of my novels, *Girl, 20*, the narrator and others visit a horrible flashy eating-drinking-dancing club of the period (early Seventies); I had to get the décor and such off my son Martin. Tony complimented me mildly for making the food at this place, to my character's surprise, 'excellent'. I had done that for, well, a little artistic reason, feeling it would have been too dull and predictable to make the food as nasty as everything else there. But he, Tony, observed that he, or perhaps his son Tristram, had in fact found the food at such a joint to be okay; I had got it right in that sense. On a later occasion, interviewing him for a Sunday paper, I asked what all that card-reading stuff with Mrs Erdleigh was doing there, meaning, ahem, its artistic function; Martin saw this point at once when I put it to him. Ah, said Tony, a lot of people had been in fact very keen on that sort of stuff at the time in question, so he had got it right.

Well, it would not do if we were all the same. One of the great strengths, and a minor weakness, of *The Music of Time* lies in its interest in families, forebears, descendants, relatives. This adds richness and scope; it can also slip here and there into something not far from mere gossip. Tony loves all that in his life and conversation, having innumerable connections, in-laws, children of in-laws. With only two cousins this side of the Atlantic, childless aunts and uncles and so on, my own life has been thin in that respect. It could be that this is reflected in a feeling of underpopulation in my fiction, only here and there, I hope. How could I tell?

My admiration and fondness for old A. P. and his writings should be clear by now. He will have to forgive me if I end this mini-memoir and tribute with a sample of yet another 'side' of his character, a faintly comic and egotistical one rarely in evidence. I had reviewed *Hearing Secret Harmonies* in the *Observer* on the Sunday before its publication on the Monday. I praised it highly, more highly than some others did, calling it a worthy conclusion to a great roman-fleuve and things like that. But I try to make it a rule, when reviewing a book by a known friend, to slip in one adverse remark. This might be compared to the habit of Arab artists and craftsmen of deliberately introducing an imperfection into their work so that they should not be thought to be trying to put themselves on a level with God. Alternatively it could be seen as the bit you put in to show that you and the other fellow are not buggering each other. I saw no reason to make an exception in this case, and after all no book ever written is impeccable.

With this in mind I said towards the end of my piece something about Mr Powell's commendable desire for brevity betraying him once or twice into infelicity, and gave as an example the sentence, 'If Murtlock liked sex at all, he preferred his own.' I added that this kind of thing had been stigmatised by the great lexicographer H. W. Fowler as 'legerdemain with two senses', and most careful users of the language, I add now, would feel slightly uncomfortable on reading the sentence quoted without necessarily being able to particularise. My review immediately went on to reiterate the merits of the work as a whole.

Evidently Tony did not share my view of the Murtlock construction. The following day, the Monday, the publishers, Heinemann, gave a lunch at a London restaurant to launch the book. Tony and I were among the first to arrive. His opening words to me were, 'Hallo Kingsley, and I think you should realise that Fowler has no authority at all and was merely expressing his personal preferences,' which he perhaps went on to stigmatise as dated, idiosyncratic or something of that sort. No doubt I babbled something back, with no way of foretelling the behaviour of Anthony Burgess on a similar occasion. That time too there would be nothing more than an oral or aural comma between greeting and ballocking. But I repeat here and now that it would not do if we were all the same, and re-reiterate the merits of the work as a whole, while not forbearing to add that I would myself go some way to avoid letting a reviewer see he had got under my skin. But again that is probably just me being lower-middle-class. (Only joking.)

JOHN BRAINE

IT WAS IMPOSSIBLE to dislike John Braine, and almost as difficult not so much to take him seriously as to be quite sure how serious he was being about this or that. He was a heavy smoker who had a small sticker made to put on his cigarette packets with the legend, CIGARETTES ARE GOOD FOR YOU – SMOKE MORE, LIVE LONGER. One would be pretty safe in assuming he did not really believe that. But did he really mean it when he announced that the sole and sufficient cause – no last straw about it – of his political conversion, taking him from a full-dress, Aldermaston-marching nuclear disarmer to an extreme right-winger it was embarrassing to be allied with, was his reading that somebody who sounds like Lord Longford had accused him, along with the rest of 'society', of being guilty of the Moors Murders? And his Yorkshire thing – more than an act, but how much more? And how like Joe Lampton, the opportunistic anti-hero of *Room at the Top*, was he really? Not ruthless and cruel, certainly, but how much of what Joe wanted did John really want? In his later life, at any rate, he was often in a state of well-controlled drunkenness.

When I met him on one of his London visits I liked him immediately. Pale, bespectacled, chubby, with a perpetual look of being out of condition – he had had a long and serious illness in childhood that gave something to his novel *The Vodi* – he had an expression of habitual gloom, even something approaching hostility, but always ready to lighten into a genial smile. Once he came to Swansea to interview me for a magazine, and was much taken with the 100°-proof bourbon whiskey in which another magazine had paid me. There was nothing well-controlled about his drunkenness on that occasion. He was put to bed in an attic room (normally that of my son Philip), there being no question of his returning to London that night as he had planned. The next morning he was found there with the electric fire full on and near enough to the bed to have caused

155

it to burst into flames had he not rendered the sheets non-inflammable. He retains the prize – a closely fought distinction – for producing the most thoroughly maltreated bedroom I have ever set eyes on.

I began to see more of him in the Sixties when first I, then he, settled in London. Well – 'I'm resident in London now, lad,' he told me cheerfully over the telephone. Good news, I replied, and asked whereabouts in London. 'Woking,' he said. Now Woking is nearly twenty-five miles from London, and to talk of the one as in the other is rather like calling Leicester part of Birmingham. A joke, sure, but on who? Anyway, from Woking, where he had secured, I learned, ideal office premises on top of a car-hire firm, he often came to the weekly 'Fascist' lunch at Bertorellis' in Charlotte Street. Seeing his moon face at the table aroused mixed feelings, of pleasure at seeing a warm-hearted friend, of resignation to hearing a good deal of preaching to the converted. Nobody at those gatherings had much time for, say, the Soviet political system, but John made certain its demerits were never to be overlooked. Taking the chair next to his was liable to bring the familiar mild discomfort of being with someone you like but find it oddly difficult to think of anything to say to.

To be sure, there were rewards. One was the Lord Soper story, quoted at least once elsewhere but never correctly or in full. The true version goes:

'I was on a TV programme recently,' said John, 'with Lord Soper, socialist, divine, and peer of the realm.' (Oh, *that* Lord Soper, I wanted to say. It was another Braine characteristic to take nothing for granted.) 'Now don't get me wrong – same programme, but different parts, okay?'

'Fine with me,' I said.

'We got chatting afterwards and he said, I understand you've just come back from the United States. I said ay. He said, What did you make of it, then? Well, I said' – and here his voice took on the bluff, puffing, impatient note he would adopt for platitudes – 'I said, With all its glaring, manifest, obvious faults it's a wonderful, free, open society they've got there, and Soper said, H'm, all right if you're not black, and I said, But you stupid bugger, I'm not black.'

The last phrase came out with real grimness, almost belligerence – no bluffness now – and was followed by a baleful stare of some duration; I, at whom he had happened to be looking, had for the moment become Lord Soper. However this may sound on paper, the reality was either the work of a highly trained jester or perfectly serious. Those who may think it cannot have been the latter were not there when he told the German-slaves story. Nor was anyone else except me and my second mother-in-law, whom he succeeded in shocking by being too right-wing, another feat unique in my experience, and by a long chalk. The scene, hard to improve on, was the drawing-room of my house in Maida Vale, where the three of us (what were we doing together?) were taking afternoon tea.

Probably munching a scone, John said, 'I don't know whether you saw in the paper recently about a woman in West Germany who'd been keeping two teenage girls penned up in her house *as slaves*. Every morning she'd let 'em out of the cellar where she kept 'em under lock and key and stand over 'em while they cleaned the house and did the washing and got the meals and that, and at the end of the day she'd chuck 'em back in the cellar, where she might throw 'em a bone or a crust of bread to keep 'em going, and then she'd shoot the bolt on 'em again. Now of course' – here came the puffing note – 'there's been the predictable prog pinko outcry from the so-called liberal Press' – his voice switched to a squealing falsetto designed to encompass all humanitarian sentiment – 'how could such a disgraceful thing be permitted to happen in a supposedly civilised country?' – back to ordinary Braine – 'but what *I'd* like to know is how did she' – fist crashed on table – '*do* it, because let's face it we've all got a servant problem and there's a woman who solved hers. Would you believe there was talk of sending her to gaol?'

My mother-in-law was sitting up very straight. 'Really, Mr Braine,' she said, 'I must say I . . . I think it is possible to go a little too . . . I hardly think . . .'

The subject passed off, God knows how. What had he been playing at? Malice of any kind can be ruled out. So, I think, crossing my fingers, can humour, as with Lord Soper. If John had been doing a Yorkshire-yobbo act he would have clowned it far more obviously than that. No, the old lad was a mystery, an agreeable one no doubt, but one I found myself feeling less and less inclined to exert myself to solve as time went by. Our almost-weekly converg-ings at Bertorellis' – he and I, along with Tibor Szamuely, were probably the most faithful attendants – came to be enough for me.

Periodically, embarrassingly, a new Braine novel would arrive from the publishers; one of them, piling on the embarrassment, was dedicated to me and my second wife. I found them all unreadable, but then as others have noticed I am a great hand at finding novels unreadable. Even the reactionary tendency of these was not enough to attract me to them. A peculiarity of them I noticed was that all the characters had names that nobody ever really has – Regilla Catamountain, Menedemus Ableport – perhaps on the advice of some libel expert on the point of emigration. But the books did go on coming out and people presumably went on reading them. I think those readers were largely of the comparatively lowly sort that enjoy stories about well-off powerful people – verbal soap-opera, in fact.

Yes, that's a nasty thing to say, but it is rather supported from the continuing success of the Joe Lampton TV series. Joe of *Room at the Top* had taken on an independent existence on the small screen, sneering and seducing his way through the middle reaches of the London smart set. One episode ended with him being turned out of the luxury flat by wife or current mistress. Letters from ladies flooded in saying he was welcome to a bed at their place any time, addressed c/o the agent of the actor Kenneth Haigh, who was very competently playing Joe, no doubt forwarded by the television company, but surely genuine death-of-Grace-Archer soapy behaviour. And . . . it goes against the grain to write this, but at least one of the last novels took a further step down.

One and Last Love – the title is lazily misremembered from a drawing-room ballad – opens with the first-person narrator, a famous novelist called Tim Harnsforth, lying in bed in a flat off Shaftesbury Avenue with his mistress. This last was a favourite word of John's in ordinary informal speech, used invariably where anyone else would have talked about a girlfriend unless the subject was Madame de Pompadour. It gave a quaintly Edwardian flavour to his talk. The bed is no ordinary bed, it is 'king-sized, with a white padded headboard and matching white bedside cupboards, with a pink-shaded bedside lamp.' The mistress, one Vivien, is a more ordinary mistress, and we get to her full but still firm breasts well after a laudatory account of Tim's body that takes up most of the first page: 'you're like a boy,' she tells him (he is fifty-six). 'You're so young, your skin's so smooth . . .' (Dots in original.) And we're immediately assured that Vivien always tells the truth. Later she tells him he's a marvellous writer, and everyone else thinks so too, bar the critics. Whether this is worse than the young-boy-body stuff, whether the pink-shaded-lamp stuff is worse than the stuff in the

Gay Hussar, where Michael Foot nods 'briefly' at Tim, I cannot decide. The book is an assault course of embarrassment for the reader.

A new peak of intrinsically Braine-type embarrassment was created and scaled on a TV show, one of William F. Buckley's 'Firing Line' efforts made in London. The line-up was clearly to have been two pop-eyed reactionaries (John and me) confronted by three fist-waving leftie heads of student unions. Some 'research' error, however, had intervened to see to it that one of the student offices had fallen at a late stage to a third reactionary, and a better-informed one than either John or me. The programme, which was and apparently had to be shot in one go, without rehearsal or retake, soon fell into a pattern.

BUCKLEY (*in the chair*): I take it that you two gentlemen [Braine and Amis] are in favour of [say] capital punishment?
BRAINE: Ay, that's the way to show the buggers and bring down the murder-rate.
AMIS: Actually I'm against it on several grounds, and I believe the figures –
STUDENT REACTIONARY: Figures from similar American states and Canadian provinces show a correlation as follows. [Correlation followed.]
STUDENT LEFTIES: Fascist crap, police-State crud, etc.
BUCKLEY: Now as to disarmament [or something] . . .

I really think it was a bit worse for me than for the others.

Politically, John's behaviour offered a choice of adjectives, among which 'naive' would be a popular choice, if perhaps an indulgent one. Anyway, he showed himself to be something like that when, acting with and for a fellow called Harold Soref, who I did not care for the look of above half, he unsuccessfully tried to persuade me to write a piece or give a lecture favourable to the South African government. On protesting that the matter was no concern of mine and I knew nothing about it, I was told that my very position of neutrality would add weight to my words, and that I would be supplied with all necessary facts. This would have been in 1970 or shortly before. The temptation scene was enacted in the Reform Club and parts of it were fictionalised, or fantasised upon, in my novel *Girl, 20*, chapter 6. (No Braine figure appears there.)

Another of John's later works was *Writing a Novel* (1974; paperback reprint 1990). He was an excellent, an obvious, perhaps the only choice for such an 'assignment' – the term seems appropriate. He sets himself the task of teaching the tyro in 150 pages how to write not a great nor even a good novel but a publishable one. There is of course much sound advice and much entertainment along the way, some of the best of the latter coming from comparison with John's own work and career: detailed discussion of the dangers of success (especially early success) and of being sued for libel, style viewed as a matter of catching 'the rhythms of speech', metaphor seen off in a dozen lines as avoidance of cliché or alternatively just plain statement. But his most interesting maxim is 'always write from experience'. Can he really have thought he was doing anything describable as that, in all his lives at the top?

Almost my last and my saddest memory of John before his death in 1986 is of what turned out to be the last of the Bertorellis' lunches. I arrived late to find only John and Bob Conquest present, with Bob looking slightly harassed, a rare state for him. John was in full spate and as drunk as I had ever seen him, frowning with earnestness as he talked.

'I've just been telling Bob,' he said, 'and I want you to hear it too, Kingsley, that the three of us are among the luckiest people alive. And in what way? In that we are free agents. We are nobody's employees. We sell our wares to the highest bidder. We receive no wage. We work as and when and where we will. We are our own bosses. Nobody tells us what to do. We have no quota to fulfil. We keep to our own hours. We . . .'

He must have gone on repeating and re-repeating statements of the advantages of the free labourer for half an hour or more. All Bob and I could, or anyway did, do was offer growingly sarcastic agreements. Eventually John must have caught some note of ridicule or impatience and said in a different voice, 'I know I'm hated. The reason being I never went to a university.'

There can be few things further from the truth than that. What he did lack, as Martin put it to me the other day, was not education but any feeling for literature. Just for possessions, I might have added. Like Joe Lampton. There was more than a joke in John's declaration that his dream of real success was of a triumphal procession through Bradford with himself at the head, flanked by a pair of naked beauties draped with jewels.

BOOZE

Now and then I become conscious of having the reputation of being one of the great drinkers, if not one of the great drunks, of our time, certainly among its literary fraternity. The original, primordial reason for this is that the hero of my first book back in 1954, Jim Dixon, drank rather a lot, in fact got drunk and showed it, which university teachers such as he were not supposed to do, certainly not while delivering public lectures, as happened to Dixon. Such a statement will seem absurd only to those, a numerous company, who are unaware of how often and thoroughly people confuse the characters in a novel with its author, even many of those people who would be regarded by themselves and others as good, literary-minded readers. Why, I even catch myself doing it.

So: I have written before how for many years I was generally thought to be a Yorkshireman because (there can be no other reason) people had it somewhere in their heads that Dixon was one; actually he is described as coming from the north-west of England, but there seems little point in calling for accuracy in delusion. To this day I am often taken for a Welshman, though I went to the principality for the first time at the age of twenty-seven and ceased to live there thirty years ago. I wrote a bit about the place, you see. And for Christ's sake surely anybody with half an ear can pick me out as a South Londoner the moment I open my mouth.

Now I know it would be no use trying to make out that my alcoholic celebrity rests entirely or even chiefly on the behaviour of my characters. But a link is set going and is reinforced every time one of my chaps raises a glass to his mouth, and I have to admit that some of them do so rather often. This is probably less an interest in drunkenness or drunks as such than a novelist's device, disguised where possible, for accelerating the story, making somebody throw a pass or insult somebody else sooner, more outrageously, etc., than they might when sober, rather in the same

161

manner that action novelists use danger or the threat of it to show us something unexpected in a person. But my chaps do put it away. And, true, I have written about booze, three little books, various articles, though that is thought to be more respectable. And in the nature of things I am to be seen actually drinking from time to time.

Some writers clearly do well out of being known as drinkers, with Dylan Thomas the great archetype. And being known to have died of drink (in fact from falling off a bar-stool) helped Lionel Johnson's posthumous reputation. If suggestions of raffishness, Fitzrovia, John Davenport can be brought in, so much the better. Other figures, without suffering anything very much in consequence, tend to be bad-mouthed in the Press. Those who do some real-life drinking in West-End or men's clubs incur the displeasure of diarists and interviewers and are attacked for snobbery, right-wingery, misogyny, etc. as well as mere drunkenness. This is especially true if the club in question, like the one I belong to, is thought highly of and regarded as difficult to get into.

Well, so be it. I dare say I ask for it a bit too, with little acts of provocation like asking for a particular malt whisky as my luxury on 'Desert Island Discs', instead of the sonnets of Michelangelo or whatever. But I have found it a little irritating in the past to be castigated in the papers for portraying some fellow as unduly drunk in tones that suggest that the critic would never dream of touching a drop himself. I would read under the name of the late John Raymond, say, a haughty rebuke to myself for being the laureate of beery Philistia and five minutes afterwards go round the corner into the Queen's Elm in the Fulham Road, that haunt of bibulous writers and artists in Sean Treacy's day, and find him incapable at six o'clock in the evening. Our dialogue on such occasions went like this:

'Hallo, John, can I get you a drink?'

'Urgh, you ff – , you ff – ' (This is intended to represent the sounds he actually made and is not a bowdlerisation.)

'Perhaps you don't feel like anything for the moment.'

'Gooh, you sh – , you sh – '

'Glass of water?'

'Pawh, you bb –, you bb – '

'Well,' I said, on finishing the quick one I had popped in for, 'next time we must have a proper get-together. Nice talking to you,' and left.

But other parts of that tale are not funny at all. John was one of the best of the old-style book-reviewers, now I think all gone, well-read, hard-working, writing with flair and vigour. But the drink took him off early, as it was to take off John Davenport, another fine critic of the same breed. And in their cases there was no reason that I know of, no escaping from the ghost of a dead talent as in Thomas's case, for instance. What is one to say? Some writers drink too much. Are there more of them in proportion than soccer players or chess masters? If it is true, as observation suggests, that actors produce more than their fair share of drunks, then this would reinforce my theory of displaced stage fright as a cause of literary alcoholism. A writer's audience is and remains invisible to him, but if he is any good he is acutely and continuously aware of it, and never more so while it waits for him to come on, to begin p. 1. Alcohol not only makes you less self-critical, it also reduces fear, which partly explains its wartime use. Just the thing for the funk at the typewriter, except that when one has one little one, one wants one little one more. The bottle on the desk is all very well, right and proper, in fact, in what used to be Fleet Street, but not for anything anybody may hope will be read more than a couple of days later.

The best treatment for writer's jitters is the one mentioned by Graham Greene, seeing to it that you stopped the previous session in the middle of a chapter or scene or paragraph and so are today merely going on with something, not starting afresh. Failing that, dredge up that dreaded first sentence not at the typewriter/word-processor or anywhere near it, but while showering, dressing, shaving, etc. The last is often mentioned as particularly useful, and one reason for the inferiority of women novelists to men, if indeed they are inferior, may well be that comparatively few of them shave with any regularity.

Whatever part drink may play in the writer's life, it must play none in his or her work, except in the journalistic circumstances I have mentioned. It does no harm, perhaps, as the supplier of that final burst of energy at the end of the day, and before I write the last few lines of this chunk I shall probably pour myself a single respectably sized glass of malt whisky. But that is the limit. There can be no doubt that, however much beer or anything else Dylan Thomas might be going to consume later – did you know that after he was married he spent not one single evening at home, always went to the pub? – he wrote his poems cold sober. Such precision required the equivalent of the utterly steady hand of the miniaturist.

Even those who, like myself, think the result is false, wrong in some way that goes right to its heart, can see that in another way it gets everything right. But, as he said, you can only work like that, properly, for two hours in the day, and what do you do after that?

It is comical and rather sad to see that restraint manifestly not being exercised. Paul Scott's Indian novels have been much praised, and with some reason, but here and there you can see the prose going to pieces as the stuff came pouring into him, then pulling itself together with a jerk as he started again when sober. All in all, the writer who writes his books on, rather than between, whisky is a lousy writer. He is probably an American anyway. But that is another, though very real, story.

GEORGE GALE

L IKE THAT OF Mr Holmes, Christopher Isherwood's schoolmaster, George Gale's glance is cold, friendly and shrewd, a difficult feat to bring off, but he manages it. In the same sort of contradictory way, his manner is bluff, gruff, even rough, also amiable. But you noticed his voice first, coarsened by the hand of nature into a sort of growl that can rise into an equally illusory petulance – a gift to imitate, as I soon found. When I first knew him and drank with him in about 1955, it used to irritate me slightly to see my own rather placatory manner with waiters or barmen bringing me ordinary service at best while this bear of a chap, uttering his wants without a please or a thank you in a kind of muted roar, should have them falling over themselves to meet them, tearing the Cellophane off fresh packets of Senior Service like men possessed. They had seen through the harsh integument to (what he would hate to have said of him) the warm gentle fellow inside.

I suppose we first met at the offices of the *Spectator*, not the present nice-enough but comparatively poky place in Doughty Street to which the magazine moved in 1975 but the grand mansion at 99 Gower Street which could and did hold half political and journalistic London at its parties. (The Doughty Street spot holds a comparable number, but has to pack them in like sardines.) Anyway, to my regret at the time, the relevant party was the one *after* Evelyn Waugh had had his ear-trumpet pinched off him by a group of girls and passed round being blown through like a serious trumpet, after which he vowed never to do any door-darkening there again. My regret passed as soon as I realised that my admiration for his works might have been seriously dinted by whatever form of social drubbing I would inevitably have got from him had we ever met. George was more worth while. So, I thought at the time, was his wife, Pat. At this first encounter we did establish that the Gales had connections with Swansea, then my home, Pat being or having been a

165

Swansea girl with a mother and a couple of sisters still living there. Soon we were on terms where a visit was promised sooner or later.

It was sooner. George and Pat came for Christmas to our house in Glanmor Road. He told me recently that he had never been in a house so awash with booze. This caused in me a burst of retrospective pride, for George had a large reputation even in those days as a formidable drinker – when the time came he was widely believed to be the foundation of the *Private Eye* character Lunchtime O'Booze. Rather as in my own case, this was only partly deserved. As I soon saw, he put it away all right, but in bursts, never missing work because of it, let alone at any stage as a way of life, and even the bursts were mild compared with what one has seen in a Raymond or a Davenport, to mention only the dead.

Nevertheless, George told one never-to-be-forgotten story involving his experiences in a train. When he was living in Staines he would find himself, more often than he cared for, getting into the train at Waterloo after a hard day at the office and/or elsewhere, falling asleep and waking up at its terminus, Reading, some miles beyond Staines. The resulting inconvenience was not great, involving merely changing platforms and climbing into one of the frequent trains back to Staines (and eventually Waterloo). After that, however, it was by no means unknown for him to fall asleep again and wake up at Waterloo, the period in toto having taken quite a bite out of his evening with zero advantage and also making him feel somehow degraded. Next time it was not going to happen. To ensure this he did not so much as rest, instead sitting forward throughout as if on the point of leaping to his feet. (Was there not at any stage anybody else in the compartment?) And sure enough, after an immeasurable interval, the lights of Staines station came swimming into his view. Only they were so to speak the wrong way round, the way you saw them when you were approaching from the Reading not the Waterloo side. So he must have . . . 'Drunks have a first-rate homing instinct,' he used to say.

I could go on with tales of the pub crawls on George's later visits, for instance the one in the Mumbles where the round consisted of double Green Chartreuses with double-gin strengtheners, but the effect would be too much like that of old warriors refighting battles long ago. The four or more of us stayed several times at Dylan Thomas's Boat House at Laugharne in what was then Pembrokeshire, through the good offices of my friend Stuart Thomas (no relation), solicitor to the Dylan Thomas estate, not of the ghastly

Caitlin. The poet had been dead only a few years then, and both house and town were much as he had left them, the former not yet the hideous 'museum' hung with daubs by 'local artists' it was to become, the latter uninfested with Dylan Bars and Grills. George was a painter himself, as I discovered when, preparing to drive from Swansea down to Laugharne, we visited an art shop to buy paints and other materials he proposed using at the far end. I remember his hands were shaking so badly I had to write out the cheque and he just managed to sign it – not so much a Sunday painter as an afternoon one with a couple of large gins inside. (He had developed a very practical drunk's signature, 'G. S. Gale' reduced to a single irregular wavy line.)

I cannot remember actually seeing George actually painting on that or any other trip, but there was no doubt that he was in some sense a bona fide painter. Years later I saw with a mild shock of surprise a large landscape, fully finished so to speak, uncamouflaged by any modernist flummery, that had come from his brush. It was leaning against the wall in a passage in his house in Wivenhoe, not even hung, nor have I ever seen any others in any position. Now I am a poor judge in these matters, but I think if I had been able to get as far as what I saw in Wivenhoe I would have gone further, developed my gift or tried to or something. But not to have done so is all too George-like.

The Welsh visits were reciprocated, with Hilly and me and some-times our children going to the Gales' in Staines. Here again the boozing was done chiefly outside the house, in the Bells pub as near opposite as made no difference and a grander establishment, the Pack Horse, where one could also eat. It was here that an American friend of mine over from Princeton once ordered a large Green Chartreuse as his main dish at dinner – that prettily coloured rocket-fuel was something of an 'in' drink for several of those years; here too that, one uncomfortable morning, I had taken a large vodka to get me off the ground and induced the kindly landlord, Ken Nias, to bring me a glass of bicarbonate of soda to reduce the painful acidity of my stomach. I drank the two in quick succession and felt no better, though markedly peculiar. 'Let's see what's happening inside you,' said George, and poured the last drops of the vodka into the dregs of the bicarb. The mixture turned a dark purplish brown and started to give off smoke.

Not long after this, though not I think as any direct result of it, the certainly kindly and genial but rather drunken and (if this is not hindsight) faintly worrying Ken Nias was taken off to a mental hospital. George, Stuart Thomas and I went to visit him there. He seemed just the same, if perhaps a little subdued.

'Giving you a thorough drying-out, are they, Ken? I asked.

'Yes, there is quite a bit of that, but it's more that I'm off my head.'

I could think of nothing to say just then, but a male nurse sitting near or next to our party had plenty, on this and related topics, letting us have it with repulsive gusto. On the whole, that 'hospital' was as disagreeable a place as any I have ever been to, featuring for instance a large entrance-hall with floor-to-ceiling murals painted, I was all too credibly informed, by a schizophrenic inmate and depicting vivid images of the sort of things you see in nightmares. I am profoundly glad that I was unaware then of what George told me only the other day, that Ken's mental disturbance first unmistakably showed itself when he was found to be painting what sounds like just the same sort of images on the walls of his bedroom at the Ostrich at Colnbrook, the pub not far from Staines where he had moved from the Pack Horse.

After saying goodbye to Ken at the booby-hatch the three of us looked around a bit and found ourselves in a large room, empty, with rows of seats like a school assembly-hall, ceiling-high pictures of worthies like Aristotle and Newton painted in a different but not much more reassuring style, and a platform at the end with a grand piano on it. Stuart went and sat down at the instrument and played 'Home, Sweet Home', not, he protested, in any spirit of mockery but merely because it was the only tune he knew. It did nothing to raise my spirits.*

Anyway, Ken seemed none the worse, at least, when he was let out not long afterwards and in due time became catering manager at Speke Airport, Liverpool. But I had better admit at this point that all this Nias stuff and its attachments is really only an interlude in a discourse on George's special relationship with pubs in general. They meant and mean something powerful to him that I could never quite share. In fact, George regards pubs as places of unique virtue, over and above their appeal to your ordinary drinking man. Part of this must be a relic of self-conscious Geordie-ism, anti-poshness, and part must have had to do with his periodic need to put some distance between himself and his wife, another part perhaps derived

*I tried to put something of the feel of the place into a novel of mine, *The Anti-Death League.*

from Fleet Street as it was, simple fondness for draught beer too, but shyness again I think comes in here. In the pub you are on neutral ground and you are never going to have to be first at the party. Whatever the exact rationale, the pub is George's place, and he must have been hit more cruelly than most of us would have been when a couple of severe heart-attacks in the last half-dozen years meant the necessity of losing a lot of weight, and so of a swingeing cut in intake of alcohol. At home or in a friend's house you can drink innocuous rubbish or nothing at all; nursing mineral water at the pub must be a grey experience.

But this is to look too far ahead, beyond for instance the Brendan Behan encounter, so to call it. John Raymond had invited for evening drinks his current girlfriend, George, me, Behan, Mrs Behan and the journalist Henry Fairlie, since denied these shores on pain of arrest for fraud for many years before his death in early 1990. Behan was well up to form, offering for instance a neat piece of bait for any taker, me as it fell out.

'I remember when I was doing a bit of painting in Paris . . .'

'Oh, I didn't know you went in for art, Brendan.'

'I don't mean painting fucking pictures,' he growled. 'I mean serious painting. Painting fucking houses.'

There seemed no obvious reply to this, nor to what he had to say a little later in praise of the Parisian attitude to the choosing and buying of wine. 'You don't catch 'em saying' – his voice rose to a squeal and took on a supposed posh English accent – ' "Have you a nice full Burgundy with a good big body?" or "Could you possibly find me a claret with some depth and plenty of tannin?" ' Back to normal: 'Christ, it's "D'ya want the ten, the twelve or the fourteen per cent and d'ya want the label with the sluts dancing or the bastard with the big hat? – what d'ya *want*?" '

As some readers will already be aware, Behan took what might be called an all-round interest in alcohol.* George was quite a mate

* When a young lady writer from the London *Sunday Times* interviewed Behan in Dublin once, he responded to the offer to name his pre-lunch drink (at Jammet's or the Shelbourne) by saying politely, 'I'll have three bottles of gin, please, and would you get two of them put in the car?' It is of some interest that, at a similar encounter the previous day with Liam O'Flaherty, all went swimmingly until the brandy-and-coffee stage, when the author of *The Informer* told the interviewer in a confidential tone, 'I've got your number now. You're a fockan agent for Scotland fockan Yard.' He was described by his contemporary Sean O'Faolain as an 'inverted romantic'.

of his, remained one even after Behan had been sick into a drawerful
of socks while spending the night at Staines, had actually gone to
stay with him in Ireland. There, as he told me some other time in
Behan's absence, the pair of them had been about to leave the pub
one evening after plenty of Guinness when Behan asked for and got
a dozen miniatures of John Power off the barman.

'That's an expensive way of buying whiskey,' George had pointed
out. 'Half your money's going on the bottle and packing and what-
not.'

'True. But there are two considerations that override that.One is
that the Irishman, though extremely dishonest, is also extremely
lazy. He'd be quite prepared to take a hacksaw to a full bottle or
even a half to get at the stuff. A miniature's too much trouble
altogether. You'll be seeing the other point in the morning.'

The morning brought George, told by Mrs Behan that himself
was stirring, into the main downstairs room to find Behan stretched
on some sort of day-bed. Two miniatures of John Power lay on the
coverlet, two on the nearby windowsill, two on a bedside table or
chair, others no doubt in other places. With eyes still closed, Behan
beat and groped about until he found one little bottle or another,
fastened on it, unscrewed its top, drained it, dropped it. In a minute
or two he opened his eyes cautiously and picked up another refresher
in no sort of hurry.

'Now you understand,' he said to George. 'If I'd had just the one
full bottle I might have put it in all sorts of places. And just you
think of looking for it.'

George shuddered sympathetically.

To cut back now to John Raymond's – the talk shifted to journal-
ism or politics or both. Behan had a hard time being consistently
outgunned by George and Henry Fairlie, both of whom knew much
more about the subject than he.

'I remember when old Tim O'Leary was foreign editor of the
Manchester Guardian,' Behan would begin.

'No, he was never foreign editor,' George or Henry would break
in. 'Worked in that part of the office for a bit, that's all.'

'The time Paddy Lewis was reporting the war in the Congo . . .'

'Paddy Lewis was never *in* the bloody Congo during that war. I
know because I was there the whole time myself, first to last.'

After a bit more of this, John said in placatory style, 'Do help
yourself to another drink, Brendan.'

The drinks table was squarely behind George's chair. Behan went

over to it, turned and gave an extraordinary exhibition of fury, easy
to imitate, hard to describe, half war-dance, half flurry of shadow-
boxing with his fists coming within an inch or two of the unknowing
George's head and neck, accompanied by frenzied mouthing and
face-making. It must have gone on for half a minute while the rest
of us watched spellbound. George sat placidly on while I wondered
what the hell he thought we were all goggling at. Then at last, to
my mingled relief and disappointment, it faded away and all was
comparative peace.

'Let's have some dinner,' said John quite soon after that. 'There's
a good place just round the corner where they know me.'

We departed in dribs and drabs, the Behans, much to my regret,
leaving the party altogether, John and his girl going on ahead in her
car, George, Henry and myself following on foot. After no more
than five minutes' walk we arrived at the restaurant. It proved to
be showing a CLOSED sign, with John and girl visible inside
studying menus. He caught sight of us through the glass door, made
a brief can't-help or perhaps won't-help gesture and returned to his
menu.

'Right,' the three of us outside said in unison, and without so
much as a glance at one another went into action on the girl's car,
unmistakable and parked by the kerb a few yards on. It proved to
be unlocked but to lack the ignition key. George or Henry got
behind the wheel and Henry or George and I started pushing. We
soon took it off the main road, which was I think the Fulham Road,
round a couple of corners and into some mews or dead end. Here
we left it with all the lights on and (my contribution) the windscreen-
wipers going at full speed, and made the best of our way to the
nearest pub. When I boasted of this exploit a couple of years later,
George Melly's wife Diana nearly knocked my block off. The car
had taken three days to find, and the delay had caused its owner,
no doubt a chum of Diana's, to miss or lose an important something-
or-other. Well, that's life, I rather thought and think. Or it was.

George and I have had our dissensions. Some of these were over
politics, in the days when I was a little leftie fart and he was what
he still is, firmly of the libertarian Right. Anything that is anti-State,
that weakens the power of the State over the individual, was how
he first put to me his general political goal, and so it has remained.
These days we are very largely at one here. Difficulties of a different
order came when my marriage to Hilly broke up and he was
unequivocally on her side. At one stage he was forbidden the house

171

as a bad influence, which from one point of view he was, though at a time when, as I now see it, I was in some need of bad influences. Now that too is resolved.

As long as I have known him, George has had a longing, doubly curious in such a sterling pub-man and foe of bullshit, for baronial grandeur. His house in Staines was, I suppose, not over-large for the size of his household, though I have wondered, as I have about his later establishments, where he got the money to run it. As his family diminished, with the children leaving home, so his aspirations swelled. With his second wife Mary he was surely adequately housed in Sawbridgeworth near Harlow, occupying a flat in a grand mansion in the middle of a gorgeous park, with two guest bedrooms and a drawing-room baronial enough for all but the likes of Welles's Kane. But at thirty miles or so (and with a good train service) Sawbridgeworth proved too far from Fleet Street. So he moved to Islington, but had not settled in there properly before he was out in a hilariously gigantic house in Tattingstone near Ipswich, seventy miles from London. Deciding after a time that with its twenty-odd bedrooms and bullring-sized ballroom it was on the large side for himself and wife and mother, he moved to a place he swears is much smaller near Alnwick, twenty-five miles or so north of Newcastle. He has always had a rural thing too.

His career at the *Guardian, Daily Express, Spectator, Daily Mail* and elsewhere has never given his talents of clear, unflinching thought the outlet they deserve. And he should have done, perhaps could still do, more and better TV, not *What's My Line?* but things like the series that never was, *The Two Georges*, with himself facing the late George Brown. What a spectacle that would have been – but they could never get Brown sober for long enough. Much more seriously, George G has had a large work of political philosophy somewhere near the verge of completion for donkey's years. It is or was to end with a long poem, which he gave me to go through and advise about, asking me to get a move on if I could as he wanted to get the whole thing off to the publisher. That was in 1967. For Christ's sake, George, *get it done*. We need it. Perhaps by the time these words appear he will have obliged;* if not, I ask him to devise a worthier and more interesting undertaking for the Sage of Titlington.

---

*Sadly, he never will now. George died on 3 November 1990.

But I cannot leave George with an admonition, however brief and however heartfelt. Let me instead tell of the time he came as my guest to a feast at Peterhouse, his old college. We got through the meal all right. Afterwards in the Combination Room (what lowlier persons would have called the common room) I introduced George to a chap who seemed to expect it, a certain Jean-Claude Simon, anyway one of those tripartite French names, the lecteur at the college, pluming myself silently on my feat of memory.

'Ah,' said George on hearing the name, or more like 'Aargh. Just the thing,' he went on, 'I've been meaning for some time to say that if there's any nation that can't write it's the sodding French with their sodding Racine and Baudelaire and what-not.'

I smiled a lot on hearing this and made faces to show how funny George was, my mind scurrying in several directions at once. Simon, much to my surprise, smiled too. 'For my part, Mr Gal,' he said, 'I have been waiting a long time to hear somebody say something to that effect.'

'*What*? All right, people talk a lot about England being the land without music, but it can't compare with bleeding France and Debussy and Poulenc and the other tone-deaf buggers.'

'If I may say so, Mr Gal, that is extremely well put.'

'*Eh*! Christ. And as for painting, France is a bloody dauber's paradise with that turd Delacroix and Manet and the rest of the sodding gang.'

'I would not change a word of that, Mr Gal.'

'Jesus, are you a man or a mouse?' said George with eyes popping. 'Here I am, denouncing your bloody nation and all its works for five solid minutes [in full it must have come to about that], and the best you can do is smile and say how bloody true. Gerh!'

'Ah, but you mistake, Mr Gal. I am not French, I am Swiss.'

I despair of rounding that off suitably, so will just say that the loudest roar and longest laugh were George's. And of course, as those who know him will not need to be told, all unfeigned. But he had a bit of luck there, n'est-ce pas?

FRANCIS BACON

W HEN PEOPLE STARTED taking notice of my novel *Lucky Jim*, which was not straight away as legend has it, the first person to write me something more than a fan letter about it, probably early in 1955, was a journalist then unknown to me called Dan Farson. Could he interview me for the *Evening Standard* (probably)? I decided straight away that indeed he could, but perhaps I should have thought about it a little longer. When you have done that sort of thing for the first time, you will find yourself doing it again, it and things like appearing on television, giving quotes over the telephone about how you will be voting at the next election or spending Christmas, helping to advertise a brand of beer, all that. The other option of course is to refuse everything for twenty years, after which you may condescend to be photographed with your face mostly hidden, preferably in a foreign magazine, and expect to be taken seriously by some sorts of people. So all unknowing I was casting a die when I said yes to Farson, but not a very important one.

Farson then said he thought Swansea was rather a long way to come (to see an unknown youngish shag teaching at a Welsh college). What about Cardiff? Any tolerable restaurants there? I thought and still think this suggestion about the venue a bit off, but was too greedy and chicken to say so, so I said instead what was true enough, that there was certainly an excellent restaurant in Cardiff, at its edge at least, in Tiger Bay, or Bute Town as the bien pensant were trying to learn to call it, Cardiff's dockland, home of Shirley Bassey, etc. I expect I met Farson at Cardiff station, whither I would myself have had to come from Swansea.

When Farson arrived he was dressed, I thought, more appropriately for some hiking or rock-climbing expedition than lunch in a provincial town, and he had someone else with him as informally dressed, smallish, middle forties, nondescript.

'Do you know Francis Bacon?' asked Farson.

174

Well, I had come across that name in the papers as that of a man just beginning to make a reputation with paintings of cardinals, or perhaps popes, screaming inside transparent boxes. 'I've heard of him, of course,' I said.

'I thought you wouldn't mind if I brought him along,' said Farson.

'Not a bit,' I said, reasoning that, though Bacon was not as far as I knew a Welsh name, he might perfectly well have had an auntie in the area, or some similar reason for making the (in those days) three-hour train journey down from Paddington. None emerged while we taxied the few minutes to the restaurant, which was called the Windsor. It gave us its usual ample and delicious old-style French lunch, kicking off with its famous unlimited and variegated hors d'oeuvres. (The place was burnt down some years later by an avenging sacked employee and never rebuilt.) While we ate and moderately drank, Farson asked me the sort of questions I was to be asked quite a number of times over the years ahead and did not strike me as very novel even then. Bacon said almost nothing, though he looked at me a fair amount, perhaps sizing me up for a drawing of me screaming inside a transparent box to accompany Farson's article.

After the meal, Farson said he would like to look round the docks for a short while if that was all right. Nothing easier, I said: a couple of hundred yards' walk would bring us to the start of them. So off we went. At that far-off time Cardiff was still a flourishing coal port, one of the greatest in the world, but when the three of us reached the waterfront we found that most of that was going on at some distance, and about all that was anywhere near us was a couple of ships, a couple of cranes and lots of reasonably dry mud. Never mind, said Farson, that would be enough for his purposes, whatever they might have been, and he climbed over a low wall and walked away over the mud. Neither Bacon nor I accompanied him. We stood side by side behind the wall rather as if waiting for the start of some sporting event. A minute or two later he stirred himself into action. He reached inside his jacket or blouse and brought out some sort of magazine, which he handed me.

'Are you interested in this sort of thing?' he asked.

It was a not very expensively produced piece of homosexual soft porn, featuring black-and-white photographs of young men in inviting or provocative poses, done in quite a refined way except for the taste in clothes shown, with nothing vital exposed or even prominent in close outline. Although needless to say unprepared for this turn of events, I was able to work out what would be the best time to spend on this vile object, not so short as to imply disgust, since I had no wish to offend or provoke Bacon, and certainly not so long as to imply any sort of affirmative to his question. After perhaps about eight seconds, then, I gave him the magazine back.

'No,' I said.

As far as I remember he said nothing to that, just nodded philosophically. Perhaps, unseen by me, he sent some signal to Farson, who at almost that very moment turned about and began making his way back to us. What among other things you might call a long shot, I mused as the three of us strolled off: a whole day ventured on the strength of – what? A newspaper photograph? Hardly. Faulty second sight? Odd, anyway.

The embarrassment that might have been expected to prevail was somehow absent, or much muted. Later we might even have had a drink with George Wigg in the bar of the Royal, but that may have been another time altogether.

Kingsley Amis in 'writer' pose (Photograph by Philip Larkin)

St. John's undergraduates in college garden, 1942

(*Below*) 91 Telegraph-Operating Section, Royal Corps of Signals, N.W. Europe, May 1945

(*Left*) Wedding of Uncle Pres and Auntie Poppy, Denmark Hill, 20 June 1914. Back row, left to right: Dadda, WR Amis (KA's father), Poppy's brother, Uncle Pres, Poppy's father, Poppy's sister Ethel, Uncle Leslie. Front row, left to right: Mater, Rosa Amis (KA's mother), Auntie Glady's, Auntie Poppy, Aunt ?, Poppy's brother's wife

Mater
(John Amis
Collection)

KA with Milton

London, 1950s: Anthony Powell, KA, Philip Larkin, Hilly (Estate of Philip Larkin)

KA after lunch
(Private photograph by
Tony Armstrong-
Jones)

Lord Snowdon
(Camera Press)

Philip Toynbee (Camera Press)

KA at the Boathouse at Langharne

KA on the rocks

Philip and Martin Amis in sink, Mumbles, 1950

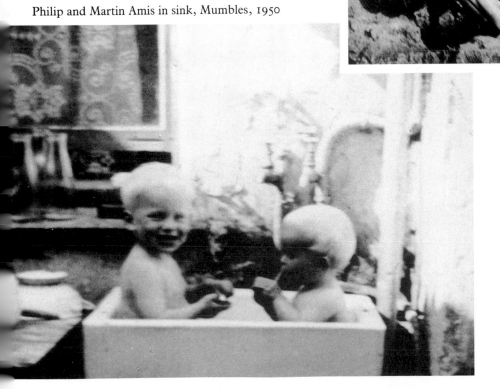

KA with Hilly and the children, Portugal, 1955 (Amis family photos)

Martin and Philip as mods, London, 1960s

KA with Philip and Sally, Majorca, 1962 (Amis family photos)

Anthony Burgess (Camera Press)

Robert Graves (Hulton-Deutsch Collection)

KA Outside the Garrick

KA and Hilly. On the left is Hilly's sister Margaret

TERRY-THOMAS AND OTHERS

I N 1957 THE film of my novel *Lucky Jim* opened – which I suppose means was the first event of – the Edinburgh Festival. A kind of skeleton crew travelled up to help in publicising the occasion: half of the Boulting Brothers and his wife, Terry-Thomas, Theo Richmond, who was then the PRO of the film company and later became a TV producer and a personal friend, my wife and myself, but not, unfortunately, the gorgeous Sharon Acker, who had played the female lead, nor, less unfortunately, Ian Carmichael, the male lead.

Unlike most comedians I have met, Terry was one of those that make you want to start laughing the moment they appear. He was not much of an actor and had been totally miscast as Bertrand, the posturing painter and leading shit of the novel, turned with some small advantage of plausibility into a non-writing novelist for the film. But the hash he made of the part was so comic that the result was a large net gain.

Also unlike many comedians he seemed just the same person in the flesh as on the screen, given to suits of an indescribable sharpness and provocative frilled shiny waistcoats. He belonged very clearly to one of two main types of professional funny man, the chap who is such a scream at parties that his friends persuade him to go public, as opposed to the performer with a probable theatrical background who has started his career in the business. At the same time Terry possessed to the full that actor's hunger for winning round, winning over an audience against indifference or even hostility, that seems by no means peculiar to comedians.

Drinks time on the first morning duly arrived. I was very happy in the bar of the North British Hotel, where we were all staying, but Terry said he wanted a beer in a typical Edinburgh pub, and soon, leaving the others in the hotel, he and Theo Richmond and I filed off. Now the pubs in Princes Street nowadays are probably models of propriety, or at least offer nothing more unwelcoming than rock music or fruit-machines, but the one we picked at random in 1957, opening straight off the main street, the city's pride, was rough at only a few minutes past noon.

I must inevitably have exaggerated the scene in memory, but I see little circles of ill-shaven red faces all turned our way with no welcoming expression at all, and I certainly hear a sudden hostile silence. The silence was not complete because Terry was still talking, talking at the top of his voice and in his most Eaton Square accent. I decided that my natural place was as near the door as possible and tried to make myself transparent while Terry went on talking as before – anecdote, imitation, full-dress story, something. Whatever it was or led to he had every man in that pub round him in a laughing semicircle in – well, rather a long time for my taste, but he got them, just like Oscar Wilde with those pompous shags at whatever club it was, and a bit more hazardous too. Strict justice would have awarded him a medium-strength kick up the arse for this display, as Theo and I agreed afterwards, but at the time you had to admire and enjoy.

Of the dozens of stories he told later, never near the point of surfeit, I think I should tell one, not, I think, the one featuring a Welshman with a speech impediment, but – 'There's a fellow called Telfer who makes more pork pies than anybody else in the bloody *world*, old boy. So the Americans went and asked him how he did it – incentive schemes, graduated bonuses, productivity scales, vacation benefits, you know the kind of thing. "No," he kept saying, "no, I never do anything like that, no, I just let 'em turn the bloody things out the best they can. Oh, now I come to think of it, there is just one thing – every so often I goes down to the yard and I bawls, 'Faster, you fuckers!' " ' Well, I have tried in this book to sort of keep things varied.

Almost our last glimpse of Terry-Thomas comes somewhere late at night with only Theo and myself present, the rest of the company having retired exhausted. Theo and I were less than bright as buttons, too, but Terry was restless, puffing cigarettes, pacing the floor. Suddenly he said, 'I'm terribly sorry, chaps, I don't want to break up the party, but I've come over most frightfully randy just in the last couple of minutes.'

'Well, there's not much you can do about it now, Terry,' said Theo.

'Or here,' I said.

'Don't you believe it, old boy. I'll just slip down and have a word with the hall porter.'

The half-dozen of us took our breakfasts as a group in the hotel dining-room. The next morning Terry arrived a little later than the others, all teeth and spotted scarf, rubbing his hands festively.

'Well, how did you get on last night, Terry?' I asked, thinking of him persuading the night porter of the North British Hotel to bring out his little black book.

'Absolutely bloody marvellous, old boy.'

'Bloody *marvellous?*' said Theo when the three of us were alone.

'Yes, you see, before I could even tell the laddie what was on my mind he'd started showing me photographs of his grandchildren and what-not and after a bit of that I found all my desire had vanished and I went straight to bed and slept like a *child.*' For me it took years, until the other day, for the penny to drop.

Peter Sellers I found the other, or another, type of comedian in several senses. The year is now 1960 and a contingent from Something Films is on its way to Swansea to do some of the outdoor shots for their version of my novel *That Uncertain Feeling*, which is set in a town closely resembling Swansea.

The film company had retitled it *Only Two Can Play*, to no advantage that I could see, in fact *Any Number Can Play* would have been nearer the mark, and filled the cast with English actors, not only Sellers but Virginia Maskell, Raymond Huntley, John le Mesurier, Richard Attenborough and somebody who was only technically if at all English, Mai Zetterling, with Welsh actors in the minor parts instead of the forefront, where I had hoped to see them. Nevertheless what they made turned out to be much better, including funnier, than the conscientiously 'Welsh' serial broadcast on BBC2 in 1986. A large part of the credit must go to Sellers.

I was eager to meet him and discuss with him what I saw as the Welshness of the main part, but he proved markedly unavailable. The Grand Hotel, Swansea, though needless to say a hellhole now, was in those days a decent, modestly comfortable provincial hotel, one that Mai Zetterling, an international star, declared at once would suit her very well. Not so Sellers, he buggered off down the coast to Porthcawl and what proved to be a measurably worse hotel, though no one seemed to mind that much. With him he had taken Kenneth Griffith, who had a smallish part in the film, fine actor and nasty little subversive creep. He would coach Sellers in the Swansea accent. Partly to my chagrin the result of this, or what Sellers made of it, was unimprovable, the precisely accurate local-university Welsh-English.

Sellers finally yielded to my importunity to the extent of giving me lunch of a sort. He told me that the whole resurgence or whatever it was of British humour had been started or invented by the Goons in their radio show of 1951-60, featuring Harry Secombe, Spike Milligan and himself, and especially Milligan and himself. Of course there were *differences*, just as there were differences between the Goons and the Cambridge Footlights people, all that, but *essentially* the Goons had started everything. It occurred to me too late that *essentially* the Goons (with Major Bloodnok) had derived from ITMA (with Colonel Chinstrap), and so had much else besides.

I would put Tommy Cooper in the same class as Terry-Thomas but saw much less of him, just a couple of wonderful but slightly exhausting hours in a Welsh train of him being Tommy Cooper. Frankie Howerd, with whom I was once a co-judge at a cheese-tasting, talked to me about Shakespeare without stopping. Michael Bentine did a something-like-ten-minute private performance of the signing of the treaty of Versailles with no one able to produce a pen that would write and no words spoken but the preliminary. 'The signing of the treaty of Versailles,' laying me flat. Groucho Marx, with whom I idiotically appeared with others on a TV panel show, was the most embarrassingly unfunny comedian I have encountered. Charlie Chester told me of an earlier and now surely forgotten performer, Gillie Potter, that he had considered him about as funny as armpits. John Cleese struck me as the most insecure of the tribe, perhaps with reason, and Tony Hancock as the misery everybody else seems to have found him.

But for an upbeat coda, may I offer a story of Hancock someone else told me? Well, many years ago another chap, a third party, a friend (or so he had thought), ran into him one evening on Waterloo Station. The two of them lived a couple of stops apart but would travel down in the same train. In the compartment they talked of this and that until the train drew up at Hancock's destination. Leaving it till the last moment, he grabbed his mate's head between his hands, kissed him passionately on the lips, said loudly, 'Good night, darling,' and jumped out just as the wheels started to turn.

The train was of the obsolete type with no corridors. For quite long enough, the mate sat with ten pairs of eyes staring wordlessly at him and said, with some repetitions, 'I don't know why he did that. I hardly know him. He's a married man with kids. So am I.

He's a comedian. You must have heard him on the radio. It must have been his idea of a joke. I'm a married man with four kids.'

Fade vision. Fade voice. Bring up noise of train.

If the fellow who told me that will apply, he shall have a large drink.

PHILIP TOYNBEE

ABOUT THE TIME I was getting going in the mid-Fifties, a small group of posh chaps had quite a lot of influence on literary developments. It included Cyril Connolly, editor of the magazine *Horizon* until it closed in 1950 and after that a principal reviewer on the *Sunday Times*, Alan Pryce-Jones, editor of the *Times Literary Supplement*, John Lehmann, editor of *The London Magazine*, and Philip Toynbee, chief reviewer on the *Observer*. All of them sat ceaselessly on award committees, contributed to symposia, took part in public discussions, etc. They were second-generation Bloomsburyites, I suppose, junior and dilute modernists. I never thought of them as opponents or obstacles, nor of myself as any kind of instrument of their undoing, but my opinion of their qualities was not high. I saw them as men of small original output and uncertain taste, owing their position to other things than knowledge or merit. (I had not yet learnt that such jobs rarely go to the deserving.)

Connolly (1903-74), the best known, seemed to me the least deserving, despite his one short, funny novel, *The Rock Pool*. Among much dubious pontification, he had said he found admirable the work of Dylan Thomas and Edith Sitwell as well as that of Auden, an impossible honest judgement for anybody with a feeling for poetry. Indeed I might have singled him out for special treatment as one of those who would never have been heard of if he had not been at Eton and Balliol, but I have no personal memories of him beyond the fact that he thought talking in a fast squeal was enough for an imitation of Lord David Cecil.

Toynbee (1916-81) was no more respectable as a critic. After finding Colin Wilson's 'study', *The Outsider*, worthy of the highest praise, he shiftily backtracked and condemned its supposed successor, *Religion and the Rebel*, as a 'vulgarising rubbish-bin', unaware that it was actually part two of the same book. His early promise as a novelist – Rose Macaulay, usually a good judge, had tipped him in 1946 – was not maintained. But I did get to know him a bit, at first because we were both writing in the *Observer* in those days, and found him, as everyone else did, engaging and enlivening company.

He was heralded, so to speak, by the once-famous Ivy Compton-Burnett anecdote, also, according to Peter Quennell, told of Peter Quennell, though, according to the latter, untruly. The accepted version has Philip resolved, perhaps even commissioned, to write a substantial article on the celebrated novelist, who kindly invited him to dinner at her house to discuss the matter. She had the reputation, merited or not, of being personally formidable. To deactivate anything like that in advance, and reckoning that he had better not count on a lot or even a little to drink when he got there, not to speak of inclination and habit, Philip tanked up at the pub beforehand.

On finally arriving he was at once confronted by two identical old ladies, one of them Miss Ivy Compton-Burnett, the other Miss Ivy Compton-Burnett's paid companion. Nearly as promptly, drinks of at least adequate strength and quantity were served. Manfully restraining his surprise, Philip did them justice. By the time the three moved into the dining-room, he was beginning to wonder if he might not have overdone either the tanking-up or the more recent aperitifs. Anyway, he got through the soup in first-rate style, perhaps helping it down with some mouthfuls of dry sherry. A fish course arrived and with it, no doubt, a Chablis or a Muscadet. A couple of minutes in, Philip passed out with his head in the fish and remained unconscious for some hours. When he awoke, with his head still in the fish, it was three o'clock in the morning, he was alone at the table and around him was evidence that a large, elaborate meal, with wines to match, had been eaten and drunk over his head, as it were. He ran out of the house and never wrote the article, but he was always not writing things without having to pass out at somebody's dinner-table to set him off.

Henry Fairlie provided me with a shorter preamble. 'Very original chap, Philip Toynbee,' he said once when the name came up in conversation.

'In what way? Not in what he writes, surely to –'

'In his life. He's an ex-alcoholic who's turned himself into a very heavy drinker. Now any fool can switch from alcoholism to total abstention – happens every day. What Philip's done shows originality. And takes style.'

183

'And some guts and determination.'

'Well, with anyone else . . .'

It must have been Philip-as-very-heavy-drinker who happened to be sitting opposite me at a generally fairly drunken dinner at the Escargot (pissily known in telephone-book and elsewhere as L'Escargot) restaurant in Greek Street, the old, nice, non-trendy Escargot with the septuagenarian waiters. Towards the end of the meal, Philip, who had been looking dissatisfied with his surroundings for some time, said to the girl sitting next to me, 'What about a dance?'

'Good idea,' she said resourcefully, 'in fact we're going along soon to a place where there's dancing.'

'Bugger that. I mean here. Now.'

'But there's no band.'

'Bugger that.'

When he was convinced he would get no further on the spot, he got up and wandered among the nearer tables, stopping at one where a sedate middle-aged trio were in the middle of eating, most likely a married couple with his or her sister. Philip urged one lady after the other to dance with him, or so I surmised from his gesticulations; there was luckily enough ambient noise to drown his words. With embarrassed smiles and blushes, and increasingly indignant looks from the man, they turned down Philip's offer. Back in his original corner, he stood with his arms raised above his head, as in a textbook photograph of a typical manic posture, and bawled, 'Who'll dance with me?' loudly enough to bring widespread silence apart from the letting-fall of many knives and forks on plates. When there were still no takers he sat mutinously down again, grumbling about mouldy buggers and, first inadvertently rolling the bottle about in a strawberry ice I was eating, poured himself much more wine.

I wondered rather what he would get up to at the place where there was dancing – it was the Gargoyle or some other unattractive spot – but by the time we got there his mood had changed. With all his yearning to dance evidently extinguished, he pressed one of the establishment's girls, a rather pretty half-caste of some sort, to come over and sit with him. And with me, not because I wanted to be around but because I wanted to dance even less and there was nowhere else to sit.

'What's it like,' Philip asked the girl in a special no-nonsense tone, 'to be a coloured person in London these days? You know. What's it *like?*'

To say that I wanted to hit him, should have hit him, should have wanted to hit him would not be enough. Over all the intervening years I have not been able to think of anything more insulting, ignorant, inept, boring, bad-name-getting, etc. he could have said in the circumstances. But the young lady talked to him, not very willingly, but she did. Bless her good nature. No doubt she was used to having strange demands made of her by visiting males.

I suppose one could salvage some sort of good or at least tolerant opinion of Philip by pointing to the naïvety he ceaselessly displayed, before shams of many descriptions as well as coloured girls in night-clubs. With all his clowning he longed for uplift, for spiritual illumination. Why he failed to end up in America I cannot imagine. No story about him, however, is more variously characteristic of him than one he told me himself. (I would give something to have been present at the occasion.) At some London party in the Fifties, perhaps earlier, Philip had picked up an attractive girl and with exemplary persistence and rashness inveigled her upstairs and into a vacant bedroom there and then. After the action, which I assumed to have been successful, his sense of chivalry emerged. Rather than reappear below at the young lady's side and thus risk damaging her reputation, he sent her down the stairs unaccompanied while himself quitting the upper storey by means of a convenient drainpipe. A little later, he would re-enter the house by the front door, having ostensibly, or even perhaps actually, gone to the pub to buy some cigarettes.

All that went as planned. After satisfying himself that this was so, and no doubt putting down a further couple of drinks, he found himself in the same situation as before, chatting up a nice-looking female with the object of . . . No sooner had he made that object clear than he took a whack across the chops – 'a real tooth-loosener' – from his unrecognised companion of maybe an hour earlier.*

The last I remember hearing of him seemed fully characteristic – I was not present, but got it from Erich Heller, once a Swansea colleague and briefly a bicontinental savant. He wrote *The Disinherited Mind*, which as you can see from the title was exactly the sort of thing that appealed to Philip.

Erich was at a dinner in London at which Philip was also expected, though like a true artist he was a couple of hours late. When he

---

*Bob Conquest heard this story too, but his recollection of it differs slightly from mine.

finally turned up, half-full of apologies, he pleaded an access of inspiration. His 'new novel' had been in desperate case until, late that afternoon, a flash of insight had shown him the way ahead. He would write it in verse.

'Oh Christ,' I said when the story reached this point.

'It gets worse,' said Erich, who was much better on this sort of thing than on Kafka or Kierkegaard. 'It was to be in blank verse . . .'

'Oh yeah.'

'. . . but he found the only sort of blank verse he could manage was the sort you get in Wordsworth and Tennyson, too regular for modern taste. So he wrote it out first in the only way he knew how . . .'

'And then went through it . . .'

'. . . making it blanker,' said Erich.

I believe in due course the result of this descent of heavenly fire was actually published, and disappeared with several successors into limbo instead of being taken, as he had fatuously intended, as 'a modern equivalent of *Don Quixote, The Prelude, Faust*, and *A la Recherche du Temps Perdu*, all in one'. Into limbo too went Philip, even before his death. To do him justice, I am not sure he would have secretly expected much different. But a good chap? Well, good company anyway, given that he might at any moment snatch a fiver off you, try to kiss you – just a surge of unpersonalised affection, not turn up, duck his round, boyishly kick a dustbin over, boyishly throw up, get arrested. A twopence-coloured mediocrity, perhaps, and so better, more fun, than the penny-plain ones who have come after him.

But I will give Bob Conquest the last word.

> You cannot, when dealing with Toynbee,
> Just pay him back in his own coin, be–
>   Cause talking such piss
>   Would come rather amiss:
> So how would a kick in the groin be?

LORD SNOWDON

In about 1958 I was invited to a rather good lunch by *Queen* magazine to discuss a project of theirs. It was, I suppose, only natural that I was included, since the project consisted of one of those multiple gossipy affairs to be called 'Top Talkers'. I cannot remember a single one of the other potential top talkers present, which may say something about my egotism but is no matter otherwise. What is of moment is that I remember the presence of a person then known as Tony Armstrong-Jones, who was there not as any kind of talker but as the photographer-designate for the feature. He was a stranger to me. All went swimmingly until one of the *Queen* girls, perhaps the editor, said,

'Actually, we've got a colour-block of Princess Margaret that's been hanging about the office for some time and we were thinking of working it off as a kind of front to the feature labelled "Top Inspirer".'

'I object strongly to that idea,' said Armstrong-Jones.

'So do I,' I said.

'What don't you like about it, Tony?'

'Well, I feel professionally that either I'm the photographer for the feature or I'm not, and it's a bit messy [or some such word] to have somebody else's work mixed up with mine.'

I sympathised with his view, but there was no time to say so. Nor was I asked what my objection to the proposed alien colour-block was. Nor again can I remember how the question was resolved, but no matter, because, trivial in itself, the incident was to have momentous consequences.

A few months later I bumped into Armstrong-Jones again, this time in connection with Long Life beer. There was to be a Press campaign showing a succession of supposed notables, including, I need hardly say, Humphrey Lyttelton, whose presence in such series is or was apparently enforced by law, all swigging away at the

187

relevant beer and crying up its merits. There was naturally another lunch, at which besides him and me there were present my wife, a couple of people from the beer firm, including one with a conspicuous beard, a couple more from the advertising agency, including a boss-eyed Australian woman, and possibly others.

After cordial greetings, I said to Armstrong-Jones, 'I see that bloody colour-block of Princess Margaret got in [didn't get in] after all, then.'

He answered neutrally and went on to ask, 'Would you mind telling me why you were against the idea of its going in?'

'Well, just that the woman obviously has no mind at all – you remember that crap of hers about it not being any good our sending the products of our minds up into space while our souls remained stuck down below in the dives and the espresso bars – schoolgirl essay stuff. I just thought she didn't fit in very well with some of the people in the article in *Queen*. That's all.'

He said firmly but without heat. 'I can assure you you're quite wrong. She is in fact an extremely intelligent and well-informed woman.'

'Oh, you know her, do you?'

Perhaps he gave me an odd look. 'I have met her on several occasions.'

'Oh, I'm terribly sorry,' I said. 'I had no idea she was a great chum of yours. How tactless of me. I really didn't know.'

I was conscious of no froideur after that. With lunch over, the party reassembled in Armstrong-Jones's studio in Pimlico. There were drinks in a drawing-room. The bearded fellow from the beer firm added a couple to the black marks his beard and general demeanour had already earnt from me by throwing a fag-end into the clean grate and following it with his empty cigarette-packet, the Cellophane off a new one and a spent match.

'Paul,' called Armstrong-Jones.

'Yes, Tony.'

'Bring a dustpan and brush, would you, and clear up the *filthy mess* someone has made here.'

The bearded bugger took in none of this, nor the clearing-up itself.

Downstairs in the studio I managed a number of sips and swallows of beer, pretended to have many more, looked at, into, round, through glass after glass of it while Armstrong-Jones photographed. After some time he showed concern.

'Don't go on drinking that filth,' he said. 'It's getting flat, too. Paul.'

'Yes, Tony.'

'Find the Eno's, would you, and stir in a little in here.'

A fine head formed. Warning me not to let the mixture touch my lips he continued to snap away. Soon the bearded shag came in, followed by the boss-eyed Australian girl. He asked how we were getting on.

'Just about finished,' said Armstrong-Jones. He paused. 'One thing, I bet you never touch a drop of your own beer. If I'm wrong you can prove it now.'

'Nah, I got a Scotch here, thanks.'

'There you are.' Armstrong-Jones looked at me. 'Never goes near it.'

'Oh, all right then.' The fellow took the glass from me, filled his mouth with a rich mixture of beer and Eno's, savoured it and swallowed. 'Right, Tony, well if you could let us have a look at the roughs by say the end of next week . . .'

Silent and straight-faced merriment for two. Jolly warm feeling.

Time was now beginning to press. It was Friday. On being asked I told Armstrong-Jones that we were visiting friends in Staines (George Gale and his wife), and would be off by taxi, thence to a train. No, he was going in that direction himself, to Bath in fact, and would give us a lift. When he had finished here. Perhaps, I said, he could take the southern road, go via Staines – no more than a mile or two further – and have a drink with our friends before pressing on. He would think about it. When he had finished here.

More time had passed before we left. And when Tony had thought about it he took the northern road via Slough after all, his customary route. Having come that far he said he felt thirsty, would like to visit a pub. We did and had a drink each, and then he said it had been fun and did the nearest thing possible to driving off leaving us standing on the pavement. My wife and I found out about the bus to Staines, waited for it, boarded it, went through Eton, Windsor and other places in it and arrived at our destination not quite an hour and a half later than if we had left when and how we originally intended.

'You've got to understand he's upper-class,' explained George. 'You'd just come in handy as a witness to that bearded berk making an idiot of himself and he felt like a bit of company for the first dull bit out of London, and you were available. Easy.'

189

'But it couldn't have taken him more than a few minutes to come this way instead. And he didn't even –'

'He's upper-*class*. He wanted to go the way he always goes and give me one good reason from his point of view why he should have done different this time.'

Not more than four or five weeks later I was reading or dozing in my study in Swansea when Geoff Nicholson, who was staying with us, came in.

'It's just been announced on the telly,' he said, 'that Princess Margaret is going to marry Tony Armstrong-Jones.'

'Look, sonny,' I said, 'try and think of something a bit less obvious next time.'

'Come out and look. It's on now.'

And sure enough, on the TV screen in the kitchen, there was the oleaginous Godfrey Talbot, always kept on hand for these do's, mouthing, 'And everybody's so delighted because this is so obviously a real love match.'

'Weren't you telling me something,' asked Geoff, 'about you telling him something about Princess Margaret being a bloody fool?'

'I expect I was,' I said. 'Anyway, I did.'

'So it wasn't just a matter of him wanting a bit of company in the car and sod you,' said George when I saw him next. 'The devious bugger. What? I mean he was paying you back for insulting his girlfriend even though you didn't know she was his girlfriend. Pretty bloody impressive, you have to admit.'

'You mean he led us that dance just because I'd said . . .'

'He's upper-*class*, I keep telling you. Which means he doesn't end up one down to the likes of fucking you.'

I still find this interpretation next to impossible to believe. (It might interest students of psychology to learn that George remains the most uncompromisingly sceptical of all the people I have told the story about the putting-down of penicillin-smuggling by female dock-workers in Naples during the war.)

Lord Snowdon (as he now was) has since photographed me twice, not counting a third time for the cover of this book: once multiply in colour, again in the *Sunday Times*, the principal picture showing me with my second wife at my side looking a good deal below her best, mildly disagreeable in fact. I wondered fruitlessly about that for a time. The second session showed me solo in black-and-white. It was to take place on neutral ground in one of those studios you hire by the hour (for a thousand quid or so). I was requested through an intermediary to bring three *complete* sets of clothing (excluding, presumably, undergarments, etc.). My imagination extended to all manner of unpredictable embarrassments and humiliations, but no. There was even a drink afterwards. The scores, if any, were presumably judged to be level.

And yet . . . It might interest students of the occult to learn that in Edinburgh in 1980, at some gigantic, amorphous gathering to do with the Festival, I found myself chatting to a very pleasant, indeed cordial fellow whose face I knew I had seen before, though I could not have put a name to it just then. Princess Margaret was known to be somewhere in the vast throng without my having actually set eyes on her. Somehow my talk with the cordial fellow drifted in her direction. I made a number of remarks about her that escape me now – it was getting quite late – except that they were to some degree derogatory. I do remember saying, however, 'Give me her sister any day. *That's* what I call first-class material.'

Some of the cordial fellow's cordiality seemed to depart and he himself did the same a minute or two later.

'Nice chap, that,' I said to someone who had seemed to know him. 'Who is he?'

'Oh, that's Roddy Llewellyn.' (Younger readers may need to be told that Mr Llewellyn had become known as an admirer of Princess Margaret after her divorce from Lord Snowdon in 1978.)

Now I ask you: I had not set foot in Edinburgh for over twenty years; there must have been at least three hundred people at that jollification, and I had to go and . . . Of course I had caught sight of the poor devil somewhere in the throng, recognised him from photographs at some level well below the conscious and brought my remarks about the Princess, whom I had never met and who as far as I know had never done me the slightest harm, up from the same low level, on the same principle that causes people to refer out of the blue to, say, gaolbirds and doing time when they would swear they had no idea that the son of the house was about to be sent down for fraud. But Christ . . .

A large copy of the published photograph Lord Snowdon took of me at the session I mentioned is pinned to the outside of my study door. It is an excellent photograph, everybody says so, I fancy it even flatters me a little, but I have been thinking it has been there long enough. Now I am afraid to take it down. I am afraid that if I do I shall go out into the street and accidentally activate the burglar-alarm on Viscount Linley's parked Aston-Martin, and who dare say what might follow from *that?*

Since first-drafting the above I have removed the photograph to forestall imputations of narcissism. Nothing significant has followed this action. Yet.

USA 1

I HAVE TWICE visited America, in 1958-59 and 1967-68. It would have been much more often and continued but for my fear of flying, and I think this deprivation has weakened and impaired my understanding of the contemporary world, not to any very serious degree but much more than it would have done before, say, 1945. I have remained strongly pro-American in my attitudes, and the 'in spite of' or 'but' clauses that protocol requires to come next have in my case little force, even after, say, a glimpse of an episode of *Dallas*, a glance at a novel by Saul Bellow or Vladimir Nabokov, or a conversation with one of those people that Americans themselves mysteriously call 'liberals'.

The fuddy-duddyness implied in my first couple of sentences should be tempered by the fact that the 'year in America' that became commonplace, if not universal, for the British writer/academic was by no means so then, though admittedly a journey conducted mainly by luxury liner, even second class, lacked something of the pioneering spirit. Anyway, on my first trip I had with me my father, widowed the previous year, and my sons Philip (aged ten) and Martin (nine), followed a week later by my wife and our four-year-old daughter Sally, delayed by Sally's recovery from surgery for the removal of a benign growth.

In those days the New York dockers were renowned for their truculence, inefficiency and sheer slowness. Four hours was supposed to be standard and we got the standard. Nevertheless, the difference from the British equivalent did not strike me as very marked, and by the time we sailed out into the dusk past the marvellously foreign-looking building-fronts of that area, recalling to me Italy or Spain, not England at all, and among the wondrous multi-coloured lights of the New Jersey Turnpike, at that time utterly unparalleled at home – by then I knew that the lefties,

193

European and American alike, were all liars and this was my second country and always would be.

It was easy enough to go on thinking that in Princeton, N. J., fifty miles to the south. The university there had bestowed on me a post as Visiting Fellow in Creative Writing. With this went a six-lecture stint in the spring, to be attended not merely by resident faculty members but by such luminaries as Mary McCarthy, Dwight Macdonald, Hannah Arendt and Robert Oppenheimer, once of the Manhattan Project.

First the four, then the full six Amises were soon settled in Edgerstoune Road, a residential bit laid out in the best posh-rural American style, with a great deal in the way of lawn, few flowers, no fences, and a patch of woodland at the back where deer would sometimes wander, just a few minutes' drive from the centre of town. This, the town, was the kind of place anyone would call pretty, bright, clean, spacious and prosperous, full of trees and porticoed wooden houses, and with an excellent train service to New York. Many commuters to that city, with jobs in Madison Avenue or Wall Street, lived there or near.

Our own house, no. 235, had been rented to us by the illustrious 'liberal' journalist, Murray Kempton, absent in Europe for the year. He had been a schoolmate of the notorious Senator Joseph Mc-Carthy, then recently dead and still much under discussion, and (according to an Edgerstoune neighbour, John McAndrew) on encountering the senator one day in some Washington corridor, had been amicably clapped on the back by him. 'You realise that means I have to get this jacket dry-cleaned, Joe,' Kempton had said, to which McCarthy, on understanding the implications, had reacted with mingled pain and wonderment. 'But you don't see the point, Murray, all that's just *politics*,' he had kept saying. 'That story tells you a lot about America,' John McAndrew declared, and I suppose it did, have always been sure it did, without ever being very clear what it told me or whether I liked it.

Edgerstoune Road was alive with neighbours, helping with the children, finding plumbers, schools, maids, mechanics, cars, talking about Europe, which they were all constantly visiting, protesting Anglophilia, inviting one to cocktails and to brunch. I soon realised that the art or custom of drinking as practised in Swansea or even London was in its infancy. Every slot was filled: the couple of hours before the football game contained a party given by the coach; Sunday brunch was not a mere gastronomic variant but a technique for getting drunk sooner than on weekdays. I had no fault to find with any of Princeton's social arrangements. Except one, often remarked on in the past as endemic to America: the absence of the male twosome. I soon dropped the procedure of saying to a colleague at the end of the morning: 'What about nipping over to the Annex [a good cheap little restaurant opposite the university] for a spot of lunch?' and getting the reply, 'Fine, and I'll call Mary, and why don't you call Hilly, and we'll meet around one.' The results of that are nice too, just as nice in their way, but a different way.

Had we any objection to coloured people, we were asked, and said no. Accordingly someone called May, a stout middle-aged black woman (as she would not have been called then), turned up to act as our maid. She was most amiable, but would not help with the children, had to be paid in advance before she would do anything, and stole our sweaters. Where she scored was with her car, in which, since we had no transport of our own as yet, she drove me to the university on my first morning. If the campus policeman found anything odd or even impressive in the sight of a faculty-aged white man being chauffeured to the Firestone Library by a negress in a pink Cadillac, he gave no sign.

By the time May was replaced, in fact after five minutes' conversation with her, I was impressed by her style of talk, which was much less like that of the vernacular black entertainers I had seen in films than the old nigger-minstrel style, full of 'If that don't just 'bout beat everything!' with eyes and teeth to match, or 'M'm-*h'm*, ain't it the truth, Mr Amis!'

This puzzled me. 'It can't be natural,' I said at a later stage to an English acquaintance, a doctor working in New York City.

'It isn't,' he said. 'It's mockery. They don't do it when they're frightened, and I quite often see them when they're frightened.' Perhaps he noticed that I was feeling quite frightened myself at the moment, having just realised we were walking out of a bar without paying. He said soothingly, 'They reckon on losing fifteen per cent this way. The boss is a patient of mine.'

'So he knows you don't pay. Told you not to, perhaps.'

'We've never discussed it.'

The Firestone Library had been built in the nineteenth or early twentieth century, when they still thought that things like universities ought to look vaguely like universities, and before buildings became statements and had to be innovative. Laboratories, halls of residence and what-not stretched away in giant shoe-box or (then) contemporary factory style, but Firestone was Gothic, on the outside at least. Inside were a lot of books, books that in a manner new to me the librarians tried to help you find as fast as possible, and a great many offices and such. In one of these, at the end of a corridor, with a view of much greenery as well as of many a structure, I was to teach Creative Writing, a subject or idea often ridiculed at that time by those who knew nothing of it.

I was more than dubious myself at first, realising that I had let my desire to get to America overrule my prudence. Was I to invent and lay down rules to a class of wondering novices? 'Before you start, make sure you have an interesting theme,' I would say authoritatively to the multitude. 'Always start off well, with a good sentence. Er . . .' As it turned out they, a couple of dozen of them, came at me one at a time for an hour at a time, to go over with me whatever it was they would have handed to me earlier for my perusal. There was one playwright, who was eventually to put together a play not only performable but performed, though not on Broadway. (I thought its main device of treating the actors as real people, who after a time start refusing to speak the lines set down for them – yes, that one – was a bit dated and boring, but had no heart to tell the author so.) There was one poet, who, on being told that such-and-such would not be clear to the reader, remarked, 'Sir, I don't pay much heed to the reader,' after which I ceased to pay more heed to him than I had to. The rest was all prose fiction.

I was bowled over by the amount of talent I encountered there, strong on subject matter, in almost every case indifferent to all tricks of presentation or to graces of style, such as to make any comparable Oxford sample, say, look bloodless beside it. After over thirty years I still remember Ochsner's accounts of life on the freight river-boats, Houghton on hunting (=shooting) and village feuds in Vermont, Collins on a father's ruthless social pushing of his son, Rose on the crew that dropped the Bomb (long before the days of 'protest'). I felt the excitement of somebody accidentally present at the first stirrings of an outburst of new talent that would surely go on to do great things.

I still think I was right to see genuine promise there in quantity, but I had underrated the extent to which high intelligence and a sense of purpose find a real but incidental and passing literary expression in more than a few young people. So Rukeyser was to become, as well as a lifelong friend, a leading financier instead of a great novelist; poor Houghton was to publish a single novel, inferior to what his Vermont one would have been, before suffering madness and an untimely death; Hirsch, the cleverest of them all, clever enough to cause me the occasional therapeutic twinge of uneasiness, managed only, I think, a single soft-porn paperback, of which I remember just one sentence: 'She tingled with erogeneity.' But this rather American-flavoured trio of fates was yet to come; at the time, Creative Writing, evidently a sad and dreadful thing now in many places, gave me a lot of pleasure and also taught me a lot about America and about literature.

Not that teaching at Princeton (if that was teaching) turned out to be all fun. Undiscovered among some small print had lain an obligation to conduct a weekly 'preceptorial' or seminar or, come to think of it, class. This was supposed to study principles of literature or some such jargon. We – the creative writers, some others and I – used a single large collection of stories by various hands. These included 'The Aspern Papers' of Henry James – whatever his merits, surely a dangerous model, especially for Americans. The story in question is the only work of his I have ever read to its conclusion. As I worked through it, I was getting quite interested in what the dead writer Aspern's papers might or might not have contained, before finding that of course we were never going to be told, and then the worse shock of having it explained that this was the 'whole point' of the story – explained by lads whose creative work had shown me beyond doubt that they were not fools. For me, I think, there began that sad rift between British and American literature which has done so much to impede our common cultural under-standing, unless that sounds too horribly solemn. More bluntly, I think most American literature is a disaster, one reinforced by its being taught in universities there to the virtual exclusion of British, even the British classics, but no doubt I would think so less ardently, or even perhaps not at all, but for my non-flying thing.

Time for a change of mood, easily achieved by a quick trip up to New York on that good train service. (No longer so?) I only ever spent a few nights in the city, but made a lot of day and evening trips and saw quite enough of the place to convince me that anyone who makes a business of hating it or being superior to it, and there were plenty then, home-grown and foreign, is a creep, and that anyone who walks up Fifth Avenue (say) on a sunny morning with-out feeling his spirits lift is an asshole. Or so it was.

On my first day I very much had somewhere to go, *Esquire* magazine, which was throwing a party for its twenty-first birthday number (with a story by me luckily in it). The card said 'Cocktails 4 p.m.,' which seemed to me a little early. I telephoned a man I knew who worked for it, Gene Lichtenstein.

'Oh sure,' he said apologetically when I mentioned four o'clock, 'but there's no need to wait till then. Come around right away and we'll have a couple of beers before the start.'

The couple of beers turned out to be three or four large bourbons, and not tremendously long after the start I was smashed, too much so to recall who else was there apart from Norman Mailer, of course, who was not stabbing anyone at the time, and who either then or on a later occasion seemed to be offering me friendship, which I instinctively evaded. Also present was the cartoonist Jules Feiffer, who left my side at once when I turned my head to utter a short phrase to a third party. I must have eaten something at some stage, because I was later in an adequate condition to be taken to the Five Spot in Cooper Square to hear my first American jazzman in the flesh. This was the tenor saxophonist Sonny Rollins, just then at the height of his powers, and the fact that these were not altogether to my taste – I was already a little old for him – mattered not at all. Outside, the city was sparkling with wonder – by then it really was sparkling with wonder a bit because the part of it I was drifting through, with Gene still, thank heaven, at my side, was putting on an Italian festival with pretty lights and dresses, dances and food and doubtless more drinks.

A remnant of sanity made me tell Gene I must be getting back to Princeton.

He looked at me. 'It's a little late for that,' he said. 'Why don't you come down and stay with me in my apartment in the Bowery?'

'Can I? Is it far? Have you got a bed?'

'Sure. Auden's bed.'

'What?'

'The bed belonging to the poet W. H. Auden.' Gene paused rather unkindly long. 'But he won't be in it tonight. Austria.'

In the sitting-room of this modest establishment I took down from the shelves a copy of Crabbe's poems, rationing myself to just one sample. 'To Wystan,' somebody had written on the fly-leaf. 'We must love one another AND die. Cyril.' Connolly, I assumed resignedly as I made for the indeed empty bed.

Partly, I suppose, as a result of contacts made that evening, I found myself with an extra job, *Esquire* critic of the Art of the Cinema. Asking what this meant, I was told just any non-American film, and by God the experience taught me thoroughly how bloody awful most non-American films were. It was especially instructive to see *Room at the Top* and be helped to notice, apart from its other deficiencies, how grotesquely it fails to portray any sort of British life. I also remember a tissue of saccharine in black and white that would have had things thrown at it if it had not been Japanese, and a surprising amount about the most boring film I have ever seen in my life, displacing *The Battleship Potemkin* after many years: the Indian director Satyajit Ray's *Aparajito*. How I brightened up at the appearance of a kind of eighteenth-century Russian Western made by Italo-Yugoslav Films Inc. with American – well, American everything that could be, authenticity being adequately supplied by fur hats, vodka instead of rye, bringing in Catherine the Great for a couple of minutes and renaming Fort Laramie Fort Raskolnikov. It also had, in Van Heflin, a proper actor in the main role, not necessarily a sound scheme. Americans, those of the greater part of this century anyway, are not much good at art, high art, fine art, but they are unequalled at art merged or hybridised with entertainment, as science fiction, jazz (until it became either a high art or nothing at all, according to taste) and films, especially the Western and the animated cartoon.

Something I had thought existed nowhere much but in films was the private outdoor swimming-pool with what some might call lounge chairs and others, more degraded, chaise lounges *and*, a vital point, a completely independent on-the-spot source of drinks, complete with refrigerator, stock of fruit, etc. An establishment featuring such a rare amenity was the home of my American agent, Alan Collins, no relation to my creative-writing Collins, in fact, though a goodish fellow and a generous host, Alan came as near being quite uninterested in writing as any man I have ever met, surprisingly then in one of his trade. As against that he made quite a bit of money for his authors.

Here, on what seems in memory like an endless succession of bright sunny mornings, my wife and I would go, always to find Old Glory and the Union Jack fluttering from lofty flagpoles and Elizabeth Bowen, another client of Alan's, sitting by the pool. She and I took to each other at once. Being practising writers we soon moved off literature, though I think we had time to agree on the merits of Ivy Compton-Burnett and Elizabeth Taylor before getting on to America, which she turned out to like as much as I did.

One day over the large bourbons on the rocks – she was a good little drinker – I said to this Elizabeth, 'Somebody called Cyrilly Abels [who edited a magazine] has invited me to lunch. Should I go?'

'Oh yes, it'll be a good lunch. Cyrilly understands writers. She's married to a very nice businessman called Oo-oo-oo-oo . . .' (Elizabeth had a small speech-defect which gave her difficulty with initial W.) 'Oo-oo-oo-ooeinstein or possibly Oo-oo-oo-ooeintraub. Something of that kind anyway.'

Without vowing never to forget it, I registered this information and the talk turned away. A couple of weeks later I stood in the deserted hall or lobby of a large posh apartment building in New York looking up at one of those directory what-do-you-call-'ems on the wall where the individual apartments are tabulated, each with its bell-push. Some of these were identified only by a number, most by a name. That of Abels appeared nowhere and I had no number. I was contemplating from a sizeable distance the prospect of ringing all the numbered bell-pushes in turn and asking for Abels, when a little voice came into my head saying 'Oo-oo-oo-oo . . .' and the name of Weinstock leapt to my eye, and within a minute I was saying how-do-you-do in the right place. There turned out to be another guest, Carson McCullers, the novelist and short-story writer from Georgia, then in her early forties, known in England for her collection of stories, *The Ballad of the Sad Café*. She was clearly ill from some wasting disease and was also, I gathered later, an alcoholic; her health was a centre of attention. The two of us found it hard to talk and significantly got stuck on literature, though neither of us seemed to have as much as heard of most of the authors the other admired.

During the meal, a black maid wearing white muslin gloves (and much else besides) came briefly into the room and warmly embraced Miss McCullers, saying in what I took to be the accent of the Deep South, or a take-off of it,

'Why, Miss Carson, dear, and just how lovely it is to see you.'

Miss McCullers replied, not in the (to me) just detectable Southern accent she had been using up to that point, but with the full treatment the maid had given,

'Just fine, Bessie, darling, and my, you looking well youself, and how you-all down back home?' – or words to that effect.

Several more such expressions went to and fro before Bessie withdrew. Not for the first or last time in the States, I had the illusion, or delusion, that a scene had been staged for my benefit.

The rest of the lunch was difficult but, thanks to the hosts, not a failure. I discovered later that Miss McCullers had written that her theme was 'spiritual isolation', so our lack of contact was perhaps not surprising. But one must not allow any sort of grin to enter here, in view of the sufferings and failures of Miss McCullers's short life; she died aged fifty in 1967, having evidently published only one book after the work I mention, which had come out when she was thirty-four.

How sad, yes indeed, and – it is almost impossible not to add – how American too. For what must be more than one reason, certainly in more than one way, writers and artists in that country seem destined to be or become stricken deer, misfits, assorted victims and freaks, drunks rather than mere drinkers, hermits, suicides. The usual explanation would make them refugees from decorum, conformity and the rest, but can they all have been? Why did some of them retreat so far? Some notoriously went almost as far in the other direction and turned themselves into bank-presidents on the T. S. Eliot model. It makes my old Dublin-born friend Elizabeth Bowen look like a paragon of moderation, of middleness, dying at seventy-four with her couple of dozen volumes behind her, the large bourbons kept for after work. (It is true that Eliot was fond of gin.)

A new-fangled kind of flight from decorum, approachable in a spirit of pure farce, was to be sampled one evening in the debating hall of the Young Men's Hebrew Association in New York. The subject, if that is the word, was 'Is there a Beat Generation?', the personnel were James Wechsler, editor of the *New York Post*, Ashley Montagu, an Englishman of long American residence whom I suppose I might describe as a social anthropologist of a popularising sort – a type of person then comparatively new to me and others – and Jack Kerouac, very famous just then as the author of *On the Road*, published the previous year, a 'semi-autobiographical novel' about idle wanderings across the country. It could be considered a landmark of sorts in the parting of literature from 'convention' towards various forms of publicity, half-baked exotic religion, drugs – a subject not to be gone into here. The audience was large and patchily enthusiastic.

After a warm-up of strumming at the back-stage piano, trying to balance a chair on his head, making faces, etc., Kerouac talked not for his allotted ten minutes but for over an hour and incoherently, mentioning Popeye, Laurel and Hardy and Humphrey Bogart as ancestral Beats and eulogising his friend Allen Ginsberg, whose raucous *Howl* had appeared in 1956. Ginsberg was himself to be seen now and again tonight in parts of the hall, though luckily without saying anything audible. When our chance came the other three of us in turn made our ten-minute pleas for reason and old stuff like that, and finally there was a discussion, which in practice meant more Kerouac and elucidated nothing. My side had won the argument (argument?) but lost the performance.

Why on earth had I gone there, one who had been trying to get away from the Angry Young Men poking his nose into something that sounded so unpleasantly similar? The usual mixture of curiosity and vanity, no doubt, with vanity coming off a bad second in the event. The Beats themselves have long vanished, of course, but they have left their mark, a bad mark, worst on poetry, helping to reduce parts of it to spoken scripts or rock without the music. But more damaging than that was the disintegrative influence of some such spirit at a higher level. Soon afterwards I was discussing the Beats with Norman Mailer, whom I had valued highly for his novel *The Naked and the Dead* of 1949 and a little-known story 'The Language of Men', confidently expecting a hearty and educated dismissal from a serious writer and getting instead a proclamation of their merits and significance. On reflection that boded worse than anything about Kerouac himself. But then perhaps Mailer had enough self-destructive impulse within him to need no outside encouragement.

But enough of writers and New York and off to Washington, where I was to give a lecture and a reading and we were to stay for some days, all six of us, Dad included, with his sister Gladys and her second husband. I had not seen her for twenty years or more on her English visit, him never before. The house was in S Street – just that; strange that a people so fond of colour and tolerant of a bit of faking should have given streets in major cities mere numbers and letters. Easier for monoglot Bohunks, perhaps.

Gladys, now a small plump bird-like woman, had had fifteen years of bringing up two children on her own before remarrying. Her second husband, not very believably, was called Virgil A. Case, about sixty-five, a flamboyant grey-haired figure in overalls and a baseball cap or sailor's cap. He at once took over entertaining the children, doling out Cokes, peanuts, chocolate bars, taking the boys to his basement rumpus room with its dartboard, ping-pong table, pump air-rifle with target, also to the beach, where he revealed himself to be tattooed from head to foot – 'nothing fancy,' said Martin, ' – just anchors and stuff.' The guys had gotten Virg drunk one time and he just woke up like it. Revealing himself to Gladys had been ticklish, because some people thought tattooing common. All in all he was an unlikely brother-in-law for my father to have, but they got on well enough. After all, Uncle Virg was used to the English. I wished he and Dadda could have met.

It was a small house and not a prosperous household. My aunt was still working at sixty-two, starting in a dress-shop at 7.45 a.m. A peptic ulcer had forced Virg to retire some time before. There was a rather dreadful prole-style parlour with heavy furniture – and no drinks in it or anywhere else on normal occasions. But they had their sun-porch and the rumpus room and plenty of parties, and in a beat-up-Chevvy, hamburger-joint kind of way they showed us something very American: what a good time non-well-off people could have.

Among my cultural treats while in Washington was to be an informal evening chat with an amiable cultural bureaucrat called Robert Richman, Walter Lippman, the renowned political correspondent of the *Washington Post*, and somebody also famous in his day, though of a very different sort, a Father d'Arcy, an English Jesuit who moved in high circles and was always said to have been the model for Father Rothschild in Evelyn Waugh's *Vile Bodies*. To my uneasiness, and also without the emergence of any clear idea of how they had done it, my father and Uncle Virg attached themselves to the party. Dad would probably be all right, but I had no idea of how my uncle would behave. He had put on a suit and a shirt that came up high enough to hide his tattoos in that area. What about his hands? I forget; perhaps they had been left unadorned.

D'Arcy was a little old thing I can only describe as whiskery, especially round the ears. Having assured himself that I was not a Catholic, he soon established that I knew none of the eminent or patrician persons in London that he himself knew, concealing his disappointment. Thereafter he said little, and that mostly about people in America likewise unknown to me. Why were the two of us there? Both British, of course. Lippman, whom I remember as large and gloomy, was taciturn from, or at, the start. A hard day round the corridors of the White House and such, I assumed, and avoided such topics. The talk languished. Then Uncle Virg suddenly said,

'Mr Lippman, I'd like to ask you something. What is your opinion of Shanghai Shek?' (He made the ruler of Taiwan sound like some-

203

body on a level with, say, Texas Dan. Uncle *Virg*, you've really done it now, I thought.)

Lippman reacted like a man given a couple of ccs. of intravenous adrenalin. 'Mr Case, that's a most interesting question,' he said, and talked for an hour or so about it without stopping much. *Of course* that was the sort of thing he wanted to talk about, not estimating the outlook for American democracy or whatever lofty turdery it was that I had been hoping to wring from him. Who cares after thirty years what he said, whether he was right or wrong? Thanks to Uncle Virg, the evening turned out to be a success after all, say ten per cent as much fun as tenpin bowling, in fact. But still thanks to Uncle Virg.

By and large, that was the most agreeable of our trips from Princeton. Though as determined as ever not to fly, I got myself and Hilly by train or car to a dozen or so spots scattered over the north-east, usually at academic prompting with a fee in prospect. I needed the cash. That Princeton stipend, known in the quaint American jargon as 'compensation', which had looked so good from Swansea turned out to be distinctly on the thin side – even when supplemented by what *Esquire* magazine was paying me for my film reviews – as soon as I started leading the kind of life the people I knew at Princeton seemed to take for granted. There were dentist's bills too. That was money well spent, on work that saved Hilly's rickety teeth, but my God it got spent all right.

I was going to write that I rather hated giving those lectures, or rather the identical lecture, 'Problems of a Comic Novelist', in all those different places. But what I probably mean is how much I would dislike having to do so now, the chronicler not being the same person as the doer, as I know I have kept forgetting. I was less troubled then than I probably would be now by the nagging neurotic fear that somebody who had heard me deliver the lecture in one place should have made his way to another and hear the same stuff all over again, complete with fake impromptus, ersatz throwaways, etc. What if somebody had, anyway? As I wrote on the point at the time, one wonders just what it is that people anywhere in the world get out of attending lectures given by literary persons. For the vast majority, I imagine, you might as well speak in Choctaw; seeing you perform, seeing you there, is all that counts. As for that potentially uncomfortable finale, the question period, the American audiences I met were far too kind to attempt any sort of going-over in such circumstances, and I would leave the stage to have the stipulated cheque ($300 was about my mark) slipped into my hand by the chairman there and then, with drinks, or more drinks, to follow. All in all it was a distinct improvement on the fiver-after-a-couple of-months-if-you're-lucky that was customary in the UK at the time, plus a free vile dinner and a bed in one of the nicer houses in South Shields.

Off I went then with my comic-novelist's problems to, for example, Philadelphia, where my most vivid memories are of the squalor of its approaches and, to make up for that, of catching a glimpse of the prettiest girl I have ever seen in my life coming out of a restaurant. We stayed with an English couple, and veddy, veddy English they bloody well seemed in those surroundings: chilly house, vicar's-daughter-type wife, caricature-of-Oxbridge-don husband who wore a bowler hat (on purpose, surely), child by the name of Jack but always called 'Boy' (aagh!). I had known hubby slightly back home and thought him a bit of a twit then, but here he radiated the quality, lowering his voice confidentially to explain that their landlady was divorced, that kind of thing, generally hamming it up.

However such behaviour might have gone down in Sydney or Perth, it was fine in Philly and elsewhere. If you were English any sort of oddity was at least explicable – Ashley Montagu had told me how, when one of his small daughters asked why he had all that hair on the backs of his hands, her sister said, 'Because he's English, stupid.' Englishness, or supposed Englishness, was attractive to Americans and remains thoroughly so, according to Paul Fussell, to the point of frequent imitation, or attempted imitation. (See his book, *Class* in USA, *Caste Marks* in UK.) When people try to ape those of another country, do they always admire and emulate the worst parts of the foreign culture? Answer, of course not, French food and drink, for instance, not being the worst things about France. But in America, sadly, quite often so, and it was not for nothing that a Princeton neighbour described himself to me as 'a horrible Anglophile'. Things took a turn for the better when, after a couple of drinks, he repeated the claim with the codicil, 'and you're trying to change me.'

The problems went also to Poughkeepsie, N.Y., the seat of Vassar College, a kind of American version of Newnham or Lady Margaret Hall, it would be, though rather less lumpish than they. I remember nothing of this trip beyond performing the symbolic-aesthetic act of kicking the metal shins of a Henry Moore statue-thing that somebody had thought worth installing on the campus. Naturally I had imagined myself unobserved, but received a full Oxbridge-class glare and admonitorily-shaken forefinger from a uniformed and capped porter pent in a little box beside the main portico, the most British moment of my stay.

The wooden spoon for these trips must, without rancour, go to the University of Champaign-Urbana, a notorious rock, to change the metaphor, on which the affection of many for the USA has come to grief. Our westward journey began auspiciously enough, with a wonderful train to Chicago, full of food and drink, and continued with a southward twist acceptably enough on the Sunday morning on a less luxurious train to a place called Kankakee, Ill., where I will confidently bet that few of my readers have been. It, Kankakee, a generic small provincial American town, was totally deserted, like a place in a low-budget film about an invasion from outer space. Matters righted themselves when it became clear that the inhabitants were not all dead or vaporised but in church, whence they emerged in time to give me and wife a magnificent lunch in a clapboard hotel. I complimented the manager on it, to be told in most unAmerican fashion that yeah, thanks, but they were used to getting compliments on their food. More perhaps than on your fucking little neon-infested glow-painted hick town, I was too polite to retort.

Westward stretched the Illinois cereal belt, or a part of it, thousands of flat fertile acres on the way to the Rockies, many times more than enough to make the heart sink a millimetre or two, to set off a brief longing for a smaller country and to suggest to the visitor, even the most eager and tolerant, that not quite absolutely everything about America was thrusting and dynamic, or even interesting. But here we were, and right on time a car appeared at a vast distance, diffusing intimations of boredom and a great cloud of dust as seen on TV. It came and picked us up and drove us a hundred miles or more across the plain to the fair-sized town that is the State University of Illinois.

In due time I acquainted them with the problems. Nothing of interest took place. It would be hard to say with any confidence when anything of interest had last taken place there. It occurred to me then, or should have done, that when a country is so rich that it can afford to send a great many or most of its youngsters to universities if it feels like it, some of those universities will be places like Princeton or Harvard, but a hell of a lot more of them will have to be like the one at Champaign-Urbana. In fact, more will mean . . . What am I saying? Fussell is good on this point, too.

206

Ah! – but I was forgetting that at the luncheon at the local hotel the next day my hangover (fair play, they had seen to it that I had one of those) not only disappeared with my first drink, but was miraculously transformed. I reached a state of dazzling euphoria, as has happened to me only three or four other times in my life, and never since. You will have to take my word for it that I was at the very apex of my form – pretty good, actually. When the party had broken up and the guests were standing about in the lobby, I heard from behind a showcase one faculty wife say to another, 'How much do you think there is in national characteristics? Have you ever met a *reserved* Englishman?' My nicest compliment. Champaign-Urbana, I take it all back.

We left the problems behind when we drove up to New Haven for what was called a three-day fellowship at Calhoun College, part of Yale University. The invitation had come from the Master of the college, a certain Archibald S. Foord, whom what with one thing and another I had visualised as a little old thing with hair growing out of his ears à la Father d'Arcy. What was my surprise when the great moulded, brass-bound door, more suitable for the House of Usher than any academic foundation, was flung open to my knock and a sports-shirted man of about forty, with one of the most jovial drinker's faces I had ever seen, punched at the air and half-shouted '*Hi!*' This was old Archie, and Calhoun College was the only habitation anywhere in which a Dry Martini was put into my hand before I had taken off my overcoat. Land of contrasts, ennit, often most marked between what you have been expecting and what you get. One thing you may not have been expecting is how polite they are, not all of them, but more than here. Everybody I met at Yale was.

On the way up to New Haven, at Westport, Conn., we had visited Peter De Vries and his family for dinner and the night. The other dinner guests included John Hersey (*Hiroshima*) and Jerome Weidman, whom I had long admired for *I Can Get It for You Wholesale*, *The Price Is Right*, and other novels. At one stage the talk turned to John O'Hara, still a great name then. On the score of early novels and novellas of his like *Appointment in Samarra* and *Hope of Heaven*, I and many others had thought a writer of the first rank was coming to maturity, but his later books showed a sad falling-off, his reputation sank, and I was fascinated to hear from Weidman that O'Hara had confided to him, 'I'm going after sales now, Jerome,' at the exact moment when he must have been embarking on his first stinker, *A Rage to Live*. You clever Americans, will you never learn?

Despite all the respect, it was hard not to feel a twinge of schadenfreude at O'Hara's fall from esteem, which had caused him profound bitterness. Weidman told a story of how a small party had been given for Ernest Hemingway at a New York tavern. O'Hara, though not invited, had typically started drinking on his own in an outer room of the same joint, presumably to depress if possible the spirits of those within and anyway make himself feel worse. In time Hemingway emerged on his way to the street door.

'Hi, John.'

'Hi, Ernest.'

Hemingway peered at something propped against the bar. 'What's that?'

'My grandfather's blackthorn stick. From Ireland.'

'I bet I could break it.'

'Well, I bet you couldn't.'

'Here's five dollars says I can.' (I am not making this up.)

O'Hara accepted the bet, Hemingway broke the stick across his own head, picked up O'Hara's five dollars and quitted the scene.

When Weidman had told his story De Vries said, 'He ought to have called after him, "I thought they talked a lot of shit about *Across the River*, Ernest," ' in reference to a late novel of Hemingway's that had deservedly done less than well. He, De Vries, whose *Tunnel of Love* and other books I had thought the funniest by any post-war writer in English, had not said much that evening. Perhaps he never said much; I had seen too little of him earlier to know. But ever since I later read his masterly and harrowing novel, *The Blood of the Lamb* (1962), about the death of a young girl from a wasting disease, told in the first person by her father, I have been haunted by the fancy that that reserve came less from temperament than from circumstances. Both Hilly and I remember meeting a thin little De Vries daughter of seven or so who might have been . . . It is not the sort of question to go about getting settled.

The productive careers, or the public reputations, of two of the American writers just mentioned went into notorious decline, that of Hemingway (1899-1961) after about 1945 no less than that of O'Hara (1905-70) after 1949. This kind of thing can happen to anyone, agreed, but many people would see something typically American about those declines, set against the examples of, say, Anthony Powell or Iris Murdoch. As can be seen, whatever it is afflicts not merely the drop-outs, the chronically sick as discussed earlier, those of slender achievement or none, but the once-established, the highest hopes of their time. Too much success, the old scapegoat? Perhaps the American fondness for size, for big books, for large statements, subjects, themes, a desire for greatness *now* rather than after a few decades of work – very demoralising and exhausting. Is it a gentiles' weakness in a literary culture more and more dominated by Jews? No to that one: for every couple of continuingly successful Jewish writers (Bellow, Roth) there are a couple of failures (Mailer, Salinger), not to speak of durable gentiles (Nabokov, Updike). But something does *happen*.

It was February, the time of the launching of the dreaded Christian Gauss Seminars in Criticism, referred to earlier, in which I was to participate, indeed orate. These were twenty-four lectures of which Dwight Macdonald was booked to deliver the first six, on 'mass culture', then a new phrase.

I had known Dwight on and off for some time, and liked him sufficiently well as a drinking companion, but I came to realise that he really was a bit of an old ass, a New York ex-Trotskyist and just the chap to fall for the kind of popular social anthropology that was starting to become all the rage in the States just then, other champions being Ashley Montagu, Marshall McLuhan and Vance Packard. The last-named was a fearless critic of American mores who had confided to me when we were doing TV in New York that he would wait till after the show before lighting a cigarette, because his mother might be watching it. Anyway, as well as mass culture ('Masscult') there was, according to Dwight, something called Midcult, middlebrowism, just as bad, or even worse in a way, because the unwary might be fooled into believing they had got hold of something good. Midcult was personified in a novelist called James Gould Cozzens (*By Love Possessed*). The way Dwight went on about this unfortunate man, you would have thought he was trying to destroy the USA single-handed or perhaps had tried to run off with Dwight's wife.

I can afford to be patronising about all this now, but at the time I was rather taken with it, perhaps thinking some of it profound because it was of uncertain meaning or relevance. Indeed, I remembered hearing one trousered matron say to another in a Princeton street, 'Did you read this wonderful book, *The Lonely Crowd*?' (by David Riesman and others, 1950) and thinking to myself that that sort of thing showed one of America's good sides, whereas of course it was not really that sort of side at all.

Anyway, nonsense or not or somewhere in between, old Dwight had clearly done some work on his lectures. So had Clement Greenberg, who followed him on modern art: I could understand that much about what he had to say. The audience too was no less McCarthy-Arendt-ridden than had been feared. I was already preparing myself like mad. My terms of appointment had offered no hint of the kind of subject I should pick except that it should be 'of critical interest' or something such. As the best lifebelt I could devise, I had brought with me my Swansea course on eighteenth-century literary theory, thinking that six lectures on that would at least satisfy the first half of what was required of me. But my audience and I were to be spared that.

There was a good French restaurant in Princeton called La Hyère's. Here, once a week or more, I would lunch with the man who was effectively my boss, R. P. Blackmur, poet, New Critic, early champion of the work of Wallace Stevens, but shifter of enough bourbon for two quite thirsty men, and smoker of enough Luckies (was it?) for several of any sort, and great teller of tales. I would invariably eat a dozen large clams and drink with them two small bottles of Foreign Guinness, a lunch fit for a king. At an early one of these feasts, Blackmur raised the matter of the Gauss lectures I was to deliver.

'I'm told you have one of the finest collections of science fiction in private hands,' he said.

'Yes,' I said. Well, he might quite well have been told so.

'I suggest you take science fiction as your seminar subject.'

It was an unexpected and enterprising choice for 1958, among the first such if not the very first academic notice the stuff had received. I took a large suitcase to Brentano's bookshop in New York and filled it with SF paperbacks and current magazines, emerging finally before my Gauss audience with six scripts. By 1960 these had become a book, *New Maps of Hell*, which was to make quite a sizeable contribution to the raising of science fiction to the status of a branch of culture, or 'culture', and so to its eventual undoing. But that would have taken some foreseeing.

Of course there were parties before and after all the Gauss lectures, in fact what seemed like most of the time. And such parties – drinking was only the start of it: you danced, played charades, played the adverb game, played hearts, took endless photographs, went on to the movies, to hear jazz, to bowl, to the football game, to sledge, to skate, into bed at 4 a.m., well into brunch by 11.30 the next, or rather the same, day. How I found time to get anything done, with creative writing and the Gauss preparation thrown in, I cannot imagine. And of course I found very little, very nearly none. When we sailed I had seven pages of my current novel and four poems to show for the whole of my nine- or ten-month stay. So perhaps this was one sort of thing that stifled American writers.

I had been offered another two years at Princeton on the same terms, and was strongly tempted to accept. I have given only part of the reason why I finally turned down the idea. Another factor was the children's education, which Hilly and I both felt we had to get them back for. In fact they would probably have done as well in America, but we thought differently then. I muttered to myself about being thirty-seven, just too old to set about becoming an American, which was what was really at stake. But I soon realised we had simply left too many friends behind, too much of everything, and wanted to get home.

What do I see when I look back at the general picture? What I suppose most people in my position would see: energy, generosity, good will, the immensity and variety of things to spend money on, which I suppose is the same thing as affluence – souvenirs, presents, clothes, gadgets, the boys' push-bikes with gears, bells, all manner of lights, electric horns, speedometers, the (to me, then) almost inordinate efficiency of capitalism, violence (I went to a party on a barge where grown men, middle-class men, suddenly started slugging it out, like one of their films), squalor and ugliness, for instance the town of Niagara Falls, beauty, for instance upstate New York, like North Wales but grander, greenness, spaciousness, tallness, bright sun on snow. How I should like to see it all again as it was then.

ROBERT GRAVES

In 1959 or so I sent Robert Graves a postcard putting him right on some mathematical point. (Not being a raving lunatic I would not have dared to try to put him right on any point of poetics.) He replied acknowledging the fault. I replied with what I suppose amounted to a fan letter. It was characteristic of him that he left this answer unanswered, characteristic, I found when I got to know him a little better, not of anything like laziness or haughtiness but of a harmless desire to be seen as the artist-man who would be compromising something if he answered a mere fan letter.

A few months later I accepted a commission from an American magazine to go and interview him at his place in Majorca. I did so first of all, I suppose, because I admired his poetry, which had had something of a following in Oxford after the war. I had at once found in it a quality it still retains for me: that of encouraging you to write a poem yourself, of almost making it look easy, though heaven knows it never was or is easy. In this his work is the complete opposite of that of a not-so-utterly-different poet, Philip Larkin, whose best poems can strike you as demonstrating the futility of ever again seeming remotely to compete. All that Muse and Moon Goddess and White Goddess stuff inspired uneasiness, but I have always found these things detachable; indeed, for me his most successful poems – 'Recalling War', 'The Cuirassiers of the Frontier', 'Love in Barrenness' – avoid such themes. For me they remain undimmed by the passage of the forty-five years or so since I first read them and the – what? – quarter of a century before that that they were written.

More immediately, what did he think he was doing, stuck away in Majorca like that since 1929 and the age of thirty-four (with ten years' involuntary absence from 1936 to 1946)? To have made a permanent departure from England was a most unusual step in those days for a healthy heterosexual not wanted for fraud. His answers, both in print and when I asked him myself, have never seemed to me convincing: he 'hadn't liked the look of the way things were going' in the England of that time – what things? He had no politics and, as it turned out, war was nearer in the place he was going to. And why Majorca? 'I didn't want to get too far off the Greenwich meridian' was the most I could get out of him on that, and I suppose it was true that the émigré queers from England (apart from the south of France, where he could never have lived) were at the other end of the Mediterranean. But I suppose I was still imaginative or gullible enough myself at the age of nearly forty to find the notion of the exiled (or anyway exotically located) poet appealing.

Our first encounter was certainly in key. Armed with not very clear directions, Hilly and I made our way round one of the coast roads of the island in the dark and then all at once – I am only piling this on a little – there was Robert Graves, there at that moment, so he said, because he had felt we were about due and had come out to the road to meet us. When I could see him in the light he made an immediate and strong impression on me: tall, beaky-nosed, a bit battered-looking, with a high forehead and lips (in his own words) full and ruddy. His often-mentioned air of authority was clearly evident but with it went an open, friendly air less noted. I soon found that, far from being an exile in any self-isolating sense, he was surrounded not just by family but by guests, hangers-on, droppers-in, including the inevitable American or two. He was clearly all for this, innocently basking in admiration and enjoying a social couple of glasses of wine – very rarely more – in the intervals of pounding away at the desk, the centre of his existence.

His conversation showed him to be humorous, inquisitive, warm and surprisingly down-to-earth, with only occasional bardic touches like the famous broad-brimmed Spanish or Mallorquin hat, and even that could go with a day or two's beard. I found it easy enough to ask him questions about those quasi-mystical ideas of his like the old White Goddess. How much did he believe in her?

'About as much as the classical poets believed in the Muses or a Christian in the Resurrection [remember this was thirty years ago]. Anyway, it works for me. It's useful.'

At another time – did he believe in the *sortes Virgilianae* or any other kind? (I suppose I must explain that this, the 'Virgilian lots' or 'chances', refers to the ancient practice of seeking guidance by sticking one's finger at random into a text of Virgil – Homer and the Bible were also used for the purpose – and trying to make useful sense of the passage pointed at.)

'Oh yes,' said Robert emphatically. He waited for what must have been a look of mild consternation to pass across my face before adding, 'Mind you, using a detective story or something would be just as good. It's nothing more than a way of concentrating your attention.'

But he was not above a bit of the old mumbo-jumbo, saying to me in his best vatic tone during a discussion of prophecy and such jazz, 'I can tell you that somebody important [meaning a woman] will come into your life some time in the next year,' and getting it right too, drat him.

He proved as unenthusiastic in private about his poetic contemporaries as he had been and continued to be in print: Pound, Eliot, Yeats, Auden, Dylan Thomas et al. Larkin? He shook his head wordlessly; after no more than the first two collections Philip would probably not have got to him by then. A pity: I should have loved to know what he thought. No, as before, only Norman Cameron, James Reeves and other lesser lights passed muster. He did not mention his sometime collaborator and even more sometime mistress, Laura Riding, whose body, I was told many years later by Peter Quennell on the decades-old information of Norman Cameron, smelt of burnt rubber. I cannot vouch for the accuracy of this information.

To resume: at the time I saw in Robert's coolness towards the names mentioned earlier some dislike of competition, and since then I have wondered whether this had played its part in his decision to leave England, where some of those other fellows would have been under his nose. He certainly liked, if not to dominate, at least to be top man. I could see for myself the attractions of giving up my academic job and coming to live in Majorca, but my (soon revoked) decision to carry out the latter part must have been to some degree the result of falling under Robert's influence, perhaps even a desire to be one of his court. It was coming to realise this, realising too that after writing one novel about expatriates in Majorca I would not easily find a subject for its successor, not to speak of a divorce still beyond the horizon, that made me change my mind, though not before I had put down a year's rent on a house in Soller just along the coast.

'Do you know Alan Sillitoe?' asked Robert, and added half-seriously, 'I invented him. He used to live in Soller in the Fifties, writing I don't know what you'd call them, fantasies about imaginary countries set in no particular period. I told him, "Alan, nobody wants that sort of stuff. Write about the life you know in Nottingham and so on." So he wrote *Saturday Night and Sunday Morning* and made his name.'

As things turned out, it was Hilly and our children, now minus myself, who lived in Soller for some months, where Robert showed great kindness to them all, including the lending of money. Later I stayed there for a few weeks with the somebody whose advent he had predicted, Jane, whom I was in due course to marry.

Jane and I saw a little of Robert on his visits to England when he was Professor of Poetry at Oxford in 1961-66, but not enough for us to set up a friendship. The last time I saw him was probably in the latter year when he appeared on television with a gang of other poets. Half of what he was saying made no sense. Robert, you're pissed, I thought, till I remembered that he was no drinker except on one of his yearly or half-yearly benders, and surely he would not have chosen this juncture to go on one of those. But I hope it was something like that and not an early glimpse of the mental decay seen in his long old age.

CAMBRIDGE

On the morning that I sat down to draft this, I read (*The Times*, 28 December 1989) that that year 'more students joined Cambridge University from state schools than from the independent sector,' after a campaign designed to show that the place was not a closed shop for the public schools. (Oxford was apparently still dragging its feet.) Oh really? There was not exactly a 'campaign' but a movement among younger dons aimed at showing something like that, in full swing when I was teaching there thirty years ago. A small admissions committee on which I was sitting had just decided that two applicants, one from the private 'sector', one from the State, were of virtually equal merit when the chairman spoke. Picking up his pen, and with that look of being sure of general agreement, he said, 'Then I take it we give preference to the chap from Bog Lane Secondary Modern.'

'Just a minute,' I said nastily. 'As I think the only non-public schoolboy present, I don't see why a chap's having been to one should actually be held against him. Can we have one more look at their results?'

They were full of remorseful consternation at their own herd-instinct and we had that one more look. I forget which chap got in after all, but never mind. The reason why State-sector candidates (perhaps) do less well at this level than the privately educated is nothing to do with . . . But faugh! And I have said it all before ad nauseam (et meam), and I have been out of the whole thing for decades. Our present educational system is in a mess, but I am going to go on leaving it alone. I will confine myself to what Cambridge was like when I was there in 1961-63. I have very little idea of what it is like now, except uninhabitable.

I had actually visited the place first in 1940, in order to fail a scholarship and meet the Norman Iles who was to reappear in Oxford. I suppose one of the things that drove me back to Cambridge in 1961 was the hope of a kind of a displaced return to Oxford, an echo of the romantic view of it which intervening time had enhanced. I should have known better, not being a young man any more and, without having realised it, expecting such different things of life. And Cambridge was flat and crowded and sort of cramped.

But it was a whole flight of steps up the academic hierarchy from Swansea (although I am still not clear how that matters, if it does) and it had Dr F. R. Leavis at it. No, this is not a work of literary criticism, let alone of criticism of literary criticism, so I will just say here that, with some patches of exception like his *Othello* lecture/essay, he now seems to me to have done more harm than good to literature, never mind the study of literature, but few scales had time to fall from my eyes in the short time I was at Cambridge, and our personal contacts were almost non-existent. I did, I believe, once have the honour of passing him, open-necked shirt and all, in King's Parade. I also heard, authentically and often, that on being told that Peterhouse had taken such and such a view of the car-parking problem, he had retorted, 'Peterhouse can't expect to be taken seriously about anything now that it's given a fellowship to a *pornographer*.' This was taken to refer to me, rather than to any of our recently appointed Research Fellows in branches of the sciences.

But a more serious disappointment with Cambridge was more directly academic. I had thought, vaguely but confidently, that its common rooms and elsewhere would abound with original and well-grounded talk about English literature. It proved hard to find. What I got was talk about intra-Faculty discord and personal quarrels, syllabus changes and retentions, the proportion of Firsts to other classes, the attendance at old so-and-so's lectures – inevitably, no doubt, but discussed far more exclusively than I remembered from my provincial days, when a not necessarily very profound remark about Traherne or Tennyson would come up now and then. A philosophy don in another college told me of how, after a year at Yale, he had come back quite eager to discuss with his colleagues what he had learnt there. They let him go on for a time and then asked him if he thought Snooks had the weight for this new Readership. 'You go south of Royston,' my informant ended gloomily, 'and you're in the outer darkness. Even some of the younger ones think you might as well have sold out to some rag like the *Times Lit Supp* or to the BBC or Fleet Street.'

Or Oxford. Anyone who, like myself, had been brought up there was likely to feel that Cambridge thought too much of Cambridge and about Cambridge. The facts of geography or economics or something stare one in the face. Oxford has had a lot of history, has heavy and light industry and is a road and railway junction; Cambridge has just the university, and with the mighty but lonely exception of Ely it leads nowhere. In particular, although the two places* are almost equidistant from London, I noticed a hostility to it in Cambridge I had never come across in Oxford. (These days, no doubt, Oxford and London are a bloody sight too close for comfort, with serving dons actually taking jobs in the metrop.)

But away with academe. What I most disliked about Cambridge, and soonest made me wish I had never left Swansea, was not academic but social. I must start by admitting that I have never liked dinner parties, and count as one of the major consolations of age the licence to answer an invitation to one with a flat 'I'm sorry, I've given up going to dinner parties.' (More shortly, 'I don't do dinners,' like a caterer.) Having a few friends round for drinks and something to eat is different, though two guests is the ideal number, four is less good but all right and six the exceptional, absolute maximum. (When you are younger, you can put up with more, though for me it has always been a matter of putting up.) Or you can go to the pub – or rather you could then; difficult now at best. Anyway, the few-friends arrangement and the pub session allow what the dinner party forbids: fairly late arrival, early departure without causing a stir, fairly manifest drunkenness, cancellation on sub-cosmic excuse. Worse, the characteristic d.p. demands that the victim should spend a good two hours trying to talk and listen to people he has never seen before, one of whom will be Sydney Smith and be heard saying, 'Madam, I have been looking for a person who disliked gravy all my life; let us swear eternal friendship.' It still amazes me slightly, on the rare occasions when I think about it, that there must be millions of otherwise normal people who like all that.

The foregoing is my way of leading up to an attack on college

*I once asked an Oxford don what Oxford had taught him and got the reply, 'Never be afraid of the obvious.' A joke, sure, but serious and important if you think longer. And Cambridge in comparison is afraid of the obvious. Contrast, as I once did, the selection by David Cecil (Oxford) of the poems in *The Oxford Book of Christian Verse* with that by Donald Davie (Cambridge) of those in *The New Oxford Book of Christian Verse*.

feasts and similar functions as I experienced them. They start by excluding women but making you put on a dinner-jacket just the same. They prolong the action by Latin toasts and having a lot of courses, often admittedly delicious, especially in Peterhouse, and accompanied by excellent wines in insufficient quantities. The hall is or was unheated. And, just in case you might have struck lucky with the stranger on one side of you or the other, when you went next door for dessert and after-dinner drinks (also excellent), they sat you down among a completely fresh set of strangers with whom you might or might not, etc.

I found that the small party, the dinner for four in the small parlour, a private room in college, did not work for me either. Our hosts could not have been kinder or more anxious that my wife and I should enjoy ourselves. The servants were fine. The food and drink were first-rate. And yet at no point could we feel comfortable, even though we wanted to and tried. Here and above I am objecting not to an exhibition of snobbery or superiority, but to a mode of social behaviour that narrowed and formalised and stiffened ordinary intercourse. No doubt you could have got used to it if you had had the heart to go on long enough. And no doubt it has all been swept away now, though I greatly doubt if anything better has replaced it.

I cannot resist adding that the moment when I decided that life at High Table was not for me came when I was dining out at – never mind where, though the detail gives me the chance to say that my own college, perhaps helped a little by its smallness, was an oasis in Cambridge of good nature and common sense. Anyway, at this other place, the talk at my end had for the first half-hour or so stuck exclusively to the paintings, drawings, engravings and what-not my neighbours had been buying. Noticing, presumably, that I had had nothing whatever to contribute to this discussion, another guest asked me, 'And what is *your* particular, er, line of country in this, er?' With Grand Guignol humility of tone and gesture, I said, 'I'm afraid I don't sort of go in for any of that kind of thing.' The other man said, 'H'm' – not a vocable in common use, but he used it. Then he said, 'I think that's a dreadful thing to say.' I went on keeping quiet for some time after that, wishing, for perhaps the hundredth time since arriving in Cambridge, that I were back in the Bryn-y-Mor with David, Jo and old Willie Smyth, or, less familiarly, that I had a ticket for Australia in my pocket.

After a spell in a pretty little mill-house kind of cottage at a place called West Wratting in the Haverhill direction, the Amises moved into a rather posh house in Madingley Road at the northern end of the city. Soon after arrival I got a letter from the writer Andrew Sinclair, then perhaps also a Fellow of some college. Although we had not then met, I knew a little of him because, without even waiting to be asked, he had sent me in Swansea a succession of his books on publication, starting with a to me unreadable novel called, I think, *The Breaking of Bumbo*. The letter politely suggested we should meet 'in this port and nuts of the soul', i.e., I supposed, Cambridge, a phrase showing signs of hard work, though perhaps not hard enough. Would I telephone and fix a time to come over to his house? Well, why not?

'Actually it's a bit awkward at the moment,' he confessed when I rang. 'We've got the builders in.'

'You come over to us, then.'

As arranged, Sinclair arrived with his wife, who was perhaps called Marianne. 'I think you will like her,' I remembered his letter saying, 'because she is so beautiful and so intelligent.' She was reasonably beautiful, sure, but not very, let alone 'so'. As regards intelligence, let us say I found her talk that evening notable for quantity rather than quality.

Describing the encounter to Bob Conquest when I saw him next, I said, 'Of course there's one rather tempting way of shutting her up.'

'What's that?'

I told him.

He thought about it. 'But that wouldn't shut her up for long,' he objected.

'Maybe not, but it would be a step in the right direction.'

That was later, however. Things went just well enough at that first meeting with the Sinclairs for me not to rule out another. I was curious to see how they lived, too. He would ring me; their turn next time.

When he rang he said, 'I'm afraid we've still got the builders in.'

I was ready for that. 'We'll go to the pub,' I said, and named my local, the Merton Arms.

'This one's on me,' said Sinclair firmly and unarguably as we moved towards the bar. 'What will you have?'

'A large gin and tonic, please.' On this point my pub code says you must balance the risk of insulting the chap by asking specifically for a double against that of being given a single. The balance this time came out as shown.

'With ice?' he pursued, inviting me to go the whole hog.

'Yes please.'

When the drinks came, Sinclair plunged his hand confidently into his top inner breast pocket. As in a dream I watched that confidence vanish in an instant, to be as quickly replaced by puzzlement, disbelief, consternation. Soon he was doing an imitation of a free-falling parachutist frenziedly trying to locate his unpulled ripcord. Finally his movements slowed, ceased, and shame possessed him. 'I must have left my wallet in my other jacket,' he said.

As when, years afterwards, James Michie just happened to have the vital photostats on him (p. 111), so now I was too shaken to fight back. I omitted to offer to lend him a few quid, cash him a cheque, ask Arthur, the landlord, to do so, and just paid up. The rest I forget, but I doubt if I ever saw the house where the builders had been. At any rate, Sinclair's books stopped arriving on my doormat.

I made little progress in acquiring friends among dons in the English faculty. All I can clearly remember of Donald Davie of Caius is his accusing me, accurately enough, of thinking him square (though I thought and think him better things besides). There was also George Steiner, now of Churchill College.

As he will be the first to tell you, George is an American, though he is less forthcoming about his early years at grade school in the USA. Since then he has done a thorough job of Europeanising himself, with a heavy German-type accent and much self-immersion in European (non-English-speaking) culture. But the latter is at least as American a trait as it may be European, and George's unspoken claim to pantophony – speaker's knowledge of every (major) language – even more so. Like his fellow-American, Ezra Pound, George is not afraid of making statements about the literature, the poetry of any and every language that *must*, to be valid, be based on knowing, say, French, German, Italian, Spanish, Portuguese, Polish, Czech, Hungarian, Russian and many more as well as he knows English. Is this likely? Once an American, always an American, in George's case a point to be borne in mind as constantly as in that of Bob Conquest, dissimilar in every other way though the two men are.

I could have put up with George's cultural omniscience more easily if he reacted less sharply to supposed slights on it. When my son Martin published a piece that found fault with his book on chess, George at their next meeting hissed at him the information that people in New York were laughing at him (Martin) in consequence. His first-ever utterance to me, made with much warmth as we walked down King's Parade after an academic ceremony, was,

'Vot iss ze metter viz zis men *Bghoeigun*? Iss he *eempotent*?'

'No,' I said, going more by instinct than Denis Brogan's own recent assertion to me and others that there were fifty states in the United States and he had fucked in forty-six of them. Distaste for the question may have played its part too. 'Why?'

It transpired that Denis, who really did know a lot, had queried, ridiculed, pissed on something George had written or said.

But what contributed as much as anything – as much as what he doubtless saw as my philistinism, for instance – to the non-flowering of Amis-Steiner friendship were the drinkless hiatuses at his dinner parties. After anything up to half an hour he would 'suddenly realise' his omission. But he was not in the same league as Andrew Sinclair, who was reputed to offer his guests tea with the Chinese meal he was serving them, subtly finessing the 'wine of the country' principle.

As time went on I found myself increasingly drawn to certain scientists, people who were not going to tell or ask me anything about the English Moralists paper in Part II of the English Tripos and who, with their love of music and interest in contemporary writing, seemed among other things to unite the Two Cultures, a controversy about the arts and the sciences just then blazing away like a fire in a gypsy's bucket. But our most entertaining acquisitions were the Burns Singers – a couple, not a Glasgow choir – whom we used to meet for drinks in Miller's Wine Bar opposite King's.

Jimmy Burns Singer, slight, even frail in figure, was a not quite unsuccessful poet specialising in unorthodox views, such as that Pope and Swift were not merely friends, as Nichol Smith had had it, but boyfriends. His wife, Marie Battle Singer, was really the better value, a very black black girl with an unreconstructed Mississippi accent who was a fully qualified psychiatrist, or perhaps psychologist, with a practice in London and an intense and vocal interest in her subject. There was something almost eerie, without being absurd, about hearing childhood regression disorders and suppressed anal eroticism having the law laid down about them in the accents of the old plantation. Sometimes the Singers brought with them the huge and often hugely drunk John Davenport, literary journalist, who lived at Duxford down below Trumpington. 'Woman desirous of being mistreated – and you know and I know there are plenty of them around,' said Marie, 'simply contact Mr Davenport and she'll get all she can handle and very welcome. I can't understand why his life seems to be so complicated.' At another time she tried, not very successfully, to lead me in the direction of the Sinophile Joseph Needham, for Marie, with all her charm, was a girl of the Left.

Not that she lacked a lighter side. As she showed more than once at our house, Marie played a fair jazz piano, though her touch with boogie-woogie was not altogether sure, and sang in quite an effective, bluesy type of voice. I remember her having a decent crack at a Bessie Smith number, 'Muddy Water', and a couple of Fats Domino tunes. (Domino was an early rock 'n roll star and as such not really 'authentic' enough, one might have thought, to suit Marie.) She also threw herself with abandon into dancing to the gramophone. When the Powells had come to stay she made a dead set at Tony, which was highly appropriate in view of his strong adherence, notorious since his youth, to the cause of racial integration. The pair were a sight to see as they danced – 'abandon' was hardly the word. Hilly reported hearing Marie say to him as they passed her, 'I sure would like to shag with you, Tony, you old belly-rubber, you' – a notable departure from the style of her talk in Miller's Wine Bar. Unfortunately, Tony's reply, even his expression, could not be caught.

I never saw John Davenport dance, but we did have him to the house, on one occasion to have dinner (and get pissed) and stay the night, reasoning cogently that Duxford was too far from Cambridge for him to put us on his list of those who might be advantageously dropped in on in future. During the evening he popped out to the outside lavatory, which was close to the kitchen. Through the window of this Hilly saw him, having quitted the lavatory, adjusting his hair, tie, etc., in the mirror formed by the window of an adjacent hut. Unknown to him, the hut contained the family's pet donkey, Debbie by name, who looked inquisitively out at him. Hilly thought she heard a faint scream as John presumably took Debbie's face for a reflection of his own. He rushed back indoors asking wildly what had happened to his face, and had to be shown Debbie directly before he could be calmed.

At some lateish hour that night, sitting in the sitting-room, I suggested we should retire. John at once got up and began taking off his jacket in preparation for spending the night on the sofa. I had quite a time persuading him that there was an actual bed made up for him, with bedclothes and everything, all waiting in a proper bedroom. If I had not been drunk I might not have felt what I did feel, a twinge of pity for one so firmly resigned to being deposited on a sofa (at best) when taking a night's lodging off somebody. But I think it was a little bit pitiful anyway.

But my most memorable encounters in Cambridge were not with any kind of senior persons but with undergraduates. My own pupils, eight or ten of them, were all polite and reasonably productive, and none was actively out to make trouble. Even so . . . I had known exactly how to deal with Mr Cadwallader when he came to my college room in Swansea and said, 'Sorry, Mr Amis, but I left my essay on *King Lear* on the bus, see, coming down from Fforestfach.' When Mr Knight came to my room in Peterhouse – actually what had once been a covered bridge between two main buildings – or the one I had later – a place like a suburban drawing-room in an apartment-house down Trumpington Street – and sat wordlessly down, and answered my question, 'Let's see, it's "The dramatic function of Lear's madness" today, isn't it?' by throwing himself at my feet, kissing the toe of one of my shoes and murmuring brokenly, 'Help me,' I was definitely nonplussed. I quite soon discovered that this was simply one of his days for being drunk, and I was eventually able to deal with that too after a fashion. But it was a pest and somehow not right.

The best or worst of these came – I think: my memory of the whole episode is patchy – on the night of a college feast. I had nerved myself for the ordeal in the customary way and had, by about the beginning of the third course, positively started to enjoy myself when a college servant, one of the porters I expect, approached me to murmur, 'A lady wishes to speak to you on the telephone, sir.' His tone and manner made it clear that there was nothing to be looked forward to in what was to follow.

I made my way to the lodge, trying pointlessly to work out how much I had drunk. A voice instantly and unshakably recognisable as a landlady's asked at a high pitch if I was Mr Kingsley. When we had been through that one the voice said, 'And you're what do they call it, you're Mr Delaney's tutor at that college.'

This was less straightforward. Delaney was indeed a pupil, no fool academically and a drunk on the whole inclined to come rather second in the running to Knight, without the other's histrionic element. Delaney was much more like the London-Irish publican's son he actually was, but no matter. The complication lay in the word 'tutor'. In the Cambridge of those days a man's tutor was not his teacher but his supposed guide and counsellor, what Oxford had called his 'moral tutor', a remote figure theoretically available at need but in practice ritually seen for two minutes once a term. And it was I that Delaney knew, or felt he knew, and he was clearly in some kind of trouble. These thoughts passed through my head as fast as I could make them, at a lumbering jog-trot.

'Are you there, Mr Kingsley? Because Mr Delaney's all soaked through from head to foot from being in the river. Went there on purpose. I'm just waiting for my brother-in-law to come round and throw him out, I'm warning you.'

After a presumable taxi-ride I was in the hall of somebody's house, not a very big house. The sense of crisis, the passage of time and so on had not sobered me up, quite the contrary. I noticed various things. There was surely a good deal more water about, chiefly but not solely on the floor, than even Delaney could have brought into the place in his clothes alone, ample as these would have been to accommodate his fat body, but if for any reason he had brought filled buckets in with him there was no sign of them. The landlady, who was also not slim and so young that for some time I took her for her own daughter, kept saying she would not have it. Delaney, red-haired, fat as ever, lard-pale, not meeting my eye, sat mutely on the stairs.

I started to speak, experiencing unusual difficulty in doing so at all, let alone making sense. What came out seemed to be all about *King Lear* and the favourable light it somehow threw on Delaney. It went on.

The landlady waited for me to finish or stop. When I did she said truthfully, 'I can't help any of that. As soon as my brother-in-law comes out he goes and no argument.'

The man was suddenly there as if summoned by being mentioned, like a demon. He took in the situation, including me, and started going for the landlady for not getting the water mopped up, sent Delaney to bed and turned to me again.

'Pissed,' he said disgustedly, referring to Delaney, then gave me another look and a rather discourteous grin. 'What's er . . . ?' he asked the landlady, pointing his head in my direction.

'Well, I wanted to complain to the college.'

'All right, you've complained. Noted. Thank you for coming out, sir, and now I expect you'll be wanting to get back to your seat of learning.' As I went out he was berating the landlady for lacking a sense of proportion.

Something like that happened, anyway. I suppose I found my way on foot whence I had come, but I am not really sure of anything beyond having finally got home without damage. Delaney apologised profusely the next day for the trouble he had caused me. He did his apologising in the sitting-room of my house, and I am not at all sure there was not a glass of something in his hand while he was doing it. The thing was that, without my much noticing, he had become a sort of friend of the family as well as being a periodic bloody nuisance and quite an interesting fellow to teach. Contemporaries of his occupied similar positions. No doubt their chief reason for dropping in was to catch some of the pearls of wisdom I might be letting fall, though the attractiveness of our au pair conceivably came into it.

(I cannot resist interrupting myself here to say that she had a steady middle-aged admirer rather than boyfriend universally known and addressed as Bummer (Scott). From his appearance onward he was as thoroughly, obviously heterosexual as any man I have ever met. He was also, though quite un-la-di-dah, posh. I mention him as the most extreme example known to me of the tendency of the posh not to give a bugger what you call them. Bummer was noteworthy too for having an accident with his car on his way home after every visit to us without exception.)

Nothing of the discredit for Delaney's walk into the Cam can be fairly claimed by me. He was the sort of young man who does that sort of thing anyway. Nevertheless, what with him and others of his kidney there could be something faintly, now and then not so faintly, disreputable about the kind of semi-open house Hilly and I kept in Madingley Road. I would offer a tentative defence of this approach as some sort of fault on the right side. I mean by this that in general the social gap between the dons and the undergraduates at Cambridge (and no doubt elsewhere) was too wide, quite inadequately bridged by the occasional formal sherry party. All the young men I asked said that the chief thing wrong with the place was this lack of contact. A 'university' is etymologically the 'whole body' of teachers and taught, and I felt there should be some arrangement to make this real. A clever person could, I think, have foreseen the student troubles of the later Sixties from the kind of thing I noticed in 1962-63.

Several considerations drove me out of the old place in the latter year. One had been incarnated in the chap who had been so shocked to find I was not a picture-buyer. Another was paradoxically what made me most reluctant to leave: teaching. Nobody who has not actually experienced it can imagine what it takes out of you if you put anything much into it. At the same time, there is no substitute for the satisfaction, almost the excitement, of seeing your pupil take your point almost before you have formulated it yourself.* What with one thing and another, after giving three supervisions in a day I would find myself fit for nothing much more exacting than playing the gramophone.

Then there was preparation. The Oxford English course, like the Swansea one, had concentrated on works originally written in English, even if in the Oxford case it was sometimes a funny sort of English. It had not occurred to me before that Aristotle was an English moralist, or that a knowledge of later foreigners and other-worlders was necessary to the understanding of the English drama, and I had to read these up. I know there are people who successfully combine a full teaching programme with a literary career, but I found it beyond me, and by now far the greater part of my earnings was coming from what I wrote. And finally, Hilly and I had just been to Majorca and got to know Robert Graves a bit there.

So in due course I found myself saying to the infinitely kind and decent Herbert Butterfield, then Master of Peterhouse, 'Sir, with great regret I want to resign my Fellowship at this college.'

'In heaven's name, why?' he asked in his unassuming way.

I gave a selective explanation, laying stress on a writer's need for solitude, being outside the hurly-burly, etc.

'Yes,' said Butterfield, having heard me out. 'Romanticism. That's what they used to call it in my day. The belief that you can help yourself to become an artist or be a better artist by going somewhere remote or in foreign parts.' But he raised no difficulties, indeed wished me well.

In the event I did not go to Majorca and lead the life of an artist

---

*I still miss those supervisions, for a rather different reason. They offered the only context I have found in which serious, detailed and exhaustive discussion of literature is socially practicable. You cannot say in your club or dining-room, 'Let's have a look at what Eve actually tells Adam about her conversation with the serpent,' without at best seeing the other fellow's eyes glaze over.

like someone of an earlier generation. I got no further than London, where I had not lived since 1940, and settled there with a new wife. I have been back to Cambridge a couple of times for a couple of hours at a time, and felt not a flicker, except of personal remorse. I should never have gone there. Well, it was partly romanticism of a different order that had taken me there in the first place, in 1961.

MALCOLM MUGGERIDGE

Given a touch of malice, not inappropriate in his case, it would be easy to present Malcolm Muggeridge in an unflattering light. His fame had little to rest on apart from his frequent appearances on television, where he helped to pioneer the probing or even hostile interview. I must admit I quite enjoyed watching him at work. I said to Anthony Powell, who had known him for years, 'He certainly gave the editor of the *Tailor and Cutter* stick the other night,' to which Tony replied, 'Nothing to the stick he'd have given an actual tailor or cutter who'd got his cuff a quarter of an inch too long or too short.' I must also admit that Malcolm was the laziest television interviewer I have ever been submitted to, letting me maunder on live for two or three minutes about my views on the Labour Party (or socialism) and then at once, with an air of cutting through all that, asking me what I thought about socialism (or the Labour party).

I once found a much less accessible monument to his laziness in an early novel of his, drawn to my attention, as they say, by Tony; I forget the title. It started promisingly enough, if not very originally, with the literary or journalistic neophyte hero being given the job by a publisher or editor of finding out what some recently deceased great man, no doubt some sort of writer, had 'really' been like. For this purpose he, the neophyte, was to go round finding and interviewing in turn the four women in his life, as it might have been his first wife, his second wife, his girlfriend and his other girlfriend. Things bowled along at a fair pace, though with rather little in the way of surprising revelations, until near the end, with one girl still to go, so near the end, in fact, that I started to get quite caught up: what cataclysmic discovery could be in store in the last dozen, ten, eight, six pages? By this stage, something of that sort was certainly needed.

The discovery was that woman no. 4, probably the other

girlfriend, turned out to be dead or otherwise totally unavailable for comment and leaving no will, final message, etc. Nobody else I know of who was writing in those days would have had that amount of cheek, to fail to come up with *anything* at such a point. Even going back to the beginning and changing all the 'fours' to 'threes' would have been more excusable, but presumably even that would have been too much trouble.

A much better book of Malcolm's, and one widely and long acclaimed, though now I think largely forgotten, was his informal history *The Thirties*. This remains quite good fun to look through, but has a pound at least of phrase-making for every ounce of fact. ' "Thou hast it now, and I fear thou play'dst most foully for it," the sacked minister might have muttered with Banquo [just to be on the safe side] as he left Downing Street' – no doubt he might, but what, if anything, did he mutter? And in any case we would rather hear what he bawled out in the bar at White's, or, better, confided later to Churchill's secretary. Of course it would take work to ferret out stuff like that. Nevertheless it must be said for Malcolm-as-journalist that he did grasp one central fact of the period: among the British correspondents in Moscow only he and Ian Fleming saw and reported that the infamous show-trials of 1935 were that and nothing more.

But this is not a book of literary criticism, or of criticism of any kind. In the early Sixties one or another independent television company (it could hardly have been the BBC) was making one of those long round-up programmes – about the state of the nation or some such jargon. It summoned everybody who had ever voiced a view on the subject to its London headquarters and got them to pontificate in ones and twos and threes in a series of short recordings it would later stitch together into some supposedly coherent narrative or argument, I imagine a newish technique in those days. In hospital or lawcourt fashion the producers made no attempt at a timetable but got everybody there at the start and called on various participants as need or chance dictated, often warning them not to go away afterwards in case a second dose of them would be required later. In practice you sat around and chattered and drank, there being nothing else to do, while every few minutes a gloomy chap or snooty girl came to summon Mr Ludovic Kennedy or Mr Bernard Levin or Mr George Gale to the recording studio.

By evening I was past my best and beginning to think of getting back to Cambridge, where I was living at the time. At about this stage Malcolm suggested that we – he and I, as I supposed – should go out to dinner.

'I'm not sure that would be a good idea after what I've already had today.'

'Nonsense, dear boy. There's the most charming girl who's dying to meet you.'

'Oh really?' I had no girl available who would be ready to come out to dinner with me at a couple of hours' notice. The couple of hours was bad in another way too, because there was most of that amount of time to be filled in before dinner could, so to speak, be gone out to.

'That's very nice but I honestly don't think I can manage it,' I said.

'She's called Sonia Orwell.'

This changed things, I am not sure how or why. Assuring me that I should not be in the way, Malcolm went off with a nudge and a wink to call on the lady before the dinner rendezvous. I must have had another couple at the studio before, via one of those instantaneous journeys through the fourth dimension familiar to drunks, I arrived at the White Tower restaurant in Percy Street. I have no idea what happened there but it cannot have been so bad, because the next time I went the place admitted me without demur. I remember Sonia Orwell only as smallish and brownish, but I may have got the brown part from the fact that she was also somehow called Sonia Brownell.* Perhaps when we were drinking our coffee I said,

'Now I definitely must be on my way.'

'Rubbish, dear boy. We're off to Sonia's flat for a last drink.'

By the time we got to the flat, wherever it was, I was still just about master of myself enough to realise that I was not going to get to Cambridge that night. I asked Malcolm to ring my number there and tell my wife this, trying to indicate that he should do so in the manner of a kindly friend saying the old boy seemed a bit too far gone to undertake the journey. Instead of anything of the sort he rapped out the bare statement that Mr Amis would not be returning

---

*This seems likely, for one who knew her better than I assures me that she was actually large, fair and, he added, cultured. He also added, without striking any chord with me, that she had been known to some as 'Buttocks' Brownell.

to Cambridge that night in the manner of a station announcer and at once hung up, his mind doubtless on other things.

What these were became clearer when he went on to say, in a similar tone, 'Come on, chaps, we're going to have an orgy.'

From this point of view we were barely quorate, being just three strong. Malcolm said that since it was his idea he would go first and disappeared with Sonia Orwell (or Brownell) into what was presumably a bedroom. I picked up a copy of the *New Statesman* and began trying to read an article on the crisis in the Clyde shipbuilding industry, I think it was, though I am not sure. I abandoned the attempt after a time because of the extremely complicated and difficult, almost Joycean, style of the piece, which I remember thinking unsuitable where such a subject was concerned. Faint sounds could be heard now and then from the bedroom next door, but nothing to arouse particular interest.

After a time I had not tried to measure, Malcolm came back into the sitting-room. His manner had lost its earlier decisiveness. He said to me without much expression, 'Afraid I couldn't manage anything in there. You go in and see what you can do.'

I did as he asked. What followed calls for no description. It has, I very much hope, befallen virtually all men, sober as well as drunk, at some time in their lives. I said some of what has to be said on these occasions, about it being me and not her, etc., the sort of speech I suppose a great many women have heard and loathed and despised the speaker for and still felt awful because of, at some time in *their* lives. More time went by. Then Malcolm reappeared, all brisk and businesslike again. Taking in the situation at a glance, an easy task, he said,

'Come along, Kingsley, you've had quite long enough, stop hanging about. Get your trousers on and be ready to leave in two minutes.' In some miraculous way he had put me in the wrong. 'Get a move on now, we're off.'

Quite willingly I did as asked. I suppose I offered poor Orwell/Brownell a further wretched apology and some sort of valediction. After another of those four-dimensional short cuts I stood with Malcolm in a largeish – well, bed-sitting-room with a lot of books in it and only one bed, a single one. My sense of curiosity, dormant over the last minutes, began to revive fairly fast. I had heard plenty of things about Malcolm but never, er, this one.

'What is this place?' I asked, or words to that effect.

'My flat.' He was on his knees in front of a hefty chest-of-drawers taking out of its bottom drawer some strips of metal that looked like components of a construction-set for an advanced child. As I watched he began fitting some of them together.

'What are you doing?'

'This is your bed,' he said, his manner lightening. 'Only take a moment to set up. Reasonably comfortable, too, or so I'm told.'

It was, so much so that the instant I had laid my head on the pillow it was morning, or rather the light was on and Malcolm was crouching on the floor near by with an electric kettle.

'I always like to make tea very early,' he explained.

Later we went and had breakfast at the Waldorf, an event which to me was almost as surprising as anything that had happened for the previous twelve hours or so, and I caught a train to Cambridge. When I got home I felt as if I had been away for some months.

'Good time had by all?' asked my wife.

'It's funny you should put it like that,' I said.

But that is another story. At the time of this one Malcolm must have been just about sixty. For years afterwards I saw little of him. It was over these years that he effected his transformation from critic of small bad bits of our society, like the *Tailor and Cutter*, to a sage or pundit (as seen on TV) criticising big bad bits like our values. In doing this he developed an amazing capacity for investing platitudes with an air of novelty and freshness: 'What we all have to realise,' he would say, screwing up his face in the familiar way that meant that something important was coming, 'is that we live in an increasingly materialistic society,' or 'All human beings need some faith to live by and our present lack of one is nothing short of disastrous.' Well, I'll drink to both. My last public memories of him are, rather sadly perhaps, of him saying things like those.

This was also the period when he became known for giving everything up: sex (of course), drink, nicotine (but that had probably been thrown out decades before), coffee (I should imagine), meat – but he seemed to be still on meat to some degree when, in the course of writing a series of articles on drinks and drinking in 1971, I entertained him to tea (naturally) at the Ritz, his characteristic choice. At any rate, he had hard things to say about those, especially among the young, who tried to keep their weight down by cutting out the veg and eating only meat. 'It makes their breath disgusting,' he said. 'Like *tigers*.' I seem to remember him giving the young a pretty bad time all round. They fornicated too much, or perhaps were just too promiscuous. No comment, then or now.

In 1972-73 I see he published an autobiography, *Chronicles of Wasted Time*, in two volumes, rather a lot of volumes, perhaps, for chronicles of such. But the title is surely a misnomer if it refers to the subject's life as a whole. Nobody who gave so much genuine and very largely harmless pleasure and entertainment to millions can be said to have wasted his time. And if that has something of a parsonical ring about it, then surely that is not inappropriate in one who finally carried what had been billed as 'an interest in religious matters' and the nickname of St Mugg to the lengths of joining the Church, and the Roman Church too, so that that 'parsonical' is not so fitting after all. And of accepting the sponsorship of Lord Longford. Sadly again, but justly, that was to forfeit any claim to be taken seriously. I prefer to think of Malcolm in the Anglican dog-collar he wore in a small part in a now-forgotten film. What I try never to think of is the fact – yes, attested fact – that his typewriter is to be seen in a glass case as part of a collection of memorabilia of various Christian writers, including also T. S. Eliot and C. S. Lewis, at the Marion E. Wade Center in the library of Wheaton College, Illinois.

The best story about Malcolm I have come across is not mine, nor can I trace it. A few years ago, the TLS reviewer of some book of reminiscences wrote that the funniest thing in it was not in it at all, but in the accompanying Erratum slip. This ran, in its entirety,

ERRATUM/Page 101, line 4 should read: At this time Malcolm Muggeridge belonged to a small club where he could always get a

Why, a ham sandwich, of course.

YEVGENY YEVTUSHENKO

I THINK LORD David Cecil might have had to agree that, when we say a man looks like a poet, we could mean that he looks not only like Shelley but (twentieth-century style) like Yevgeny Yevtushenko. So it seemed to me at least when I met the latter in Cambridge in 1962. He was then twenty-nine years old and known to me and many others, more or less vaguely, as a sort of rebel against the Soviet system, especially as it had been under Stalin. Nor was this view unfounded – but I propose to tell this part of the story as I saw things then, without benefit of hindsight or further investigation of how justly he could be called a rebel, though with very considerable benefit of an article I wrote a few weeks after our encounter in Cambridge, where he had come to give a reading of his works at the Union.

Those looks of his were the most immediately striking thing about him. His clothes reflected perfectly his elegant and casual demeanour: light-grey silk suit with variations in tone that did not quite constitute a pattern, navy-blue brass-button shirt with a vertical chequer-board strip running up and over the right shoulder. His hands looked strong and deft, like a precision mechanic's. But his face held the attention. With its clear blue eyes, thin upper lip above delicate teeth, and generally flattish planes, it was both grim and gay, seeming to hold both these qualities at once when in repose and lending itself to swift alternation between the one mood and the other.

No photograph of Yevtushenko could do justice to any of this, to the directness of his gaze or to his personal magnetism, a quality I had hardly cared to believe in before I met him. The prospect of several hours' conversation through interpreters with a literary Russian had not thrilled me much, but when I arrived at the lunch and was introduced to him, all but one of my reservations vanished. The remnant was slight disquiet at the notion of being cross-examined

235

about Russian and other foreign literature. This foreboding was justified: I ended the day feeling ignorant, which I imagine does one no harm occasionally.

We began well. Through one or other of the interpreters, who were both British, Yevtushenko complimented me on my novel *Lucky Jim*, which he said had been well received in Moscow. I said truthfully that I was pleased to hear this.

'Since the appearance of *Lucky Jim*, some people have found they've had to take up a new position,' one of the interpreters said.

'People in Russia? Good God. Tell him –'

'Er, not quite,' the other interpreter said. 'What Mr Yevtushenko wanted to know was whether, since the appearance of *Lucky Jim*, you've found you've had to take up a new position.'

'Oh. Well . . . not really.'

'But you've come to Cambridge. Won't that make you change your line? Do you like it here?'

'Oh yes.' This was not the time to discuss any dissatisfaction with Cambridge life I might have felt. 'It's not too bad.'

'It's bourgeois, though, isn't it?'

'Yes, I suppose it is. But the people are quite pleasant.'

When this reached him Yevtushenko looked disappointed: I had become corrupted, perhaps, or else had just clammed up on him. He switched the talk to politics.

'In many countries,' he evidently said, 'there is a conflict between the bureaucrats, the philistines [that's as near as I can get, it's got a broader meaning in Russian], and the people who want to live ordinary private lives.'

'Between the power men and the sensualists?'

'Possibly. There are really two international nations in existence, each with its own interests in common, and these override national interests.'

He developed this neo-Marxist thesis for a time, but always in general terms. In an attempt to give things some sort of concrete trend, I mentioned the power man's supposed indifference or hostility to bodily enjoyment, and instanced the tale that Hitler had abominated smoking, feeling myself on safe ground here with one so clearly committed to the cigarette.

'Hitler's cigarettes were the chimneys of the extermination camps,' was the reply. There were more such *sententiae* later, all as hard to answer as this one.

'What do you think of *Dr Zhivago*?' I was asked.

'I haven't read it. I don't know Russian.'

'It has been translated.'

'I know.' I thought of doing my piece about an interest in the paraphrasable content of literature being an anti-literary interest, but refrained. It felt too boring in anticipation.

After lunch we went across to King's chapel. Yevtushenko's height and youth and foreign look gave him an authority which had nothing to do with arrogance. In the way he looked about him I thought I detected the courteous interest, the concern to see but not to make comparisons, of a man looking at something impressive that the Other Side had done.

'You atheist?' he asked me in English.

'Well yes, but it's more that I hate him.'

I felt he understood me very fully. He gave his delightful grin. There was in it a superiority impossible to resent. (It might have been real.) 'Me,' he said, pointing to himself, then gesturing more vaguely towards the roof, the other people there, the Rubens, but also seeming to include the being I had just mentioned; 'me . . . means nothing.'

Outside again, we walked towards the river. 'You like Kipling?' he asked. 'Kipling . . . good.'

'Isn't he an imperialist?'

He gave a brief shout of laughter. 'Oh yes. But . . . good. Russian translator Shakespeare . . . good. Translator Shakespeare translator Kipling. Good.' Then he declaimed something I can only represent as:

> 'Boots, boots, boots, boots, koussevitsky borodin,
> Boots, boots, boots, boots, dostoievsky gospodin . . .'

and so on for another two or three couplets.

'It sounds good,' I said.

On the way up in the car we noticed some uniformly clad figures flitting about beyond the trees. Yevtushenko turned round animatedly. 'Football,' he said.

'Cricket, I think.'

'Football.'

We stopped the car to prove it to him. He turned round again. 'You like football?'

'Well, not soccer so much. I prefer Rugby.'

'Roogbi,' the interpreter said. 'What else can I say?'

237

Yevtushenko did his disappointed look.

When we stopped finally he leaned over and grasped my wrist in the way he had – I forget what led up to this – and spoke with great earnestness. 'I am only a writer by coincidence. My readers would write exactly as I do if they wanted to write. They created me, I didn't create them.'

We got out. I indicated my house. 'Bourgeois?'

He gave another shout of laughter. It had no edge to it.

The Press boys were waiting. Yevtushenko refused brandy, said unavailingly, 'No photo,' and went and sat down on the lawn. A sort of interview developed. I found it natural to look at the interpreter when I was talking and also when he was talking. Yevtushenko, however, looked at me more or less throughout, so that he could put his points with maximum conviction and then, while these were being translated, be on the alert for each fresh access of bafflement or horror as it dawned on my face. He always did this, I was told later. It disconcerted me a little at the time.

He was rather severe, for him, when I expressed indifference to the work of Henry Moore and added lamely that I preferred something I could make a bit of head or tail of. 'There is an old Russian proverb' – I gazed unbelievingly at the interpreter – 'which says that some kinds of simplicity are worse than theft.'

'Yes. Would you ask him who are the readers he writes for?'

'Russian writers have always written for the people. Some of my poems are for the workers and soldiers, others for the intelligentsia.'

'Doesn't he find it hard to be two men at the same time?'

'There's no difficulty. The bonfire is the same even though the flames fly out in different directions.'

'Does he feel his primary responsibility is to literature or to the Russian reading public?'

'To both.'

I left it. Hereabouts the interpreter explained to me that time was getting short: Yevtushenko was booked for his reading at the Union in an hour and a bit, after an undergraduate tea and a game of ping-pong – he had to have that before he read.

When he had said, 'Some poems are like some children: the ugliest are the best,' we wrapped things up. A little of the damp from the lawn had transferred itself to the seat of the poet's trousers. He cured this himself, politely taking an electric iron off my eight-year-old daughter and vanishing into the play-room. It was all over before the photographers could do anything. 'That's the shot of the year gone,' they said morosely.

Rather as earlier, the thought of a poetry recital in an unfamiliar language had not greatly excited me. The reality was for long periods absorbing and at no time dull. Yevtushenko's voice, leaning hard on vowels not at the beginning of a syllable but an instant later, ranged from sad quietude to sonorous declamation in a way that perhaps suggested a good Russian actor reciting Shakespeare. The renderings were evidently word-perfect* and under complete control. Everybody listened intently.

Each poem was preceded by an admirably un-'poetical' prose translation. The evidence of these would have convinced me, had I needed to be, that the man before us was not a charlatan. But I wondered, trying to allow for my ignorance, whether I was right in detecting a lack of the power of statement. The 'They' whose presence, expressed or unexpressed, can be felt in Soviet verse seem hostile to the very quality of that verse by pushing it into dealing with pluralities and abstractions. Is it a bourgeois or other prejudice to feel that poetry had better deal with the particular, with the concrete, with the present indicative and the preterite rather than the durative present and the imperfect? And similarly, that if poetry is pushed too far away from statement in one of two opposite directions – towards fiction or towards symbol – it may be weakened? Anyway, if there really was a lack of statement in Soviet verse, I would have backed Yevtushenko as the man to put it there. In his words, 'One day it will be normal, not courageous, to write the truth.'

The reading was a great and genuine success. Afterwards we took our leave in what seemed to be the Russian rather than the English manner. That was all right with me. Yevtushenko went off waving his joined fists in the boxer's gesture. He was the first completely good reason I had met with for liking the USSR.

Except for changes of tense, that last sentence is what I wrote and how I felt in 1962. Now, of course, I know that neither Yevtushenko nor anybody or anything else ever could have been an even

---

*I was told afterwards that at one point Yevtushenko got a line wrong and instantly improvised a following line that both rhymed and made sense – a convincing example of the professionalism that marked his whole performance.

partially good reason for liking the USSR. But I undertook at the beginning to tell the thing as it happened.

In the autumn of 1968 Yevtushenko came back into my life, though not in person. His name was put forward for the then about-to-be-vacant Chair of Poetry at Oxford University. At first, remembering our Cambridge meeting, I was all for this. Reflection and a little investigation changed my mind. The year after that meeting he had been reprimanded by the Party leadership at home and relapsed into what Robert Conquest has called 'well-rewarded collaboration' with it. While continuing to be a sort of liberal – the sort that prefers suppression and repression to be carried out with as little brutality as possible – he had become a servant of the régime. I did not then know that he was one of the very few Russians with a proper passport, instead of having to obtain separate permission for every trip, but I did know that he had made trips, not only to England, but also to Cuba, Italy, the United States, Spain, Australia, Senegal, France, Denmark, Mexico and Portugal. During these missions on behalf of his government he had shamefully attacked Sinyavsky, Daniel and other writers who really were liberal in outlook and had suffered for it, and on more than one occasion in the West had remarked of Olga Ivinskaya, Pasternak's mistress and heir, imprisoned on a trumped-up charge of illegal dealing in foreign funds, i.e. Pasternak's royalties from abroad, that he, Yevtushenko, was not interested in currency smugglers.

In spite of all this, in spite of the endorsement of his candidature by the Soviet Embassy in London, which for anyone with a tittle of wit ought to have been disrecommendation enough, there began an apparently concerted campaign in the British Press to get the Chair for him. It included *The Times*, the *Sunday Times*, even the *Spectator* (then under the editorship of Nigel Lawson), as well as avowedly leftist organs. If successful, it would have installed a trusted ally, if not a total minion, of the Soviet régime in a highly sensitive and influential spot. Support for Yevtushenko went wider than that, was common form among those who might have called themselves progressive. Why? To answer that in full you would have to know what makes an intelligent person progressive.

Bernard Levin and I, at first separately, then in concert, did our best to fight back, but it could hardly have been our efforts alone that caused Yevtushenko to lose the Oxford election by a barely satisfactory margin. In the years that followed he continued his activities on behalf of the USSR, including numerous attacks on the

West, especially America. Then, according to Conquest, in the early 1980s we find him urging upon the Soviet leadership a greater respect for historical and other truth. 'We might yet accept,' Conquest concludes, 'that in Soviet circumstances his record, with all its shifts and compromises, may merit, on balance, a positive assessment.' And none of us, I think, can be sure how honourably we would behave 'in Soviet circumstances', at least as they were until recently.

PETER QUENNELL

For years, starting I suppose in the Fifties, Peter Quennell was just somebody one ran into at parties, or more likely saw at a distance. Having been born in 1905 he was not of course very old at that time, and nowadays it seems rather more extraordinary than it would have then to pick up a volume like *Georgian Poetry 1920–1922*, published in the latter year, edited by E.M. (Edward Marsh, I imagine), and find in it the name of Peter Quennell and four of his poems – remarkably assured and accomplished, too, for a schoolboy's work – alongside the likes of Harold Monro (ob. 1932), John Drinkwater (1937) and W. H. Davies (1940). With his essay, *The Pursuit of Happiness*, published in 1988 and book reviews in 1990, Peter's must be about the longest career of any writer of this century. He has started a new work on the connections between literature and pictorial art.

In the Sixties I would see him occasionally in El Vino's, the wine bar in Fleet Street frequented by writers in those days. 'See' was again the right word; wearing a battered hat, an equally battered briefcase in one hand and a glass of (probably) hock in the other, he would nod unsmilingly at me and make for one of the alcoves, there to correct the proofs of the next number of *History Today*. I put him down, quite off the mark, as a grim sod.

Then, about the end of the decade, he unexpectedly approached me and asked, 'Does the name Marilyn Kerr mean anything to you?'

'Yes,' I said, feeling like a character out of *A Dance to the Music of Time*. I had known Marilyn in Oxford after the war, when she had been going about with a college mate of mine, Mervyn Brown (now Sir Mervyn, our sometime High Commissioner in Tanzania and Nigeria, Christ), but not since then. I explained some of this to Peter.

'Well, I'm married to her now' – as his fifth wife, I was soon to discover. 'She was saying she'd like to see you again.'

So it was arranged. Marilyn was still one of the most beautiful women I had ever met, hardly at all changed from what she had been a quarter of a century before at the age of seventeen. On the outside, that is. Otherwise, from being meek and mild, almost silent, she had become a bit manic-depressive with a fondness for vodka and very far from silent. I found myself cast in a role I have had to play too often, especially of late, that of confessor, lay (and unpaid) psychotherapist, and/or pretty unwilling listener to egotistical female outpourings. Luckily I had also become a friend of Peter's, so foursome gatherings also took place. First with Jane, then in the middle Eighties with Hilly, I would go down for dinner or Sunday lunch to the Quennells' rather irritatingly pretty house next to Carlyle's in Cheyne Row in Chelsea.

On the Sunday midday dates Hilly and I would usually pop in for an early quick one at the pub with the two names on the corner of Cheyne Walk. Every other time we would see Peter there similarly occupied, but he would never see us, greeting us warmly instead when we got to the house, coming downstairs to do so as if he had been up top all the morning. I dare say my characterising the ambient prettiness as irritating would strike other visitors as eccentric if not rude, but it is perhaps a defect of mine that I hate having to notice and perhaps admire others' possessions on display, or just prefer to have as little to do with houses as possible, though I can see the point of living in one. I once most rewardingly disconcerted some elevated and well-off fellow who asked me, in a tone that expected an affirmative answer, if I would like to 'see round' his rather grand house by replying with a tolerant smile, 'No thank you.' But I digress.

Originally there were, I think, no fewer than three cats at the Quennells', all Burmese or Siamese or one of those. Although admittedly nice to look at and often engaging in their behaviour, these exotic animals generally are in my experience unreliable: one can never be quite sure they will not sink their claws into the hand that strokes them. But Peter fussed and fusses over his no end, actually buying their food himself, unlike most married cat-men. Here he may be consciously following the example of Samuel Johnson, on whom he is an authority. It will be remembered that Johnson's policy was intended to forestall any resentment on the part of servants who he thought might take it out on his cat if they had to shop for him. Anyway, the Quennells are more or less at one over these cats. It would be fair to say that this is one of the rather few matters so describable.

I was delighted when in 1986 Peter and Marilyn gave up their Chelsea house and moved to a smaller one in Chamberlain Street, only a couple of hundred yards from my own house in Regent's Park Road. Since then I have been able to see him three or four times a week, her a little less often, there or here or in the Queen's, the pub on the corner of Primrose Hill. The two are on the whole better met separately than together. Viewed at closer quarters than before, their marriage revealed itself as one of those where bickering is endemic and on occasion quite sharp stuff, with wife the more loudly abusive, husband more offensive though quieter; favoured outsiders like myself seem welcome to join in on either side, sometimes are drawn in willy-nilly. It takes a little longer to become aware that with it all they are devoted to each other and in total accord over their son, the steady and shrewd Alexander.

Luncheon at no. 2 Chamberlain Street is seldom altogether straightforward, though Marilyn is an excellent cook on her day and the booze usually all right or better. Hilly and I were once invited to partake along with Paddy Leigh-Fermor, with whom I was anxious to renew acquaintance, and his wife, whom I had not met. When we turned up we found out quite soon that the Leigh-Fermors would not be doing so, because Peter had got muddled about dates on the telephone, and not long afterwards that Marilyn had forgotten that anyone at all had been invited to lunch. There was loud music from the record-player, first the Gipsy Kings, as I gather they are called, then some monk-like chanting (Marilyn's choice). Spectacular artificial flowers were arranged with great style all over the place, not least on the dining-room table, on which lay also two cats and a lot of valuable or valuable-looking plates and silver.

After what had been a long wait and, for once, not much to drink the meal arrived. It consisted of a sunken or squashed quiche lorraine, a salad of lumps of tomato and onion, and ice-cream with mangoes. At the end I made some mildly derogatory comment.

'You're a great fat bum,' said Marilyn. 'What you write is a load of rubbish and you can't even speak French. You are extremely boring and very rude and who the hell do you think you are anyway, I'd like to know.'

I managed a laugh at this, and stayed on. Hilly walked out.

Either that evening or the next they were round at my place for drinks.

Sometimes, in slightly different vein, Marilyn would talk about her life before Peter. She had known Evelyn Waugh.

'Horrible little man. What I couldn't bear about him was the way he arse-crept rich and important people. He wouldn't just say something about the house looking very nice. He'd say, "I do hope you and Cedric realise how much all your friends admire you for the wonderful things you've done to this room. That *ceiling* is a dream. And the *orangery*, which I saw this morning, it absolutely took my *breath* away." Little fart. You know I used to be Lady something. Nobody could have made more fuss of me while I was. And nobody could have started ignoring me quicker when I stopped being it.'

But I must not let Marilyn walk away with what is supposed to be Peter's piece. I have met few people who really deserve to be called charming, but he does. As I write he will be eighty-five in a few weeks, but is still very recognisably the handsome chap to be seen in his early photographs, some of which Marilyn put into a pretty collage the other day. He has kept most of his teeth (I have not counted them), enough of his hair not to be considered bald, very nearly all his hearing, that most precious of faculties. He uses it, too, showing an attractive interest in the doings of others whether or not they might be of concern to him. There is nothing to beat his welcoming smile and handshake, his reliable cheerfulness undimmed by some nasty surgery a couple of years ago and its continuing effects. Tall, erect, wearing always the same dark suit and tie, topped by an unbattered black broad-brimmed hat less flamboyant than that of Robert Graves (only ten years his senior), he has already become a familiar figure in the neighbourhood, moving at a reflective pace towards the pub, Tony's off-licence (even nearer), the cat-food shop, or just occasionally the Underground station at Chalk Farm en route for White's.

As his work on Byron, Boswell and many others will show, Peter's interest in literature and in writers is mainly biographical and personal. This bias is reflected in his conversation. Time and time again I will try to keep the focus on, say, *The Village* and Peter will shift it languidly but inexorably to Crabbe's opium addiction. I am usually content to let the talk stay in such areas and to leave most of it to him. After prolonged exposure I nominate him as the best storyteller one is likely to meet, always funny or surprising and to the point.* I have known some of his favourites to come round more than once, but you get that with anybody who opens his mouth at all frequently, and from all points of view, compared with whoever you care to pick, Peter is staggeringly unrepetitive. There is nothing of its kind to beat the experience of sitting with him in the alcove at the top end of the Queen's and letting him have his head; what if he does go on about the French a bit?

It would be too dull and cowardly to call a man a good talker and not give a sample, so here goes. It seems Peter was drinking in a café in Paris with, among others, the poet W. H. Auden and a boyfriend of his, an English public-schoolboy type. When the time came to pay it emerged that nobody had any money. Auden gave a sharp command and the boy at once stood up and started to take his trousers off. Peter felt uncertain of the outcome, and of much else, until it was revealed that under the boy's trousers was a second pair of trousers, from the pocket of which he drew a satisfactorily full wallet. Security, you see. It also turned out, for good measure, that the lad was the possessor of the head which had once been laid sleeping on the poet's faithless arm.

Written in December 1989

---

*I have also known his sense of chronology to falter, as when he asked me if I had ever met D. H. Lawrence. I answered good-humouredly that I had been only eight when Lawrence died. I mention the good humour because when Peter recounted the exchange to a journalist, the man naturally wrote that I had turned purple in the face with rage at the suggestion.

ARNOLD WESKER

In 1962 I wrote a thoroughly nasty review of a number of Arnold Wesker's plays, based not on seeing any of them but on reading them in published form. (At that time I was never going to the theatre except to see Shakespeare; some years later I was to see a Royal Shakespeare Company's production of *Hamlet* that failed to make me want to cry in Ophelia's mad scenes or laugh at Osric, so now I never go at all, but that is by the way.) I spent most of my review saying horrible things about the dialogue, instancing lines like 'You're just drowning with heritage, mate!' and 'I suddenly feel unclean,' but I need not go into that now either.

Anyway, some time later I got a letter from Arnold that said, politely enough, that he knew I had no very high opinion of his work, but he was convinced that I could not fail to like his then new play, *Their Very Own and Golden City* – despite its title, he might have added, though that would have been asking rather a lot, I do see. What he did add was that I had only to name an evening and he would have a couple of tickets waiting for me at the box office. After a good deal of groaning, swearing, etc., I rang him up accepting his invitation for self and wife, with the proviso that I should pay for the seats, adding jocosely that I would expect him to lay out his cash for my books and not require free copies. All was agreed along those lines and a date fixed.

When we got to the theatre on the night we found ourselves in excellent seats at the front of the stalls and next to the playwright Frank Marcus, who had the actress Kika Markham on the other side of him. He and I, previously unknown to each other, soon established that all four of us were there under the same conditions, Marcus apparently being no more, or insufficiently more, of a Wesker-admirer than I was. We wondered how many others in the audience had been summoned for the purpose of undergoing conversion.

247

The curtain rose. In my charitable way I had been secretly a little worried lest the play should turn out, against all the odds, to be some good, but the first few minutes put my mind firmly at rest about that. The dialogue preserved in full that 'air of being hastily translated from some other tongue' that I had noted in my review. The story was about the efforts of a young architect or planner, seemingly entrusted with the construction of a whole new town, to get this done in a style worthy of the decent, ordinary, working-class human beings who would be living in it. The action revolved round the struggle of various bad people, 'vested interests' of the expected sort, to frustrate the young man's intentions. I fancy he lost the argument and a repulsive, repressive, greedy, corrupt, reactionary city was to be put up instead. But I really forget almost everything but the main theme, except how boring the whole business was.

And enough of one speech to give a short paraphrase of it. Asked by his faithful girlfriend some question like, 'But what will it be like, Gerald, this city of which you dream?' the young man, his eyes appropriately bent on vacancy, said something like, 'Ah, Brenda, my city will be a city for the young and for the old, for those who are surrounded by those close to them and those who are lonely, for the happy and for the sad, for those who have found love and those who have missed it . . .' And for those who like drinking their draught bitter out of a tankard and those who prefer a straight glass.

When, several days later, the curtain fell for the last time, either Marcus or I said to the other, 'You know, we're not going to get away with this indefinitely – sooner or later he's going to get us to say what we thought of it,' and hardly had he or I finished speaking when a man who looked like a soccer player in mufti had come up to the four of us and said, 'Mr Wesker's car is outside waiting to take you up to his house for supper.' So off we went. What would you have done?

I am not much good at houses at the best of times, so can say of Arnold's only that it seemed large – larger than mine – and well appointed without being showy. He presented us to his wife, Dusty, whom I greatly took to and who had cooked a splendid meal she was unnecessarily anxious about. (In a later decade she was to assure my son Martin that the Wesker holiday journey to Andalusia by train would be comfortable enough because they had reserved courgettes for the whole trip, as half the wives I know might have put it.)

A few minutes into the food, feeling that someone had to start somewhere, I said, 'Arnold, I'm afraid I didn't like it.'

'Well, I didn't expect you to,' he said with a smile, rather negating the message of his letter. 'What didn't you like about it?'

A full list of the attributes of any and every play was what I should have given him, but after a few lies about having thought the character of the old trade unionist was well done, I told him, 'I don't know anything about architects, but surely the first things they go on about are how much money they can spend, the position about water, practical stuff, not about it going to be a city for the young and for the old and, er, and things of that sort.'

Before I had finished he was laughing and shaking his head. 'The trouble with you, Kingsley,' he said amicably, 'is that you don't know anything about the theatre. I tried it the way you're talking about, in fact I took six numbers of *The Architectural Review* to check, but it just didn't work *dramatically* like that.'

'But surely you needn't have – '

It went on for a good half-hour, probably more, with Marcus coming in on my side with different arguments, me getting a bit heated, Dusty looking more anxious, and Arnold altogether unshaken, in fact cool as a cucumber, rather disappointed of course with me and the others that we had kept missing his point, at no juncture taking the smallest offence.

'Pretty impressive, you have to admit,' I said to Jane as, in *New Yorker* style, we drove home discussing the party. 'I said some things back there that would have got me not far from throwing me out of my house, and he just sat there and took it all on the chin.'

'Impressive in what way?'

'Well, for tolerance. Good temper. Grown-upness.'

'You're wrong. It was conceit. He's so sure he's marvellous that it wouldn't matter what anybody in the world said to him.'

'Not even someone he really respected?'

'He wouldn't respect anyone who didn't think he was marvellous.'

Well, that was roughly what she said.

It must have been quite soon after this, still in the 1960s, that I ran into Arnold again, at an evening party at Martha Crewe's house in Primrose Hill. In those days of abundant spare vitality, everyone happily settled down after supper to a session of The Game. Originally, I think, devised in America, this consisted of a series of turns in which members of one team were to convey to their mates a succession of phrases devised by the other. The phrases could be titles of books, plays, films, etc., well-known quotations, sayings in common use and I dare say other things. No words were allowed in transmission, only mime, with a system of agreed signals representing 'This is a book-title', 'I now propose to mime the first syllable of the second word', and so on.

That evening, Arnold and I happened to be on opposite sides in The Game. When it came to his turn to perform, he drew out of a hat the slip of paper on which I had written, 'Oh, what a rogue and peasant slave am I!' – *Hamlet* II ii, I should perhaps add here. I had not thought to puzzle the opposition for long, much less defeat them, merely to enjoy the spectacle of someone being a terrific rogue and peasant slave before the company. My hopes were exceeded.

After reading those few words with as much concentration as if he had been translating them into Hebrew off the cuff, Arnold promptly started being a voiceless rogue and peasant slave to the best of his ability, making impassioned gestures of self-loathing, writhing about on the floor, looking really fed up. His team-mates were baffled. 'What *is* it, Arnold?' they kept asking. 'A play or a proverb or what?' For he had not made any of the preliminary signals that communicated such data, nor did he do so now. After a bit he answered these questions with a silent but unmistakable Don't Know. (I forget the upshot.)

Among the spectators, I drew in my breath sharply. Jane, at my side, sent me a warning glance. What with one thing and another, it was not until she and I were as before on our way home that I said what I had not stopped ardently wishing to say. I will not transcribe it here, but it indicated among other things that Arnold had apparently clean forgotten the first line of the second-best-known soliloquy in *Hamlet*. That thought set my mind running on those writers, notably poets, who on the evidence of their writings, are not interested in the literary medium they use – no art, just 'statements'. Many of our cultural troubles start there.

The last time I saw Arnold, who was now wearing his hair down to his shoulders, was in a large room at the top of the London Hilton hotel, where he, Margaret Drabble, Jane and I had agreed to harangue several hundred Japanese teachers of English. Why does one let oneself get drawn into these things? Conceit, of course. It may or may not be a more amiable form of conceit than the one that keeps you away because you consider yourself above such trivia. Anyway, these were my first Japanese and throughout my allotted ten minutes their reactions might exactly equally well have been covering the thoughts 'Isn't he marvellous?' and 'The next time he says "tradition" we all rush up there and tear him to pieces.' End of story. Oh, except that when it came to Arnold's turn he went on for forty minutes instead of the standard ten. But then I expect he could tell they all thought he was marvellous.

TIBOR SZAMUELY

It was in the middle 1960s that Bob Conquest introduced me to somebody he had described as a mysterious 'Hunk' or Hungarian, a refugee from the Other Side whose name had already begun to appear in right-of-centre periodicals in this country. For some reason I visualised this unknown as a figure of grace and suavity, though I might have thought differently had I known of the connection of 'Tibor' and 'Tiberius'. The reality was a shock to all at least who have written about him, a very short thick figure, square of face and frame, heavy, with a distinct lurch in the gait, a fierce curved pipe on the go at the corner of the mouth, a 'foreigner' if ever one was to be seen among English people. In fact he told me that, on settling in London and starting to find his way about it, very sensibly, on foot with a street-map, he had soon had to take to going into a telephone-box to consult it, before some friendly stranger, spotting so obvious and complete an alien, should come up and offer manual directions.

Despite this and the many other differences between us, I doubt if I have ever taken to a stranger so quickly. He could not have been said to have an attractive mouth or a sweet smile, and his eyes were small, but remarkably direct. We were soon meeting often, most regularly at the 'Fascist' lunches at Bertorellis' described earlier. No one turned up more regularly and enthusiastically than Tibor.

By degrees I learnt parts of his history, some of it a matter of record, some of it probably never committed to paper. He was born in Moscow in 1925 into a well-known émigré Hungarian political family with some sort of status in the city. I am not sure of all that that 'political' means. Certainly his uncle and namesake, a 'hero' of the Hungarian Revolution of 1919, was a famous associate of Lenin's, and Tibor had a framed photograph, prominently displayed, of the two monsters standing side by side facing a crowd

252

from a platform. Tibor's father abruptly ceased to be noticeable in 1936, during Stalin's Great Purges. There may have been more indirect connections. Tibor hinted broadly to me at one time that his mother-in-law's relations with Mátyás Rákosi, Hungary's Stalinist dictator 1949-1953 and later, were or had been uncommonly close.

Tibor's privileged position had taken him to England and Bertrand Russell's Beacon Hill School for a year or two in the 1930s. Here he learnt to speak perfect English both formal and informal, though he retained a slight accent. He came to write the language like a master, better than most of those whose native tongue it is, and soon dropped the traces of 'heavy Central European irony' Bob had noticed.

In due time Hitler invaded Russia and into the Red Army Tibor went. On his way home from the front at the end of the war, he noticed that, at the border with the Ukraine, the train in which he and his mates were travelling was having fitted to the front of it armoured coaches covered with machine-guns and low-calibre artillery. It was understood, though not of course proclaimed, that these were there to deal with the Ukrainian nationalist guerrillas (rather well-armed guerrillas, evidently) who were in a state of war with the Moscow government. Until recently the same men had been fighting the Germans, whom they had once for a short time greeted as liberators. It took Stalin over a year to put them down by his customary methods, including village massacres, etc. Tibor would have approved of my inserting this digression as a reminder that anything Stalin took so long to suppress will need more than a touch of *glasnost* to smooth over.

Back in Moscow, Tibor took his doctorate at the university, and at this period was outwardly an active servant of the régime, though he had already, he told me, made up his mind that it was going to be England for him, however it could be managed and however long it took. Not only for him: in the early Sixties, leaving their two children behind as hostages, he brought his Russian wife, Nina, on a trip here to make sure she liked it too, as he did. That insistence on a joint decision was characteristic; I think they were the most devoted couple I have ever met. Anyway, come they would one day, with the children.

Their route was roundabout in the extreme. Besides his more orthodox academic activities in Moscow, Tibor taught at a secret but official 'university', actually a training-school for Third-World subversives. It was a rule of this institution that nobody knew

253

anyone else's name. One of the 'students' took a fancy to Tibor. He told him, 'My country is an imperialist colony called the Gold Coast at present, but one day it will be a free people's democracy, and then you must come and teach at it.' Tibor said he would like that very much, and there the matter rested for some years.

In this interim he got into trouble with the authorities. The position of his house and his work timetable meant that when arriving home for lunch he was liable to see at close quarters the substantial figure of Georgi Malenkov (Prime Minister of the USSR, 1953-55) getting into his opulent official car and being driven off for a no doubt opulent lunch. Irritated by this recurring sight, Tibor told somebody he thought he could trust that he was fed up with running into that fat pig Malenkov every day and could not wait for the vacation. After a due interval, a couple of fellows turned up at Tibor's place at three o'clock in the morning and took him away. His last words to Nina were: 'Write to your mother,' which perhaps ties up with my earlier remark about Rákosi and with what was to happen later.

'Slandering a member of the Soviet government,' or words to that effect, turned out to be the charge. (Another one, of plotting to assassinate the said member, was based on the discovery of an overlooked World War Two cartridge somewhere in Tibor's belongings, and was soon dropped.)

'Ah,' said Tibor, when enlightenment eventually dawned, 'I see there has been an unfortunate misunderstanding. Slander? What I actually said was that I was delighted to see Comrade Malenkov looking in such good shape and obviously enjoying life.'

The interrogator laughed merrily. 'Nice try, Comrade,' he said. 'Eight years.' This was his educated expectation of Tibor's sentence when he came to trial, and it was to prove entirely accurate.

The above account is not as bizarre as it may appear to some: after all, they could get you for anything they fancied any time, or for nothing at all if they were so minded. But it may well not be complete. Tibor never said – he was secretive over parts of his life, as anyone is likely to be who has been brought up in that kind of society even when he has got out of it, and I soon learnt when not to press him. Any kind of personal malice or envy, quite possibly something deeper and more ordinarily 'political', might have criminalised his remark about the corpulence of Comrade Malenkov.

The camp they sent him to was a well-known one at Vorkuta in NE European Russia, not one of the strict-régime sort, where they literally work you to death. Before we get to it, however, it may be worth pausing over his (and others') remark that the worst prison is better than the best camp. At some early stage, Tibor was one of the several dozen occupants of some cell doubtless built by the Czarists for a smaller number, and a privileged occupant. The big daily event in a Soviet gaol is the delivery of the copy of *Pravda*, and it was Tibor's right and duty, as the Professor, to read the contents out to the cell. I wish I had by me the account he wrote of the reception of one particular item of news.

It appeared that Stalin had protested *in person* to the UN or one of its offshoots about the inhuman conditions under which some Greek Communist prisoners were being held at the end of the civil war there – inadequate exercise, meagre rations, food parcels only once a week, gross overcrowding on a scale comparable with (say) Czarism, insufficient visiting, and suchlike enormities. After a moment's stunned silence, every prisoner broke into hysterical laughter, the tears running down their faces, embracing, rolling over and over on the floor, old feuds forgotten, for minutes. Indeed, the mood of euphoria lasted not for minutes but, in short bursts, for days. A careless spray of urine over one of the sleepers nearest the bucket would bring not the usual howl of rage, or worse, but a cry from the offender of, 'Now, now, Comrade! Remember the sufferings of our Greek fellow-fighters for peace against the Western oppressor!' and an answering guffaw.

Nothing remotely like that could have happened where they took Tibor to serve his sentence. What that camp was like I never heard, nor how long he served in it, but it was not, probably no more than a fraction of, the full eight years; long enough, though, for Nina to find out what was entailed by going to visit him there. But, one gathered, she had written to her mother as instructed; something presumably passed from mother to Rákosi and from Rákosi to Stalin; certainly a letter passed from Stalin to the commandant at Vorkuta, ordering that Comrade Szamuely be released immediately. This kind of personal intervention from the top was very rare, so much so that Tibor was given to boasting that he was the only person ever let out of any form of custody on Stalin's specific instructions. (He used to pretend to be fond of Stalin on this account, and also for his having killed more Communists than any other man.)

It now appeared that Stalin wrote the commandant a *second* letter, emphasising that 'released' meant not what it usually meant, viz. 'released from there but sent straight to exile in Siberia for ten years or so', but 'released, returned to Moscow and rehabilitated'. This virtual amendment caused a minor administrative crisis. When Tibor arrived at the local railway station, bound, as he thought, for Siberia, he found a repentant KGB man on the platform.

'A repentant KGB man?' I asked. 'How did he express his repentance?'

'By kissing my shoes.'

'Come on, Tibor, what did he really do?'

'I told you, he *kissed* my *shoes*. Then he bought my ticket to Moscow.'

'Royal treatment.'

'More to get his hands on my money. They give you back most punctiliously everything you had with you when you were arrested. I saw this chap put half of the cash I gave him into his pocket on his way to the ticket-window.' (If Tibor were here now, I suppose I might ask him how he happened to have had on him at least twice the railway fare from Moscow to Vorkuta when they arrested him.) 'Then, when the time came, he put me on the train for Moscow.'

'The least he could have done.'

'Not quite in the sense you mean. Putting someone on a train in Russia doesn't consist just of opening the carriage door for him and handing him his luggage and newspapers. You have to trample underfoot all the old ladies who've been waiting longer than you have, and sometimes clobber a sturdy peasant in the process. Then the passenger has to be found a place. My chap got me a very good one, a piece of corridor all to myself where I could stand all through the days and nights back to Moscow.'

Tibor found himself so thoroughly back in favour that he was allowed to resume his academic duties and eventually to go back to Hungary, becoming Vice-Chancellor of Budapest University in 1958. One day there came to see him the pupil of his at the secret 'university' who had promised him that Gold Coast job.

This time I thought I had really caught Tibor out. 'You told me before that nobody knew anyone else's name at that place. How did he find you, this chap?'

Tibor snorted. 'All he had to do was come to Budapest and ask who is very short and very fat and smokes a pipe and speaks English! Anyway, he told me his country was called Ghana now, and their invitation to me to come and teach still stood. Accompanied by my family, of course. Of course.'

At that time Ghana was a pro-Soviet dictatorship, though still with some British links. Tibor told me that in the university Combination Room after dinner they drank vintage port with the sweat pouring down their black faces, but I regard that as fantasy. But I certainly wanted to believe Nina's story that when the family visited the glorious Atlantic beaches there, they were the only people on them. Nobody had remembered to tell the black attendant that it was no longer necessary to see to it that all the black bastards were kept away from nice places like that.

Those British links meant that, when his leave came round, he could go to London to do historical research at the British Museum. Accompanied by his family, of course, but not his library of God knows how many thousand books, most of them in Russian and irreplaceable anywhere. Accordingly, he said, when he got there he went down to the harbour in Accra and found an American who undertook to send them to England by sea. In due course they all turned up, a priceless archive. It was one of Tibor's boasts that no prodigious talent was needed to get oneself out of the USSR, a good deal more went to getting one's wife and children out as well, but to get one's entire library out on top of everything called for genius of a high order. Anyway, here in 1964 he was, already on his way to becoming established as one of the world's most authoritative historians of modern Russia and commentators on the contemporary Soviet scene, a lecturer at Reading University and a tireless contributor to learned and journalistic periodicals, soon comfortably settled in West London with his family in a house in Sutherland Place.

Among the newspapers he took regularly there was *Pravda*. This reached him under a pseudonym, which I will preserve protocol by not revealing even now, though it was a long way from 'Tibor Szamuely'. He himself was quite often mentioned in its columns, though never under any name, only as 'a well-known enemy of peace and freedom' or 'a notorious reactionary writer'. After all, he explained, considering the heroic status over there of his uncle and namesake, to be more specific would be rather like having *The Times* refer to 'the international criminal Winston Churchill'. Tibor read *Pravda* constantly, claiming that it was possible to obtain an exact and detailed picture of life over there by doing so. Its denials about the occasional larger matter, by being taken back to front, could be informative also.

It is often forgotten in the West that one important feature of *Pravda*, as the organ of the Communist Party of the Soviet Union, is constructive criticism. From it, Tibor used to say, patience and some schooling in reading between the lines would provide you with full information about what the régime subjected everyone to, not just its prisoners. One chronicle, rich in incidentals, has stuck in my mind and may be worth recounting at length. But I can give no hint of the boyish gusto with which Tibor would deliver such accounts.

'Difficulties of a Motorist' the piece was headed, and it was prominently displayed. The writer, whom I might as well call Boris, evidently a prosperous Moscow office-worker, had planned to take his annual holiday not in Czechoslovakia, which for a West European would have been like choosing the south of France, but down in the Crimea – more patriotic and in a way more adventurous. To start with, he would drive rather than take the train, which was certainly adventurous because he had no map. No maps are supplied in Russia for civilian use, because that would make it easy for ordinary people to find places and go there when they liked. But after some inquiry, Boris heard of someone in Moscow who had acquired a map, and at the price of the customary half-litre of vodka this person allowed him to trace the maps and parts of maps which would guide him to his destination. Off he went then, with the back of his car full of tins of petrol, because there are not many (if any) filling-stations in Russia outside the large towns, and he had something like a thousand-mile journey ahead.

All went tolerably until he was almost in sight of his goal, when the main driving-shaft of his car fell into the road. For a couple of half-litre equivalents he got a tow into some sort of garage or repair-shop that supposedly dealt with vehicles. Here it was explained to him that the piece of machinery was damaged beyond repair. Nor, although there are only a half dozen types of vehicle in the USSR, was there a spare available. I forget the immediate sequel to this, but the next event of significance was Boris coming across a news-paper report – in *Pravda*, presumably – to the effect that a car of the relevant type had been burnt out in an accident near Smolensk west of Moscow. The condition of its driving-shaft was not mentioned. Boris had no way of finding this out from where he was, because he could not have got through by telephone to anyone who might have known, because he could not find out anybody's number, because no telephone-directories are supplied to private persons in Russia, because if they were you might start ringing people up, arranging to see them, etc. How British Telecom must envy their Russian colleagues!

Boris accordingly got on the train back to Moscow, no doubt taking the damaged shaft with him should its presence be required or its existence have to be proved at some later stage. In Moscow he changed trains and set off on the mere 250-mile hop to Smolensk. Here all went swimmingly: the driving-shaft of the burnt car, though perhaps a little stained with soot, was otherwise in excellent condition, and, no doubt after doling out a half-litre or two, Boris sailed triumphantly back to the Crimea. Here it proved that the garage had nobody who could fit the shaft, but a fortunately passing truck-driver and a half-litre soon took care of that, and in due course Boris was back in Moscow, just in nice time to be sitting in his office chair on the morning scheduled for his return to work, and that was his holiday. Surely, he finished his letter – and I wish I could have caught the tone, but that would have been too much to ask from Tibor – something could be done towards improving matters should anything similar arise again.

'That's the sort of thing people in the West should know,' said Tibor. 'Of course they should know about the famine too, and the purges and the camps – all that – and quite a lot of them do in a way, but for some of them it's too much, too big. They might find it easier to take in that in Moscow you can't get an electric-light bulb or a bar of soap.'

Pravda was not quite the only periodical Tibor discussed with his British friends, nor politics his only topic. He had a good knowledge of British and American literature, a predictable liking for Kipling (also popular in the USSR), a more unexpected one for the works of Anthony Powell. The two got on well together, and, seeing them chattering at the lunch-table in Bertorellis', I sometimes found it hard not to feel like someone out of Surtees or Dickens pluming myself on having such interesting friends.

Tibor fitted quickly and uncommonly well into the London life of his time, intellectual, academic, literary, even public – he was a vigorous controversialist, often appearing on TV. Nevertheless in one deep way he never could settle completely, perhaps never would have. I would sometimes telephone the house to confirm his intention to turn up at some lunch or other, learning to leave it as late as possible because I knew how late he liked to sleep. Once I complained to Nina about her husband's morning lethargy (though his output of sheer words over the weeks was immense). 'Why can't the silly sod go to bed earlier?' I asked.

'Well . . .' she said, 'sometimes if it hasn't been a good day he sits up late, reading away of course, but not just for the reading. It's more that until he sees the first signs of dawn he can't be absolutely certain that they won't be coming for him that night.'

'But this is England,' I said. 'And he knows that.'

'Oh yes, he knows that all right, and you wouldn't call him neurotic, would you? But in spite of everything he still can't be *absolutely* sure until that time has come.'

I forget what I said then.

Eventually, on the first available day, Tibor's naturalisation came through. There was of course a lunch-party at Bertorellis'. It contained an unforgettable moment when his plateful of roast beef – what else? – was put in front of him, and the waitress innocently responded to his request for mustard by asking if he wanted English or French. 'English!' he bawled in his semi-falsetto, with an exactly calculated mixture of real and simulated indignation, full of joy. When the time came we all congratulated him on membership of his new club. 'There's one thing I want to say to you about that.' There was nothing but seriousness now. 'You got what you have as a birthright, a gift, willy-nilly. I chose it and went to some trouble to acquire it. I think that ought to make you a bit prouder of it.'

On a later occasion he said to me, 'You know, this [naturalisation] means I have no more worries. Nothing matters to me now. Not even dying. I'll be able to say to myself, well, at least it's in England.'

After only a couple of years he needed that last comfort, and I hope he found it. He died of cancer at the age of forty-seven and was buried in Kensal Green Cemetery.

Within another year, Nina too was dead of the same disease as Tibor at the same site, cancer of the bowel. I remember Bob Conquest saying to me, 'Science doesn't recognise dying of a broken heart. There has to be a disease for you to die of.'

Nina had turned to the Roman Church at the end of her life, and my wife and I had banked at least on a proper funeral, though what we got was the modernised liturgy with traditional trappings. But none of that was anything after one of the most harrowing sights imaginable, that of the two young orphaned children, Helen and George, there at the top of the church steps to greet the mourners, standing completely alone, with no kin in this country and none anywhere else in the world they could go to.

I am not qualified to comment on Tibor's work, except to praise its style, the English of an Englishman with a profound appreciation of the language, free of the jargon that can afflict writing on his chosen theme, free of any earlier mannerisms. He successfully completed his magnum opus, *The Russian Tradition*, published posthumously in 1974 to much acclaim.

I have had seven great friends in my life. Three are dead. Tibor and another still living have been the only two people with whom I have ever formed the habit of talking on the telephone almost every day, not about anything in particular, just talking, 'like a couple of bloody women' as he was fond of saying. Of my seven, Tibor was the last I met, the one with whom I grew intimate most quickly, and the one I knew least long. There was nobody like him for so many things, most of all perhaps for steady underlying cheerfulness and optimism, which it is tempting to think of now as a conviction that the world would one day begin to haul itself up out of the mudhole it had sunk into.

SIR JOHN BETJEMAN

IN WRITING HERE about John Betjeman I am in a difficulty that has come up more than once in these memoirs. It is that my attention and emphasis tend to go to those people, and those characteristics of theirs, that are suitable to an anecdotal or at least a narrative approach, as in a novel. Those who are merely good chaps, or fairly good chaps, with whom I have enjoyed some drinking and yarning, perhaps self-restrained chaps or even secretive by nature, or just less given to colourful behaviour, get fewer pages from me. So with John, which is partly a way of saying I wish I had known him better.

I came across the work long before the man, when I was still at school. In 1936 or so it would have taken a very unusual or much more privileged schoolboy than I was to have known John's first and then only book of poems (*Mount Zion* of 1931), and what I got hold of, in the school library, was *Ghastly Good Taste* of 1933, 'a depressing story', it subtitles itself, 'of the rise and fall of English architecture'. In those days I was trying to find out about all sorts of things like 'modern' music, art, poetry, ballet, 'cinema', architecture and so on, or would have said I was. My interest was mostly so superficial that I managed to mistake Betjeman's multi-pronged attack on modernistic, stolidly antiquarian and playing-safe styles for an exalting of the new, and therefore 'modern', over the old. In maturity I was to share the view of one of my characters, who reflected that he would have liked to see architecture 'all done away with'. John did once take me on an educative walk round a bit of Barnet, however, pointing out some new horrors and a couple of survivals from a less flashy era, but the lesson failed to take.

In poetry, which really did interest me, I cottoned on to Betjeman as soon as I saw him, at Oxford, in the pages of his second and third collections, though I must somehow have come across in *Mount Zion* the little poem that made me feel at once, and justifiably as it turned out, that I understood what sort of poet he was, how he saw and portrayed the world. I was first drawn to it by its title, 'Croydon', the name of what was once a country town in Surrey but long since suburbanised to London and, in my boyhood, a place where my mother would take me on bus-outings, as to Streatham or Brixton on the London side of where we lived in Norbury. The poem is probably short enough for me to quote it here in full.

> In a house like that
>   Your Uncle Dick was born;
> Satchel on back he walked to Whitgift
>   Every weekday morn.
>
> Boys together in Coulsdon woodlands,
>   Bramble-berried and steep,
> He and his pals would look for spadgers
>   Hidden deep.
>
> The laurels are speckled in Marchmont Avenue
>   Just as they were before,
> But the steps are dusty that still lead up to
>   Your Uncle Dick's front door.
>
> Pear and apple in Croydon Gardens
>   Bud and blossom and fall,
> But your Uncle Dick has left his Croydon
>   Once for all.

I hardly dare say that I too knew Coulsdon Common and was *nearly* a pupil at Whitgift School, for fear of falsely personalising my reading of the poem, doing my bit to de-universalise its appeal and its meaning in the old biographical style; perhaps I can be forgiven under the plea that even so tenuous a link is rare enough in one's experience. Anyway, the astringent revelation that we are not after all being presented with an affectionate album-picture of Edwardian suburbia, with even a touch or two of pastiche, is characteristic of both poet and man. He is always taking us from the reassuringly familiar, sometimes bland, surface of things to the unpleasant underlying facts of death, loss, pain, illness, grief. In this his work resembles some of Philip Larkin's, despite great differences in other respects, and a corresponding likeness of temperament and outlook can be seen too, reflected in the congenial way they got on together. Both lived sociable lives with plenty to do and plenty of friends, and an abyss of hopelessness never far away, perhaps a little nearer in Philip's case.

John was cheerful enough, almost vivacious, the first time I saw him in the flesh, at the English Society in Oxford in 1941 or '42, talking about Tennyson. Half accustomed as I was even then and there to critical analysis, if not limiting judgements, I was first surprised, then delighted, to find him talking about *Tennyson* and what he was like as a man, how he behaved and misbehaved. John never wanted to talk about texts; even to an audience of one he would say no more than, 'You know, old Lionel Johnson's really quite *good*,' or, less often, 'Just got through the whole of old Lewis Morris. Nothing there, absolutely *nothing*.'

This kind of thing of course turned up later, actually quite a lot later when I got to know him in London in the Sixties, visiting him at his house in Cloth Fair in the City and finding him surrounded with young women, lunching at the Tate Gallery Restaurant, whose Dry Martinis he much admired ('I don't think one is really quite *enough*, do you?'), or the Charing Cross Station Hotel, a favourite haunt bedecked with copies of the poems and other Betjemaniana, going for drinks or drinks-and-dinner with him in Radnor Walk. He listened quite as much as he talked, his eyes, his whole attention, fixed on the speaker.

His habit of doing so brings up the difficulty of defining the Betjeman face. In the words of Philip Larkin, whose article 'It Could Only Happen In England' is the best account of the man and the work:

Above it [the face] the extraordinarily powerful skull, like a Roman bust. Impossible to characterise such features: the top half is authoritative, perhaps a famous headmaster, but lower down is the schoolboy, furtive, volatile, never entirely at ease.

Never? Well, not very often. John suffered chronically from embarrassment, though that may be putting it too strongly: I mean no more than first-degree embarrassment, social discomfort. I only once knew him to make any kind of counter-move, when at that hotel restaurant the head waiter launched into a long ingratiating monologue about the deep honour of a visit from 'Mr Betjeman' (who had been knighted a good couple of years before).* John retaliated with a simultaneous monologue of his own, most unflattering to the waiter, delivered sotto voce. So I put it, but whether intentionally or not it came out a good deal less sotto than I cared for, and although the victim's eyes did not quite flicker it was a nearish thing. I have heard from others that John was not always polite to his inferiors.

Embarrassment in its purest form radiated from him on the well-intentioned and somehow inevitable occasion when a score of assorted poets, each bearing a poem specially written for the event, descended on him at his house in Radnor Walk on his seventy-fifth birthday. They took him by surprise among the television cameras. Although he was not the only one afflicted with embarrassment that day, everything naturally passed off all right. I knew very well that he was saying to himself, among other things, 'So kindly meant' – like the hideous tie in 'Christmas'.

More discomfort was to be seen in John on other bits of TV, though only when there were other people about – he made an exception for Philip. As a solo performer he was, or seemed, 'entirely at ease', because he had only the camera to talk to, and *it* was not going to ask him how he rated Sylvia Plath or if he thought a poem was an exclusively verbal construct. Ah, but here I cannot resist adding that I once heard a young man on some panel say he thought something similar, to be buried for the rest of the programme under John's enthusiastic response, 'I say, I think that's *frightfully good.*'

Shy people probably enjoy company more than anyone else when the company really suits them. John was for small gatherings, old friends and a sufficiency of drink, such that a couple of bottles of wine would turn out not to be really quite *enough.* 'I *am* enjoying myself,' that great phrase of his at such times, was heartfelt. And there would be his famous laugh, sudden and total, beautifully caught by Jane Bown in her *Observer* photograph of 1972. One moment he would be listening closely, even seriously to whatever was being said, on the alert, not quite sure where things were going; and then, in a flash, the jaws sprang apart, the nose crinkled, the eyes disappeared and he was transformed, a different creature from the grave, slightly formidable-looking person of two seconds before.

*I have known even the most unassertive of knights to become huffy when they experience this solecism.

This too was spontaneous, so full of rejoicing as to obliterate as if for ever the sudden look of profound dejection that, even when all seemed at its best, it was possible to surprise on his face.

I cherish a portrayal of John as seen by my old friend Susan Allison, for many years his part-time secretary and, more lately, mine too. She describes how his statutory mid-morning half-bottle of champagne could be brought forward to eleven a.m. with the aid of an elaborate display of casualness on his part or deferred by her dangling the completion of another horrible couple of letters. He would dictate all of these straight into Susie's typewritten text, sending her a devious look when he came to a hard word, breaking off every so often to leaf through *Who's Who* or *Debrett* and read aloud 'the hobbies and habits of one or another usually eccentric, always indigent Irish peer, embellishing his reading with some scandalous titbit from memory or mischief.' I find it obscurely significant that he bought all his stamps in the Isle of Man.

At the end, John was finally incapacitated by Parkinson's Disease, and that incomparably expressive face became set into a mute unchanging mask. I went and read poems to him, some of them by his much-admired Newbolt, not 'Drake's Drum' but later pieces like 'The Nightjar'. His stare remained as blank as before but I know the words reached him.

CZECHS

IN 1966 I was invited by the Cultural Attaché of the Socialist Republic of Czechoslovakia here in London to visit that country. I had never done so before, but had so to speak nearly done so in 1948, having been twice interviewed for a post teaching English literature in Prague. In that year, newly married with a small child and another on the way, I would have accepted a post anywhere, even, as can be seen, in a country a thousand miles away that had suffered a Communist coup in the February of that year; how little we knew then, or cared. I have sometimes, but not often, wondered what would have happened to my life if we had gone to Prague instead of, as came along in the October, Swansea.

At first the invitation puzzled me. If I was known anywhere as anything political at all, it must have been as some sort of anti-Communist, certainly since 1956 and the Soviet invasion of Hungary, certainly not a grata kind of persona to the Czechs who had invited me. Then I realised, or was told, that of course to a Communist bureaucracy working at normal speed I was still an Angry Young Man, a malcontent like old John Osborne and the others, one who had been patted on the head in *Nový Mír* in Moscow as one 'yet to take the full step to full socialism, but whose works contain sharp criticism of bourgeois reality.' So I got a fellow from their Embassy to come and see me.

He was called Peter Pujman, I remember, not only a nasty little man but one of a type almost instantly recognisable to anybody who has had to deal with that sort of person, not only so much of a faux bonhomme that you thought at first he must be trying to be funny, but also an exuder of equally false, and clearly false, decency, reliability, and just the right amount of sympathy for Western ways. I, plus wife, was to be the guest of the Czech government for six days, during which I was to give one lecture and talk to a student or so. Nothing else. The rest of the time was to be spent seeing

267

whatever I wanted to see, said Pujman. Guides and an interpreter would of course be provided.

Now as to the lecture – what should be its theme? 'I was thinking perhaps . . .' I said.

'Yes?'

'Perhaps something like . . . "The Literature of Protest in Great Britain"?'

After a moment's pretended consideration, Pujman said enthusiastically, 'Is good subject.'

And so it was arranged. We entered Czechoslovakia by rail from West Germany. At the frontier, I watched unbelieving as a steam locomotive with a red star on its front chugged up out of a twenty-year-old Yugoslav movie and a squad of lesbians, in blue uniforms to match their chins, barged in to do the documentation, holding well back on the affability. At Prague station we were at once identified by our interpreter, a strikingly handsome man in his thirties called Karel who at other times lectured in English at the university. 'Welcome to Prague, Mr and Mrs Amis,' he said in excellent English; 'I will attend to your luggage, and when we reach the car, please remember I am not the policeman, the driver is the policeman.' He added that the driver affected not to understand English, but of course did so in fact.

It was quite a short drive through Prague, a city of something under a million inhabitants, remarkable for its splendid baroque churches, castles, old bridges, gardens, tanneries, breweries, chemical works and other industrial installations all jumbled up together, so that the architectural beauties, virtually undamaged by war, are (certainly then were) polluted by soot and fumes. The place, especially for instance in its public transport, has also the heaviest general concentration of body-odour I have ever come across. This is not, I think, because Prahans are particularly dirty, but because they have bourgeois tastes and prices are high, so you buy your ticket for the well-staged opera before you go on to the lousy dry-cleaner's. We were booked in at the Yalta Hotel, probably selected less for its comfort, though it was perfectly adequate,* than for the

---

*It showed no sign of the lavatory-paper shortage said to have afflicted Prague for twenty post-war years. (Before the war Czechoslovakia, with all those trees, was a major producer of paper, with sixty factories turning out the stuff.)

efficiency of its bugging. ('*Comparative* efficiency,' insisted some-body who was listening to this explanation.)

The next morning came the official welcome. On the way to it, Jane and I were struck by many attractions, but also by how drab the general effect was, defining drabness for the moment as absence of colour, of bright colour. We were stumped for why or how until my eye happened to be caught by a forlornly battered and dust-covered vertical row of faded green letters reading MARTINI. So what I was missing was all that vile garish corrupting advertising we never let up about when we, and even more the wicked Ameri-cans, go in for it! Shame filled me until a sense of proportion returned.

We reached a grand public building and were shown into a State apartment instantly recognisable as too imposing for the reception of a single non-governmental non-VIP and his wife. After a marked delay, a stout elderly lady entered with an aide or two. An unnatu-rally large visiting-card was laid in front of me, bearing a couple of names rich in consonants and diacritical marks. The English of the oral follow-up was not good, and it was only by degrees that I was able to place her nibs as a veteran Bolshevik who was probably Minister of Culture. (I should perhaps have made it clear earlier that the ruling dictator at the time was Antonín Novotny, predecessor of the 'liberal' Dubček.) As had already happened and was to happen often again, the sight of the lady gave me a feeling that the various players had been selected by a Hollywood casting director of the period or the one immediately before, rather unimaginative in taste. This was one of the old Red Guard and by Christ she looked and sounded it.

After it had been explained at some length that the room we were sitting in held some special historical significance, though neither of us understood exactly what, we signed some sort of visitors' book and were escorted out. Only later and after some digging did it emerge that the room must have been the one in which President Beneš received the British and French ambassadors in 1938, to be told he would have to give up the Sudetenland to Hitler. So Jane's and my intended mini-humiliation had been a flop. They never get *anything* right.

At intervals over the next days Karel showed us round the city. He was not in some ways my cup of tea, but he was a decent and serious man who uttered no word of complaint or apology and was going to make the best life he could in his city without coming to more than a minimal accommodation with the people who were running it. It disconcerted me to find how quickly one came to understand and take for granted how life worked here. (In the car) 'What building is that, Karel?' – 'One of no historical interest,' i.e. police barracks, etc. Subject at once dropped. (In the hotel, to a writer) 'Come up to our room for a drink.' – 'Thank you no, but the bar is all right.' And, somehow most repulsively: the three of us visited one of the castles, where behind the man giving out the tickets stood another, a living cliché in raincoat and trilby, who looked us expressionlessly up and down one after the other. Just that. When we had moved away, Antonin said to me, 'Did you see him?' with more bitterness and disgust than you can easily imagine going into four words and a glance. Yes, I had seen him.

At one point Karel said, 'Mr and Mrs Amis, I would like to show you the flat where I live. I think it would interest you to see the kind of living conditions experienced by a lecturer at Prague University.' He took us into an apartment building and, with an explanation that his wife was out working, into a room measuring about 25 feet by 20. Speaking this time with total impassivity throughout, he said, pointing to each corner in turn, 'That is the study, and this is the living-room where we are standing, and that is the bedroom, and that is the dining-room. Over here is the bathroom,' which actually contained a sitzbath, at the moment overflowing with books. 'And here is the kitchen,' a place about the size of an old-style British railway compartment, 'which is also my mother-in-law's bedroom,' and impossible for even three to have sat up to table; that must happen in the dining-room, if anywhere. Then at once, without mentioning children, sparing us the necessity of any comment, he repeated something about typical accommodation and led us off to our next appointment.

I have to hand it to Them that They let us meet a number of writers and let us talk to them unsupervised. Such talk was less of the state of Czech letters than of the idiosyncrasies of the régime and social detail of life in Prague. The most sought-after occupation is, or was then, that of taxi-driver, still granted, under some administrative anomaly, a measure of self-employment. The next best is that of driver of a confectionery delivery vehicle. You get your truck to the chocolate factory as soon as it opens, fill it up and park it outside a suitable pub, where you keep it till just before the relevant retail shop is due to shut. When not drinking in the pub, you have been mixing up together all the sweets of all prices. The retailer has no time to sort them out again and gives you a price above what you would get if he bought them grade by grade, willingly enough because the next day he will be selling everything at a price fixed above the average for the entire load. If you have a private car, and a reasonably well regarded novelist, say, would in those days have expected to command something small and unsmart but perfectly drivable, you will need a mechanic. A mechanic in a truly socialist society is not a mechanic, but a person who drives one of the many types of State vehicle. When you find that, say, a sparking-plug in your car has gone wrong, you seek out your mechanic, who swaps it for a part-worn one of similar type in another State vehicle, in as it might be the television company car-park, and charges you twice the price of a new one, a fair bargain with new ones unobtainable without an incalculable delay. From top to bottom, the socialist state is not just alleviated by corruption, it consists of corruption. And by the way, the ten-per-cent 'service' charge on restaurant bills and the like, which in capitalist times had stood some chance of reaching the employees, is still there, but as a mere managerial surcharge.

I have not forgotten about the lecture which had been the whole raison d'être of my visit to the city. Its structure and theme were simplicity itself, no more than pouring brief doses of contempt on a David Storey or a Michael Hastings or two and saying that a country like Great Britain gave them little of much substance to protest about. I fancy Colin Wilson came into it too, as he did into most things in those days. The British contingent just sat through it without showing what might have been unsporting signs of satisfaction. The three men in raincoats in the middle just sat. In a sort of muted, filtered way, the questions at the end were uniformly hostile to anything that could be associated with protest in the West. Most of the audience were doubtless young teachers of English. One such came up to me afterwards and, with the show of serious concern I was already starting to recognise as a local habit, said he had been interested to hear my less-than-high opinion of the plays of Arnold Wesker. 'In Prague,' he told me, 'they could not now be performed.'

I turned on the caution at once. 'Is there some . . . restriction?'

'No!' he shouted, almost screeched. He was a red-haired young man with eyes that seemed to bulge behind his glasses. 'Nobody would be fool enough to turn up to see them! They are too political! We can get all that at home!'

Nevertheless, the Czechs had published *Lucky Jim*, the first

Eastern Bloc country to do so, for a decent sum for the time, too, in three figures, and the only money ever to reach me from the other side. The sole exception was the £50 for their TV adaptation of it. I was far from being the first Englishman to feel a quick sympathy with the local form of straightfaced irony, handy for deflecting officialdom, and used to amuse myself with a private imitation of the conference selecting *Šťastný Jim* for TV adaptation: 'And how can such a show be justified ideologically, Comrade?' – 'For its portrayal of bourgeois philistinism, Comrade.' Hilarity was possible in that unhappy city; there was jazz; there were our friends Johnny Dankworth and Cleo Laine, coincidentally in town; there was an elaborate enactment by Dankworth and myself of Lord Halifax acknowledging the salute of a policeman that caused consternation among the waiters at the Yalta. Now and then I even regretted missing that job in 1948.

Not keenly. One of the novelists said, 'It is better here in Prague than anywhere else behind the Curtain; it is better now than at any time since the coup – and look at it!', which was very Czech and very ironical and less than half funny. It was not funny at all to be told by the young British attaché that three years was going to be enough for him, three years of being able to talk freely with his wife only on Sunday afternoons, when they walked in the park. The last irony of all was when the outward train stopped at what turned out to be the first station across the frontier, and the name I read, with relief, was Nuremberg.

They had given us what gifts they had that we would have wanted, including a jazz record that I still cherish – Dixieland, mainstream, Sixties, what you will, a band that included a trumpeter no other non-American known to me has surpassed. To hear him and his friends letting go with *Rag Javorové ho Listu ho Ustu* ('Maple Leaf Rag') or *Kdybych Mohl Být s Tebou* ('If I Could Be with You') gives a pleasure that for me could never possibly be purely musical, nor purely pleasure. Though I can tell that they are very good.

That is the proper end to this piece, but I cannot resist adding a coda featuring the first and only Czech writer I feel I dare name, Josef Škvorecký, who is safely out, not only out but deprived of his Czech citizenship and now a Canadian citizen instead, sitting prosperously in Montreal, novelist and publisher too, among much else publisher *in Czech* (there are a lot of Czechs in Montreal) of Martina Navratilova's memoirs – 'one-third tennis,' he imparted to me when we lunched in London, 'one-third girlfriends and one-

272

third attacks on Russia – what could be better?' He also told me the following story which brings my own information up to date, or near enough, indeed it needs telling more now than ever.

I have said that Josef was deprived of his Czech citizenship, having displeased the régime in various ways. At some later stage, his half-sister applied to join him in Canada. Although they had never been particularly close, she was an old woman otherwise alone in the world, having nursed through a long illness her late husband, who had been a good Communist, such a good Communist, added Josef, that he had kept his job when Dubček got the boot. Needless to say she was unversed in nuclear physics or anything else of interest to the West. Her application was turned down in Prague. Why? Partly to remind Josef through his half-sister that he was still an enemy of the Czech State, partly just to show her.

'It's worth remembering, Kingsley,' said Josef, 'that it's not just awkward, noisy fellows like me they'll persecute, but also ordinary, loyal, deserving, totally unimportant little people like my half-sister. Anybody. Everybody. Why not?'

There is not just one or half a dozen but a thousand things that must never be allowed to happen again, and we must make sure of them all.

ANTHONY BURGESS

I HAD READ a couple of Anthony Burgess's early novels before I met him in the mid-1960s: *A Clockwork Orange* and *The Wanting Seed*, both published in 1962 – the dating shows the frightening fecundity that has remained a feature of his career. Both, especially the first, struck me as highly successful works of science fiction, imaginative and inventive excursions into the future, based, in the best traditional style, on visible features of contemporary society, youth violence and over-population respectively. Both, especially the first, made effective and funny use of plays on language: 'bolshy great yarblockos to you' as a piece of plausibly russified teenage cursing, and 'It's Sapiens to be Homo' as a government contraceptive slogan stick in my mind without having to be looked up. I apologise for all this literary talk, but my relationship with the author, such as it has been, has been more to do with books than most of such, as will appear.

When I met John Burgess Wilson (the Anthony, he writes in his autobiography, was added at his confirmation) it was natural to call him John, as his wife did. Nothing could be more characteristic of him than that there should be some sort of linguistic crux about his name, nor that he should go on to write that 'Anthony Burgess' shows 'the carapace of my nominal shrimp, the head and tail I pull off to disclose the soft edible body' – God knows what that last phrase refers to. Anyway, 'John' he was and is to me, though it was not long before I heard cultural climbers referring to old Tony Burgess.

Attempts were made to set up a friendship. I was attracted by John's air of independence, of being completely his own man, above the literary or any other arena (I was not to know then that this went with a deep inner solitariness, as his huge output might suggest) and by the gleams of humour that lit up his air of slight solemnity. He took my wife and me to lunch with his wife Lynne at the Café

Royal, the latter lady being a bit pissed and rather spoiling an occasion he had clearly wanted very much to be a success. I invited him and her to a drinks party at my house in Maida Vale. She was pissed again.

'John, there's a horrible man in that conservatory being horrible about you. You ought to go out there and bash him.'

'No no, darling, it's only old Terry [Kilmartin], only old Terry. He means no harm at all.'

'But you've got to stop him saying . . .'

I moved off. Later, when most of the other guests had left, John was fussing about the non-appearance of his driver. He brought out the word in such a way as to lead me to expect the eventual arrival of a fellow in gaiters, peaked cap, etc., but it was only a hairy sod in jeans out of a minicab who finally rang the doorbell. Perhaps it was raining; anyway I invited him indoors.

'Would you like a drink?' I asked him drunkenly.

From where he was standing Mrs Burgess could be seen accepting her second drink in a couple of minutes from the drunken hired butler. 'No thank you, guv,' said the driver; then, after a second, closer look, he made me feel as if the two of us were taking part in some black-and-white comedy film by saying, 'Could I change my mind? I'll have a small brandy if I may.'*

John took me to a pub one time, a grim barrack-like place in some unglamorous purlieu like Kilburn or Hammersmith. It was possibly the first time we had been alone together for more than a couple of minutes and he proved, though amiable enough, to have little in the way of small-talk. It was as though he was so far above the hurly-burly that he habitually occupied some private strato-sphere. But he did tell me something about his wife's rape by some GIs during the war, and went on to say that he was on the look-out for a sword-stick – he had with him a stout but conventional walking-stick – from which if ever menaced by ruffians he would draw and brandish the blade, shouting (and he shouted in illustration), 'Fuck off, I've got cancer!' Yes, I thought uneasily, seeing the look in his eye, you bloody mean it.

It cannot have been long after this that John left England more or less for good, moving about a bit at first, settling for some time in Monaco, now I believe Switzerland. But he was in London in

*A version of this incident comes near the end of chapter 15 of my novel *Difficulties with Girls*.

1968, as by coincidence were a number of Czech writers in flight from the Russian invader. I asked him and his new wife, Lynne having died, to a modest lunch I was throwing for some of these writers. I had next to me a pleasant fellow called Igor Hayek, the editor, or ex-editor, of a literary magazine whom I had met on my 1966 visit to Prague. He asked me apologetically if I could give him any help in finding 'the obvious thing', a small place to stay that should be not too expensive and not too far from the centre. I said I would get my wife, who was good at that kind of stuff, to have a go. When the time came to make our farewells I said to Hayek, to show I had not forgotten his request, 'Right, Igor, I understand your problem.'

'What-a do you mean-a,' said Mrs Burgess (name of Liliana or Liana) with a strong Italian accent, not unexpected in an Italian, 'you understand his-a problem?' and went on to ballock me (from a left-wing point of view) for presuming to claim I understood the problem facing a Czech Communist or Marxist or whatever whose country had been occupied by the USSR.

'No no, darling, Kingsley only meant he understood Igor's problem about finding accommodation.'

Etc. Well, I thought to myself, people do go *on* about men, some men, marrying the same woman over again. Then I thought that that was reading too much into it. He, not I, was the one to see significance in the similarity of names, Lynne – Liana.

Over the years, starting with *Tremor of Intent* in 1966, I went on not being able to read John's novels – too much wordage, word-play, wordiness and not enough character, story, etc., to suit me. In fact the severance in what we had had in the way of a friendship could be traced to my failure to write to him when he sent me an inscribed copy of *Tremor*; I could neither have said I had liked it, nor, surely, could I have opted for any of the bullshitty alternatives about looking forward to reading it when. I naturally avoided reviewing it or its successors. Over these same years John reviewed either all or nearly all my novels, every time in the most glowing terms. Naturally I was delighted, but proportionately embarrassed. I did make an exception by reviewing his *1985* when it came out in 1978, but with all the will in the world could not be much more than lukewarm about it.

Then in 1987 there appeared *Little Wilson and Big God*, the first volume of John's autobiography. This I asked to review with some confidence, out of a kind of conviction, which I still hold to, that autobiographies are not really serious in the way novels are. There were sure to be good bits which I could praise extravagantly, and to call the book outstanding in its genre would be all right, would not offend the Muse. I found I had been right about the good bits, but there were also bits I found I had to quarrel with, such as those about music (a large part of John's life and, it seems, of his output too). Handel and Schumann were all very well, for instance, but they 'were saying nothing about the modern world'; it took Stravinsky, Schoenberg, Hindemith to do that. So? Then came Joyce, the writer who had shown how to produce in prose an equivalent of the complexities of a modern composer's score. And, John might have added, the introvert with the size of talent to inspire other introverts, or one at least.

The next and most recent time I met John in the flesh was later that year at the Book Fair in Olympia where I and many others were signing copies of our works. He appeared at my side with some suddenness and instantly said, 'Hallo Kingsley, I was sorry you couldn't find something a little kinder to say about my autobiography when you reviewed it. After all I have been extremely kind about your novels in the past, you must admit.' I admitted it, tried to apologise, babbled away, taken aback not so much by what he had said as by the instantaneousness with which he had got round to saying it – not even a token stab at the 'My God, it's been a long time' (like nineteen years) kind of thing one might perhaps have expected. After a couple of minutes, during which nothing of consequence passed, he said, 'Oh, and by the way, I'm certain I'm right about servicemen taking MBE as standing for My Bloody Effort,' not My Bum's Everybody's as I had – certain now as then that *I* was right – put at the end of my piece in a well-meant effort to lighten it up. End of conversation. Exit.

And then he was as nice as ever, as nice as pie, about my next novel, published in the following year.

A few weeks ago as I write this I saw John on the Terry Wogan show. Part of the reason he was there arose from the then forthcoming stage version of *A Clockwork Orange*, updated to the year 2004, at the Barbican Theatre. He said, as he had before, that the phrase enshrined in the title came from an old cockney expression,* 'queer [i.e. odd] as a clockwork orange', and added with

*Unknown to me, a Londoner (John is a Mancunian), and unrecorded in Eric Partridge's monumental (1065 pp.) *Dictionary of Historical Slang*.

characteristic characteristicness that 'oran' was Malay for 'man', so his title could alternatively be taken to mean 'mechanical man' and refer to what his hero, Alex, was finally turned into. I would say from a position of utter detachment that to love language is one thing, to be infatuated or obsessed with it another. But none of us can do anything but write as we must.

In his autobiography John remarks touchingly – of his army service, but with a wider application – that he was never one of the boys. For my own sake I am sorry to think that.

USA 2

I HAD ENJOYED my first trip to America in 1958-59 so much that, when a second chance came along eight years later, I failed to do what I soon discovered I should have done and drop it like a hot potato. While at Princeton I had grown friendly with a New Yorker called Russell Fraser, a professor of English who at some stage in the late Sixties had become head of the English Department at Vanderbilt University at Nashville, Tennessee, an institution known, unironically I suppose to some, as the Athens of the South. Russ now wrote to invite me to teach modern British writing there as a visiting professor under his auspices.

I set about devising the shortest possible polite refusal. What, visit the home of lynchings and all that, of a particular sort of horrible popular music (though I may be a little misled by hindsight here), and of all those Southern writers, starting with Truman Capote? Then I noticed that the invitation was only for a semester or half-year, a period of something over four months from October to mid-January, and that the teaching load did not look heavy. Russ, a reliable fellow, affirmed too that the place in general was not like what they said and, more cunningly and tellingly, that no English-man was ever seen in those parts. I was soon won round by the thought of a comparatively remote, still quite romantic-sounding part of America unpolluted by the kind of Brit they think you must be pining to see but actually loathe and dread. Off I went, with a different wife this time, just the two of us, in the old *Queen Mary* on what I fancy was her last transatlantic voyage.

Arrival in New York was a quicker business than before, and instead of tipping the porters for shifting your luggage it was more a matter of paying them to get it back off them. I spent two days at the famed Algonquin Hotel with a stiff neck, one of those comic ailments like lumbago and gout that is deeply unfunny to its suf-ferers. Now and then I tried to talk to Fred Pohl, Robert Sheckley and other distinguished science-fiction writers. Thence for a few days in Princeton, where the friends I had made those years before proved not to have abated their drinking-rate in the least. The ones we stayed with had moved to a pretty little newly built house that had a delightful, copious stream or rill chuckling and purling through its grounds. Asking where it rose, I was told that this took place in the air-conditioning unit of the gigantic supermarket recently constructed off the main square. That's the old America. You wouldn't get such imaginative energy today.

Travel by train, except either locally or across most of the continent, proved difficult, pestered by doglegs and zigzags. The trip from Trenton, N. J. (the State capital) to Nashville involved a stopover at St Louis, where I thought with due reverence upon Louis Armstrong, Bessie Smith and other luminaries, but missed the famous arch, and forgot all about T. S. Eliot until we were clattering south again. In those days the trains themselves were fine. The trick was to find one that would put you down at a junction that had a redcap, not a military policeman but a porter, to hump your luggage. They were as rare as water-diviners, though probably no less helpful. Anyway we got there, not knowing that at some point we had crossed a frontier from old to new.

Russ's wife Phil met us at the station and drove us off at speed into, well, into a very lifelike version of what you see every time you put the TV on and are shown a main street in a standard US town put up or redone since I don't know when – 1950? I can spot no real differences between what I saw there the other night and what I saw in reality in 1967. To evoke it you need not a description but a list, or the mere start of a list, and one that everybody knows. Start where you like, with hamburger joint or gas station, you get through all the ones that matter soon enough. That list has been compiled by a thousand more energetic pens than mine, though in a case here and there they may have left out all those horrible towering silver-grey poles and the brilliantly offensivised greens, reds and yellows and *nobody on foot*.

But this sketch is not about any of that, nor the Grand Ole Op'ry where I never went (*me?*), nor the Parthenon that unlike the one in Athens, Greece, has a roof on it, nor the roadside Holy Family that changes colour all the time, so that with an unusual dose of luck you may see the green Holy Family as you approach, the purple Holy Family as you pass and the yellow Holy Family as you leave it behind. We have been there, all of there, before.

One sociological note I will contribute because it now belongs to history is the State ban on liquor by the drink, as it was rather mysteriously called. A dying Bible-Belt flicker meant that you could buy as much booze as you could pay for from sundry well-stocked liquor stores, but not to drink then and there. Before you took off the seal, you had to be on private premises, or in a public bar or restaurant licensed to let you drink in it but not to sell you the stuff. So you took your bottle of gin and your bottle of vermouth along to a place called a bar. Here they would sell you set-ups, in other words provide you with ice, a glass, an olive or twist of lemon-peel, a spoon, a chair, a table, all that, and leave you to it, though how drunk you were allowed to get I never discovered. Habitués were permitted to keep their bottles in the bar. The same rules applied to restaurants, of which there seemed to be only two (in a town of nearly half a million), one providing bad, the other very bad food and service, but united in accepting no bookings. There were bars where you could drink glasses of gnat's-piss beer to your heart's content.

Not only in its user-unfriendliness but in its elaborate quasi-logic, this seemed to me a thoroughly unAmerican arrangement. I would have expected it more of the British Army or some municipal body in Wales. Towards the end of our stay, but not I think on that account, it was revoked and normal procedures instituted. This seemed to bring no attendant changes.

I will add a meteorological note, because it will not be in the lists and because its content got us down as much as anything else about the place, which is saying a – but I will not anticipate. Always one to look things up, I had noted that Nashville was on the latitude of Tangiers and Crete, giving me expectations of brilliant sunshine for some, perhaps a good deal, of the time we were going to be there. What we got was a lot of hot sun certainly, but well offset by smog and humidity. It was odd to walk at a reasonable pace under a sky and in a light comparable with those of a slightly hazy English June and find oneself pouring with sweat. It was odd to walk there anyway, as I found the time I walked, the only pedestrian, along a couple of hundred yards of pavement at ten in the morning, and found a prowl car keeping pace with me in old-movie style.

It was, I think, during our second conversation by ourselves that Russ let fall that, contrary to what he had told me in his letter, but not to my surprise, Nashville was rather like what they said after all, though there were good bits if you knew where to look for them.

281

The good bits I found were Russ and his family (whom I had, so to speak, found already), a lecturer in German called Dick Porter and his wife Brigitte, born in the Federal Republic, quite a few of the students, Seagram's gin, the squirrels that leapt about the trees surrounding the house we had taken, and a chipmunk we persuaded to come to the windowsill for a saucer of milk in the evenings. Poor Russ himself found one of the worst bits of the lot in being nearly thrown out of his department over some administrative matter in circumstances not to be gone into here.

Like what they had said . . . Well, after twelve years in the business – in Swansea, Princeton and Cambridge – I still thought that inside the portals of the university it would not be like that; the values of the society outside, which certainly sounded deficient, would be ignored. I can no longer remember what first showed me the reality, but those very portals made a good start.

On them it stated that Commodore Cornelius Vanderbilt (1794–1877) had endowed this institution with the object of 'strengthening the ties that should exist between all parts of this our nation'. I read this as we drove in for the first time and have often thought it over since, without ever making out much more than that there were some guys who wanted ties strengthening, and other guys who were not sure there should be any ties at all.

Anyway, it set up an uneasiness in me, which sharpened a little when I asked somebody if there were any – I think I said 'coloured' – students in the university.

'Oh, certainly. He's called Mr Moore.' (This was and is not a joke.)

'How's he, er, getting on?'

'Well, funny thing, when he first came here a couple of years ago he seemed to enjoy it, but now, he doesn't seem to like it so well.'

From there I can cut straight to a dinner party at the house of a professor of English, the very man, in fact, Walter Sullivan by name, author of several novels, whose place I was in a sense taking during a period of his leave. From Princeton, from all other American universities I knew of, a professor on leave was in Tokyo, Lima, Sydney, London, Bodrun, Naples, where you will, by the first available aeroplane. Walter's sabbatical trip had been all of twenty miles cross-State to where he lived the rest of the year, there to continue work on his current novel or piece of academic shit or, for all I knew, to shoot bears.

At first, as ever, all was well. Drink, conversation and cordiality flowed, with one or two not ungraceful compliments to my homeland thrown in, the Old Country from which so many of those around me ultimately derived. (As my stay in Nashville wore on, I began wishing more and more ardently that a few more Albanians or Irish or Dyaks had had their share of responsibility for what I saw about me.) The food was good and ample, but I have forgotten if there was any wine. Then, at about the stage of the second highball after dinner, as always, we got on to the staple subject. They, or some of them, started making remarks about the mental, moral, social qualities of black people that it would probably be illegal to print here and I would shrink anyway from putting on the page.

It is worth trying to get straight the kind of remarks that were made and the kind of tone they were made in. Individually they were often mild, no more than patronising, with points awarded for supposed black virtues of loyalty, obedience and so on and disapproval expressed of attempts to advance the black beyond his station. (The very familiarity of a lot of this made it the more disagreeable.) Some indeed were damned if they were going to see any more steps, or any steps, taken in that direction. With the couple of exceptions just mentioned, I never sensed, let alone heard, any disagreement from the consensus of irremediable and universal black inferiority, perhaps to be alleviated here and there but never altered, and the important thing was keeping 'em down. And Walter and his mates went on about it all the time. So much for illusions about those old academic portals, inside which half of those present belonged. Not that being outside those portals would have excused anything much.

Walter himself summed it up. (Remember he was a university teacher.) Whenever I tell this story, as I frequently do, I give him a Dixie chawbacon accent to make him sound even more horrible, but in fact he talked ordinary cultivated American-English with a rather attractive Southern lilt. Anyway, his words were (verbatim), 'I can't find it in my heart to give a negro [pron. nigra] or a Jew an A.'

There was a short and curious silence, which I almost broke by dropping in a sociable laugh and saying, 'You do it marvellously, Walter – for a moment there I thought you really . . .'

The others were not saying that. They were saying it was real good to hear that said, time people faced facts, they wouldn't stand for being pushed any further, *thank you* for saying that, Walter. The feeling in the air was reverential as well as tough, loyal, united, etc., rather as if an Englishman among friends had said he thought we hadn't made such a bad shot at running the jolly old Empire after all.

What should I have done when Walter and his mates said things like the one quoted? Burst out into real laughter? Tried to lead them along the path of reason? Had a fist-fight? Had an argument shortly leading to a fist-fight? Walked out? Every time, every night? Never gone out again? For four months? Resigned? For what I heard people say when I wasn't working? What I did do was what almost everybody else would have done: kept my mouth shut, avoided assenting to what could not be assented to and made the most of the good bits, human and other. And, of course, had the notebook at the ready. John O'Sullivan has described how the loony liberal utterances he was always coming across in Washington, New York and various universities constantly visited him with the fear that he was on 'Candid Camera'; I had the same thing the other way round.

There was in Nashville, not I think associated with the university, a body called something like the Institute of International Relations, designed to meet the needs of the four or five people in the city who could show some sort of interest in places like Venice, Hungary, Philadelphia, Easter Island, London and other exotic locations. As a visitant from the great world outside I was invited to one of its dinners, in fact one with a special interest for me because the guest speaker was another person from the United Kingdom (made to sound like the United Arab Emirates' next-door neighbour). During the pre-meal drinks – never any trouble there – a small ugly man who looked like, and by now I am pretty sure was, though he need not have been, a senior truck-driver in his best suit was produced and at once said,

'You from England?'

'Yes.'

'Boy, you-all got yourselves a real packet of trouble there.'

This line calls for a footnote of Shakespearean length. Harold Wilson was our prime minister at the time and George Brown foreign secretary, and it crossed my mind that a general attack on the British government might be on the way, arousing a difficult question of loyalties. Forget it. The point of real and great interest was of course that of you-all, pronounced yawl by yobboes of this stripe. Every native said it. Even Dick Porter, as civilised and unaffected a man as I have ever met, used to kick off a conversation with 'How you-all bin?' It took getting used to. The children naturally said it, those children now in their thirties. Do they still? You bet they do. Only possible in serious talk if you switch off the outside world. And that condition applies. Not important, but more interesting than just a local mannerism.

Anyway – 'What were you thinking of?' I asked.

'I mean all these coloured people yawl letting in.'

'Well, we're not letting them in quite as –'

'But yawl letting 'em *in*,' he said, making a wondrous polyphthong of the adverb.

'Well, there were these agreements –'

'D'you know' – and it was here that I started getting worried about the Candid Camera cameras – 'there are machines that measure the human brain?'

'Really?' I said, trying to think, looking for help.

'And according to the most scientific tests that can be devised, the brain of a black man is smaller than the brain of a white man?'

'I have heard that said.' I spoke as coldly as I could.

This he took for agreement with his thesis. 'Sure, everybody knows it. So have yawl gone mad in England, letting all these coloured people in?'

Yes, I know that then I really should have walked out, but at that moment the chairman-figure called, 'Would you-all kindly take your places for dinner?' and the tension was broken. And well, I wanted something to eat, though admittedly not as much as something to drink. But I had the presence of mind to call after the savage before he disappeared, 'Excuse me, but what line of work are you in?'

'I'm in labour relations.'

I took that at the time for a great ha-ha, but that was before I found out that, at that place and time, black people were not allowed to join most trade unions, so my yawl specialist was as round a peg as ever plopped into a round hole.

The speaker was a Labour MP called Ivor Richard, whom I had met before, on what I took to be a kind of ill-will tour. His line was that the British were becoming much more interested in Europe and much less in America, so any special relationship there might ever have been was going or gone. When he had finished, the chairman turned to me and said, 'We have *another* gentleman from Britain with us tonight,' displaying the modest pride of a provincial zoo official who reveals its possession of not one but *two* Arabian oryxes. Would I like to say a few words?

I spoke briefly to the effect that Richard's view was all balls and the British for their part were as firmly attached to America and Americans as ever, not at all the good-riddance message I might have been tempted to deliver any time in the previous weeks, especially fresh from a dose of the black-man's-brain expert. Evidently my pro-Americanism was too powerful for even Nashville to shift. Or my common sense. Richard bore me no malice and we got satisfactorily drunk afterwards.

Some Southern encounters were quite funny. There was a do at the house of the Professor of Iberian Languages. Of my host I remember nothing, of my hostess among other things that she had the biggest pair of knockers I had ever seen in the flesh and still unequalled. When you stood at an ordinary conversational distance from her, you found you were standing too close to her. I know it sounds puzzling.

'Did you happen to see,' she said in her no more than averagely unbelievable tones, 'the movie Surr Laurence Oh-livyay made of Shakespeare's *Oh-thello*?' – lately shown in the States. (There are times – yawl is another – when you have to relax your rule against speech-spelling.)

'Yes,' I said, fighting for concentration on more than one front.

'And what did you think of it? – I don't mean so much the movie itself, I mean *him*.'

'Well . . . I thought he was very good.'

'You mean the way they made him up to look?'

'Well, yes, that too.' There was by now general silence. In my mind's or memory's eye a hundred Western barkeeps reached for the shotgun.

'But they made him look like a black mayun!'

'Yes, they did, didn't they?'

'But he even toked like a black mayun!'

'Yes, perhaps a bit –'

'But he even *woked* like a black mayun!'

'Yes,' I said, lying in a good cause, 'I thought that was the most brilliant part of his whole performance.'

They had not allowed for anything like that, which went down like the appearance of a US marshal. Only Mrs Iberian Languages said in melancholy defiance, 'But how could a real lady fall in love with a man like that?', thus reviving Thomas Rymer's objections to the fable of *Othello* as set out in *A Short View of Tragedy* (1692) in a way he could not have foreseen. I shirked the task of explaining about him and the conversation moved away from black men, as I recall for the best part of an hour or more. I would lay out a dollar or two to hear what Knockers and her pals, not to speak of their husbands, had to say about the black actor Willard White's appearance as the Moor at Stratford-on-Avon in 1989.

This makes a slot for a point that should have come up before. However many times it may have been asserted and disbelieved, and whatever you say about it, the Southern white had not then lost (has he lost it now, twenty years later?) his sense of being sexually threatened by the black male. I heard it or a whisper of it or a mere echo, saw it in a glance or a nod of the head, mistakenly fancied its presence I dare say a hundred times for every time it came out fully formed: *Can't you see it's our women they after?* There seems little chance of saying anything useful on the point after all these years, except perhaps to insist to some sceptics who have not encountered it that it is real, not a metaphor, not a figure of speech, not an interpretation. And has anybody thought to ask the women how they feel about it? I might add that there are few things to beat the discomfort of sensing its presence and its possible expression the next moment.

I was never at all clear just what it was in practice these people so much feared, or at any rate disliked the thought of, nor did I feel up to questioning any of them. An attempted individual or mass rape? Surely they would have rather enjoyed dealing with that. Could they have imagined that 'their women' all secretly preferred the thought of a nigra, and would have gone off with one if other things had been equal? What would a man's life (or his wife's) be like if he went round with that in his head? No, they merely felt menaced and insecure, and if sex gets a chance of entering such feelings it will, and, as is common in all human affairs, a fear is rendered the more oppressive by being vague and elusive. They just didn't care for the way they sometimes saw a black man look at a white girl, or fancied they did. But the violence of their emotional reaction remains interesting (I hope I am using that word appropriately for once) long after the crap about *them* having bigger ones than ours has fallen out of mind.

After the *Othello* party I had a severe hangover. I say this with such confidence through no feat of memory, but because I always started the day at Vanderbilt with one. You had to, to have got through the day before. I don't drive, thus evading more than one reason for my possible violent death at Nashville, getting out of our car (with wife at the wheel) some yards inside the good Commodore's portals. This, the getting out, invariably caused me an audible and painful shock as I earthed the static electricity my clothes had picked up from the plastic upholstery. Waiting for me here was a graduate student called Don Schultz, officially known as my reader, actually my guide and general helper, dough-faced and inept but willing and efficient enough. Greetings and information, if any, were exchanged. Then I walked through hot polluted sunshine to the lecture theatre and faced the class.

This regular event, which with questions went on for over an hour, made up the most consistently bearable part of my Vanderbilt stint. The class was about the best I have ever taught: punctual, polite, attentive, ready but not overready with questions and objections, containing that ingredient essential for a decent course of lectures, however much the lecturer may squirm at its presence: a couple of students of whom he is very slightly afraid. The subject was The Modern British Novel, of whose exposition I will say no more than that it was much what you might have expected from somebody in my position in 1967.

At the end of the course I took a vote, asked the students to put the novels we had read in their order of preference, not of their notions of importance or value but of liking, enjoyment. The clear winner was *Decline and Fall*, by Evelyn Waugh. I remembered that I had taught a course on similar lines in Swansea in 1959-60, and that *Decline and Fall* had come top then too. This no doubt says something about my own preferences, but I think it says more about the book. One group of mainly lower-middle-class provincial youngsters, and another lot from four thousand miles away of whom not more than a handful could ever have been outside their home State, had appreciated it. And it had been written before any of them could have been born.

After the lecture it was home nine times out of ten, and a large Dry Martini at least as often. Then to prepare tomorrow's lecture, and not just bloody notes either – your script is your lifebelt if nothing else. During this part the mailman would come, often bearing the *Daily Telegraph*. I used to feel very colonial fetching this in from the box, like a Maugham rubber-planter picking up his copy of the *Penang Times*. I also felt frightened, as Major, the huge snarling mastiff-type dog who lived next door, tried to get over his little gate and come and tear my guts out. It was a fraction of an inch too high for him, but every day he thought that *today* he was just going to be able to manage it. So did I, and very much needed the ensuing Martini.

So then more drinking, more working, even some TV – and if American TV has become better than British TV it must have taken some gigantic strides. An occasional sharp pop sounded as one of Ivar-Lou's jars of pickles or preserves exploded in the cellar-basement. I once explored this dark, low-ceilinged place, in which the network of shelving and ranks of various food-containers helped to reduce visibility, and found there enough decaying provisions to have supported, once upon a time, a full platoon of Confederate troops for some days before they died of various toxins.

Ivar-Lou, the Scandinavian-American lady who rented us the house, was of parsimonious bent. She had tried to charge me for using her husband's typewriter, a measure he vetoed. I only met her once, for the necessary exchanges, but was reminded of her appearance as often as I liked by a large, dreadful portrait of her in oils that dominated one end of the living-room. I have forgotten why I never took it down, but I never did. It was not exactly the way the paint had been put on the canvas, nor so much what was portrayed there, but the . . . All I can say is that if, as I now and then fancy in my own case, you think you don't greatly care about art, pictorial art, a few minutes looking at that picture of Ivar-Lou Duncan will persuade you that you care a very great deal.

Major came into my life again, and as before, every time I had to haul logs from their shelter in the yard into the house. He was no learner, that dog. As the autumn evenings settled in, the deficiencies in the central heating of the building became apparent. The living-room was really comfortably warm only with all the radiators on and the fire going. But the logs were so damp that they had to be part-dried off by being laid along the radiators, and then made hot enough for combustion by an hour or more in the grate, so that it was really only the top log of all, just under the chimney, that could really be said to be *burning*. Among faint wreaths of smoke, and to the accompaniment of a continuous, less faint hissing sound as the damp boiled off, I sat drinking large Dry Martinis, telling myself I really would do something about finding a source of dry logs in the morning, and sneering at the local TV. About two evenings out of three, the chipmunk turned up for his milk.

If I have somehow given the impression that, dealings with students apart, I found pleasant more than a few minutes here and there, or a very few longer periods, of the time I spent in Nashville, I have signally failed in my intentions. In fact to remove any lingering doubt I would put it (that period) second only to my army service as the one in my life I would least soon relive. Of those students I will single out one. She was called Julie Smith and she was then, I suppose, nineteen or twenty years old. It is not relevant that she was one of the most beautiful girls I have ever seen, this in a place as rightly famous for female beauty as it once was for roast 'possum and bull-whipping yourself a coon. In fact if things had been different, things might have been different. Along with her looks and splendid carriage, she was intelligent, conscientious, interested, inquiring, all one asks for from a good student. She did not need the kind of support her parents gave her by taking Jane and me out to dinner, and did not hide all her embarrassment at the occasion.

The party at the sorority house promised far better. There is a lot that is too obvious to need saying for being the only man in a large roomful of young women. But a sorority house is a dry house, or this one was. The organisers, who I think included Julie, somehow felt I would not give of my best in such a house. With characteristic tact and intelligence glass jugs of drink were produced, most of them containing one cola or another, but a couple Pimm's No. 1, which it resembles to the eye. They were jugs of respectable size.

All seemed well, with Julie and Jane across the room having quite a chat. Then it, the chat, took an apparent turn for the worse. I assured myself that this time the issue could not be to my detriment. Then afterwards, after a good party of its unusual kind, I said to Jane,

'Jolly nice girl, that pretty one you were talking to.'

'Julie something? She's certainly very pretty, with lovely manners. In fact I thought at first she wasn't like the others.'

My spirits sank a little. 'You don't mean about colour?'

'Yes. She seemed so sympathetic and open . . . I said I'd noticed from the newspapers here that there seemed to be a lot of trouble with coloured people in the Northern States, whereas in these parts one never seemed to come across anything like that. And before I could ask why, she'd given a sort of chuckle and a wink and said that up there they didn't know how to keep 'em down. And I'd thought she was so nice.'

Me too. Keep 'em down. That was where they were to be kept. In that tiny reported remark I found and have never lost a not-so-tiny disappointment. I realised that just as inside those portals it was not like what they said, so without conscious thought I had fancied the youngsters would have got over all that crap. Russ, Phil, Jane and I were in our mid-forties; Walter himself (who, I forgot to say, had like many of his neighbours thrown a party when Kennedy was shot) and the other Walters half a dozen or more years older; the people actually at the top coming in sight of the particular compartment of the dustbin of history where they belonged. If Julie thought like her parents or grandparents, how long was it going to take before people forgot about keeping 'em down? I still remember the instant in the supermarket when I saw real fear flash in the eye of a black mother when she snatched her harmlessly wandering toddler out of the path of what looked to me like a placid, indeed unaware Southern matron. I am not quite sure what you say about that sort of thing, except that the place would not be really all right till it would or could never happen, and that might take a long time. Perhaps Julie's children are free of it.

Plenty of troubles elsewhere, sure, and it is patchy, like everything in America. In A-town they had to get the National Guard in to enforce the desegregation of schools; in B-town, twenty miles down the road and no different to drive through or eat a hot-dog in, it got past on the first morning. Nashville itself, or a lot of it, is probably fine now, but I won't be back.

We made a few trips, one to a gorgeous place called Standing Stone State Park where you lead a brief pseudo-log-cabin existence among stunning wild scenery (a version of it appears in my novel, *I Want It Now*, under the name of Old Boulder State Park) – the air was supremely clear. It took some imagining to see it must all have been like that once. On another occasion Russ and Phil took us across the State border into Kentucky, into Bourbon County no less, where I drank a certain amount of fine old corn whiskey and felt very authentic, like a pundit supping cognac in Cognac, and followed up with some moonshine, not very much really, after which I fell asleep for two or three hours. Our host, a quietly genial fellow in his fifties, committed suicide the following week for no reason I ever heard.

Russ's and my furthest expedition took us to the southern part of the State, to Lynchburg, Tenn. I am nearly sure I once heard Walter explain that this was the 'wrong' Lynchburg, understanding by the 'right' Lynchburg probably the one in Virginia, from which the famous mode of applying justice took its name, but the origin of that mode is so fiercely contested that the issue is uncertain. The Lynchburg Russ and I visited is beyond question the seat of the distillery of Jack Daniel's Sour Mash whiskey – correctly labelled a Tennessee whiskey, not being made in the state of Kentucky, let alone Bourbon County, though the styles are similar.

Lynchburg, this Lynchburg, turned out to be a pitiful hamlet of barely three hundred souls existing for little but to make whiskey. We, some dozens of us, were taken round the place at a fair clip and amid a tremendous din, part of the latter being, it was easy to see, a way of getting back at Whitey. But then two important people like college professors were obviously going to get heavily entertained for lunch in the boardroom and filled up with the fifty-year-old, weren't we? No, we were taken to Madame Bobo's Boarding House (I swear), a place that set you thinking unwillingly of the earthier works of William Faulkner, and given cold meats washed down with cold tea, for Moore County, where we were, and never mind all the liquor produced there, is a dry county, or was then. Departure, at least across the county line, became a high priority, but we, the two of us, were held back for an audience with the chairman. He had obviously decided that the delivery of a diverting anecdote would pain him least as a means of getting through the five minutes' chat required by protocol. With small preliminary he told Russ and me something like the following – I have normalised his speech in the interests of general sanity, though his polyphthongs ('hayyut' for 'hat', 'bawun' for 'born', etc.) were of the rarest quality.

'I guess as how you saw that statue of Jack down by where the stream comes from under the cliff,' he said, and went on, 'All of us around here are real proud of that. Well, one time a couple of nigras were trimming back some of the trees growing around there, and one of them was real careless, and he cut away a bit of branch that fell down and took a chip out of the brim of Jack's hat. Of course we could get it put back but he did take out that chip.'

Russ and I tried to show how serious we could see that was.

'Well, when Mr Motlow [the then proprietor] heard about that it made him real mad – of course, he was in his wheelchair by then. Anyhow, he had them nigras in and he opened his desk drawer and he took out his six-shooter and he emptied it right on the spot and them nigras wasn't seen in Moore County no more.'

He means he fired into the floor, I told myself. To keep the conversation going I asked, 'When was this?' 1911, perhaps. Or 1923, when King Oliver started recording. Or into the ceiling.

'1952,' he said. At least I think he said that. It could not have been more recently than 1956, I have discovered, because in that year the reigning Motlow sold the business.

The university had telephoned the distillery to tell it about the two professorial visitors and their importance, and we each got our bottle of the Black Label on leaving. And as our first drink of the day we took a good slug out of paper cups in the car outside the first drug-store in the next county. That strengthened a tie that should have existed all right.

The months passed. When not telling me about experiments proving the inferiority of black intelligence, my colleagues, if the expression can be used, were explaining how they were all giving up, had probably already given up, teaching English or British literature in favour of the American variety. This raises several large subjects, to one of which I can add here perhaps a couple of specks.

Americans as a whole do not really care for poems or novels or plays as such, as individual works of art each of which is to a certain extent self-contained and autonomous. They like the generalisations that can be drawn from them or put into them, the messages, the bits of uplift or downpush, the statements, the large imponderables reached as soon and as directly as possible without niggling, limiting, specialising detail (seen in things like character, story, setting, motivation, etc.) and proclaimed as loudly and eye-catchingly as possible. The tendency was inaugurated by a fellow who wrote about death, horror, etc. whenever he could, Death, in fact, if not DEATH, *DEATH* and as much more as the printer could run to in the way of Gothic, blackletter, bold and the rest of it. This fellow was E. A. Poe, the first distinctively American writer and 'by the same token' (whatever that means exactly) the first positively bad one in the language. The results of American literary elephantiasis can be seen in curiosities as diverse as Saul Bellow's reputation and James Dickey's belief that Larkin's poems are by or about somebody who hates his record collection. (Actually as can be seen in the poems Larkin rather liked his record collection, but then.)

I might not have bothered to go into this but for my desire to record the solitary small victory I reckon I won at Vanderbilt. It arises, rather indirectly perhaps, out of the point just made. Allen Ginsberg had published his once-famous poem *Howl*, a wonderfully characteristic piece of flatulent, fraudulent 'message' and 'statement' in 1956, but it had taken a dozen years to trickle down as far as Nashville. Anyway when, acting as directly against my better judgement as I have ever done in my life, I agreed to serve on a

Poetry Brain (*sic*) Trust on campus, alongside Russ and I think Dick Porter and another, the entire hour-plus was devoted to Ginsberg and *Howl* Nobody and nothing else interested anyone, and none present, as I remember, took any but a pro-*Howl* view.

Argument or reason of any sort proving out of the question, I suppose I fell back on personal scurrility, laying stress on the poet's self-assertiveness, hauteur, etc. And by the merest chance a verbal success fell into my lap. 'You're all wrong about Mr Ginsberg's personal attitude,' said someone, 'he's a very modest man,' and I, quoting unbeknownst to all what Churchill had once said about Attlee, snarled on, 'with a lot to be modest about.' Small, indeed, and not my own, but neat and shitty, and boy, were those several hundred kids annoyed, enough to make it all worth while. That occasion, I mean.

This seems an appropriately peevish and trivial note on which to leave the Athens of the bleeding South. A couple of weeks later Jane and I were on another train, all the way down from St Louis over the Rio Grande to Mexico, where they had their problems too, but none that had anything to do with us, and everything looked much nicer, though I soon established that tequila does you much more harm than bourbon.

Note: I noticed at the time that there were round the place monuments to the battle of Nashville, but felt too lethargic to discover details. I have since found with some satisfaction that, fought in December, 1864, between a Northern army under G. H. Thomas and Confederates under J. B. Hood, it ended in victory for the North, Hood's forces being almost annihilated. Apparently it was one of the most decisive battles of the Civil War, or the War between the States, as semi-moronic descendants of the original rebels no doubt still call it.

ELIZABETH TAYLOR

I KNEW ELIZABETH Taylor for a number of years before her death in 1975, when she was living in Penn in Buckinghamshire with her husband John, a businessman. Jane and I quite often exchanged visits with them, mostly weekend lunches, when we had a house in Barnet. Although she had published four novels by 1950, two of them as good as all but her very best, I had not come across her work until that year, when I noticed her *Palladian*, the second to be published, on the shelves of a subscription library in Swansea. I had never heard of her and took the book down on the very long odds that the author's name might have been that of the other Elizabeth Taylor, the actress everybody had heard of. On reading I found it extraordinary, novelettish in some parts, something a good deal more down-to-earth in others, a bit like *Jane Eyre* with scenes in the pub, real scenes based on experience. She was already showing one of her great gifts, that of getting thoroughly inside characters quite unlike herself.

By the time I met her, years later, the novelettish part had gone – I doubt if it had ever been detectable in her behaviour – but the pub was still there. Though we drank in one another's houses I bet Elizabeth was always inclined to pop into her Penn local for a gin and tonic. She had wanted to be a painter, she was politically on the Left, but I found out these things about her after her death, not from her. She never discussed them, any more than I ever heard her discuss literature, even on the have-you-read-X's-latest level, though I have heard she would talk about it with Ivy Compton-Burnett and Elizabeth Bowen. What she was fond of was chatting, a good gossip. From my experience of her she was just what you would expect a nice, lively, bright, comfortably-off Penn housewife to be like, except that she wrote all those marvellous novels and stories. She gave no interviews that I know of, never reviewed a book, nothing like that. She had no interest in 'the literary world'.

One thing I did get from her first-hand was that she was a rationalist, an unbeliever, and this hardly came up until she fell ill with cancer. We visited her several times during what was not a long illness. She knew all about her condition and prospects and her equanimity was exemplary and wonderful. She had chosen to be cremated. When the time came I officiated at the brief ceremony and read out the short-winded atheistical salutation to the dead that she had also chosen. It is none of my business and not my point to comment on that, but to me the ceremony was in no way suitable to the departure of one of the finest novelists of her and our time. Nor were its accompaniments, such as Press coverage. The neglect of her work continues to this day, and it is not uncommon to talk to someone who professes an interest in modern literature and has to have it explained that it is not Elizabeth Taylor the film star who has entered the conversation.

She would probably be embarrassed if she could know that I was using this brief tribute to her and to her work as a way of drawing attention, if not to her, then to it and its quality, but not having been the kind of person who resented things she would not, I think, be resentful. It is a sad and awful comment on our culture, on the way we regard our writers in general, that what has led to the neglect I mentioned, to the fact that when people make lists of leaders in the field her name rarely comes up, is that very self-effacement described earlier. Even in her day (her first novel was published in 1945, her last posthumously in 1976) it was necessary to be a sort of semi-public person, to get your name in the papers and your face on the screen, in order to be heard of and so to be read. The alternative, to cultivate an Olympian detachment, to become known as the writer nobody knows, was equally foreign to her company-loving and humorous nature.

The years since her death have seen here and there a stir of interest in her and her work, welcome but still inadequate. The trouble with that work, in the sense of the barrier to its full recognition, is that in summary, or read hastily and superficially (as most work is read), it can seem like something fit for an old-fashioned women's magazine, something about husbands and wives, parents and children in the commuter belt, something trivial. Yes, trivial in the way John Betjeman's poetry is trivial, seen at a second glance to be concerned with themes like loss, grief, disappointment, loneliness, hope, love, death. But never gloomy. And, at times, sharply funny, caustic, enchantingly catty in a style that is all her own.

In the 1980s Virago Press republished most of her novels and books of short stories and in 1984 her masterpiece, *Angel*, was chosen as one of the Book Marketing Council's 'Best Novels of Our Time'. Paul Johnson, normally a sensible enough critic, complained that it was not 'important' enough to be selected. Important! Fearful contemporary word, smacking of the textbook, the lecture-hall, the 'balanced appraisal'. So-and-so may be readable, interesting, entertaining, but is he important? Ezra Pound may be pretentious and dull, but you've got to admit he's ever so important. What? You haven't read Primo Levi (in translation, of course)? But he's *important*. As the philosopher J. L. Austin remarked in another context, importance isn't important. Good writing is.

ENOCH POWELL

IT IS NO part of my business, here or anywhere else, to discuss what gets politicians into office or debars them from it, but in the case of two noteworthy contenders of our time, J. Enoch Powell and Anthony Wedgwood Benn, the reason for their failure to reach the top is surely obvious. They both look barmy. I understand this as an elastic term which would include Benn's appearance of general dislocation as well as Powell's of more specific derangement. Please be clear that I say nothing about the reality, only the impression.

Benn I have run into only once, early in his career, when by a misunderstanding he arrived on my doorstep expected but not heralded by any name. The door was one of those with a glass panel affording a preview of the caller. At the first sight of the present arrival the thought flashed into my mind, 'Who is this English cunt?' The distinguishing adjective is important. There are Scottish cunts, there are even Welsh cunts, and God knows there are American cunts, but the one in question could have come from nowhere else but this green and pleasant land. Something about the set of the lips.

Other guests arrived at the same time and my silent question went unanswered for the moment. I offered drinks. Someone asked for a gin and tonic. I turned to the cunt. 'Same for you?' He reacted much as if I had said, 'Glass of baby's blood? It's extra good today,' and somehow in that moment I knew him, recognised him from television. He settled for bitter lemon, 'with plenty of ice,' he added firmly. (I once heard him say unequivocally, also on television, that his sole interest in life was and had always been politics, which to my mind should debar anybody from standing for Parliament. Even Ted Heath has his yacht and his choirs.)

Benn at any rate gives an impression of physical harmlessness: he would never, you feel, go for your throat. Not so Enoch Powell. He merely looks definitely but mildly barmy when looking straight

298

ahead; it is when he moves the pupils of his eyes into their corners that he looks, to me, physically dangerous. He makes me think of a book on how to learn to draw I had when I was a boy, in which the artist had cleverly shown how the expression of a face could be transformed from meekness to brooding ferocity by this one change. Powell was affable enough on our first encounter, merely addressing me and one other as if we were a public meeting, as politicians will, for a couple of minutes before switching to informality with startling speed and thoroughness – 'But we don't want to go on nattering away about boring stuff like that, surely to God,' or words to that effect.

Powell and I had a more prolonged and testing session at a small dinner party given in about 1970 by Ralph Harris (now Lord Harris of High Cross) and his wife José at their house in Hadley Wood. Among the other guests were my old friend Colin Welch, then in a senior position on the *Daily Telegraph*, and his wife Sibyl. I was on my hostess's left, Powell on her right, so that we faced each other at the end of the table. All went normally, at an easy pace, until I remarked to José Harris,

'Yes, there's obviously going to be [or has been] considerable Soviet impingement in the Middle Eastern countries.' Well, one has to show willing.

Powell, who had been paying attention but not contributing much, at once showed a lively interest. 'Impingement, Mr Amis,' he said. 'May I ask you: whence do you derive that word?'

'Well now, Latin *impingo, impingere, impinxi, impinctum*, meaning something like "I shade in",' I said, never having come across any such verb in my life (nor does it appear to exist), but feeling I was doing pretty well for ten o'clock or so at Ralph's table, which was never frugal.

'Alas no, Mr Amis,' said Powell, shaking his head regretfully, but smiling in appreciation of a nice try. '*Impingo, impingere, impaxi,*★ *impactum*, "I strike . . . a *blow*",' and he struck one, quite a hard one of fist into palm. His eyes were gleaming, but not in their corners.

'I obviously must concede the point to you, Mr Powell,' I said, feeling like someone in a costume drama, and a prat too.

★*Impaxi* is my recollection, but so impeccable a classical scholar as Enoch Powell must surely have given the form correctly as *impegi*.

'Yes, I think you must.'

Well, there we were, but not for long. Powell, as if charged up by his linguistic triumph, after a minute or two leaned across to Colin Welch, who was sitting next but one to me. 'Mr Welch, may I ask you a question about the conduct of your newspaper?'

'Of course.'

'I am curious to know why the intention of the Right Honourable J. Enoch Powell, P.C., M.P., to give a speech in Brussels [I think] attacking the proposal that the United Kingdom should apply for membership of the European Economic Community should have gone unreported in your columns.'

'Well,' said Colin in a conciliatory tone, 'I had no direct hand in that, Enoch, but I imagine it was felt that we'd wait until we'd read what you actually had to say before we went into the matter.'

'Ah,' – this defence had been foreseen – 'but surely the *known intention* of the Right Honourable [etc.] to give a speech attacking [etc.] was an event in itself worthy of record in a newspaper such as the *Daily Telegraph*.'

Colin apologised, promised to do better in future, etc., and I fancy, though I would not swear to it, that the matter was allowed to drop there. On chewing things over afterwards, I reflected that if I, like who knows how many other people, had heard or read that to refer to oneself in the third person is or may be a sign of paranoia or one of those, then surely a man of the education of the Right Honourable J. Enoch Powell must have come across the same information somewhere. Or had he stopped reading after mastering the principal parts of *impingo*? Or . . . I gave it up.

My last meeting with Powell, and I mean last, as the reader will see, took place at the *Spectator* party in 1988. I spotted the great man standing by himself, wearing his familiar look of slightly resentful slight bafflement, went up to him and said, 'Hallo, Mr Powell, it's Kingsley Amis,' all unaware that I was about to receive the most economical put-down of my career. So far. Julian Barnes, who was standing next to me, confirms that I pronounced my name loudly, slowly and clearly.

Powell pursed his lips like a flautist's. The notation does not exist that would indicate how short a time it took him to pronounce his next vocable.

'Who?'

'Kingsley . . . Amis,' as before or more so in all respects.

'Oh.'

That was it, and no wonder that within the next three seconds I had spotted someone I knew standing near by with whom I simply had to go and have a word.

Again, what can one say? Probably the less the better. It does seem, I think, that nothing personal was at stake. But it also perhaps needs saying that the world is built on people babbling things like, 'Of course, my dear fellow, how very absurd of me not to have recognised you,' when they have no idea whom they are talking to, and if you are going into politics with hope of success, instead of some obscure branch of the truth-at-any-price business, you had better come to terms with that widely grasped fact. And of course he knew perfectly well who I was, and if he was not prepared to put up with such possibly disagreeable encounters, what was he doing at that party? I like to think he had not forgiven me for coming as high as second over *impingo*.

JUDGE MELFORD STEVENSON

His honour judge Melford Stevenson had an impish sense of fun which could sometimes be mistaken for, and occasionally really was, the voicing of outrageous expressions or opinions, the deliberate saying of the unsayable. What a judge says in court is privileged, not subject to the law of libel, and a newspaper that prints what he has said is protected by the same privilege, which explains how I came to be reading this story. Many years ago a Jamaican worker on a building site was accidentally picked up by the leg by some piece of machinery, carried some distance through the air and dropped to the ground, sustaining serious but not fatal injuries. He sued the construction firm and, rightly it seems, won the suit. When the facts of the matter were explained to the learned judge (Stevenson), he said, 'Ah, clearly a case of Eeny Meeny Miny Mo.' (Just for this half minute I am like that fellow in Berlin all those years ago, a camera with its shutter open, quite passive, recording, not thinking.)

My acquaintance with Melford was really confined to the Garrick Club, where he would tell stories, tell them in a style and with a stylishness suggesting the sense of drama that is inseparable from the law and makes lawyers' stories the best, better than doctors' or journalists', good as these can be. Once I ran into him in the Garrick bar the day after the conclusion of a successful libel action brought by Telly Savalas, of *Kojak* and other fame, against a British journal that had represented him, I had better say misrepresented him, as having screwed and boozed his way all over West Germany during the making of some film there. I asked Melford what he had thought of Savalas.

'Well, frankly I was quite bowled over by the man. He was charming, a perfect gentleman, his evidence was a model of concision and clarity, I was delighted at the way things turned out and they tell me he's also an extremely promising actor.'

I had, I think quite successfully, told or retold this story several times before seeing that it carried within it an innocent little joke at cunts like me who imagine that judges really don't know who people like Telly Savalas are.

Later or another time I fortunately mentioned to Melford the Bodkin Adams case, a famous one of the 1950s in which an Eastbourne doctor had allegedly poisoned an unknown number of his elderly and ailing female patients after inducing each of them to leave him a smallish but useful legacy. He had been charged with two of these supposed killings, presumably the 'best' ones from the police point of view, yet had got off. A lot of people had thought at the time and still thought he was as guilty as hell. Melford's attention sharpened immediately at the name: as a barrister he had prosecuted the doctor in front of the magistrates.

'How many did he do?' I asked.

'The police knew he'd done thirty-two,' said Melford firmly. 'There was some doubt about number thirty-three, his mother.' He gave the last two words a weight and a kind of disgust of which no description would be adequate. 'There were parts of the evidence given in court which would have interested you particularly, or should have done.' Interested *me*? Should have? 'There was an occasion when the doctor visited one of his prospective victims and was admitted at the front door by her much younger sister, who led the way upstairs to the sick-room. She had gone less than halfway when from behind her she heard Adams call out something and at the same time a kind of crash or thump. She turned to see him prone on the floor of the hall. According to her evidence he explained he had knelt down on a mat to pray for the sick woman's recovery when the mat slipped from under him on the highly polished floor.

'Counsel asked her, "Could you make out what Dr Adams called out as he fell?"

'The witness, who must have been an unusual type of person, said, "Yes. He shouted, 'Oh fuck.' " ' As before his deep, well-modulated voice lent the last word an authority and resonance it rarely receives. 'Now *that's* the sort of thing you novelists ought to be going in for. It could be the foundation of a striking little paragraph.'

He had not quite finished with the good doctor yet. 'When the man was released he took a house in Hove, not very far from where I live. I happened to be passing one day,' – you bloody old liar, I thought, I bet you went specially to have a sly look – 'and saw he had installed a brass plate outside his door that read, "John Bodkin

Adams, MD, etc. At home 5 p.m. to 7 p.m." As if he were inviting the world in general in for a glass of sherry. Somehow I've never been able to bring myself to accept.'

One Saturday I found Melford and myself part of a small company lunching at the club common table – Saturday lunches were always thinly attended at that time and have since been discontinued. An actor called Rowland Davies was sitting next to me. Opposite us were Melford and a guest of his whose introduction I had missed or failed to understand, someone clearly concerned with the law but detectable as belonging to a lower level than that of judge or silk. Melford was in ebullient form, telling us how, in the only parliamentary election he had fought, he had inserted in every speech a strong denial of rumours that his Labour opponent was a practising homosexual. Shame on us, no doubt, but Rowlie and I and others laughed at this. Just then I happened to catch the guest's eye and it was very stony. Undeterred, I laughed at Melford's next sally too and this time guest was relaxed and friendly and continued so. When he had finally left, Melford explained that the chap had once been his clerk in chambers (seemingly an official distributing work among barristers occupying a given building in a legal Inn). So, as Rowlie and I worked it out, his first stare had meant, 'Don't you dare laugh at my judge' and his subsequent amiability arisen from his seeing that our laughter was with, not at. I thought all this spoke rather well for Melford, who was just then (probably) saying,

'On Monday I shall be trying a libel action George Wigg is bringing against Nigel Dempster, and I must say I've seldom approached a case in such a spirit of complete impartiality.'

Melford's house in Brighton was called Truncheons, much to the delight of many. At his death in 1987 only the *Daily Mail*, I think, had the honesty to observe that the place was called that before he moved there, though it would be hard to maintain that he had been simply too lazy to change it.

ROALD DAHL

I HAVE ONLY once met this renowned children's author. It was at a party in the 1970s given by Tom Stoppard at his house in Iver, Bucks. This may or may not have been the one at which Stoppard himself so memorably wrong-footed me over greeting procedure. On our second or third encounter earlier he had embraced me in full Continental style, which I tend to dislike a bit when it comes from a man outside the family. Oh well, I had thought, the chap was a Czech, after all (though none of the other Czechs I knew went on like that), and obviously no queer, and it would be churlish to back off. So for the next couple of times, resigning myself, I had got off the embracing mark simultaneously with him. Then this time, or one like it, he stepped back from my outstretched arms with a muffled cry of shock or distaste. Awkward, you know. And why?

The Dahl occasion may or may not also have been the one at which the actor Michael Caine had demonstrated that he put exactly the same amount of feeling, no more and no less, into his ordinary chat in the flesh as he did on the screen when saying things like, 'I just want you to know you mean more to me than anything in the whole world' and 'Would you bring the car round to the front of the hotel in ten minutes?'

Anyway, on some such occasion, Dahl was invited and duly arrived, late, after everybody else was there, and by helicopter. I could not imagine why this form of transport had been thought necessary on a perfectly normal fine day, a Sunday as I remember, nor was any explanation proffered. At some stage, not by my choice, I found myself closeted alone with him.

First declaring himself a great fan of mine, he asked, 'What are you working on at the moment, Kingsley?'

I started to make some reply, but he cut me short. 'That sounds

305

marvellous,' he said, 'but do you expect to make a lot of money out of it however well you do it?'

'I don't know about a lot,' I said. 'Enough, I hope. The sort of money I usually make.'

'So you've no financial problems.'

'I wouldn't say that either exactly, but I seem to be able to – '

Dahl was shaking his head slowly. 'I hate to think of a chap of your distinction having to worry about money at your time of life. Tell me, how old are you now?' I told him and it was much what he or anybody else would have expected. 'Yes. You might be able to write better, I mean even better, if you were financially secure.'

I was hating to think of a number of things, but one that eluded me was how to turn the conversation. I must have mumbled something about only knowing how to write in the way I always had. Never mind – what had *he* got on the –

He was shaking his head again. 'What you want to do,' he said, 'is write a children's book. That's where the money is today, believe me.' ('Today', as I said, was quite some time back.)

'I wouldn't know how to set about it.'

'Do you know what my advance was on my last one?' When he found I did not, in fact had no idea, he told me. It certainly sounded like a large sum.

'I couldn't do it,' I told him again. 'I don't think I enjoyed children's books much when I was a child myself. I've got no feeling for that kind of thing.'

'Never mind, the little bastards'd swallow it.'

Many times in these pages I have put in people's mouths approximations to what they said, what they might well have said, what they said at another time, and a few almost-outright inventions, but that last remark is verbatim.

'Well, I suppose you'd know,' I replied, 'but I can't help feeling they'd see through me. Children are supposed to be good at detecting insincerity and such, aren't they? Again, you're the man who understands about all that.'

When he seemed to have no more to say for the moment I went on with more on previous lines, boring him a good deal, it seemed, but that was perfectly all right with me. At length he roused himself.

'Well, it's up to you. Either you will or you won't. Write a children's book, I mean. But if you do decide to have a crack, let me give you one word of warning. Unless you put everything you've got into it, unless you write it from the heart, the kids'll have no use for it. They'll see you're having them on. And just let me tell you from experience that there's nothing kids hate more than that. They won't give you a second chance either. You'll have had it for good as far as they're concerned. Just you bear that in mind as a word of friendly advice. Now, if you'll excuse me, I rather think I'll go in search of another drink.'

And, with a stiff nod and an air of having asserted his integrity by rejecting some particularly outrageous and repulsive suggestion, the man who put everything into the books he wrote for the kids left me to my thoughts. I felt rather as if I had been looking at one of those pictures by Escher in which the eye is led up a flight of stairs only to find itself at the same level as it started at.

I watched the television news that night, but there was no report of a famous children's author being killed in a helicopter crash.

A. J. AYER

It is no secret that Freddie Ayer, while he may well have been one of the greatest philosophers of our time, was certainly one of its greatest egotists. I take leave to add my mite to the rich treasure-house of stories showing this trait in him, though before doing so it is only fair to assert that I liked him personally, despite his lack of small-talk – to him all talk not somehow connected or connectable with philosophy was small – and was always cheered by the sight of him and his extraordinary nose.

To begin with one I heard from a relative of his and have seen misquoted (for the worse, as always): when someone looked up from the paper to say, 'I see poor old Philip Toynbee is dead,' Freddie's response was, in full, 'Ah, he wrote a very nice notice of my first book.' Which could be taken not so much to show a want of feeling as at any rate likely to be truer than the pieties being simultaneously mumbled at a thousand breakfast-tables up and down the land, as well as approaching the condition of verifiable statement. Crappy, though.

When I saw him last he was gravely ill though still quite mobile, in fact arriving almost simultaneously with me in the vicinity of what already looked like being, and turned out every whit to be, a decidedly stuffy lunch in a private room at Wilton's in honour of the unavailingly unstuffy Peter Quennell. Happy to see what is often called not very accurately a friendly face, and without thinking, I called, 'Hallo, Freddie, how are you?' and I suppose rather deserved to receive the reply, 'Absolutely terrible, dear boy – in fact the moment this is over I'm off into hospital. Can't breathe. Simply unable to breathe.' There may well have been more in the same strain. Well, I had known he was not well. But then again.

Another non-secret is that, besides his distinction as philosopher and egotist, Freddie was also – well, remarkably keen on female company and good at acquiring it. The second half of this was demonstrated in my presence on and after a television chat-show. The participants, apart from him and me, were Bernard Levin and a then (fifteen years ago or more) moderately celebrated feminist called Juliet Mitchell, a rather pretty blonde girl, or woman as she would no doubt have insisted on being called; the duration, an hour; the conditions, recorded quasi-live earlier in the evening of the transmission. So for an hour the four of us sat before the cameras discussing questions of the day and the rest of it. Nothing any of us said struck me as very thrilling, but one hardly expects that of any such programme. When we had finished, the producer, the amiable Eddie Mirzoeff, came in to us smiling and shaking his head. 'Sorry,' he said. 'You'll have to do it all again. The whole hour.'

Execration burst from us, but Eddie got his way – of course he did – and we did it all again. Gallingly, we found ourselves admitting it was better the second time. Well and good. But we were now faced with a small time problem. If the first recording had been pronounced successful, we should have been able to have a drink at the studios afterwards and be taken off at leisure to watch the transmission at our own firesides, basking in the admiration of our families, guests, etc. This would not now be possible. Eddie suggested we should move to a viewing-room in the same building and watch the thing go out from there, while drinking the drinks and eating the sandwiches he would provide. All four of us accepted.

The available viewing-room proved to be rather small for five plus others concerned in the production. Eddie did his best to arrange the seating. Very soon the broadcast began. I at least concentrated reasonably hard on it, though I did notice at one point that Juliet Mitchell, who had been occupying a not very cramped-looking chair at one side of the narrow room, was now sitting on the floor with her back against the edge of Freddie's chair and, so to speak, between his thighs. At the end, amid much mutual congratulation, Eddie was busily arranging taxis to take the performers where they wanted to go. Freddie intervened benevolently in this process.

'It seems Juliet and I are going in the same direction, Eddie,' he said, 'so we can share a taxi and make a bit of a saving that way.'

When I got back to my house in Barnet I found waiting for me, as I had expected, the couple I had invited for the weekend, the day being Friday. The man was my Australian friend Jim Durham, a rare kind of fellow in several ways, not the least that of being about the only sane and sensible psychiatrist I have ever met – he now runs an enormous madhouse in Sydney. He had watched the programme, as we had planned to do together. When I had apologised for my absence (I hope I had thought to ring up earlier to explain), he said,

'Just confirm, would you, that Freddie Ayer went off with that girl after the show?'

I stared at him. 'You bastard,' I said. 'You haven't got second sight as well, have you?'

'I didn't need it. When that fool bitch made one of her more outrageous remarks, you and Levin quite properly went for her like a pickpocket. Not Freddie [whom he knew, at least by repute]. *He* was saying, "I think Juliet's raised a very important point," or "Juliet's question needs very careful answering," ingratiating crap like that. And it was getting through to her too, you could see. Didn't you notice any of that? Even when you watched the transmission?'

'No,' I said.

'No, it was obvious to me, but while you were performing you were too busy seeing you got your word in and not saying fuck, and while you were watching it you were making sure you looked right and were making reasonable sense. Never mind anyone else. I don't suppose you remember much about what you said yourself, do you?'

'Not really.'

'No. You were pretty good. Especially about education.'

So there may have been no more than one great philosopher and one great cocksman on that show, but there was certainly more than one egotist.

TOM DRIBERG

IN THE MID-1970s, when Oxford Books still counted for something, I was commissioned to edit *The New Oxford Book of Light Verse*. One of the principles that guided my selection was, not very surprisingly, to include a fair proportion of the unfamiliar, the unexpected, where appropriate the unpublished. So alongside, or rather after, Lewis Carroll and W. S. Gilbert I prepared to put Robert Conquest, under three pseudonyms, Wynford Vaughan-Thomas, Alan Bennett and a poem by Anthony Powell previously printed only privately. But I had heard that a famous group of poems neither I nor anyone I knew had ever seen, the Constant Lambert limericks, was in the possession of Tom Driberg, ennobled as Lord Bradwell either just before or just after, whom I had never met. Accordingly I wrote to him explaining the circumstances, asking to be allowed to look at these limericks and some other stuff by Auden also said to be in his possession, and referring him to Christopher Hitchens, whom I knew he knew and whom I had met through my son Martin, if he wanted to be assured that this was not a frivolous request. I also offered, as fee, dinner at a restaurant of his choice. My motives were of course a mixture of legitimate editorial inquiry and a rather vulgar inquisitiveness about, desire to meet in the flesh, well, have a look at, a man famous both for the ferocious vigour and glaring conspicuousness of his homosexual activities and for the complete and baffling immunity he enjoyed from the law and the Press to the end of his days.

In due course Hitchens reported back to me, already chuckling before he started to speak of the matter in hand.

'Okay about Tom,' he said, 'but you ought to hear this bit first. A couple of years ago, something like that, Tom said to me, "Martin Amis, now. You know him, don't you? What a charming boy. I thought I might ask him out to lunch." – "You'd be wasting your time, Tom," I said. "What, not even five per cent?" he said. "Not

311

even five per cent." – "Oh dear, how frightfully disappointing."
End of scene. Then he got your letter the other day and said to me,
"Kingsley Amis, now. Tell me, is he as charming as his son?" '

At this point Hitchens broke into open laughter, in which I joined
after a short interval. Perhaps I should have mentioned that I was
then a comely lad of fifty-three summers or thereabouts.

'So I said,' went on Hitchens, ' "Yes, Tom, absolutely, but –
how shall I put it? – he is old enough to be Martin's father," and
he said, "Oh dear, yes, I suppose he must be." '

It emerged that the restaurant of Driberg's choice was to be the
Neal Street Restaurant, actually one of my own favourite spots, but
the dinner was to be preceded by a visit to a terrible 'club' in an
upstairs room in Soho, the sort with a white baby grand piano and
millions of signed photographs of rightly forgotten people, seemingly
unchanged since the Raymond-Davenport days of the Fifties when
I had visited it a couple of times and no doubt for longer than that.*
The sense of history it diffused, the history of legions of spongers
and hopeless drunks, depressed me quite remarkably in the short
time we were there, and Driberg himself seemed dissatisfied with
it, though when we got to the restaurant he seemed dissatisfied with
that too; perhaps it was just his habitual expression. Our party, by
the way, had turned out to include Hitchens and Martin, not that
I had any memory of having invited either of them. The Neal Street
place was (and is) quite expensive and as I write these words I am
nearly sure, to my chagrin, that I forgot to claim, or to try to claim,
the considerable cost of the meal back off the OUP.

They gave us a decent enough table about halfway down the
room. The Hitch too had noted Driberg's discontented glances about
him and muttered to me, 'Complaint coming up.'

'Eh?'

'He has to find fault with something to feel properly settled in.'

Sure enough, within a couple of minutes Driberg was asking the
manager to have us moved to a quieter part of the restaurant, though
it was not very noisy where we were. We were duly moved to a
temporarily quieter part, which as the restaurant filled up over the
next twenty minutes naturally became as unquiet as where we had
been. Driberg said little. I have since thought he might have been

---

* A version of the place appears in chapter 10 of my novel *Difficulties With
Girls*.

ill, since he was to die within months of our meeting. Martin did not exert himself. Hitchens did – he could be relied on for things like that. I gabbled away. I always tend to fill in conversational gaps, merely to avoid general awkwardness, a trait that has brought me from close-mouthed buggers cheeky accusations of being a chatterbox.

Eventually we reached Driberg's flat in the Barbican. When some rather good whisky had been produced, the Lambert limericks were brought out and I could see within a couple of minutes that they were no good for my purposes, perhaps for any. Written out in an unattractive hand, they featured one at a time all or many of the diocesan bishops of probably England and Wales. Each limerick had e.g. the Bishop of Truro in its first line, a limited amount of technical ingenuity and an obscenity of some kind, usually mild. Nothing else of significance, for example humour, was anywhere present. However, I read them through with simulated care and interest before saying with pretended regret and real evasiveness that I was afraid they would not quite do for the OUP. The Auden poem – there turned out to be only one – ruled itself out even faster than the limericks by being a long and detailed account of an act of fellatio told by the fellator in the first person. This too I politely kept my eyes on for some time.

While I was doing so, Martin asked if he could ring a minicab. The telephone was in the bedroom and he disappeared into it. A little later I became vaguely aware that I was sitting alone with Hitchens. A little later still Driberg was with us once more. And a little later again Martin reappeared, the driver of the minicab I had ordered that afternoon turned up, I told Driberg that unfortunately the Auden poem would not quite do either for the OUP, issued thanks and goodnights and left. A wasted evening.

More than I then knew. The next morning Martin rang me up and showed no taciturnity at all. 'A fine fucking father you are,' he said half-humorously. 'The slag at the cab firm told me to hold on a moment, please, caller, and in no time bloody caller was holding on with one hand and beating Driberg off with the other.' Driberg was several sizes larger than Martin. 'We must have gone round the bed about five times before he clapped me on the shoulder, said "Fair enough, youngster" in a sort of bluff style and buggered off.'

'That was sporting of him,' I said. 'Anyway. You should have taken the Hitch into the bedroom with you.'

'Maybe. And maybe not.'

Perhaps exhaustion from chasing Martin round that bed hastened Driberg's demise. The idea does not displease me much.

MARGARET THATCHER

I AM A political supporter of Mrs Thatcher, but this essay is not about politics. It just so happens that I was lucky enough to be able to inspect the lady at close quarters without having to go through any of the usual channels. Some time in the interval between her becoming leader of the Tory party and winning the election of 1979, Robert Conquest was staying with me in Hampstead while I was temporarily on my own. Invited by Mrs T to dine at her house in Chelsea, he explained my position and she very decently invited me to join the party.

No. 19 Flood Street is one of those neat little joints between the King's Road and the Chelsea Embankment, comfortable but ungrand and decorated in a boldly unadventurous style. (That is about as far as my natural observation of domestic interiors normally takes me, and were this fiction I should have to call in females to assist me with the furniture, etc.) Besides Bob and me, the company comprised just three Thatchers including Mark, and Professor Julius Gould, sometimes described as the only right-wing sociologist in captivity, a saturnine fellow I had known thirty years before in Swansea.

I was rather overcome with the occasion and the fairly close propinquity of Mrs T, who had been before 1979 very much a new face to me as to most people, too much so to take in a lot about the fare except that it was properly unimaginative and, as regards drink, ample enough. The hostess wore one of those outfits that seem to have more detail in them than is common, with, I particularly remember, finely embroidered gold-and-scarlet collar and cuffs to her blouse. The same attentiveness had gone into the construction of what was asking to have itself called a coiffure. That sort of styling happens not to appeal much to me, but it undoubtedly made a plausible and in its way impressive harmony with the rest.

But this is not an appropriate tone to go on about one of the best-

315

looking women I had ever met and for her age, then over fifty, remarkable. This quality is so extreme that, allied to her well-known photogenic quality, it can trap me for split seconds into thinking I am looking at a science-fiction illustration of some time ago showing the beautiful girl who has become President of the Solar Federation in the year 2220. The fact that it is not a sensual or sexy beauty does not make it a less sexual beauty, and that sexuality is still, I think, an underrated factor in her appeal (or repellence). Envy of it among women, consciousness of its unavailability among men, retains power even when advancing age should have disposed of it. But Mrs Thatcher's enemies cannot admit it in those terms and call her cold, unsympathetic, schoolmarmish, suburban, etc. Of course the clothes and the hair and so on are part of it; what would you expect? To look like a caring, compassionate female politician, ordinary physical ugliness is a great help, and should it not be available, as in the case of Shirley Williams, say, then make sure your hair looks as if it has not had a comb through it for days and you have just got off a train that has delivered you an hour late (because you missed the one before).

Mrs T's voice is, I admit, rather another matter: I mean her public voice. She has softened it over the years, but I still find myself saying to her televised image, 'Maggie, please don't be so monotonous [in the literal sense of staying on one tone or note] – it can't help giving some sort of ring of petulance or superiority when I trust you enough to know you're not feeling either.' But there was none of any of that in the way she spoke to me that evening in Flood Street, though I was too much interested in the content to take much notice of the manner. The bit that stayed with me most ran roughly,

'People have always said that the next election is going to be crucial. But this one really will be, and if it doesn't go the way Denis and I want then we'll stay, because we'll always stay, but we'll work very hard with the children to set them up with careers in Canada.' This crystallised my impression of a truly tough-minded person.

I said as much to Julius Gould as we waited to pick up a taxi in the King's Road afterwards, rather a long wait as it proved, some of which he used, disagreeably to me, by asking how I had managed to 'stand it' all those years in Swansea, 'a town redolent of fish and chips'. More to the present purpose he endorsed my feelings about

Mrs T, adding that he had been impressed by her readiness to be interrupted, an uncommon trait, as he pointed out, in politicians.

A couple of days later I had the chance of repeating some of these praises to a young man in the Travellers' Club who said Bob had told him of our Thatcher evening. 'I'm very glad to hear that,' he said with what seemed to me undue emphasis before withdrawing.

'Who's that young shag?' I asked.

Bob mentioned a name. 'He's Mrs Thatcher's personal private secretary,' he added.

I had been lucky. If feeling below my best, or finding the young shag over-earnest, I would have been quite capable of a sharp sentence or two complaining of Mark's over-attentive conduct of his lighter or Denis's deference towards his wife, even though on the second count I had thought at the time and still think that it would be very hard to suggest an improvement on his version of the behaviour appropriate to the difficult and vulnerable function of the husband of a prime-minister-to-be, at once respectful and ready to argue, and natural too, just what I would be looking for in her shoes to greet me after a heavy day in the House. I may have said some of this too to the young shag.

So far so good, then. I was appointed CBE in 1981.

But then things took a small turn for the worse at a later evening of a very different sort, in one of the rooms at the House of Commons in fact, at an informal meeting to which had been invited various known Conservative journalists and miscellaneous sympathisers like myself, with a number of back-bench MPs thrown in. The speaker was Margaret Thatcher, now Prime Minister and already, after a couple of years, making both a success and a stir. Questions were naturally asked for. The first, from a well-known journalist of – what shall I call it? – unimpeachable loyalty, made the point that, despite the great support she had attracted and optimism aroused, some of her supporters were worried about her ability to secure a second term, because so much of what she had in mind for the country was going to require more than a single one. What kind of prospect could she offer such people that such a second term would be forthcoming, because things might go badly awry should it fail to materialise?

'If that's your attitude I wonder you haven't emigrated already,' began Mrs T in her best high-handed, planking, unreconstructed style. Oh God, I thought, never forget she's a bloody woman with the rest of them, one who had encountered what she took for opposition. It was an unfortunate question to open with, it had perhaps been delivered in an irritatingly pompous way, the tone rather than the words of the reply had been off, and a smile would have done more than save the day. All fair enough, but she had treated her questioner not as one of her supporters but as someone on the other side at a public meeting. The Mrs Thatcher I had admired at Flood Street would have come up with something more like, 'I acknowledge that as one of our toughest problems', and won the respect of everybody in the room at once instead of bit by bit, as she did in the course of the rest of her reply. I am still devoted to her, but the fact remains that in even the best of us there is something for others to put up with, and I feel an occasional moderate twinge of sympathy for those in her own party who may think it necessary to disagree with her over this or that.

To a party at 10 Downing Street in 1980 – not one of the big affairs, just a few hundred close friends and kindred spirits – I took a copy of a novel of mine, *Russian Hide-and-Seek*, a science-fiction story, you must know, about a future Britain under Russian occupation. It had been published that very day, which I considered must remove any imputation of arse-crawling from my having inscribed that copy to Margaret Thatcher. (The inscription mentioned things like respect rather than undying passion, etc.)

'What's it about?' she asked after thanking me.

'Well, in a way it's about a future Britain under Russian occupation,' I said.

'Huh!' she cried. 'Can't you do any better than that? Get yourself another crystal ball!'

It was an unimprovable put-down in being unfair as well as unanswerable. No amount of explanation about science-fiction writers not being in the prophecy business would have cut any ice here, not to speak of there being no time for such casuistry. Meanwhile, I was told later, Denis Thatcher was telling Philip Larkin about the current Test series without possibility of interruption. Well, I suppose that's Downing Street parties for you.

My devotion to Mrs T retains something of that initial physical bowling-over, in fact she has replaced the Queen as my dream-girl, using this phrase in its more literal sense of the female who, more than any other, tends to recur in my dreams. The last time she (Mrs T) and I met there it was in 10 Downing Street again, but a transfigured 10 Downing Street, in that mysterious way of dreams known to be that building without physically resembling the reality. She drew me apart, came close, came closer. This was going to be the big one.

'You've got such an *interesting* face,' her shade murmured with a softness I had never heard her use in life or in any broadcast. Even as I dreamt I admired her charity and cunning in hitting on about the only epithet still applicable to my face that might be considered neither unkind nor blatantly untrue. Then, alas, in that other way of dreams, her image faded.

But the devotion remains serious too, so much so that I will have to indicate its limitation and abandon my original undertaking not to write about politics in this piece – well, not exactly politics, about which I probably know no more than any other newspaper-reader or bar chatterer, but education. In this one field I find the policy of her governments wrong in an important respect, anti-educational in fact. There is education as social engineering, and she has rightly and effectively worked against it; there is education as vocational training, and that is necessary and she has rightly promoted it; and there is education as education, definable as the free pursuit of knowledge and truth for their own sake, and this, I hate to say, the effect of her governments' policies has been to weaken and undermine.

LEO ROSTEN

AT SOME STAGE in the 1970s at some party in London I ran into
an American called Leo Rosten, who turned out on investigation to
be the author, under the pseudonym of Leonard Q. Ross, of a
number of stories (reprinted from *The New Yorker*) in the now (and
even then) long-defunct British magazine *Lilliput* in the war years
and after, comic genre pieces about one Hyman Kaplan, an Eastern-
European immigrant to America, and his attempts to learn English
in night school in New York. I remembered having thought them
genuinely funny in a closely observed verbal way, and when Rosten
amiably proposed throwing a quadripartite dinner including wives
I gladly accepted.

Alas! I had infringed the old rule that lays down, *Never accept an
open-ended invitation from a stranger*: when one who seems interesting
and possible asks you out to dinner, say you have time for an early
drink on Tuesday before a firm dinner date. If he still seems all
right after an hour or so of early drink, say you reckon you can put
this guy off. When you have gone through the motions of doing so,
remember to mutter stuff about having to be home or in bed early.
Then, and only then, you may go off to a place of your choice and
dine with him.

It was arranged that Jane and I should turn up at Rosten's flat at
some time like seven and go off to a restaurant from there. On our
arrival Rosten presented his wife, name of Zimmy, a pet-form, so
I gathered, of Zimmermann, her maiden name. Being at once burly
and flat-chested she did not appeal to me visually, but she was
anxious to be agreeable. Rosten poured us all some very small
drinks, an unusual performance for an American, at that time
anyway. I seem to remember they were Bloody Marys about the
size of a fairly large glass of sherry. We drank ours up rather fast
and got another of the same size. He said he would take us to eat
at what he called his local. I had been looking forward to something

a little fancier than a snack at a pub, and was relieved to find in due
course that, mistaking a British usage, what he meant was a nearby
restaurant. Anyway, in a little while he telephoned it from across
the room.

'Hallo, Mario,' he said vivaciously. 'Buona sera . . . What?'

Having already begun to dislike him I was pleased to hear him
getting to the end of his stock of Italian with such promptitude. He
continued his conversation in English.

During it, Zimmy noticed that Jane's and my glasses were again
empty and, lowering her voice, asked us, 'Would you like another
drink?'

She had not lowered it enough to escape the attention of Rosten,
who slapped his hand across the telephone and said with some
emphasis, 'They've had two! They've had two!'

'I just thought . . .' said Zimmy apologetically before shutting
up, and there was a brief embarrassed pause until Rosten finished
at the telephone and, doing a lot of laughing to show he had only
been joking a moment before, came and poured us all a further
diminutive drink before departure.

The local turned out to be indeed local, less than a hundred
yards off, and a standard and perfectly acceptable trattoria-type
establishment. Rosten put on a revolting pseudo-Italian show of
delighted cries and embraces with the proprietor and the waiter and
doubtless others too. The four of us sat down at a rectangular table
with Jane facing me and next to her Zimmy facing Rosten. Despite
earlier talk about how he loved England and how often he came to
London, he was turning out to be nearly the sort of American who
tells you that in the United States of America we have this man we
call the President. Not quite. He began doling out information about
his life and works while the food began to arrive. It turned out to
have been ordered in advance. This practice is surely a bit off,
destroying as it does part of the point of going out to eat in a
restaurant. What they brought us, however, was palatable enough.

Rosten went on with his narrative to me. The successive episodes
were not very varied and they all shared the quality of showing him
in a uniformly favourable light. Across the table Zimmy seemed to
be delivering a similarly unbroken monologue to Jane, who looked
as if she was enjoying it about as much as I was Rosten's. At one
point he said,

'In our high schools and colleges back home in the United
States . . .' Here he paused, no doubt to debate mentally whether

he needed to explain to me what a high school was, but, evidently deciding this would be unnecessary, continued, '. . . we have something we call Commencement.'

'Yes, I know about that,' I said; 'in fact we use the –'

'It's our name for the end-of-year ceremony of conferring diplomas and degrees. We call it Commencement to show it's to be regarded as the beginning of something, not the end of something.'

'Oh, I see.'

'Well, during the ceremony we get the Commencement Address, and the faculty, the professors and whoever, like to invite some kind of –'

No single noun would come near doing justice to the mixture of self-deprecation, amusement, worldly wisdom, mockery, vanity and shittiness with which he spoke the next word.

'– *distinguished* guy to deliver it. Well, one time when some school couldn't get hold of anyone better' – chuckle – 'they came to me. So I just told the kids,' and he told me a certain amount of what he had told the kids, eventually reaching the peroration, ' "But all this learning and knowledge and hard work and dedication and so on is of less importance in the end than one other thing, which is sincerity. And if you can *fake that*" ' – he did a wink involving most of his face and held up a crooked forefinger – ' "you'll have the world at your feet." Well, some of the high-ups and stuffed shirts didn't care for that *at all*, not *one little bit*, but the kids just *loved* it. They simply *exploded*. They *went wild*.'

I have forgotten what else the kids did. Somehow we got to the end of the meal. After a glass of grappa, which I greatly appreciated, the bill was settled and we were outside and making for the Rostens' flat. No thank you, we would not come in for a final drink.

'When do you go back home?' I asked.

Rosten named a time forty-eight hours ahead or so.

'Oh dear,' I said as insincerely as I could – 'we won't have time for another get-together.'

No, we would not. When the other couple were just about out of earshot Jane said to me, 'If you fancy that woman I'm leaving you.'

I reassured her most vigorously on that point.

'Well, that's something.'

I could not see what more there could be of that, but said, 'You know, I can't help feeling a bit sorry for old Zimmy even so. Married to that – '

'I can. I don't. She's a revolting creature.'

322

'Well yes, but –'

'You saw how she was going on at me. Do you know what it was about? Just what a drag it was, going to see her mother in an institution every Monday. She doesn't like doing it, you see. Just think of being eighty-something and having that as the one event in your week.'

The following week I entered the Garrick Club and the first person I saw was Leo Rosten, sitting writing at the writing-desk. Expertly converting my yell of horror into a cry of delighted surprise, I said, 'Leo! I thought you said you'd be back in New York by this time.'

'Well, I kind of . . . decided to stay a little longer.' At Windsor Castle, or perhaps Chequers.

We chatted for a moment. I considered asking after Zimmy, but soon rejected the idea. I noticed he had a couple of books with him on the desk and, going by the principle that you can find out something about a man from his reading, unobtrusively took in what they were. The top one was called *Selected Short Stories of Leo Rosten*, and the one underneath, different in size, shape and jacket-design, was called *Selected Short Stories of Leo Rosten*. I hurried off to the Gents.

If you should ever feel you may be getting complacent, or too complacent, look up Rosten in *Contemporary Novelists* (St James Press, 1972), a most useful compilation. In his entry, Rosten includes among the posts he has held ones like Consultant to the Commission on National Goals, 1960, and Member of the Educational Policies Committee of the National Educational Association; no lie-abed or recluse he. He writes of his writing: 'I write as my interests guide and seduce me: see the preface to *The Many Worlds of Leo Rosten* [by Leo Rosten, 1964] . . . The titles of my works indicate the range of the nets I have cast into the sea of my fancies.'

And to think the bugger has probably had a better time of it than you and I.

THE BOOKER PRIZE

In 1986 I won the Booker Prize for Fiction with my novel *The Old Devils*. With that substantial exception, I found the occasion of the award a horrible one. It took place in the London Guildhall, a splendid building for many purposes but not, in its stony vastness, one to hold a dinner in. And of course the dinner was a public affair, i.e. scores, hundreds of people were present, thereby guaranteeing my discomfort. The food I thought was worse than is inevitable with a gathering of that size, though in the circumstances, with my book on the short list and the winner to be announced after the meal, I might have found it hard to eat anything. And like all the other male guests I was wearing a dinner jacket (with my feet in brown brogues because they would no longer go into my smart patent-leather half-boots).

They sat us as usual at round tables serving about a dozen. I had brought my old friend and ally Mavis Nicholson along to ride shotgun with me, but they had stuck her on the far side of my table, out of my hearing in the general din. All the others were Booker shareholders, as far as I could tell, certainly unknown to me personally. I was slotted in between two middle-aged females. One was mostly silent, which was fine with me, the other was American. After I had done all I felt like doing with a small torpedo of was it veal, the latter said to me,

'Do you mind if I smoke?'

'Not a bit. Go ahead.'

'Would you like a cigarette?'

'No thank you, I don't smoke.'

'But you don't mind if I do?'

'Not a bit. Smoke away.'

'Are you sure you wouldn't like a cigarette?'

'Absolutely certain.'

After another couple of the same, the lady said, 'Isn't there any-thing I can do to please you?'

'Actually there is – you see that opening at the far end of the room there, that's called a door, and you can please me no end by going out through it and staying out,' was what I felt like telling her, but being far too nice and cowardly by nature I made some other, innocuous reply. In fact now that the dreaded announcement was drawing near I realised I was becoming as much bothered by the prospect of making a fool of myself in public as of not winning after having been the clear favourite. So I thought up a funny thing to say if I won, and another funny thing to say if I lost. Having done that I felt much better.

The short list of six had been reduced to five without, so to speak, a shot being fired. One chap had made it known that he would only attend the dinner if he had won, or was going to have won. Other-wise he would go home, and had been told he had better go home. Here and now a TV camera was pointing directly over the head of another chap, so I felt he could safely be forgotten about too. But it was quite tense enough to suit me when the Booker chairman, who had some name that someone else had, like John Lennon or Genghis Khan, got up and introduced the chairman of the judges, Anthony Thwaite, another old chum of mine, of which you may make what you will.

Anthony said, as he had to, how good everyone was and then named yours truly as the winner. The American female grabbed me first and embraced me like yet another and closer chum. Soon, without having fallen down on the way, I was on some sort of podium speaking towards the camera. I divulged both the funny thing I had been going to say if I won ('How do I feel? Sick as a parrot, Brian') and if I had lost ('Oh, over the moon, Keith'), and other boffs of that nature. I also said, grinning from ear to ear to show I was joking, that until just now I had thought the Booker Prize a rather trivial, showbizzy caper, but now I considered it a very serious, reliable indication of literary merit. (This remark was to turn up again in a television round-up of events of 1986, reshaped into 'Kingsley Amis won the Booker Prize, the importance of which he had previously disparaged.' Memo to writers and others: Never make a joke against or about yourself that some little bastard can turn into a piece of shit and send your way.) Soon after that I happened to notice a non-dinner-jacketed man standing near the camera rotating his fist, and duly wound up.

325

After that came interviews. The first was with Hermione Lee, invisible at the far end of the hall. Anybody who has to make his way that far under those conditions, between quite closely packed seated groups, inevitably has to weave to and fro a little. I certainly did, and the commentators all said or hinted that I was pissed.*
Later there was a moment when the runners-up had the opportunity of congratulating me, should they have felt so minded. Only Kazuo Ishiguro took it.

So there I was, £15,000 the richer, though I bought nothing specific with that money, which merely slimmed down my overdraft, and really benefiting from increased home sales, foreign advances, etc. There was naturally some comment on my win, much of it naturally hostile. The media or something correspondent of the *New Statesman* complained that I had been given a marvellous chance of appraising the role and status of the novel as an art-form and in our society, and had thrown it away by making jokes instead, 'mainly at the expense of football managers'. My, that had rankled, rather strangely considering the writer was a woman. No, I did not say 'of course' there.

How good a thing are literary prizes? Are they perhaps not a good thing at all? Well, they are obviously all right when I win one, and obviously I should not have agreed to serve as a judge on the 1988 Sunday Express Prize committee if I were not generally in favour. I notice too that nobody seems to have a word to say against the Prix Goncourt, the Pulitzer Prize and others set up before the era of book hype, before, that is, the era of absurdly large advances to authors and the treatment of books as little else but saleable commodities – all that. In fact it could be argued that the institution of the prize, by at least in theory rewarding excellence, works against the mere consideration of future profit. Nor have I any time for the view that the existence of the Booker encourages the writing of 'Booker novels', designed to tickle the palates of judges rather than appeal to ordinary readers; I doubt if anybody but a non- or failed novelist would seriously think of that. (Though it is true that some pretty weird and unreadable stuff has in the past captured the Booker before sinking from sight.)

With all this said, I no longer regard it and its fellows with the unmixed approval, even enthusiasm I showed when, for instance,

---

*So I was, of course, but not to the extent suggested.

having some years ago got on to the Booker short list and failed to win, I defended the prize in general – aforementioned little bastard, kindly note – against Robert Robinson, who at the dinner of that year was taking the unexpectedly leftie line that it was all a matter of conscience-money put up by the firm, then supposedly exploiting Caribbean workers on its sugar plantations. I would now argue that, however real the plea of rewarding excellence, the prize is drawn willy-nilly into the hype machine. More particularly than that, it deforms the yearly publishing pattern and it works against the good writers who will never win anything and of whom there are always too few. And I think it cannot help working against the young writers who are trying to start their careers. Perhaps a way could be found of devising a different kind of award, even a new scheme, though not an Arts-Council-type straight hand-out, which would help such people on their way. They need it now more than we did then, when I was getting going.

Income-tax relief, any kind of pension scheme, etc., for old writers are part of a different but important subject.

A PEEP ROUND THE TWIST

THAT DAY IN 1982 I had attended the annual lunch of the Society of Snuff Grinders, Blenders and Purveyors at the Institute of Directors in Pall Mall. Although chronic hay fever had put paid to my snuff-taking years before, I was still an associate member of the Society, which on this occasion was as generous as ever with its hospitality. Even so on the way home I paused at my club for perhaps an hour's relaxation with friends. When I did get home I added a few lines to my current novel, drank some gin, ate supper, watched 'Minder' on television, drank some whisky and, having taken a sleeping pill, one of the Mogadon group, eventually retired upstairs. Not an altogether exceptional day.

I was coming out of the bathroom on to the awkward little stairhead when I lost my balance and, instead of sensibly letting myself fall, thrust my right foot out and down hard at an unaccustomed angle and broke my leg standing up, a feat presaged in different circumstances in my novel *I Want It Now*. Help was luckily to hand and quite soon I was in the Royal Free Hospital in Hampstead waiting to be operated on. I had never had an operation before, and I had last had a general anaesthetic in 1934 for a tooth, but the fear of the situation I had sometimes feared never turned up.

The next morning I came round with some crafty little pegs in my shin and a feeding-tube in my arm. The latter arrangement means you lie there hour after hour without feeling hungry or wanting to shit. You want to pee, though. But that is another story. For the moment all that concerned me was that I had woken up in a strange but warm and comfortable place. There was a nice lady there who explained very clearly where I was and what had happened. That was fine, but I noticed something odd about her movements, especially those of her hands. While being entirely normal and familiar these movements struck me as somehow sudden and fluid, decidedly out of my control. Or so it seemed to me. Soon I put the matter aside and went to sleep again.

I had plenty of opportunity to dream and took it. Other people's dreams are boring, or so at least we are constantly being told, though in my experience they are no more boring to hear about than anything else. However, over the next two or three days and nights there was some material that impressed me at the time and seemed to throw light on my waking moments.

Games, table games, are the very stuff of dreams, as Alice reminds us, and I was not surprised to be introduced to a chessboard with mobile squares and an unexplained relation to astrology and sequences of numbers. To be faced with a mystery, not to understand what something important signifies or to be able to fathom what is really going on, may well be the repeated experience of every dreamer. I certainly keep having it and had it a lot then.

There was a good sequence about drink. After a short episode in which some minor ordeal was inflicted or problem set, we cut to a scene in which, supposedly awake now, I chatted about it with friends over drinks. Ah, but – the management explained – I was no longer in a position to drink when awake, so the scene could not have taken place in that form. A notional corrected version of it followed in which my glass and its contents were visually wiped out. I suspect that, in the way dreams have of instantly rewriting or even inventing earlier matter, the first two sections were a mere pseudo-memory slipped into the invisible-glass passage.

A closely similar device of dream-production is to introduce into an ordinary one-off dream a pseudo-memory alleging that the dreamer has been this way before and is actually experiencing the latest run of a recurring dream, a device evidently aimed at making sure he remembers afterwards what he has dreamed, or some of it. I certainly remembered a good deal of my Kenneth Tynan dream and also retained for a short time the strong impression that I had dreamt it, or another rendering of it, before.

In the dream in question I came across after the lapse of ten years or so a folder of papers in which were a Press cutting, part of a lawyer's contract and a typescript. (So to describe the objects that seemed to be there in front of me is, of course, to make the sort of hopeful approximations forced on a xenologist investigating an alien planet.) The cutting told me that Kenneth Tynan, one or other of my sons and I were to collaborate on a political-historical work for the stage, part factual, part imaginative. The contract I took to refer to this project. The typescript seemed to be part of its text and was set out as verse.

I am constantly coming across reading-matter in my dreams, most often poetry of some kind, sometimes fiction, always a work of great moment, as a sleeping brewer no doubt conjures up fabulous best bitters, a pathologist malignancies beyond compare. For me the most precious find of all is naturally my own lost, forgotten masterpiece, if not to be bodily repossessed on the instant then to be remembered by a choice phrase or two, at least to be read through. But, this time as every time before, not one word could I make out, and I was never to know so much as the subject of that Tynan-Amis-Amis enterprise. It would have had to be his idea, therefore in some way left-wing, and yet acceptable to me; perhaps a musical about George Orwell.

That shows part of the absurdity of the whole thing, and the chronological details show more: I had not even seen Tynan since 1970, when I was still the only writing Amis. It was absurd of me, too, to go on being undecided whether literary Martin or quite non-literary Philip might have been involved. But the dream had been not so much vivid as penetrating, enough to convince me that there might be truth in the story, enough to induce me to ask the boys about it when they visited me a little later. No, they said without premeditation, nothing of the sort was known to either of them. No, they added rather disappointingly at a later stage, they had seen nothing mad in my question or way of putting it.

But of course I still was a bit mad, though less so by then than I had been. To the shock of the accident and operation had been added the abrupt cutting-off of alcohol and nicotine after forty years of indulgence and, per contra, a powerful input of antibiotics, pain-killers and sleeping-pills. As it happened I was also ill, suffering from 'flu or something similar with the classic symptoms of sore throat and pains in the limbs, which I disregarded at the time as part of the package. Afterwards I looked in my charts for those days and found one high temperature reading – only one, but all in all I was probably as well set up for a touch of madness as I will be for the foreseeable future.

When very tired I had had hallucinations before, and found that the aural sort were partly subject to the will. In fact I could create in my own ears the sound of music playing just audibly, no louder, and make it go through whatever tune I fancied. On the first after-noon in the ward I lay listening not very alertly to the daytime hospital sounds, which consist of voices, footsteps and things being dropped. The voices seemed to swell, and I wondered if I could make somebody say something. Sure enough, within a few seconds a young girl seemed to say, in clear upper-class tones, 'Mummy, haven't they got that old fascist Kingsley Amis in here somewhere?' I smiled with amusement, also with satisfaction at having brought off a kind of technical feat.

Abandoning that, I turned my attention to the cats in the ward, or rather to what I knew to be the hallucinated shapes of my own two real cats from home, Tina, a tabby, and Sarah, a white cat. The motionless image of Tina was provided by part of a blanket or other bed-covering. Looking at this through my long-distance, 'television' spectacles revealed the image as more of a first-rate optical illusion than a true hallucination; as I had expected, I saw a bunch of material. However, a similar look at the supposed shirtsleeve that was doubling as Sarah showed me Sarah still. At this I felt mildly surprised and tickled.

The cats, though not I think the old-fascist moment, could have been a dream. What happened next, a couple of minutes or days later, was probably not, because Mr Elliott, the unexcitable ex-schoolmaster who occupied the bed next to mine, told me he had had the same sort of thing at about the same time. To be on the safe side I asked him just before leaving hospital if he would say so again and he did, mentioning as before all those drugs we had been given.

What happened to me was to be trying to read a book and at the same time to be aware of its text being uttered in the form of a conversation. More exactly, at least two such conversations were going on, one involving me and some vaguely located persons in front of me, another taking place over my right shoulder. For a moment I seemed to be where I could not have been, on my feet near the foot of the bed and with my back to the window. From time to time I made what I thought were appropriate comments, audibly too, for Mr Elliott heard me say one thing he regarded as very odd, odd not so much in itself as in the fact that I had said it; after all my pleas he could not call it to mind. Nor could I remember the general topic under discussion.

The man in the bed opposite mine seemed very inactive compared to Mr Elliott, who showed an admirable capacity for making the best of his situation. The other fellow, Mr Stephenson, simply stared undeviatingly when not asleep, and our relative position meant that

he stared towards me, indeed, as I began to notice after a time, at
me, and with impassive hostility. After he had done this for a time
he discussed me with some other person whom I never saw distinctly
or even glanced at. I could hear little of this but, having mentioned
my possibly tolerable qualities when younger, he did clearly and
forcefully call me 'a *vicious* old man'. I was quite dashed by this at
first, but had stopped believing in it, and had realised that his staring
had only been at vacancy, by the time he died in the ward while I
was on a visit to the X-ray department.

The room I was in had just the four beds in it. It was about
twenty-five feet square with a plain brown lino floor, a creamy wash
on the walls and a ceiling of large square off-white tiles. One side
had a large window looking out high over the houses and blocks of
flats on Haverstock Hill and beyond, with an adjacent wing or stub
of the hospital projecting at right angles to it. The opposite side of
the room was open, revealing a counter, offices, telephones, files,
notice-boards, a wash-basin, pot plants and a curve of corridor with
a day-room seen opening off it and the sense of another room-for-
four just out of view. In every direction there was a lot of bare metal
in the form of ventilator gratings in the ceiling, plates in the walls
for switches and plugs, the understructure of the beds and the rails
on which the internal curtains ran, the ones screening off each bed-
area at need. In these surroundings the washed, shaved and evacuated patient, put out on a chair with his breakfast beside him, might
fancy himself to be among the nickel and fake marble of a small
old-fashioned Belgian café.

That was the best time of the day, full of light and activity. Or
rather it came to be so. During my earlier, less animated moments
I probably had those curtains drawn a good deal of the time. They
were pleasant enough in themselves, their brown-and-tan colours no
doubt chosen by environmental psychologists with their minds on
things like warmth and cheerfulness, but even by day, even after I
was quite myself again, to be enclosed by them for long had a
disorientating effect on me. What they enclosed was not a small
arbitrary space round a bed, chair, table, cupboard, light, bell and
window. I sometimes found it easy to forget that, when the curtains
had been pulled back again and the 'room' had vanished, I was still
sitting or lying where I had been and not elsewhere.

Usually, as when I thought I had left pen or sponge-bag 'behind',
the particularity reminded me at once of the true state of affairs.
Now and then during the first days I stayed confused for rather

332

longer, not actually believing I was in a different place, just under a light unexamined impression that I was. The 'conversation' Mr Elliott heard part of, for instance, seemed to be carried on in something like a study, rather square and cramped, and the Tynan discussion in a lounge rather than a café, one with the kind of pale-orange lighting I associate with cinemas. Of the two I was much nearer my usual state for Tynan but I think I should have been disconcerted to learn I had not moved from my physical starting-point.

I suppose I was furthest out the first evening and night. There was no supper for me – all I needed had come straight into my bloodstream – but it would have been after the others had eaten theirs, towards seven o'clock, that the curtains were drawn round me for some sort of wash or tidying-up to be administered. When they had been removed I soon found I was 'off' somewhere new. For a time all sense of being in a hospital was lost. I had arrived in a brightly lit, tallish room, much longer across my front than the one I had left. Just out of sight round the corner there was an outside door by which parties arrived and left from time to time. (The shifts would have been changing about now and the last visitors getting on the move.)

At first there were a great many people about, talking noisily, nothing to do with Mr Elliott or me, well, me at least, because he had been there before – I very clearly remembered thinking that – and knew something about the place. I tried to ask him whether he thought they would look after us properly here, but I doubt if I got my question across. By this stage I was beginning to conclude that a party was under way, though not one to which I was invited. What sort of people were these? In silence I heard, unnaturally amplified for my benefit, the voices of a young man and a girl talking pure N.W.1 party chatter, faltering, shutting up. The whole thing must have come out of my own head, but less consciously than the old-fascist line.

To my growing bewilderment was added disapproval. These were irresponsible people, none of them doctors or nurses or anything like that – so the hospital was not quite forgotten. What was going on? Mr Elliott's curtains were briskly drawn together. Bodies bumped against them from the inside. There were shuffles, scampers, giggles, whispers. A bed creaked. 'What's going on?' I called several times. It must have been about then that I saw a man in grey overalls coming through a door in the wing outside the window and entering the ward. This scared me, as well it might have in a way, for as I established a day or two later such a move is impossible.

Actually what went on scaring me as I lay there was something that seemed much more practical. By now I was fully 'back' in the hospital, though not yet quite the hospital as it really was. In the last few minutes things had quietened down, but that was just a stratagem. Whatever was going on or about to go on, sex orgy, drugs orgy or something unguessed-at, I and probably I alone was outside it. My knowledge of it would be dangerous and would have to be prevented, and here most conveniently (this was real enough) came the pill-trolley on its late-night round, doling out dosages to the helpless patients. Nothing would be easier than to slip me something lethal. With what I still think was impressive self-command I had thought myself out of this notion by the time the dispensing nurse approached me. Murdering a patient would cause a terrible stink – the idea was ridiculous. Knocking one out good and hard for a few hours was another matter. I turned down the offer of a sleeping-pill and pain-killer, at least I meant to.

'All right, this one's just an antibiotic.'

'No thank you very much.'

'You're supposed to take it, you know.'

'Nurse, what's going on in this ward?'

'Nothing,' she said, as one asked such a question every day for years.

'There was a man in here from the wing next door.'

'Oh yes. Lift up and I'll do your pillows.'

'I wish to speak to the sister.'

'Sorry, I'm afraid she's off now. She'll be here in the morning.'

2400 hrs Magnapen refused by patient, notes my record. Well, it would presumably have noted something more if I had said and done more. Thinking it over afterwards and since, I came to the conclusion that mental afflictions, or the visible part of them, which is the same thing, have to do with your temperament. We all know some people who on hearing the nurse's soft answers would have insisted on seeing the sister, the matron and everybody else up to and including the Minister of Health, as in saner circumstances the manager, the chef, the captain. It is they, and not the ones who have the same fancies but shut up about them, who get called mad, and quite right too. My other reflection was that the whole thing comes from self-created fear, and that what the outside world calls madness is the victim's attempts to give that fear a shadow of external justification. Some victims, of course, never make any such attempts and are known as neurotics or phobics. But this is a large subject.

No doubt half-reassured by seeing that some civilised restraints were still in place, I went to sleep – I think I must have had that sleeping-pill after all. The next morning I was still a bit off my head, deciding now that what had taken place was a drinks orgy, imagining that everybody had turned up late on the job in consequence and dropping unnoticed snide remarks about some people needing to make up their sleep, etc. Nevertheless the fit was passing. At this stage the Tynan chat and other touches must have been still to come, but I was beginning to slip comfortably into the passing show of ward life – Big Kay with her dinner-waggon and tea-waggon, the surly Spanish cleaning-lady, the old bag who wordlessly and not very tunefully sang 'The Lincolnshire Poacher' fourteen hours a day, the succession of colonial doctors and therapists who X-rayed and discussed and looked at my leg and otherwise forwarded its cause, brisk, sweet little Nurse McKee, strapping Nurse Cotton with her appearance of pink-cheeked depravity – alas, unexplored by me, and the rest of that casual, decent, lively band, daughters of the London lower middle classes every one of them that I saw, very much like their elders as I remember them forty years ago.

By the middle of the second week the room of the four beds was staying the same all round the clock – its diversity held out longest in the evenings, when it briefly took on a rustic, almost barn-like air. One puzzle persisted. On the wall opposite me, between beds 17 and 18, was a picture done in some quick-drying paint, the representation of a bathing scene in strenuous blues and turquoises on about the stylistic level of an up-market Bulgarian cigarette-packet. Its continuing presence had at any rate the value of reassuring Mr Elliott and me, if no one else, that we were in our proper station and none other. Sometimes I thought that it could only be there for that reason. Then on my very last morning one of the sisters told me that others not so much unlike it hung in every room of the ward, perhaps of the whole enormous hospital, there in fulfilment of an Arts Council scheme intended to supply a new picture by a living artist every week but at once lapsed, leaving the first of the series in place for ever. Ah, the Arts Council! Even here, O Lord . . .

To the end of my stay – a bare three weeks – I found the nights not altogether easy to get through, long and undiminishingly overheated as they were. Once my first unconsciousness was lost I had trouble staying convinced that nothing was required of me during the hours of darkness, nothing had to be thought of or written, I had only to go on lying parallel to the side of the bed and the room would start up again of its own accord when the time came. A really good sleep was not to be looked forward to until the night was over, the nurses began to steal about, the early-morning pill-trolley slid into view and the flats in the distance glowed like logs in ash.

INSTEAD OF AN EPILOGUE

To H.

I

In 1932 when I was ten
In my grandmother's garden in Camberwell
I saw a Camberwell Beauty butterfly
Sitting on a clump of Michaelmas daisies.
I recognised it because I'd seen a picture
Showing its brownish wings with creamy edges
In a boy's paper or on a cigarette-card
Earlier that week. And I remember thinking,
What else would you expect? Everyone knows
Camberwell Beauties come from Camberwell;
That's why they're called that. Yes, I was ten.

II

In 1940 when I was eighteen
In Marlborough, going out one winter's morning
To walk to school, I saw that every twig,
Every leaf in the vicar's privet hedge
And every stalk and stem was covered in
A thin layer of ice as clear as glass
Because the rain had frozen as it landed.
The sun shone and the trees and shrubs shone back
Like pale flames with orange and green sparkles.
Freak weather conditions, people said,
And one was always hearing about them.

337

III

In '46 when I was twenty-four
I met someone harmless, someone defenceless,
But till then whole, unadapted within;
Awkward, gentle, healthy, straight-backed,
Who spoke to say something, laughed when amused;
If things went wrong, feared she might be at fault,
Whose eye I could have met for ever then,
Oh yes, and who was also beautiful.
Well, that was much as women were meant to be,
I thought, and set about looking further.
How can we tell, with nothing to compare?

INDEX